Entrepreneur to Megapreneur

Publishing Details

Title: Entrepreneur to Megapreneur - Why they did what they did, and how they did it.
First published 2019
Second Edition 2020

Publisher: Powerhouse Productions Australia
Editor: Pickawoowoo Publishing Group, Eddie Albrecht
Interior and Cover layout (Paperback/Ebook) Pickawoowoo Publishing Group

A catalogue record for this book is available from the National Library of Australia

ISBN:

ISBN 978-0-6485971-0-0 (hardback)
ISBN 978-0-6485971-1-7 (paperback)
ISBN 978-0-6485971-2-4 (e-book)

Permissions

PerthNow Story: ©West Australian Newspapers Limited 2013
Andrew Pritchard Photography
PremiereVision and Fashion Network

Entrepreneur to Megapreneur

Why they did what they did, and how they did it.

Lesa J Hinchliffe

Powerhouse Productions Australia

In memory of my great friend
John Vogel (1942-2015)

And for the lights of my life, my two beautiful sons
Alistair James and Julius George Hinchliffe

Megapreneur is a word that does not currently appear in any recognised dictionary however, its definition may, for some, require no explanation. For the sake of this book Megapreneurs are entrepreneurs who, with a desire to build a business, start small. Through hard work, perseverance and a preparedness to take a risk based on extraordinary determination and unquestioning belief they build those businesses into large, often global enterprises. They can be well known, well respected; most are highly private individuals.

Contents

"That some achieve great success,
is proof to all that others can
achieve it as well."

Abraham Lincoln

Foreword

Entrepreneur to Megapreneur is a powerful book. It has the capacity to create a change in the mindset of people who never dare believe that anything is possible. It is written with unexpected honesty and simplicity about business owners largely unknown and stories previously untold. This is a book that everyone who ever had a dream should read.

Western Australia is a unique State. From the foundation settlement in Albany in 1826, Western Australians have a record of developing small to medium size enterprises iconic in character. Conceivably the adversities of geographical and environmental conditions confronted by our early settlers engendered the development of a unique and determined spirit. That spirit has been transmitted to modern day business pioneers.

In my public life I have had the privilege of meeting some of the outstanding businessmen and women who have collectively shaped the economic and social landscape of Western Australia. They are the industrial and commercial pioneers. The creators of the iconic enterprises which in part badge our State enhancing our distinctiveness.

We live in economically challenging times. Almost every Australian, no matter how successful, is feeling a strain – some of course far greater than others.

That is why, in times like these, a book like this is so compelling - it is a book of hope, no matter what your situation in life. It clearly demonstrates that if you have a dream, unyielding belief, a fierce determination, and a willingness to work hard you have what it takes to achieve great business success. This book is testament that anyone who has a dream to be in business and to do it successfully can ultimately live that dream.

While the obstacles are endless and the risks substantial, the desire to achieve great business success is evidently motivation enough judging by the ever-increasing number of entrepreneurs emerging daily onto our economic horizon. Despite their determination and courage, it will not lessen the enormous challenges they will inevitably confront.

Lesa Hinchliffe, by writing this book, has given us an extraordinary insight and an opportunity to learn from the fascinating real experiences and lessons of 8 very successful businesspeople. The point of difference in this book is in where they all started – some literally had nothing, not even an education. Theirs are stories of hardship, sacrifice, collapse, courage and ultimately the reward for never giving in.

The people depicted here emerged from ordinary families. For most there were no books to guide them; no one to learn from – they had no choice but to learn on the go. Each undeniably took risks but subsequently the lessons they now share in this book are invaluable tools for people going into business. Their lessons form the basis by which you can plan your own path forward – the things you have to know, the things you have to do, and the things you should never do.

As Lesa says life is too short to make every mistake, so better and wiser to learn from those who have been down the path before us.

In chapter 1 Lew Beale despite being in business for more than 4 decades makes the comment, "I've learned to admit I don't know everything and as such continue to ask questions and seek advice from people who do." Or from chapter 2 Kylie Radford shares, "When it comes to advice, my advice to others is to really think about who is giving advice and only listen if they have knowledge about what it is you are trying to achieve."

These comments from two enormously successful business owners are why every business owner or aspiring entrepreneur should read this book.

Peter Cumins in Chapter 4 begins with, "To build an empire you have to build on solid foundations, if not it will crumble in 5 – 10 years. Have a clear idea at the beginning what you want to achieve and build it accordingly – don't underestimate the significance of this." Great words, great advice. This book is full of such intelligence, lessons and tips for building a better business.

From the moment we take our first breath we start watching and learning from the actions of others. It's how we grow. The same is necessary to develop a successful business. So as Lesa would suggest - don't stop learning, don't stop listening, don't stop reading – begin right now with chapter one.

The Honourable Kim Beazley AC
Governor of Western Australia

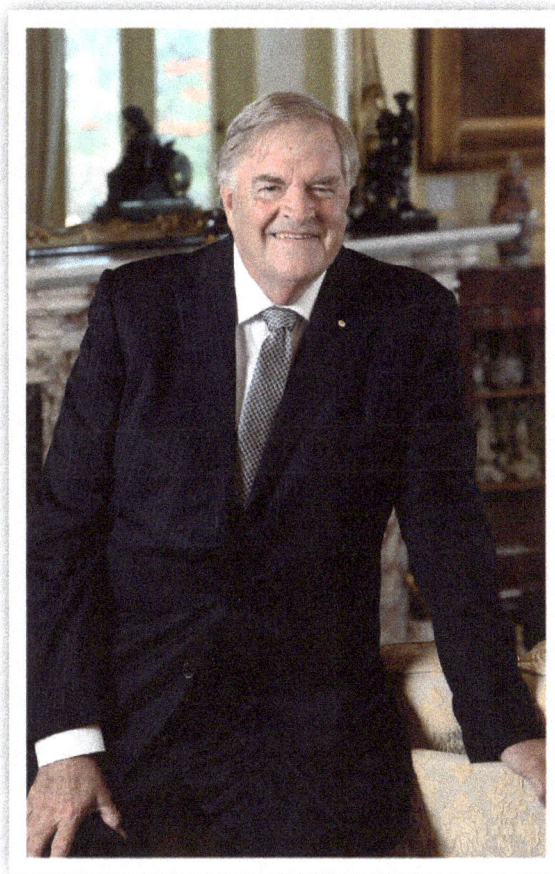

Preface

It's an amazing feeling to write a book – it's exhilarating to finish writing one. This is the first book I have written, and so after taking nearly three years to complete, typing the final words was quite an emotional experience. I'd achieved my goal. But it was more than that. I had also changed as a person and, over the process, learned how to attain my own goals. However, with that realisation came regret. If only I had written this book or read one like it when I was 18 – just as I was embarking on the journey of adulthood. How different my life might have been. C'est la vie.

Nothing can change the past but if you are like me, driven to learn about what it takes to succeed in business, then reading this book and acting on the suggestions within may well bring to you, as it did to me, the realisation that anything is possible.

Have you ever read Napoleon Hill's Think and Grow Rich? Although it was written in 1937 it's a great read because the messages are still so relevant. I was 16 when I first read the book and ever since I've had a curiosity and a desire to achieve business success. It was why, at 18, I started to look at buying real estate. I also had some good business ideas over the years and I gave a fair amount of time to each but I never totally achieved my goal and success was only minimal. I never gave much thought as to why that was, I just gave up and went on to the next idea. But that was part of the problem. I now realise it's not the idea that guarantees the success, it is the execution of it and the driving it through to completion.

So, what are your goals? For most of us, unfortunately, that's where it gets difficult.

Reading Think and Grow Rich at 16 had led me to believe I would have great business success if I wanted it badly enough. But, in what seemed like a few quick heart beats, I was 54. I hadn't achieved what I wanted to achieve or expected to achieve, but I had reached that moment when I suddenly understood how short life really is.

So why not? Why hadn't I had success? These were the start of many questions. Why do some people make it and others don't? What do they do differently? What if those trying to achieve business success had the opportunity to learn first-hand from those who had already walked down the path before them? What would the outcome be? Would achieving success be that much easier and that much quicker? I wanted to know all the answers. That's when I decided I would write a book. It would be intimate, informal and straightforward about the journeys of a select few who had started life with very little - some with nothing not even an education - and go on to achieve great business success. Similar books had been written before but some are difficult to follow. So, I decided to tell this story differently, in a way that would be both easy to read and absorb, and most importantly, would clearly demonstrate why a journey from ordinary to extraordinary is one we all have the potential to make.

I started on my book writing journey in late 2015. At the beginning I was naïve; I had no idea how amazing but difficult it would be, or how long it would take. In the first 18 months, my inner critic was relentless. For 18 months I listened to that voice. However, the power of the stories I was being told and the strength of my goal compelled me to write every day – even when I didn't feel up to it or capable of it. Then, almost subconsciously, I started copying the behaviours and the habits of those within this book, and that was when I started to feel and see a difference. I started to believe in myself, my inner voice fell silent and with that, the writing became easier. With the silencing of those negative inner monologues I was able to finish the book and through the process finally recognise why my success had only ever been minimal. That understanding has irrevocably changed the way I live each day.

Not surprisingly, my writing style also changed over the journey. I considered going back and re-writing it all but only for a moment. It showed a transition, and any change that occurs on a journey to achieve a goal delivers both a lesson and a triumph. As this book is about achieving success, I decided, therefore, to leave it alone.

So, as you read you might notice the transition in structure and style; I hope you do because that would indicate I have grown as a writer. But what's more important, I believe, is to understand what triggered the transition that enabled me, after all these years, to achieve one of the most significant goals I had ever set for myself. I have absolutely no doubt it is because of the people in this book and the stories they shared. They gave me courage, direction and the wisdom to accept that the only way to achieve anything in life is to simply start somewhere and not stop until you have accomplished what you set out to do. And that's what I did.

I hope by reading this book you too will find the forward in your path.

So, let this journey begin.

Acknowledgements

I would like to acknowledge eight amazing people; Lew Beale, Kylie Radford, Rick Hart, Peter Cumins, Sasha deBretton, Murray McHenry, Peter Hodgson and Lorraine Hodgson. They gave so much of their precious time to share their triumphs and their disappointments in order to inspire others to begin, to keep going, to be resilient, to expect the inevitable challenges and then to conquer them all. They know that the reward of pushing through far outweighs any of the adversities one is likely to encounter along the way.

Thank you to each of you from the bottom of my heart for your trust, patience and generosity.

Sincere thanks also to those friends and colleagues who gave me the courage to keep going and the belief that I would get there. You know who you are.

To Clare Aisthorpe, for the hours upon hours you spent transcribing interview recordings – thank you.

To Judith Darlington, for your unwavering friendship, immense support, extraordinary assistance and constant encouragement – without you, the journey to achieving this goal would have been longer, even more challenging than it was and certainly far lonelier. No words can express the depth of my gratitude.

Finally, my heartfelt thanks to those who believed in me – my partner Rick Hart, my sons Alistair and Julius, great friends and sounding boards Anthea, Alison, Claire and Karen, and last but never, ever least, my wonderful Mother and Father, Elaine and David Allen.

Thank you to each and every one of you.

Introduction

Entrepreneur to Megapreneur follows the lives of eight entrepreneurs who started with nothing but an idea. They were ordinary people who, for reasons made clear in this book, achieved what so few do – they turned an idea into a hugely successful business. Not one of them had an easy ride but the lessons learned along the way were vital to their success! For the first time they intimately share those lessons.

If you are driven to succeed in business then their lessons may well help you turn your idea into reality. The principles shared are simple and you will have heard many of them before, but what is crucial is to understand that their simplicity is what makes them so easy to dismiss as unimportant. However, by not applying them your chances of success will be greatly reduced.

I define success as the reward, for achieving a goal, gained as a consequence of the actions taken over the journey to attaining that goal. The incentive of the reward is the reason one makes the journey [without that incentive, few would begin] however, it is the management of the journey that determines the magnitude of the reward.

Therefore, to achieve great success, we must focus on the journey not the destination, and that is why this book has the capacity to have enormous impact. It details the journeys and the methods employed by these entrepreneurial eight that ultimately led to their success. Each story is remarkable.

If the mountain of success you are climbing appears to have an ever-rising summit, then this book could well be the trigger you need to conquer it. It is likely you will find many parallels in the journeys of these people who were born ordinary, people who didn't really begin with a goal, people who didn't really know where they were headed, people who simply made the decision to do something and were determined to do it. They have each become extraordinary as a result of that determination. However, what is more inspiring is their 'ordinariness' – it is one of the greatest indicators that exceptional success is within reach of us all.

So, for now, don't worry about the destination, just begin your journey because you may well find yourself on the peak of a far higher mountain than you ever thought was possible.

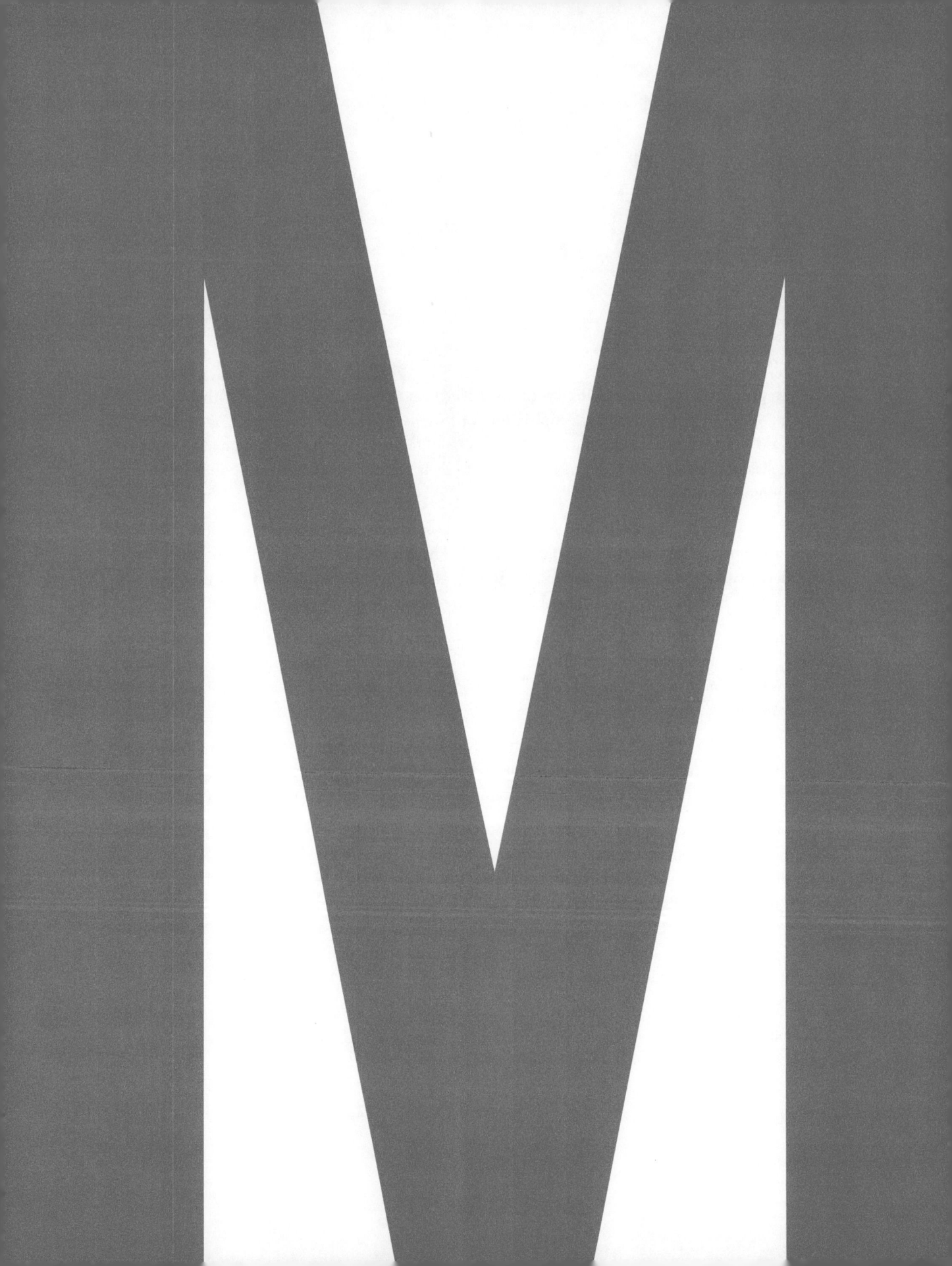

1

Pursuing Excellence and Unrivalled Outcomes

[Dedicated to the memory of Ben 1970 – 2017]

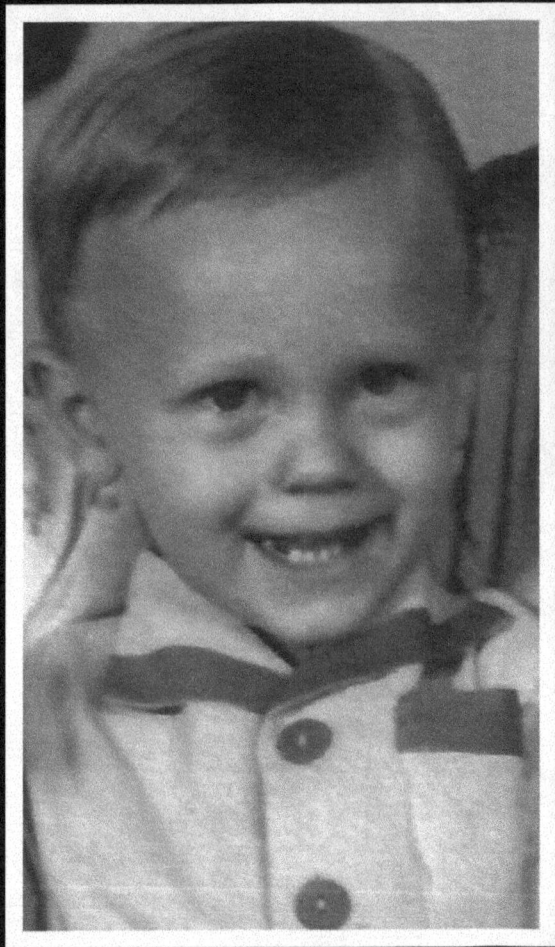

"Don't be afraid of the unknown - each day is an unknown."

You probably wouldn't know this man if he passed you in the street. He flies under the radar and he's perfectly comfortable with that. He is just as comfortable with the knowledge that financial success was never a priority – but being the best in his chosen field, was. However, in his quest to be the best he created one of the finest swimming pool manufacturing companies in the Southern Hemisphere, if not the world and so financial success was simply part of that package.

For him wealth was purely a means to an end; to do what he wanted to do but also and more importantly, to work every day with his children who under his guidance, developed into industry leaders themselves. Together they built a business without peer, anywhere in the world. It was that opportunity and achievement that brought him his greatest joy. But it didn't come without its challenges and disappointments. Only sheer will and ability allowed him to traverse the highs and lows he encountered on his journey to achieve great business success. Nothing it seemed could dull his spirit and determination… until heartbreak drove him to his knees.

He is a proud family man, he is a shrewd businessman, a thinker, an entrepreneur; he is the man behind Aqua Technics, Buccaneer Swimming Pools and Sapphire Pools, he is…

Lew Beale

Lew was a man born ordinary into an equally ordinary Australian family but the events that led to the birth of that family were far from ordinary. They were events based on panic, devastation and despair – the far-reaching consequences of the Great Depression of 1929. That was the year that crumbled hopes, shattered dreams and ruined lives. But if not for the adversities generated from those turbulent years, Wilhelmina (Willa) O'Rourke and Lewis (Lew) Dring Beale may never have met.

Far from the suavely suited brokers of Wall Street, the people of Perth, Western Australia were being drawn into the vortex of the greatest stock market crash in world history. To escape mounting unemployment and poverty many people headed to the north-west of the country in search of work. For that reason it was in Wyndham, a coastal town in the Kimberly, that Willa and Lew senior first met, fell in love and became Mr and Mrs Beale.

Their daughter, Robin, arrived first and then, six years later, on the 15th of June 1946, Lew made his entrance into the world. Both Willa and Lew senior were great role models for their children, and whilst they had limited education, the couple were determined to build a good life.

Lew senior took work wherever he could find it; hauling sides of beef on his shoulder from the cool room down to the state ships berthed at the Wyndham Jetty; or on road maintenance, manually loading and unloading his old Side Banger Ford truck with heavy blue metal, made hot from the ferocious Wyndham sun. It was hard manual labour. Watching his dad struggle in the heat taught young Lew a valuable lesson – never shy away from hard work. Equally ingrained was his father's frequently voiced statement, "It's better to overwork your brain than your back." Lew was equally influenced by his mother, a very determined and capable woman. Willa taught him the enormous value of developing your skill set to optimise your opportunities and role in life. As a wizard on the manual typewriter with 120 words a minute, she acquired the auspicious role of personal secretary to the general manager of the Wyndham Meatworks. She was smart and astute and very proud of her claim to not only be the first woman in Western Australia to receive equal pay to a man, but just as significantly, the first woman to go to work without stockings. A courageous act for the era!

For the first six years of his childhood, life for Lew was idyllic. His favourite memories are of the wet season. There were exciting trips to Perth aboard the state ship Koolinda that connected the North-west to the outside world and gave families the opportunity to escape the uncomfortable conditions of the season. Thanks to his mother's work, the Beale family would house sit the general manager's mansion when he was away. Lew remembers it was an old stately home with a bowling green, tennis court and full-sized billiard table – certainly something a young impressionable lad might aspire to.

The mansion still stands today, but in the 1980's crocodiles became the new residents of the gardens and the old tennis court when the grounds became home to the Wyndham Crocodile Farm. Crocodiles were abundant in the area, so perhaps it was the crocodile infested waters that surrounded Wyndham that sparked Lew's interest in swimming pools; a thought not beyond the realms of possible.

School life began in Wyndham at the local primary school, but just as Lew was about to enter Third Grade his family packed up and headed for the big smoke. Lew's first experience at school in the city was at St Patrick's, a graceful building which once stood proudly at the end of Perth's Murray Street (it has since been demolished). It was then on to Christian Brothers College (CBC) set on the corner of St Georges Terrace and Victoria Avenue, Perth. CBC was a big change to the small school in Wyndham – but Lew fitted in wherever he went. He would no doubt have finished his schooling at CBC, however, Perth City Council had other plans for the prominent corner site.

Perth had been selected to host the Empire Games in 1962. In preparation for this major event the council purchased CBC in 1961 to enable both roads abutting the school to be widened. Subsequently the school, its staff and students were relocated just down the road to a site with considerable open space and a spectacular position on the banks of the Swan River. The new location, brand-new buildings and facilities called for a new crest, a new motto 'In Nomine Domini' and a brand-new name. On the 25th of March 1962, the very modern Trinity College officially opened its doors and welcomed 830 schoolboys, including Lew.

Lew was a naturally clever student. He does wonder however, if he had bothered to open a few books every now and then, how much better he might have done. But school didn't particularly interest Lew – attendance was simply to pass the exams and to have a good time. Regularly his parents' voices played over in his mind – "The sooner you start the sooner you finish", or "No task is insurmountable". However, for Lew, like so many young men before and since, his parents' words were largely ignored. Many years later he realised how much truth was in them and again wondered – what if he had listened?

Lew's school days were soon drawing to an end. Being 'one of the lads' was still paramount, so Lew had given little thought to what he would do next? Not an unusual position to find yourself in at 17. Fortunately, as somewhat of a mathematics and science whiz, studying the two at the University of Western Australia (UWA) seemed like a natural path to take. Good grades were all he needed to be accepted.

Lew achieved what he needed to gain entry into UWA but surprisingly, considering the effort he put in, his grades were also good enough to earn him a Commonwealth scholarship.

It was a great achievement; however, the scholarship was means tested. Lew was shocked to learn that, with both his parents working, he was ineligible to receive a living allowance. That meant his fees would be paid but there would be (in Lew's words) no beer or car money. That was not going to work for Lew – he had to find a solution. He did. Lew discovered that if he studied to be a teacher, he would receive a teacher's bursary. The bursary would support his social life, car and studies – in that order of priority. While teaching wasn't on Lew's list of preferences it was a solution to what would otherwise be an unendurable lifestyle. All he had to do was attend Claremont Teachers College and UWA at the same time. It was an easy decision and once made, his tertiary life began.

Again, achieving good grades came with relatively little effort. For Lew it was as had always been his practice, get the job done as quickly as possible and move on to the next thing.

> [Lew] I became excellent at most things, brilliant at none and that was cool for me. But I always knew I had fuel left in the tank and now on reflection, look back on what could have been if I had applied myself totally to one chosen field. In my early years I never pushed myself through the pain barrier.
>
> In my last year at school I remember being at athletics training. We had the 800-metre trials but I was a sprinter and so 200 metres was my mental limit. We had a state champion in our class for the 800 metres and I was pitted against him for this race. I idled around the first 400 metres and ended up nearly 50 metres behind him.
>
> As I was running, I thought to myself should I give this a crack – then launched into sprint mode. I chased him down and almost caught him, only to fall short by two metres.
>
> I fell to the ground exhausted; unable to walk. I never raced over that distance again but I was so close … and just maybe. It still haunts me today. Should I have had another go?

It still haunts me today. Should I have had another go?

What might Lew have achieved if he had gone back and had another go? What if he had applied himself fully to one chosen field? Clearly, he will always wonder. Regret is something most of us experience at some point in our lives. Why? Why do we make the choices that don't sit quite right with us? Is it that life gets so busy that we don't stop to think about our actions or why we are taking them?

As Lew reflected on his past, I was reminded of the phrase, 'If only I knew then what I know now', and wondered why it is that when we are young, we don't often listen to those who have been down the road before us. What might we achieve if we did?

However, for Lew there were simply too many distractions in those heady days of uni, too much fun to be had, girls to be wooed and beer to be drunk. There was also sport to be played. Lew was fit and fast; a bit like a roo dog is how he describes his younger self. Athletics was his choice of sport until he became bigger and stronger and more prepared for the physical contact of team sports. Today golf is his chosen sport and apparently, he is just as competitive now as he was back then.

On the day Australia switched from the imperial system to metric, Lew took his first step as a teacher into his classroom at Northcliffe Junior High School. It was the 14th of February 1966.

[Lew]   I knew absolutely nothing about teaching. I thought the training we received at Clare-mont Teachers College was futile as it concentrated on aims and objectives. If you did not pass the spelling test you did not make it to the classroom. What about teaching us how to teach?

Luckily, I knew the metric system backwards and I was given the task of introducing and educating the entire senior school on the metric system. It was relatively simple to comprehend so it was an easy topic to begin my days of teaching.

Lew's classroom was the school's washroom. A blackboard ran down one wall, hand basins ran down the opposite wall and in the middle were enough desks to seat 15 pupils. After two weeks of teaching himself to teach, he had it mastered – or so he thought. However, the teaching inspectors and superintendents didn't agree with Lew's opinion of his teaching ability.

[Lew]   I never liked being told what to do by my superiors, which was clearly evident when my teaching was being adjudicated. I was probably very annoying to them, but I felt, who were they anyway, their opinion was not important to me. It was probably this attitude that was the driving force that compelled me to become my own boss; where I could be accountable only to myself and the laws of society.

Over the next two years Lew taught mathematics and science at a level never before attempted at Northcliffe Junior High, achieving 100 per cent pass rates. He was clearly a great teacher and he loved it, but something was missing. As the days rolled on, Lew became more and more restless. Not only did he find surviving on $45 a week a near impossibility (his love of the good times hadn't diminished), but also the mathematics senior master was having a defining influence on how he saw his teaching future.

[Lew]   The senior master was a really nice person, a very contented man. He would arrive at school each day dressed in a white shirt with a tie, a grey cardigan and carrying a brown paper bag filled with two sandwiches for his lunch. It was the same every day. He was meant to be my role model, someone I should aspire to, but even though he was a nice man, the thought of me ending up like him really scared me.

One day I was sitting in the staff room looking around at the other teachers, when it hit me that if I worked really hard this was as good as it was going to get. Maybe I might become the mathematics senior master, maybe the deputy-headmaster, or if I finished my degree the headmaster – 30 years down the track, that is.

The knock of dull monotony and lack of opportunity was getting louder and louder. No more than a week after his staff room pondering Lew made a life changing decision. He resigned from the Education Department. With that resignation came the eradication of any possibility of a grey cardigan ever making it into Lew's wardrobe.

Learning to listen and act on your gut instinct usually comes with age and experience but for Lew it came at 23.

Not long after he resigned, teachers' salaries increased by 20 per cent and within three years, went up a further 30 per cent. If teachers' salaries had increased during his time in front of the classroom Lew may well have continued in the role.

But it seems destiny had other plans. In his first year after leaving the teaching profession he had more than doubled his previous salary – and he had a company car thrown into the mix as well. Perhaps there is something in those words – life begins when you step outside your comfort zone. For Lew that certainly was the case.

In his early life to earn a bit of extra cash on Saturdays and during school holidays, Lew had worked in a car wrecking yard. So, with that experience and no other opportunities in sight he went to work for his brother-in-law, Peter Gardner, in his house demolition and car wrecking business. It wasn't ideal but from the day he started, Lew never looked back.

> [Lew]   It was a good steppingstone that allowed me to move on. It certainly gave me great product knowledge and taught me some valuable management skills that I have applied ever since, but it had limited opportunities not to mention it's a dirty, piecemeal business.

It was during his time in this industry that Lew learned a truly valuable lesson – what not to do in life and in business!

> [Lew]   You meet all sorts in motor wrecking, but I remember this one chap. I won't mention names, but he turned out to be a really shady, unsavoury bloke. I guess you could say I had a short-term glimpse of the dark side and I didn't like what I saw. Some of the things he did were very wrong. I knew then without question I would never get involved in issues outside the law and would always make sure everything I did was upfront and honest. So, as much as I didn't like it, it was a good way to learn a lesson – not by getting into trouble or doing anything wrong, rather, learning from observing other people's actions and how I reacted to them.
>
> I'd had a good Christian upbringing and knew right from wrong, but I also think about karma – that one day, if you do something wrong, it's going to come back around and bite you on the backside. Some people don't think about that, they don't care, they have no conscience. Some of them make a lot of money doing the wrong thing – but are they happy with themselves? I don't know.

So, car wrecking wasn't to be Lew's lifelong career, it didn't inspire him, but it did provide a platform for insight and knowledge that proved enormously beneficial in his next career move.

> [Lew]   Everything I have done taught me something that enabled me to move to the next step – that's why I believe you should always be open to every opportunity that comes your way. I have always been a bit of an opportunist ready for the right break in life, and it's proven a worthwhile trait.

Lew left the wrecking business to take a job at Repco Carbon Brakes, Perth's biggest brake, clutch and automatic transmission repair organisation. With the knowledge gained from his previous employment he took to the job quickly and within 12 months was managing Fremantle, the largest of the branches.

Everything I have done taught me something that enabled me to move to the next step - always be open to every opportunity that comes your way.

[Lew]   I found management quite easy, so it must be somewhat of an innate thing as I'd had no formal training. I've since learned that when it comes to good management skills it's really important to be a good delegator – it's the only way to have people working consistently under you. Delegation came naturally to me!

Some people don't trust others to do the job well, so they don't let go. But you have to get past that. Give others a go, set someone the task, keep an eye on them until you are 100 per cent sure they can handle the job, and if they can't, address it immediately. You also need to be able to identify what the job will entail and then put in the practices and procedures that enable it to progress efficiently – on time, on budget – that sort of thing. And ensure that you have the resources to complete the task.

You must have the vision of where you need to get to – sometimes it's not going to be your vision if you're working for someone else, but then it's your duty to understand and implement their vision, the same as if it is your own business.

While working at Repco, Lew's brother-in-law sold his successful car body building company to Bell Brothers. He subsequently purchased a company located in Kenwick that was in liquidation. The name Sydren Pty Ltd, gave no indication they were manufacturers of one-piece, hand-made fibreglass swimming pools so Peter was quick to rename the company Sapphire Plastics Pty Ltd, trading as Sapphire Pools.

In November 1973 Lew left Repco to work for his brother-in-law as an installation supervisor. It didn't take him long to work his way up to installation manager.

It was at this time that Perth was becoming the choice destination for migrating Brits. With pre-approved house and land finance packages, they arrived ready to spend. It was a great market opportunity for any business ready with a product to meet the needs of the new arrivals. Sapphire Pools not only had the product but they had just opened a new display centre in High Road Willetton. The centre was around the corner from the suburbs of Parkwood and Lynwood, the major nesting ground for the new British migrants. It wasn't easy to adjust to Perth heat, and so installing a swimming pool in the back garden was the perfect solution to surviving the hot Australian summers.

[Lew]   In those days we could install a small pool in your backyard for around $1,000 to

$1,500. With their finance already organised, we almost couldn't keep up with the demand. We sold and installed thousands of pools in the area. Talk about being in the right place at the right time.

In opposition to Sapphire Pools was FON Pools, named after a legend of the swimming pool industry, Frank O'Neil. In 1976 two of FON's ex-employees went out on their own and started a company they named Aqua Technics. It started small but they were soon manufacturing more than 50 pools a year.

In 1978 Lew's brother-in-law sold Sapphire Pools to another company, Taylor Made Pools. After the sale, Lew stayed on for a further four months, but without any allegiance to the new owners he was open to an approach by Ross Townsend and Andy Niikkula of Aqua Technics.

[Lew]   Ross and Andy asked if I would join them as a minor shareholder. They were keen to have my experience in operations, sales and marketing which I had gained from being with a much larger company. I knew and respected them both. Ross was an engineer and Andy a genius with fibreglass – there wasn't anything he couldn't do with it. Their skills together with mine made for a good combination and so I felt it would be a great partnership.

Being the person I am, I probably would have moved into my own business eventually anyway, but this was a perfect opportunity to get involved in a very new venture whose future would depend on how well I applied myself. In fact, it felt really awesome to think that I finally had the opportunity to use everything I'd learned and apply it to a company that I had a personal interest in.

It was immediately evident to Lew that there were two areas within the business that needed significant improvement – sales and product range – both needed to be increased. He worked out a plan of how to make that happen and then executed it with precision.

[Lew]   We upped the advertising in press and radio. I employed a full-time salesman to effectively work on the leads that were generated from the advertising. At the time we had two pool shapes. From one of those, the 24-footer, we extended to 29 foot because our opposition already had one and it was very popular in rural areas. We made our pool a better design, it had more features, was structurally sound and technically superior – when it hit the market it was a huge success.

Advanced Technology in Fibreglass Swimming Pools was a motto we used – we pushed it from day one. None of our opposition had used that approach, they only came from a price-based position. In order to extrapolate yourself from a price-based product you need to offer a better quality product, better quality service – we did that and we were only a fraction more expensive than the rest of the competition.

It's easy to build the best pool in the world but what's the point if no one can afford it.

It was paramount to get the advertising right. As Lew points out advertising was and still is essential in their business. You can have the best product and facilities but if no one knows about it, it's pointless.

> [Lew] We've been the industry advertiser for at least 30 years and over that time we've come to realise that whilst we can't capitalise on 100 per cent of our marketing dollar, we do know that if we stop or reduce our advertising, then sales leads reduce and consequently the business suffers.
>
> The swimming pool industry has always been a very tough and difficult industry. What I did come to understand during those early years was, to really survive not only do you have to be the best at what you do, but you also have to be the market leader. So that was my goal. Now we believe we are the best and we are definitely the market leaders. This is a great position to be in – leading the way is so much better than following, waiting for others to come up with the ideas, the technology, the innovations.

To really survive, not only do you have to be the best at what you do, but you also have to be the market leader.

Fresh ideas and innovations often evolve from a crisis into an opportunity, but for that to occur you have to be aware and prepared to find the solution to the crisis. Lew was always prepared and aware, and in this next instance – pun intended here – he paved the way for others to follow.

> [Lew] When brick paving became very popular around pools it butted up to the fibreglass edge beam. It looked awful, so we introduced two-toned pools, where the pool itself was blue but the top was an ivory colour; it then blended beautifully with the paving and became very popular. That idea was born from a problem we were confronted with when we sent a blue pool north to the Pilbara. The Pilbara's red pindan soil is magnificent, but it penetrates everything – your car, your clothes, your fibreglass swimming pool! The pindan was staining the top of the pool and we couldn't get it out. So, we experimented by sending up a pool with a two-toned edge beam to blend with the pindan – it worked. So, what was a problem, turned into marketing opportunity – we do that all the time and it's that kind of thinking that has positioned us as market leader.
>
> We introduced steps, ribs and racing lanes – no one else did those extra little things. We also introduced the first fibreglass kidney shaped pool into Western Australia. There were a few peanut shaped pools available, but they weren't balanced correctly and so were not appealing. Being a mathematician, it wasn't that difficult to get the correct radiuses and balances, so I came up with a couple of really good designs. These days everyone is saying how ghastly they are and ripping them out, but in the '70s and '80s they were all the rage. Every landscaping book you picked up was full of rock waterfalls and lagoon pools surrounded by Toodyay stone – oh and always a few palm trees. We've now destroyed the moulds but who knows maybe they might want them again in 20 years!

We turned a problem into a marketing opportunity - that kind of thinking has positioned us as market leader.

Lew was constantly on the lookout for new ideas, new trends or, if there was a problem, the solution. One such problem was the quality of the raw material used to manufacture early fibreglass swimming pools. The technology and structure of the pool struggled to withstand the rigorous attack from pool chemicals and pool water, and often "osmotic blistering" was an unsightly and unacceptable result.

[Lew]   There was a method used to build a pool, some still use it, but it's 30 or 40-year-old technology. We wanted to be able to manufacture a pool without all the problems like osmotic blistering. So, we invested heavily in research and development whilst knowing we had to avoid our costs escalating or we wouldn't be able to sell our product. We found the solution. We completely changed the way we built the structure and the technology without overly increasing our costs. We were then able to offer a better pool, one that didn't blister, one that would last longer, with extended and better warranties but at the same price as the lesser quality of our competitor's pool.

This technology gave Aqua Technics the edge. As a better pool at a competitive price it met with approval from the male buyer. However, Lew was aware he needed to offer "that something extra" to satisfy the female side of the decision-making process.

[Lew]   Women have a very big influence in buying pools so if you can relate to the feminine aspect – the aesthetic qualities – and meet the functionality and price expectations of the male then you are more likely to secure a sale. You should always know who's making the decision to buy your product – in our case it's often the female. We realised that a pool would keep the kids at home – just where the mum likes them to be. We've seen this time and again over the last 40-odd years. By putting a swimming pool in your backyard your kids are happy to stay at home rather than go to someone else's place where they might not be supervised.

You should always know who's making the decision to buy your product.

It was the determination to identify and understand their customer that drove Aqua Technics to have the largest range of finishes and colour options of any pool company in Australia; brilliant colours, marble, granite, quartz finishes, and pavers that sailed over the edge of the water to create a truly magnificent finish. No longer could fibreglass pools be considered boring. Aqua Technics had taken the backyard pool from being purely functional to be the central focus and feature of a garden.

In Lew's view, if your goal is to be a market leader then you need to be the one setting the trends. You also need to be five steps ahead of your competitors in ideas and innovations, live and breathe your business and read and watch everything about your industry. Making that effort will give you the best opportunity to become completely in tune with your product, your customer and their decision-making process. No doubt a few personal strengths don't go astray either.

[Lew] It's easy to build the best pool in the world but what's the point if no one can afford it. So, during those first years of growth it was imperative to provide the very best quality product at a very competitive price. That's what we focused on and that's what we achieved. We also knew we needed to improve our service but at the time we had to accept we just couldn't afford to. There was no money to put on that extra PR person or extra serviceman – we had to do the best with the resources we had. But despite our efforts, sometimes that wasn't enough. We were expanding, and any spare capital went back into the business and into development.

Ours is not a business where you simply buy something and then resell it with no expenses in between, other than marketing. Ours is a capital-intensive business, where we do everything from concept to manufacturing the raw materials, manufacturing the prototypes – everything – all the way to servicing the finished product in the field.

Clearly the fibreglass swimming pool industry is not for the faint-hearted and over the years Aqua Technics has seen plenty of the competition come and go.

[Lew] Perth, as one of the world's most isolated cities, has a small population, but it's a Mecca for owner-businesses and entrepreneurs wanting to have a crack. So, competition is fierce for those dependent on that one small market for survival.

If you have a great concept here in WA, within 12 months the market is swamped with similar concepts. So, you have to be constantly innovating and evolving and you have to be the best. My philosophy by necessity in those early days was to be as good as you can be – failure was never an option. Just quietly, fear of failure was a major driving force to being successful. The great Harold Clough once said to me – Nothing motivates a man more than the needle of bankruptcy in your butt.

For Lew, like so many great achievers, it was never about the success of reaching the destination, it was about surviving the journey – to survive he had to become better than all the opposition.

In 1984 the company, in its continued drive for excellence, set out on the quality management path. After a mammoth input of time and resources they achieved the ultimate recognition. Aqua Technics became the first fibreglass swimming pool company in Western Australia to have a quality endorsed product certified to Australian Standards. It was a great achievement and perhaps why part owner, Ross Townshend, chose that same year to sell his share of the company to Lew and head off overseas on a new venture.

The business continued to improve and grow, as did Perth; becoming better known as a great place to live and do business. It was the era of the entrepreneur. In 1983, Alan Bond and his wing-keeled,

Australia II, had taken the America's Cup from the clutches of the New York Yacht Club (NYYC). The NYYC had successfully defended and held the cup for 132 years and as such were unaccustomed to defeat. They launched a full-scale challenge. By 1987 the challenge was in full throttle in the port city of Fremantle. Dennis Connor, skipper aboard USA's Stars and Stripes, fought to win back the cup he'd lost four years earlier. By February he had achieved his goal with a 4-0 win, but despite the disappointing outcome for Australia, Perth was forever changed.

The America's Cup challenge made 1987 an unforgettable year for so many West Australians but for Lew it will be always remembered for other reasons.

On the last race day of the America's Cup, the 4th of February 1987, Lew married the love of his life, Lesley. It was a momentous occasion, but the year had even more to give. A few months after their wedding Lew took over full ownership of Aqua Technics when Andy Niikkula, Lew's only remaining partner, agreed to sell his share of the company.

It was a significant milestone for Lew who, through hard work and extraordinary determination had achieved a momentous outcome – his own family business. It was May, and for Lew at that moment, 1987 was establishing itself as a very good year. That was until Monday the 20th of October dawned.

In Australia it would be remembered as Black Monday. The day Wall Street went into meltdown, when the Dow Jones lost 22.6 per cent of its value, or to make it easier to relate to (perhaps) $500 billion. Panic and fear spread as global stock markets opened around the world. By the end of the day the Australian stock market had plummeted 25 per cent leaving the country in shock and in fear.

Having just taken over the business it was the last thing Lew expected or indeed was prepared for. The impact on sales was horrendous. Fortunately, the downturn was relatively short-lived and while many other companies did topple and sink, Aqua Technics continued to swim towards the '90s, albeit into shark infested waters.

By 1989 for many, the crash of '87 was a distant memory. Australia had all but recovered and was enjoying the spoils made possible by the banks' eagerness to lend. In an attempt to slow a fast-moving economy, the country saw cash rates rise to over 17 per cent, pushing overdraft interest rates for some to more than 22 per cent. When you consider what they are today (the cash rate in January 2019 was 1.5 per cent) you have to wonder how any business managed to survive. No doubt for many it was like living on the painful edge of a very sharp knife; something had to give. It did. By late 1990 Australia and the rest of the world was well and truly in the depths of recession. It was triggered in part by the excesses of the '80s, high debt and the pressure of high interest rates on businesses mortgaged to the hilt. Australia's treasurer, Paul Keating's famous phrase, "It's the recession we had to have", rubbed salt into the already deep wounds of those unable to meet their loan repayments, as companies fell, and unemployment rose to a staggering 10.8 per cent.

[Lew] The swimming pool industry, like so many others, is market sensitive so when customers find themselves in the middle of a recession, buying luxuries like a swimming pool is the last thing on their shopping list. For business owners it becomes about making it through the hard times.

"Don't be in a business if you can't be in it by lunchtime," was a very wise statement made to me by a well-oiled American in the '80s. Luckily, I had taken his advice on board and concentrated heavily on Western Australia. We were, therefore, somewhat prepared for the bad times – like in the recession we had to have. I had observed many high-flying companies that were so successful but came apart at the seams because they were too highly leveraged or grew too rapidly and didn't have the resources to manage their growth. That's why I believe it is so important not to leverage yourself or your company beyond your serviceable limits – but it's where people go wrong, time and again.

> *Don't leverage yourself or your company beyond your serviceable limits - it's where people go wrong, time and again.*

It's during these times that advertising becomes even more important. Even though you might be hurting, as we were amidst the recession, you have to be very careful about cutting it back altogether as some do because it's essential you continue to show a presence. When the market returns, those who have maintained their presence in a depressed market will be top of mind and recognised – to have survived the tough times they must be good. But it's also important not to overspend on advertising during these periods – it needs to be managed very carefully. Discard anything peripheral like sponsorships or branding exercises and advertise very specifically in a way that offers your customer a return on their spend. If you just wave a flag saying, "Here I am", they will simply say, "So what" and turn away. Give them something in the tough times and they'll respond.

Despite careful management and control, Aqua Technics, like most companies during the recession, lost money. How could they not when interest and overdraft rates were crippling. Again, it was sink or swim but Lew, who had always been hands on, managed to steer the company through the murky waters into 1991. The year when two of his greatest joys in life were finally ready to join him at the helm.

[Lew] My children Ben and Lynley used to come in after school, on weekends and during the school holidays to earn some pocket money. They both took a real interest in what was going on which made me very happy. In 1991 after completing his degree in business and commerce at university, Ben joined the company. I couldn't have been happier to have him on board. His exceptional negotiation skills enabled us to secure some very good deals to freight our pools around the world, an essential aspect of our business. Lynley was still at uni but regardless of her workload she was still very involved and interested in what was going on in Aqua Technics.

One day Lynley said to me, "Dad, everything about this business is in your head but no one else knows what's in your head so we need to get it down on paper."

Lynley's comments started a paper-intensive pursuit to become a quality endorsed company. Unlike their earlier endorsement this included both the product and the company. In 1992 they became the first fibreglass business in Australia to be a quality endorsed company with a certified quality management system known as ISO 9000. It was a mammoth undertaking and achievement and for Lew it was an acknowledgment of his years of relentless pursuit of excellence and technical expertise. For Ben and Lynley it meant all Lew's business secrets, technology and processes that he had stored for so long in his head, were now safely on paper for them to both understand and implement.

By 1994, Lynley, having finished uni, joined Lew and Ben, and by the mid-nineties Aqua Technics had firmly taken its position as market leader, where it remains today.

"Dad, everything about this business is in your head but no one else knows what's in your head so we need to get it down on paper."

[Lew]   Ben and Lynley bought to the company university degrees in business and commerce along with modern techniques of applying marketing and business management, commerce and HR. With the application of their knowledge, together with mine, we refined the company to what it is today. They took on the day-to-day aspects of running the business enabling me the freedom to concentrate more on the development side.

One of the areas I was very aware needed improvement was in service because ours simply wasn't good enough. Word of mouth is so, so important. In those early days people used to say they were very satisfied with the product but the service was lacking. At that time, we were just scrambling to do what we needed – so there wasn't any surplus cash to spoil our customers with – like a bottle of champagne, half a dozen beach towels or pool lounges waiting at the end of the contract. However, as the business got bigger and better and we started making money, we were able to reinvest it back into the service we provided.

Constantly seeking improvement and a desire for excellence, we found a very useful tool within the ISO 9000 management system – a process called Continuous Improvement. It's a reporting system through which if a mistake, a loss or wastage occurs in the field or in the factory, a staff member or contractor submits a report, so the problem can be identified, addressed and corrected.

One of the things about a quality endorsed certified system is that you can guarantee if you are making a mistake, you will continue to make that same mistake, because it's embedded in the system. That's why the Continuous Improvement aspect really works because it allows you to quickly identify where the mistakes are being made and address them.

Two months after introducing the system we hadn't received a single report, so we called a meeting. We found out that no one wanted to 'dob in' a work mate for screwing up and costing the company money. I completely understood. We made a few changes that allowed staff to report how and where the system was failing and not the person. From that moment on we were swamped with reports.

As a result of Lew's awareness and empathy with his staff he understood that the phrasing of the system was where the issue lay. By changing a few words, reapplying its direction and providing greater clarification, they were able to craft a very rewarding and successful system. More importantly, it engendered a more responsible, united and loyal workforce.

[Lew] A lot of companies don't go down the quality endorsement path because it is such a paper intensive process and many simply don't have the resources to do it. So, while I understand the limitations, I believe unquestionably, every company should make itself aware and apply the basic principles of the system – whether you become fully certified or not.

One of the most significant lessons Lew learnt along the way occurred in the mid-nineties when the company, now known as Aquatic Leisure Technologies, purchased a gelcoat manufacturing facility in Villawood in Sydney.

[Lew] Our intention in purchasing the gelcoat company was to compete with large suppliers, but the business model was doomed from the start. Perhaps I should have listened to my own advice as the business was in the western suburbs of Sydney, and being a remote business, I could not be there by lunchtime. It was a struggle for a number of reasons. My partner in that business was making some bad decisions. Unbeknown to us both at the time he had a brain tumour and eventually left the business. We were giving credit when probably we shouldn't have, but you try to make these things work. We ended up shutting the business down in 1998. We then brought the skeletal remains back to Perth where we set up our own gelcoat batching facility. We were able to add value to the business and be more unique in the Western Australian market by producing our own extensive range of colours and textured finishes. Rather than just buy our gelcoat from a restricted range, as was being offered by the suppliers, our product was freshly batched every day and we were unlimited in what we could offer. It was possible to design a new colour and have it in production within a week.

Once we had established the new gel coating batching facility, we started making our own gelcoats and colours. We did everything in-house, and because we weren't relying on outside suppliers to give us the materials, we were able to increase our range to 60 different colours. We might have failed in Sydney but if we hadn't gone there and learnt the art of manufacturing and batching for ourselves, the technology would never have been exposed to us. That experience has been of inherent value to our company, as was the decision to stop manufacturing and to stop supplying our opposition and other gelcoat users. By taking those steps we have created a business without peer – it might never have happened if not for the failure of the Villawood facility.

We have created a business without peer - it might never have happened if not for the failure of the Villawood facility.

Stock market crashes, debilitating interest rates, recession and business failures would, for many, lead to enormous stress and sleepless nights. Not so for Lew. It is an ability to sleep, regardless of the level of stress one is enduring, that appears to be a shared trait of the truly successful entrepreneurs.

[Lew]   I always sleep well. I can take a nana nap just about anywhere – which I think really helps keep the mind clear. I can also handle a degree of stress – a bit of stress is good. The saying, 'Don't sweat the small stuff', is so appropriate. In times of adversity I tend to work better because I'm forced into doing, into making things happen. That is so much better than just floating along in the good times because that's when you become complacent – and one thing I know for sure, you must never become complacent. You must always be looking to improve your business, looking ahead to where the company will be in the years to come. You have to have growth, because if you don't, it will just plateau and after a period of plateau it will decline – so make sure you or your business are never in that situation.

It was with his understanding of the need for growth that Lew decided to deviate from his core line of business and enter the marine industry. It was 1997.

[Lew]   This decision to deviate from our core business evolved from us believing, if we could successfully manufacture fibreglass pools then we should be able to successfully manufacture fibreglass boats. However, that's just the beginning. Making a boat is one thing but then you have to sell it. Ninety per cent of the market is on the east coast of Australia and we didn't have any expertise in selling over there. Dealers were reluctant to help as they had sweetheart deals already set up. They would only buy if the price was well below par. Eventually, we purchased a small marine business ourselves through which we could market our own product. That business wasn't big enough, so we had to build it up.

To do this we acquired big agencies in the US – Sea Ray Boats and Boston Whaler Boats. At one stage we were the biggest Boston Whaler dealership outside of the US. To acknowledge our position and to say thank you, Boston Whaler took Dean (my son-in-law and manager of Challenge Marine) and I to Costa Rica on a fishing trip – we didn't do very well with the fishing but as father and son-in-law and in business together we had a really great time.

The perks of being in business for yourself! Entering the marine industry was, as Lew described, 'right at the time', but why you should never deviate from your core line of business is one lesson he would prefer not to have learned in the way he did. But more on that when we reach 2007. Right now, it's 1998 during which Lew makes another purchase – and a very sentimental one at that.

[Lew]   Sapphire Pools, the company once owned by my brother-in-law and where my pool presence had begun, was in financial decline. So, in 1998 I decided to buy its assets and integrate the company into Aqua Technics. Lynley and I spent many long hours negotiating the acquisition.

It was good to be in a position that enabled us to take under our wing what was once our family company, plus it increased our market share by 10 per cent. We then acquired, in 2001, Buccaneer Pools. This again increased our market share by a further 10 per cent.

We kept both names. Some people asked why we didn't change them to Aqua Technics, but you would never do that. Why would you change something you've just paid a huge amount to acquire and where millions of dollars have been previously spent on marketing and branding? Football legend-cum-radio and TV personality Wattsie did a commercial for Buccaneer Pools: "Where's your Buccaneers?" was incredibly well known, and then there was the slogan: "Wouldn't you rather be in a Buccaneer pool?" Everyone knew them. So, if we had gone in and put Aqua Technics' signs over the top of Sapphire and Buccaneer, it would have been meaningless. The cumulative benefit of the three companies would have been far less if we had joined them together rather than leaving them separate.

Why change the name of something you've just paid a huge amount to acquire when millions of dollars have been spent on marketing and branding?

In Western Australia the bottom dweller tends to pull the top ones down. We didn't want that to happen – we would rather lift them up than pull the good ones down. The Aqua Technics pool is the highest selling pool, so we elevated Buccaneer and Sapphire with quality advertising, we improved their shapes and designs and the quality of the pool itself. Now we have 50 per cent of the total fibreglass market. Fortunately, our market opportunities are always expanding because there are more homes built in Western Australia than swimming pools installed.

The main opposition we now have is with what people choose to spend their money on – home theatres, travel, air conditioners, second car, a boat – it's not a matter of if you want a pool, it's where does it fit on the list of priorities.

The buying spree continued. Aqua Technics had introduced the first range of spa baths to the West Australian market back in the early '80s so it seemed like the right decision to purchase the very well known Jadan Spas when it went into administration in 2003.

[Lew]   It was a "just okay" business but it was diminishing, and we saw that pretty quickly. The Chinese had a big influence over the market and we ended up having our spas made in China. We then transported them to Australia where we sold them with a 30 per cent greater margin than if we were to manufacture them here ourselves.

During this period the pool business was as strong as ever, but a change to pool fencing regulations was causing a few ripples in the industry. By 2006 anyone with a pool in their garden was required, by law, to install barriers to restrict access. This significantly impacted on pool sales as people adjusted to the idea and the expense of installing compliant fencing. It was just another challenging encounter and Lew had experienced plenty of those.

However, it was the next line in the list of challenges that had a far greater impact.

It was December 2007 when suddenly retail sales in Western Australia fell dramatically. A new prime minister and four interest rate hikes were held responsible. Kevin Rudd had just taken over the reins of Australia. By 2008 the Global Financial Crisis (GFC) was in full force and leaving a trail of destruction as it spread across continents.

In the tough times you must react very, very quickly and make the hard-hitting decisions. The company must survive because a lot of people are relying on it.

[Lew] Interest rates went through the roof – again – because that's how they handle monetary policy. I remember our sales in the marine and pool business were the worst we'd ever experienced. Australia was on its way into a retail recession before the GFC really hit in 2008, so it was like a double whack with a sledgehammer, especially after the excesses of the boom times in 2005 and 2006.

The US economy had crashed, and thousands of fire-sale boats were being imported into WA. Suddenly, sales in our marine business fell by 80 per cent but we were locked into international dealer agreements and costly land leases that were impossible to maintain in the economic climate. The business never recovered, and we systematically reduced our stock levels until we could afford to liquidate it all – a nasty hit to take in an already depressed market. We gradually paid off all our creditors and closed the business down while holding our heads high knowing that we did not leave anyone, other than us, out of pocket.

Marine business – SOLD!!

The spa business was much the same dropping to 25 per cent of its previous turnover. Lew believes that whilst China was a major contributor to the futility of the spa business, it was 'Kevin 07' and the GFC that pushed the business down the proverbial plughole.

Spa business – SOLD!!

[Lew] Never think just because you excel in one business it will give you a free passage into a similar industry – it simply doesn't work that way.

Their core swimming pool business was able to carry them through the losses. However, the horrendous cost and destruction of the GFC as it careered around the globe, eventually engulfed that company too and that was when the bleeding really began.

[Lew] It all happened so quickly; we started losing lots of money. We had no choice, we had to dramatically reduce our staff and workers. It was awful. Some of these people had been with us for years and we didn't want to let them go, not just because of their knowledge and experience but also their loyalty and friendship. But when the market disappears you have to take drastic measures.

The hardest part of making so many people redundant at the same time is the redundancy packages – the cost is enormous. How do you manage works in progress, coming down from an industry high to a Global Financial Crisis? In retrospect we didn't cut numbers quickly enough, but we still had a huge number of works in progress that needed completion, so we weren't able to immediately drop off the 80 people. Sadly, in a crisis you can have no mercy – you have to save the company.

Ben and Lynley had never seen anything like it before, I had of course, a few times – but nothing as bad as this. It took us 12 months before we were able to stop the haemorrhaging.

The lesson I learned here was – never put your head into too many nooses because it's really hard to handle when they all tighten at once.

Another, and probably the most powerful lesson we learned as a result of the GFC, was to always have an exit plan. During the resources boom of 2006 I had fortuitously asked some of my managers how we would extricate the company from failure if the market was to collapse. I had no idea at the time how important that question would prove to be. The majority of managers thought there wasn't any chance of the market collapsing and that we should move ahead with gusto to take advantage of the boom. I wasn't so sure and subsequently we had started to reduce our vulnerability prior to the collapse. It would have been prudent to do the same with the marine business.

Always have an exit plan.

The lessons were learned and recovery was slow but with both the marine and spa businesses gone, full attention could now be given to their core business of swimming pools. Lew's drive for technical excellence had withstood the turbulence and was as strong as ever.

[Lew] In 2009 we invented a world first – Pool ColourGuard®. It's a revolutionary manufacturing process that prevents pools from fading, which until we introduced it, was a real problem for the industry. We have now patented the technology with approvals in 27 countries including Australia, New Zealand, Japan, China, South Africa and India. We've also patented it for the marine industry. Our competitors can't offer anything like it so we have a real marketing advantage. Pool ColourGuard® was acknowledged with product excellence at the Australian

Business Awards, so we are very proud of what we've achieved as a consequence of wanting to be the best in the business.

Lynley is quite amazing with her never-ending quest for excellence. This became even more apparent when she implemented Lean Manufacturing, an educational process, teaching people to minimise wastage and maximise results – a very real issue for companies like ours. She then went one step further and introduced the ALT Business Excellence Initiative designed to embed a 'Think Perform' cultural change across the business.

I would urge any company to consider this initiative. It's had a huge impact on us in terms of cost and labour reductions. Our people are now so much more aware of wastage; they care more and take responsibility for what they do and what they can do themselves – they own their position within the company.

I would urge any company to consider this initiative.

That loyalty, respect and responsibility became significantly more apparent in 2014 when at 10 am on the 16th of October, Lew received an urgent call to get to the factory. When he arrived, the building was well and truly under the control of massive flames. The heat was so intense firefighters could do little to stop it.

[Lew]   Standing there watching my business going up in flames with so many devastating thoughts going through my head was one of the lowest points in my life. Fortunately, through the diligence of our staff the fire was contained to a small section and the damage was minimal relative to what it could have been.

For Lew, a great believer in making good out of bad, the aftermath of this devastating event evolved into what became one of the most rewarding experiences of his career.

[Lew]   Our management team and our staff just launched themselves into the rebuilding process. To be a part of the team that resurrected our company from the ashes to be manufacturing again eight days later was a truly amazing experience. But the journey with my family and my staff over the 12 months after the fire was the proudest and most rewarding period I have ever experienced in business.

Lew had been through enough of the tough times to understand and believe that when you are faced with adversity you must look to find the positives. Already planning to move the factory into new premises, a call was made to the builder to fast-track development. Over the next 12 months at a cost of $12 million, a world class, purpose-built manufacturing facility was constructed in Jandakot, just south of Perth. In February 2016 as an acknowledgement of their drive to deliver excellence and for their outstanding contribution to the State, the then Premier of Western Australia, Colin Barnett, officially opened the factory. It was an incredibly proud moment for business partners Lew, Ben, Lynley and all their staff.

The lead up to the launch had taken a momentous effort. It was yet another united achievement and had a tremendous impact on everyone involved. Staff, contractors and suppliers got down to work immediately while Lew, Ben and Lynley worked tirelessly to build and forge new markets. It was soon very clear the business was headed in a strong upward direction.

It was at this time that Ben decided to take part in the Royal Queensbury Championship, a charity, white-collar boxing match to raise funds for sick and disadvantaged children. His oldest son, Mitch, had survived a form of bone cancer at 16, and so this was Ben's way of giving back.

Ben gained enormous fitness and lost 9kg in the lead up to the big match scheduled for the 12th of May 2017. Lew was amazed but not surprised at Ben's level of commitment and proudly watched his son reach new heights, both personally and in business. To not only see Ben achieving his dreams but also to see him so happy bought Lew immense joy and pride.

But on the 24th of April 2017 everything changed.

Ben was in Dunsborough, a picturesque beachside town close to Western Australia's Margaret River region. He was holidaying with family and friends, doing his usual thing – having fun. It had been a big weekend for them all and so the decision to take it easy was the play of the day. But not for Ben – he was on a mission to win the big charity boxing match. So, a jog before meeting everyone for breakfast was how he chose to start his day. Jogging was something he did often, so, it was just a quick 'see you soon' to Sarah, his wife, his children and best mates as he strode energetically out the front door.

Everyone was saying he had never looked better – but that was on the outside. Internally and in silence his heart was fighting for life. No one, least of all Ben, had any idea. So, on that Monday everyone was carefree and happy as they went to meet him. Suddenly, the sound of ambulances and police sirens broke the tranquillity of the morning. A crowd had gathered around a fallen figure. It was Ben. As he ran, a catastrophic heart attack had struck without warning, driving him motionless to the ground.

Those who gathered around desperately tried to save him, but they could do nothing – and the life, that only moments before had been bursting with enthusiasm and joy, slipped silently away.

With Ben's death the writing of this story stopped as shock and pain descended on all who knew him. For Lew the loss of his son was brutal. It took more than a year for him to be able to continue his story, his grief and pain still so unmistakably present.

[Lew] Lynley, Ben and I had an unbelievably loving bond that had held us together over all the previous years. We were not only family, we were business partners, confidants and best friends who loved to work and holiday together. The three of us knew each other inside out and drew on each other for strength and guidance. We had each other's backs. It was a partnership made in heaven but alas not meant to last long enough.

The loss of a child is something a parent dreads more than anything in this world. There are no words to explain the devastation, horror, pain, sorrow and loss that you experience and there is no respite. I've slowly learned how to park my emotions to enable me to get from moment to moment, only to be swamped with another wave of sadness at the sound of his favourite band, U2, playing or walking past his empty office. Ben's office remains the same today as the day he left it, with one exception – an empty seat once occupied by the most loved and beautiful son and brother.

That seat can never be filled, however we have had to move ahead and regroup after this tragic loss. Once again, our faithful staff has come through showing their true colours. Experienced members have stepped up and we have reassigned many positions to enable the company to move forward as smoothly as possible. While I should be retired and looking for mundane activities to fill in the voids of life, I am once again going into work every day. Life has never been busier but I'm loving it. I'm grateful to be spending time in the business that was created to enable our family to be together.

Ben would be so proud of what everyone has achieved in his honour, but he would be particularly proud of his little sister. They thrived working together in the family business whilst bringing up their children.

Lynley is now managing director of the company. Every day she amazes me as she continues to work tirelessly in the business finishing off many of the works initiated by Ben earlier. There is a constant tear being shed as milestone after milestone is reached as a result of the integral part Ben played in its evolution.

When we moved into our facility at Jandakot, we decided to extend our penetration to the east coast. Prospective dealers would come over and visit us and once they'd seen what we had to offer – the world's best manufacturing facility for fibreglass pools – they just fell in love with the concept. Now we have twelve dealers in Victoria plus, as the result of a recent pool and spa show two more are coming on board. We also have six in NSW and six in Queensland.

We have two logistics depots; one is in Victoria where we have at least 150 pools in stock at any one time. We have to fund the stock of the pools ourselves because the dealers are not in a position to buy them. Our Queensland facility was initially in a small yard, but it wasn't working so we moved to a much bigger, much better facility. Finally, at the beginning of 2018, it started to evolve and now we're stocking it up to a ready supply of 150 pools.

It was Ben's initiative to set up the stockholdings and logistics yards in Victoria, and once we were able to stock the pools over there, the business model really took off. So, what Ben set up Lynley has followed through and brought home to roost. It's very exciting and rewarding and we would love more than anything for Ben to be here to enjoy what we have achieved together.

The fire was devastating but it was the catalyst for building our state-of-the-art facility. Having that facility has enabled us to grow exponentially. Today, nobody has what we have, nobody has a better product. Our pools are made better, the models and shapes are consistent and true; we have our patented Pool ColourGuard® system; they're all made to set formulas plus, everything is done correctly.

At any show where our pools are displayed, there's an obvious difference between the quality of our pools and others. Then you see the reactions of prospective pool buyers when they come into those shows, it's quite plain to see. The dealers can see it too of course and then, once they go through the facility at Jandakot and meet the family, they're hooked and say, "We'd like to get on board".

We'd been through some really hard times – some horrendously challenging periods – but none more so than 2016-17.

The hard work that went into the expansion has paid off because over 2016-18 the West Australian marketplace was horrific, and without the support of the east coast it would have been extremely difficult for us to survive. We had previously been through some really hard times – recessions, crashes, global catastrophes, regulatory changes that overnight wiped 25 per cent off our business, interest rate hikes and the GFC. These were all horrendously challenging periods but none more so than 2016-17 with the end of the mining boom in Western Australia and subsequent retraction of buyers from the market – not just in the swimming pool industry but in all luxury, non-essential items. And we lost Ben.

Ben and Lynley hadn't known what to expect from the GFC, but they learned from it and before Ben passed, both he and Lynley got it. You have to react very, very quickly in the tough times, and sometimes you have to make some very hard-hitting decisions that nobody likes just to get through.

The most important thing is for the company to survive. It supports hundreds of families; it's not just our family that needs bread and butter on its table, it's also the 200-plus other families that we support, it's the hundreds of businesses, the subcontractors and all our suppliers that rely on us as well.

The lessons we learned helped us endure 2016-18. In late 2017, the business plan that had been forming over the previous three or four years finally came to fruition and is still evolving.

But...nothing is the same nor will it ever be again. Since losing Ben...it's been hard to keep going but the world has not been so kind as to stand still and allow us to grieve. Life moves on.

Sometimes you think about where you've come from and of the people who rely on you – it's very sobering.

So, it has been a long and winding road to get to this point. Regardless of the challenges and the good times, it's always been very important to me to be a man of integrity, to be able to hold my head high. Sometimes you think about where you've come from and the people who rely on you – it's very sobering. Some of those people will be with us until they retire, and I feel it's very important they are looked after until that time. The reality can be quite stressful, and over the years I've had to work hard at not letting the pressure get to me.

For some people success appears to come easily, but for the majority, me included, it comes after many years of hard work, stress and relentless dedication. I must admit I don't think about my success but sometimes I do have to pinch myself and soak up the reality of what has been achieved. This leads me to question when do you reach success and how much is enough? Mick Jagger must have considered the same, when he sang, "You can't always get what you want but if you try sometimes you get what you need". Appropriate and a great song to boot.

I am proud of what I have achieved but it didn't come without its sacrifices. My marriage and my children suffered as a direct consequence of me running the business, but I always tried to mitigate the damage as much as possible. It is so important to be aware and make time for your family, but that can be such a challenge because you have to focus on the business, particularly when you first start out. This is also when you sacrifice your own personal wellbeing by working long hours at a very stressful pace. You think you are invincible, however in later years you regret having put so much in without reflecting on your own person.

In saying that, having a successful business enabled my family to be together and have a great lifestyle. Sure, it does have its drawbacks, but the positives far outweigh those. I've also learned so much along the way – never to be afraid of the unknown – because each day is an unknown. I've learned to admit I don't know everything and as such continue to ask questions and seek advice from people who do. I've learned the value of having a university degree, even if you don't know what direction you want to take, just pick a field that interests you – I believe it puts you ten years ahead of those who do not. There are, of course, exceptions to both sides.

But one of the greatest things I've learned is the importance of surrounding yourself with good people and to draw on their experience and skills. I've been very fortunate to have so many good people working with me.

Having a good team has enabled us to be creative, to think outside the square, to have a united vision and by doing so become market leaders. We have totally changed the industry and the way fibreglass swimming pools are made, but we have also changed the cultural way we all think about the business; how we go about any activity within the business. To get to that point has been an expensive process but it's been worth every cent and I can comfortably say I'm very proud of everything we've achieved.

But my greatest achievement and my greatest joy in life was to be able to go to work every day, and with the aid of my children build something rare and special. Every day was such a pleasure to guide and watch as both Ben and Lynley developed into industry leaders and to know that without them our company would not have developed into what it is today.

No father could be more proud of his children.

There are so may beautiful memories of Ben that trigger our emotions. Only now can I empathise with those who have experienced a similar loss, and now have some understanding of how they were feeling and what they were going through. We have been so lucky with our extended group of family, friends and business acquaintances who have stood by us and comforted and nurtured us through these needy times.

So, life has changed dramatically for Lew and his family, but he continues to look forward with hope, and as always is ready to impart some great pearls of wisdom.

[Lew] Enjoy your family and close friends. Search for better health and wellbeing and smell those roses whilst you still have the chance. Give your support and unconditional love to those around you and those that need you. Be thankful and grateful for what God has bestowed upon you and be prepared to help those not so fortunate as yourself. And enjoy the journey of greatness in others.

Thank you, Lew.

Postscript

[Lew] After Ben died one of his friends said that Ben had told him we were his heroes.

That was so lovely to hear.

Ben, you are our hero and I only wish I could aspire to have all the beautiful attributes that you brought into our lives during the 47 years you were with us.

Rest in peace my beautiful boy.

Mr and Mrs Beale with Robin and Lew

Robin and Lew

Lew with Ben and Lynley

Lew and Lesley's Wedding Day 1987 with Lynley, Ben and Lesley's son Andrew

Lew and Lesley

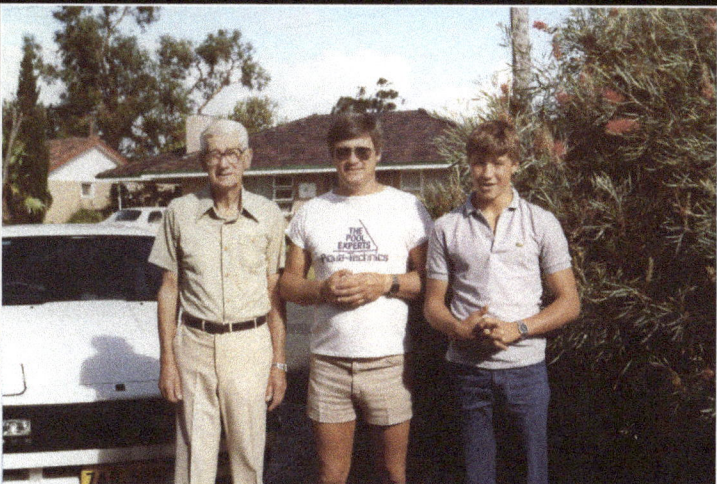

Three Generations of Beales Lewis Dring, Lew and Lew Benjamin

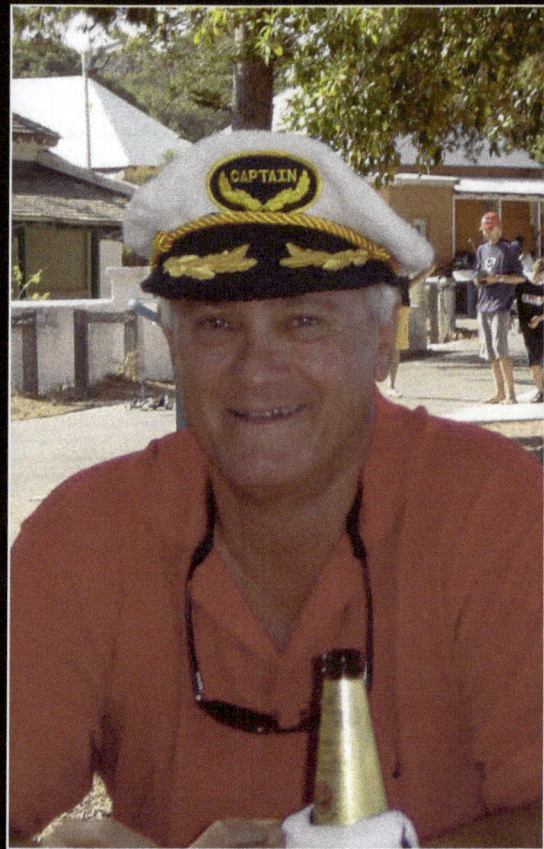

Taking a break on Rottnest Island

Lew with his catch of the day

Lew surrounded by his favourite males

Winners - 1996 Telstra WA Small Business Awards

The Jandakot facility under construction 2014

Another win - Award for Excellence 2016

Lew with business partners - his children Ben and Lynley

Lynley, Lew, Premier Colin Barnett and Ben at the opening of the Jandakot facility (2016)

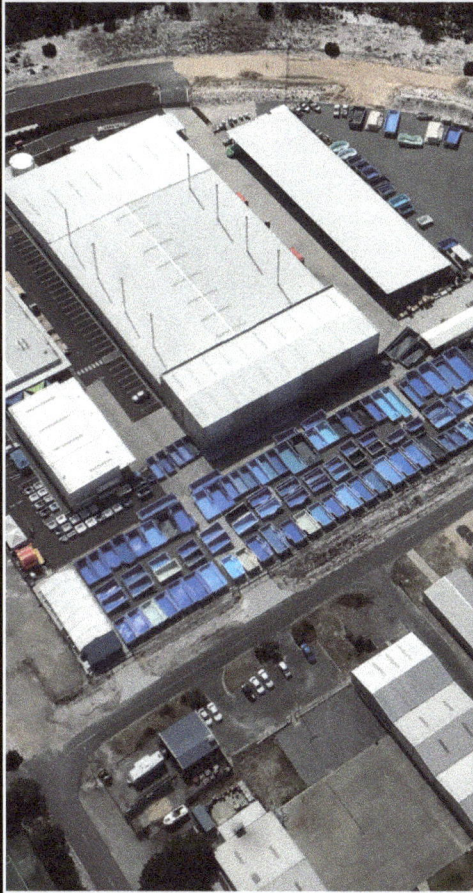

Aquatic Leisure Technologies Jandakot

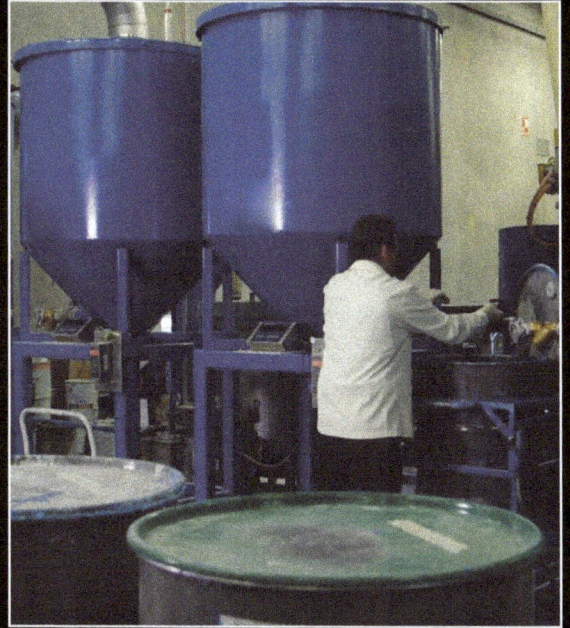

The mixing bay at Jandakot

Aquatic Leisure Technologies - the whole crew

From Here

To Here

The Beale family

Lesley and Lew

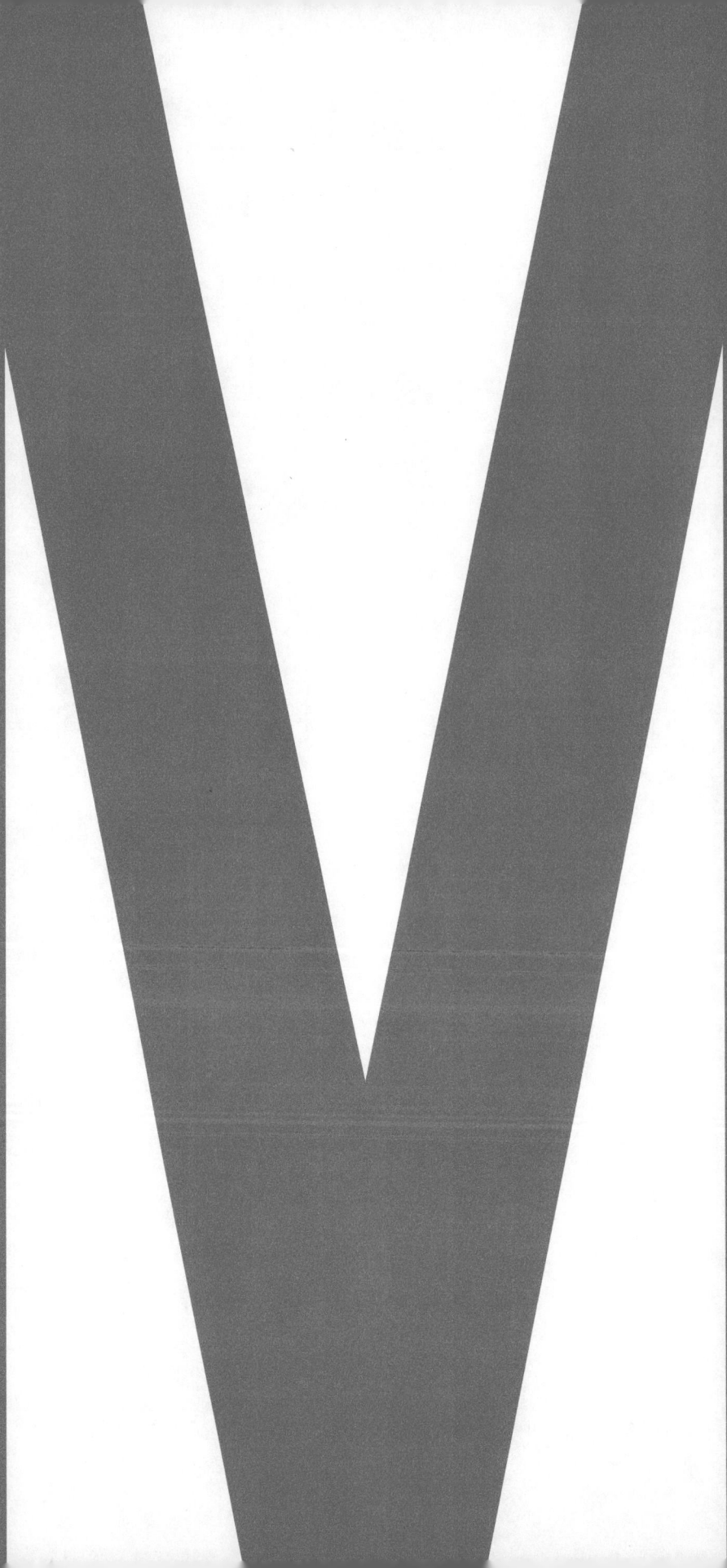

2

The Vision, The Passion and The Style

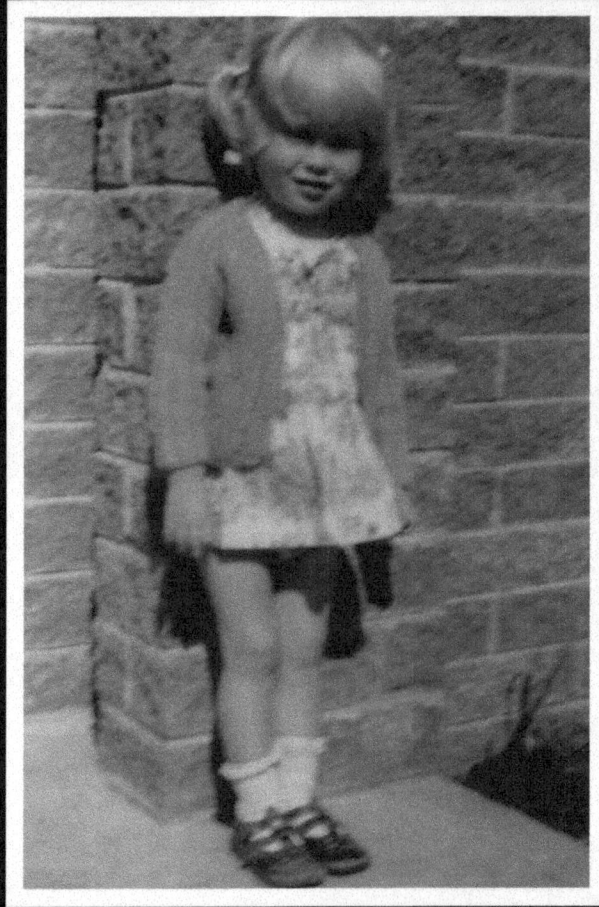

"There's opportunity everywhere, you just have to go out and look. Don't just sit around waiting for it to come to you because if you do, life will just pass you by and that's when you live with regret."

She is a woman of great substance, strength and determination, who from a pair of pyjamas and a beloved dog, created an empire. At 21, with a leap of faith, her journey began.

She left the only home she'd known and travelled more than 4,000km to the other side of the country. She arrived alone, in a city she knew little of, with $40 in her wallet and a vacuum cleaner in her suitcase.

As a woman with integrity, ambition, humility and courage there would be no looking back – life was about to change. Her days of ordinary were now very much numbered as the businesswoman in her began to emerge.

The love of the company she created came second to none until the arrival of her children – then she had it all. As a mother and a businesswoman driven to be the best at both, life became demanding and spiritually confronting. But over time she learned to trust, above all else, her intuition and her own voice. The challenges most women face when they live and breathe for two worlds were immense, but courage and the dawning of a greater wisdom gave birth to the woman she was destined to become.

This woman is savvy and smart and also beautiful but that is one attribute she places little importance on – although lives in a world that does. The world of high fashion, catwalks, lipstick and cameras is her day-to-day reality. She has cut the pattern of her life from an innate sense of style, elegance and quality, sewn together with a desire for simplicity and a clear understanding of what is good fashion and what isn't.

She is a megapreneur in the very best sense of the word; she is fast becoming an Australian fashion icon; she is the woman behind fashion label, Morrison, she is…

Kylie Radford

May 23, 1973 was an unusually cold morning in the picturesque city of Launceston in northern Tasmania. As one of Australia's oldest cities and where the North and South Esk Rivers meet to become the Tamar, it is both historic and spectacularly scenic. The surrounding mountains that rise from the floor of the Tamar Valley in which Launceston sits, are a majestic sight from the city's hospital. Robyn Radford was in hospital on that cold autumn morning. She had just given birth to her daughter Kylie. Their bond was immediate and over the next 18 years, the two would rarely be separated.

Kylie's family were honest, hard-working people. Her father Kevin, a panel beater, worked for others until he decided it was time to go out on his own – and probably from whom Kylie picked up her inherent business sense. Her older brother David now runs their father's business. Her mother Robyn worked just as hard as a waitress. She would go to work at night while her children slept, so that she could be with them during the day. Eventually, Robyn left waitressing to take up a position as a sales representative - a role she was far happier in.

[Kylie]   Mum worked hard in her new job but she really enjoyed it. No matter how devoted or hard Mum and Dad worked they would, without fail, take four weeks off every year to take us camping. We always had the best time. I just loved getting dirty, eating campfire food, sleeping in the tent and fishing with Dad – it was so simple and wonderful.

The family lived in a small three-bedroom suburban home. There was a granny flat out the back for Kylie's grandparents, and the next-door neighbours were Robyn and Kevin's best friends. They were the typical 1970s Australian family whose lives were simple but special.

[Kylie]   Our house was in an area where there were groups of kids that were pretty rough and so I experienced a few hard knock situations. I'm sure Mum would say, "What are you talking about Kylie, we lived in a wonderful area," but the fact is, it was a bit rough and if anyone picked on you, you would just – just punch them, you would just deal with it and move on. I was a bit of a toughie myself, a bit of a tomboy. I remember my brother getting into a fight and there I was hanging off the other guy's neck. My brother was always there for me and still is – we are very different, but we are very loyal to each other.

Mum and Dad taught us so much – like working hard. I'm sure a lot of people think if you come up with an incredible idea, you'll make lots of money. That's not necessarily true – you can – but you have to work really hard to succeed at anything.

They taught us about respect and loyalty and just keeping it real – if someone is speaking bull-shit, they are just speaking bullshit and I have no tolerance for that kind of behaviour... people who talk non-stop about themselves – just like I'm doing right now (laughter). You don't cheat, you don't lie. My Mum said, "Kylie if you ever steal anything, don't come home – she didn't really mean it but she was very straight with that sort of thing and I've picked that up from her.

Her parents' guidance had a huge impression on Kylie, and she continues to live her life around those learned principles. Worryingly, she sees those values slowly disappearing in the workplace and is fearful even her own children will pick up on the current mentality of expectation; 'I deserve this – I deserve that', without giving anything extra.

[Kylie] I've told them they will be buying their own first car and they will get a job when they're 15. My son Baxter did the paper round when he was nine for about eight months but I pulled the pin on that because when young kids do paper rounds you have to do it with them and I didn't want to do it anymore – but it taught him quite a bit and he saved every cent.

Kylie never expected anything from her parents; they had taught her that if you want something in life you have to work for it – so she got her first job at 14 in a supermarket.

[Kylie] I really wanted that job but you couldn't get one at 14 so I had to say I was older – I was so happy when I got it. I loved it – serving people and chatting to them – it was just a great first experience. I worked really hard and so got on well with management. I also made sure that everyone was doing their bit 'cos I didn't want to be a part of a team where someone was going to slack off. So, I'd confront them. I have girls in the team at Morrison who would do the same and I just love them being that way. Some people simply have an understanding of busi-ness and what needs to be done. I got it from watching my Dad run his panel beating business and now as a business owner I look for those traits in my own staff.

Perhaps it was her work at the supermarket that changed Kylie's thinking – maybe the responsibility of having a job pushed her to thinking about her future despite being so young. Kylie was in Year 9 and, according to her, a very average student. She doesn't remember doing her homework or anyone checking to see if she had; she didn't read out loud to her parents before going to bed and they didn't often read to her. A little different to the parent of today. Despite her shortcomings and disadvantages (tongue in cheek) Kylie knew she wanted something different. Almost overnight she made a decision – she would go to university.

[Kylie] No one on the Radford side had ever gone to uni and when I found that out I wanted to be the first. I'm competitive like that, although if I don't think I'm going to win or do well at something – I won't do it. I may have had no idea what I was going to do when I left school but there was never a question in my mind – I was going to be successful!

Then a careers councillor at school helped me decide what I should do but not because of her suggestions. She told me I should do hairdressing and I got a bit pissed off about being told to do that – you won't tell me what to do. I'll do what I want to do...I know – I'll do law! I chose law purely because I thought it was an important position. I was aiming high. It could have been medicine but I knew I wouldn't get into that (laughs) 'cos that was way out of my league. But I thought, well lawyers are really important people and everyone looks up to them – they are smart and earn lots of money. It wasn't really about the money it was more that I just wanted to make my parents proud – I always have and still do.

With her goals firmly set Kylie fiercely embraced homework – still no one checked on its completion but now with a purpose, Kylie was driven. Her grades improved and so did her confidence – confidence often comes from having a few wins along the way. Years 11 and 12 saw a move to a different school in the middle of Launceston, or the big smoke as Kylie called it back then. It was here that she really got down to work, doing little else other than sport and study. The outcome was worth it. Kylie was accepted into law. It was a momentous achievement marred only by the reality of what years of study would mean. Funds would be very tight. So, a job in the lead up to commencing her law studies was the only way Kylie would get through.

[Kylie] One of the girls I worked with at the supermarket was also managing a bar on a Tuesday night. I wanted to work there too, but you had to be 18, so I lied about my age – again. I got the job and started saving for uni which was in Hobart. Once I was there, I got Austudy (a student allowance) but basically lived on nothing. Mum and Dad who had separated by then, paid my uni fees, although Mum, bless her, was only on a part-time wage so she rented out the spare room at home. My Nan would save 50¢ pieces and then give them to Mum in bundles – all just to get me through uni.

I had attended the same school from kindy through to Year 10 and was used to that security. So, the first year being in Hobart was really hard because I'd never been away from Mum for long periods of time and I was very homesick. By the middle of the year I realised law wasn't for me – I didn't fit in – too many words. I didn't enjoy it and knew I wasn't going to be successful. So, as I do, I stopped putting in the effort but managed to finish the year. I shifted to political science, psychology and sociology. It was more creative and I enjoyed it but I didn't work very hard because by that time I discovered there was a big world out there and was far more interested in having fun.

I got my arts degree and although I would have been really disappointed in myself if I hadn't finished, it hasn't made a huge difference to my life. In saying that I'd love my kids to go – not just so they can say they've got a degree, but to experience it. University life is special and fun and where I met some of my best mates – I wouldn't want my kids to miss that.

Many of the friends I met at uni were from affluent families and so headed off overseas when uni finished. I wasn't in a position to do that; it was out of my league. Instead, I got a job in this little Mexican restaurant. I also went back to uni part-time and studied commerce but I think I only did that so I could work in the restaurant without being too disappointed in myself.

It was the owner of that little Mexican restaurant who taught me so much about business — he was such a great operator. It was only a small business and yet he made a truckload from it. It was all to do with him calculating the cost of everything, making sure his margins were right, making sure the staff hours were right and in line with what they needed to be. He even had the kitchen staff working like a great machine — everyone knew what they had to do and when. Very quickly I became the restaurant manager and from that experience learnt the value of having good procedures, policies and processes in place.

Managing the business gave Kylie the confidence to make a lifechanging decision - to leave Tasmania. Most of her friends had already moved away and were living in Sydney and Melbourne. Robyn, Kylie's mother had been to Perth in Western Australia to visit her sister and had loved it. So, Kylie at 21 years of age decided to make the move to Perth.

[Kylie]   I arrived with $40, a credit card with no money on it and no plans. I rented a car using my empty credit card which I couldn't return until I'd made some money. I got a job at the Mexican Kitchen in South Terrace, Fremantle. Eventually, I made enough to return the car but not enough to buy furniture for the little one-bedroom unit I'd rented in Osborne Street, East Fremantle — so I slept on the floor. I did have a vacuum cleaner that I'd bought with me from Tassie — and no, I'm not a clean freak, but it was all I owned and it fitted in my suitcase. So, there I was with $40, an empty unit and a vacuum cleaner. It was perfect and I loved it.

Eight months later, drawn to the beauty of the Swan River and the buzz of working behind a bar, Kylie went to work at the historic Left Bank in Fremantle. It was here she met a group of friends and so checked out of her own little apartment and moved in with them. Kylie thrived on their energy; life was fun and Fremantle it seemed, matched her enthusiasm and love of life. But that ever-present ambition was calling her to take charge of her life and financial position — it was time to earn some real money.

[Kylie]   I always had ambition but I had no idea what I was going to do, only that I would one day run my own business. Whenever I visualised anything of my future, I never saw myself as an employee. For some reason I just knew I would control my destiny, my life, my job, and maybe for that reason I rarely hesitated or qualified anything in my mind. I just went with my gut and did it — I didn't think too far ahead.

I knew I would control my destiny, my life, my job, so I rarely hesitated or qualified anything in my mind. I just went with my gut and did it.

[Kylie]   A close girlfriend from high school, Natalie Weaver, was working for Yellow Pages and was earning really good money, so I thought that's what I need to do. I knew I couldn't keep working in hospitality – the money just wasn't there, and as much as I enjoyed it, it wasn't for me.

When I went for the interview at Yellow Pages, the guy asked me, "What are you going to do if you don't get this job?" I said, "Ring you every day and hound you until you give me a position!" I'm sure I got it because they thought; well she's determined, we'll give her a go.

Working at the Yellow Pages was better money, but it was in an office environment which just didn't suit me. Even now I don't like sitting in one spot looking at a screen. The job was in sales and as much as I like sales, I didn't want to sell an ad.

Kylie became very unsettled and uncertain of what to do but of one thing she was sure, her days in front of the computer screen and on a telephone, cold calling were numbered. She considered her options. Should she stay in Perth or should she move back to Tasmania? How different her life might have been if she hadn't had a conversation with a friend working for a recruitment company. It was a sliding doors moment.

[Kylie] I remember Amy telling me about her job in recruitment and I thought to myself, I'd be good at that. So, I did up my resume and got an interview with Choice Personnel Group on St Georges Terrace in the city. Mum gave me her credit card number and off I went to Picnic and bought myself a new outfit. I thought Picnic and my new linen wrap skirt were so high end. I got the job. I felt really good in that outfit and that was when I first thought about the impact clothing can have on your self-confidence.

Kylie enjoyed recruitment and made some great friends, including a girl named Ros Spann. At around the same time she met a man. Very nice thought Kylie. His name was Richard Poulson. In time, Richard would come to play a major role in Kylie's life and so, on a personal level, life was good. On a business level however, Kylie was restless. Ambition had well and truly settled in and with it came the realisation that recruitment was not for her. Kylie wanted something more. She wanted her own business. And so, the research began.

Her investigations led her to Peter Alexander, the sleepwear king. He inspired a vision in Kylie. The iconic business, named after himself, had grown from humble beginnings at his mother's dining table into a hugely successful brand. His story inspired Kylie, but it was her belief Peter Alexander could do with some competition that compelled her into action.

In late 2000 Kylie together with her new wingwoman, Ros Spann, launched a business. Max was Ros's cat and Morrison was Kylie's beloved Kelpie-Lab cross – but together they were the inspiration for the name of their new unisex pyjamas business - Max and Morrison.

[Kylie] I had been reading a lot about Peter Alexander's success and because he didn't seem to have any competitors, I thought we could give him a run for his money. What could be so hard about making pyjamas? I had no idea how to do a pattern but I did sewing classes at high school and enjoyed it, so I thought, yep, let's do it.

We knew absolutely nothing. I found a pair of pyjamas I liked and someone made up the pattern, and because we didn't have a clue about fabrics, we contacted every fabric agency and asked loads of questions. I've learned it's so important in business to never be embarrassed to ask questions of people in the know, and don't think you have to pretend you know what you are doing. Sometimes what seem to be stupid questions are often the best.

We advertised in Country Style magazine and people would ring us to place an order – we couldn't wholesale because the margins weren't there. We'd box them up and send them off in the mail – that's how Peter Alexander was doing it and we were modelling ourselves on him. I can't stress enough the value of modelling yourself on a successful business, getting good advice and having a mentor – it just saves making too many mistakes.

So, the business was moving forward – albeit a little slowly for Kylie – unlike her relationship with Richard Poulson. Six years after meeting him, on St Patrick's Day, the 17th of March 2001, amongst the vines in Western Australia's Margaret River wine growing region, they married. For the next 10 days they celebrated but then, in true Kylie style, it was time to get back to work.

[Kylie]   Ros and I were working hard, but Max and Morrison just wasn't making any money. We were selling and covering costs but we had no capital to promote it. We needed to have a retail presence and so leased a little shop behind the Post Office in Claremont. We chose Claremont because we thought being an affluent area, people would spend money on pyjamas – $66 and $88 a pair and $44 for kiddie's ones. We built up a customer base but the location wasn't in a high traffic area. It was fun at the start but then it got monotonous – we weren't moving fast enough for me.

Disenchanted, Kylie did some research. She decided what they needed to do was diversify their stock – stay with their sleepwear but also buy in an eclectic mix of product. She also believed that Fremantle, where retail was booming, would be a wise move. Driven by gut instinct Kylie decided that Market Street was the place to be – it had shop vacancies - but more importantly it had a high level of walk in trade.

[Kylie]   One night, Ros and I were out at dinner with our husbands and so I took the opportunity to talk about moving to Fremantle. While Ros and I were great friends we were very different. She declined the idea and with that we agreed to go our separate ways.

Kylie was ready to start afresh but with no money it was time to take a leap of faith. Richard's $4,000 ski boat and their $4,000 Honda Civic were sold. Equipped with those funds and Richard's support, Kylie followed her instincts and found a small shop in Market Street Fremantle. She dropped 'Max' the cat leaving only the name of her Kelpie-Lab to fill the sign above the door. In 2002 'Morrison' opened for business. Kylie was 28 years old and the dream of running her own business was finally a reality.

[Kylie] From my research I knew I had to diversify. Mum lent me her credit card – again – with a limit of $3,000 on it to buy stock. When you first go into business it's not easy to get terms and I had to be quite strategic but I did manage to get them and that made a big difference to how I bought stock. I bought in some really cool stuff that you couldn't find anywhere else in Perth – home wares, jewellery, and I still did the pyjamas. We also brought in a really funky and cute underwear brand from Melbourne, called Sabi, it was an absolute hit for us – I learnt then, the value of being different.

We opened the doors to the shop at 1pm on a Sunday – by five o'clock we had taken $590. It was amazing and every day after was great – I was so excited. For a long time after leaving uni I'd floundered, never quite sure what I should be doing. When I opened the doors of Morrison and people wanted my product, I knew I'd got the mix right and I felt incredible. I thought, this is me, I have found exactly what I want to do.

I learnt then the value of being different.

Before I opened Morrison a lot of people told me not to go ahead, saying it was too risky. I got to the point where I actually wanted to prove everyone wrong. Over the years I have found people can be negative and try to stop you, but I now understand that sometimes that's just their fear talking – fear of the unknown and fear of stepping out of a comfort zone. But I've never liked being told what to do, or what I can't do. I remember years ago my poor Nan organised for me to attend a birthday party. I was only eight at the time but I thought, how dare she do that to me, accept an invitation on my behalf, without asking me first! I had to go to it but I'd never been so angry in all my eight years!

With that strength of character and determination it was not surprising that back on Market Street Morrison had hit Fremantle with gusto. Customers loved everything Kylie presented. But she knew she had more to give and this is where Kylie's innate business sense started to come to the fore. She identified there was a need to offer something more, something of higher value, something that was unique to her, something you couldn't get anywhere else. Little did she realise that 'that little something' would lead to the creation of an empire.

[Kylie]   I already had sleepwear, I had leisurewear but I decided I needed something casual that people could wear out, something that was unique to Morrison; so, I designed a really cool pair of black pants. I found the fabric, got someone to do the pattern and someone else to make them. Once the Morrison label went on, I hung them on the rack. They were an instant hit. And that was where and when Morrison really started.

They were an instant hit. And that was where and when Morrison really started.

Looking back Kylie's mother, Robyn, remembers her young teenage daughter altering her clothes to make them different – cutting the straps off a dress to make a skirt, finding a nice piece of fabric to make into a top or simply wearing things a little differently to everyone else. Perhaps if courses in fashion had been available in Tasmania, Kylie's talent and creative potential may have been discovered years earlier. Was it destiny, fate or providence? Whatever it was Robyn, despite Kylie's love of clothes, never dreamed her daughter, the little girl from Launceston, would one day become one of Australia's leading clothing designers.

Kylie was now putting in seven days a week in the store. It was her business and she loved everything about it so it didn't matter there was time for little else. Opening boxes of new stock when they arrived, working out the margins over and again to make sure they were correct – it didn't matter, she just loved her business and loved making the sales. However, her greatest satisfaction came from talking to her customers.

[Kylie] By working in the business, particularly when I first opened, and by talking to the customers I knew what they wanted. I got to know what was selling and what wasn't or what was missing and what needed to be bought in, in order to add to a sale – I would have missed that if I'd employed others to work for me. Customers would say things like, "This fabric is too heavy," or "I need a top to go with that." I got to know very quickly if they were there to buy just a skirt or a whole outfit. But it was very different back then – if people wanted something, they just bought it, they would just spend. It was fantastic – there was no online shopping, and everything unique or interesting was a hit.

Now I always tell my staff, listen to your customers 100 per cent, find out what they want because if you don't know, you won't sell anything. I believe my job in fashion is to inspire my customers and offer them something they didn't realise they needed or wanted before they came in.

At the end of the day the most important thing is sales. I talk to the young designers that come in here wanting to be purely creative and I tell them, "Yes you can be creative, that's wonderful, but you need to be able to sell it." They talk about getting a PR company almost before they've begun and so I always remind them, that whilst I'd had the business for years, I'd only just got a marketing manager. You have to sell your product...really, that's the only thing that matters, everything else is secondary.

Working in the business and talking to the customers you get to know your business, what your customer wants and what is selling and what isn't. That's invaluable. I would have missed that if I'd employed others to work for me at the start.

By Christmas 2002 it was clear to Kylie she needed help in the store. She asked a friend to help her on Sundays hoping it would bring a little balance back into her life. But it wasn't long before even more help was needed. Despite the extra support, every day was equally hectic, the uphill pace relentless and the learning curve immense. There was no choice but to learn along the way, which meant Kylie grew as the business grew; her knowledge and business acumen building with every obstacle she encountered. It was invaluable experience; a priceless education that gave her a confidence and understanding of her business from the bottom up. Her everyday presence in the store is probably linked to Kylie's belief that, 'Understanding your business is not rocket science'. In contrast, those who employ others from the beginning of a business and are not so present in it, may well find that running their business is indeed rocket science. When a business grows so quickly, it's very easy to get lost or behind, particularly with those unavoidable but fundamental tasks. The tasks that are often put in the 'do tomorrow' basket, such as paperwork. This is where the Touch it Once principle is so vital to success and one that we should all apply if success is our intended destination.

Keeping on top of everything meant Kylie would often do her paperwork (balance the books or pay the bills), while sitting at the store counter – but she was never alone. To keep her company there was the ever-loyal Kelpie-Lab cross, Morrison lying at her feet.

While the rapid growth of the business was exhilarating, the pressure and growing demands on Kylie were huge. Consequently, eight months after opening, a major decision was made and actioned. Richard closed his advertising sales company and joined Kylie at Morrison…

And so, then there were three – Kylie, Richard and Morrison, their Kelpie-Lab cross.

[Kylie] Richard believed, as much as I did, that the business would work and was a great support all the way through. He's an amazing salesman and an entrepreneur, and although we're relatively different we both have a lot to contribute – so we make quite a team.

The black pants that had started Kylie on her path as a designer, had become known as the 'good butt pants'; and as we know anything that makes a woman feel good about her butt naturally sells like hotcakes – 23,000 pairs to be precise. With that came the confidence to design additional pieces until Kylie was creating full season collections. This was a girl with no qualifications in fashion design, just a passion and a belief in what she was doing.

[Kylie] I found our customers just wanted more and more of the fashion items I was designing. We still had the home wares but our margins were much better in fashion and so it just evolved to the point where we bought less and less of the other stuff. It happened so quickly. Within two years we had wholesale accounts and an agent. I was designing almost full time to keep up with demand.

A lot of our customers are curvy and want something a bit different, so I was designing garments for the not-so-perfect body, the more curvy. Before Morrison opened there were very few stores where women could find something a bit funky, not dowdy, and something that wasn't in every shop. I recognised there was an opening in the market for that. We entered the market at the right time and were lucky the retail climate was perfect for us. To be honest, I don't think it would be as easy now.

Even though we were doing really well I was saving all the money we were making. I picked that up from my Dad who always ran his business conservatively. When you make a lot of money one week you don't take it all out and spend it on a holiday the next. Yes, it may be your business but that doesn't mean all the money you make is yours – there has to be enough to sustain the business and your staff. A lot of people in this industry don't survive because they don't have that balance right. In retail it's easy to get really excited when you have a good week but then it can die in the arse the next – then you have nothing. So, you must put back in so you can grow. Growth is essential in any business.

In retail it's easy to get really excited when you have a good week but then it can die in the arse the next – then you have nothing. So, you must put back in so you can grow. Growth is essential in any business.

With sustained and targeted reinvestment Morrison's growth continued and in so doing attracted the attention and respect of the broader business community. Within their first two years they received numerous local business awards. Similarly impressed was the Fremantle Chamber of Commerce. They acknowledged Morrison's hard work and subsequent success with a regular show of support for Kylie, Richard and their growing team. In 2003 they received the accolade of Fremantle Business of the Year and then in 2005 Kylie was named as one of WA Business News' 40 under 40, business achievers. Kylie shrugs off the significance of those achievements. She is clearly proud and grateful for the recognition and humbled by it too – but for Kylie designing fabulous clothes, building a great team and a great business is simply her doing what she loves. She does admit however; public accolades are great for business.

By this time Morrison had a full-time accountant, an administration receptionist and two girls covering the wholesale division; all driven from the storeroom above the store. There was also the immensely loyal Renata, Kylie's pattern maker of 14 years (who only left the company to return home to Austria). Renata initially worked from her own home due to a lack of space in the office. To create a more conducive working environment for her team Kylie leased an office above the Commonwealth Bank, just around the corner from the store. However, that still wasn't enough and within months they'd moved again. This time it was into an even larger space in High Street Fremantle which not only became their head office but it finally meant samples could be made in-house. It was that move that took Morrison from simply having a retail presence to being a recognised label.

[Kylie]   I think it was at that point I knew I was in control of my own destiny. I remember chatting to Rich about it and saying we were onto a really good thing – that we'd hit the mark and needed to look after it. What we were doing was really working and that was exciting. I felt empowered and confident. However, we were building a business on stock generated from wholesale sales and the Fremantle store, and I knew that if Morrison was going to be a serious label we would need to grow and present ourselves quite differently. I recognised it was time to take the next step.

Even with the success of Fremantle a lot of people were still very negative. Thankfully, I didn't listen because if I had we wouldn't be where we are today. My advice to others is to really think about who is giving advice and only listen if they have knowledge about what it is you are trying to achieve. One of my girlfriends, Sasha, who I worked with at Yellow Pages, has done incredibly well. We are both equally proud of each other's achievements. I believe being happy for others creates success for yourself. So make sure you aren't the one dishing out the negative comments and don't ever let anyone hold you back – dreams are for living and Morrison was my dream – and no one was going to stop me.

I probably got that determination from my Mum – she is very loving but she didn't mollycoddle me – instead she would always push me and say, "Go on darlin', you can do it, off you go". She was a go-getter and if she'd had an education, I'm sure she would have done amazing things herself. She always did Dad's books as I was growing up. She's written a book of poetry that she self-published, she is still president of her social committee and has a great social life – she's got spark, she's hilarious and she's a great friend.

When it comes to advice, my advice to others is to really think about who is giving advice and only listen if they have knowledge about what it is you are trying to achieve.

As Kylie talked about her upbringing it became clearer as to why she has become such a successful woman. She learned very early on that if she wanted something, she had to work hard to get it. There was no room for laziness, lack of drive or doubt that she would achieve success (despite not always knowing what path to take). Nothing was freely handed to her and that probably made her stronger and more independent. It makes you think about how much is too much when it comes to our own children. How best to talk to them – how to encourage them, how to protect them and yet push them at the same time. It's a fine balance especially when most of us just want to see our children happy and therefore believe that by giving them everything they will be happy. But if we give them too much, protect them too much, it may hinder their drive to reach their full potential and quite possibly breed that sense of entitlement and expectation that helps no one.

[Kylie] We got an opportunity to open a store in Claremont but this time we did it properly with a professional store fit out company – no Ikea furniture in sight. The result was amazing and so we decided Fremantle should look the same...that was when we made a big shift in our profile.

The Claremont store opened and was an immediate success. So now with two successful stores they started to investigate potential locations for their next. Bold thinking took Sydney's Paddington to the top of Richard's list. However, there was no time for following through – a life changing experience was afoot and one that Kylie was totally unprepared for – the arrival of their first child.

So then there were four; Kylie, Richard, their newborn son, Baxter, and Morrison.

[Kylie] I left work the day before I had Baxter. I'd started losing weight and after a scan was told he needed to be delivered within two days. So, I was like, OK, I'll just get as much done before I go in – I wasn't even thinking about after. Being the person I am, I thought everything would be fine, but when I arrived home with him, he was so tiny and cried a lot. I remember thinking, oh god, this is my life, what has happened, why can't I control this? I didn't even know that babies cried that much, I thought that when you put them down, they went to sleep. I tried taking Baxter to work with me but he screamed the whole time we were there.

I just became numb, a robot trying to be a good mum but totally anxious all the time. I wanted to be the best mum but also, I wanted to be at work, still doing what I had always done. To a certain degree I felt the pressure that I had to be there anyway because we were building the business. I was doing design and production and covering a huge amount, so there was no way I could step back. I had never experienced that level of stress and I certainly didn't know how to handle it.

Looking back, I should have been more organised. I should have had people in place, recruited, handed over some responsibilities, planned when I was going to start back at work, but because I had no idea what to expect I wasn't organised. I totally underestimated the impact of having a child, working and trying to build a business at the same time. It wasn't easy.

No more than six weeks after the arrival of Baxter, Richard's vision of opening in Sydney's Paddington became a reality. Kylie's gut instinct had told her they shouldn't go ahead, that they had too much going on. However, struggling with a newborn baby, still designing full time and dealing with the demands of growing a business left her no energy to disagree, and so Oxford Street in Paddington became Morrison's third store.

[Kylie] It was the only time Richard and I had ever really disagreed on anything. I felt it was the wrong time, there was so much going on here and I believed we should just concentrate on what we had. I'd just had Baxter; I was exhausted and I couldn't think clearly – it was a terribly stressful time.

Oxford Street was once considered to be a great shopping destination in Sydney but that had changed – there were no people walking past. The local council had stopped cars parking in the street so everyone stopped shopping there – it was dead. We didn't do enough research, we didn't have a marketing person or a PR company to promote the brand, we didn't have a customer base because Morrison wasn't known on the east coast and so it was an absolute disaster.

We had $400,000 worth of stock just sitting there with no one buying and no one to motivate the staff because we were on the other side of the country. It was very difficult to manage. We had to stay because we had a lease in place. But there was a positive – we started to build our customer base.

I learned so much from that experience. I learned not to open a store where people aren't walking past – to actually listen when somebody tells you an area is hard work. These days Richard calls other brands and ask questions. That might sound bizarre but a lot of them ring us too and most of us are happy to share. We no longer allow emotion to get in the way of making decisions – we are more calculated. We no longer try to manage our stores from afar; we have managers living in those states. We now know where our customer bases are, so that's where we position ourselves. These days we like adjacency. We make sure we situate our stores near other brands that we align ourselves with...if they're not there, we're not there, it's just too risky.

I learned not to open a store where people aren't walking past.

I also made mistakes, particularly after having Baxter. I remember finding this great print mill in Germany and ordering all these prints, but I ordered too many, just too much print – it was disastrous. I don't know what I was thinking – I call it baby brain because there is no doubt having a baby did impact on the way I handled things – but a mistake like that isn't just a matter of saying, oh well, you've ordered a wrong print. NO, this was $200,000 worth of fabric! When you first start out you only order a few metres of fabric at a time, but when you grow like we had, our orders were for 5,000 metres – that's expensive. So, if you make a mistake it can take you years to recover.

After that episode I realised I needed help with Baxter. So, when he was six months old, I engaged a nanny – Jill, or as Baxter called her, Diz. She had a huge impact on my life. She taught me how to be a mum, she really cared for our whole family, cooked beautiful meals for all of us and with her help, and knowing that Baxter was in great hands, I was able to get a little more organised.

So, 2005 was a big one for Kylie – a year of both great joy and great stress, but the year wasn't over – there was still Premiere Vision to attend. Premiere Vision is one of the best textile and fashion fairs in the world. It's where the likes of the John Galliano and Yves St Laurent teams are seen; a place where the entire fashion industry comes together. If you're in fashion it's the one you shouldn't miss. Of course, it is held exactly where you would expect such a trade fair to be held – Paris – the fashion capital of the world. So, with baby Baxter in tow, Richard and Kylie set off for Premiere Vision.

[Kylie] We flew into Paris – I was so excited but when I got there I thought, oh my gosh, what am I doing here, look at these people, look at what they do – what am I thinking? I was gobsmacked. It was incredible and intimidating but I just walked around asking loads of questions – and to a certain degree, I did lead people to believe we were a bigger company than we were just so they took us seriously.

Back then people were still allowed to smoke at the fair, so there were all these very stylish people walking around smoking looking at fabrics or sitting at tables, cloaked in white cloth, having lunch and drinking wine – very different to the Melbourne fabric fair where you stand in line to get a pie or a sandwich.

Paris is an incredibly stylish place, the women and men are just amazing in the way they put things together, the style in the streets – there's no other place like it. All of those environmental factors can have an enormous influence on your creative outcome. At the time many French brands were only available in France so that was exciting to see, but now you find them in Australia. When I go to Paris now, I can honestly say that if we had one of our beautiful Morrison stores in a shopping district of Paris, it would be one of their best.

But no matter where you go, when you travel you find inspiration. These days the online trend-forecasting sites are great and so we don't travel as often, but also, we know our brand really well now and are better at what we do, and we design our collections around that understanding.

The following year saw Kylie and Richard's entrepreneurial spirit acknowledged with a nomination in Ernst & Young's (EY) Entrepreneur Of The Year. If that wasn't indication enough of where this company was headed, Morrison also received a Rising Stars Award in that same year.

The awards continued to arrive: BRW's 13th Fastest Growing Australian start-up business; finalist in the Marie Claire Retailer of the Year – for anyone in fashion to receive this kind of acknowledgment from such a publication is a huge accolade. It didn't stop there; another award was waiting in the wings and this was a big one – WA Fashion Designer of the Year.

[Kylie] I was so shocked – I had no idea or hadn't even given thought that we might win. The first thing I did was text Mum and said, not bad for a little girl from Lonnie. I had to get on stage and make a speech – I hadn't done any public speaking and I was so nervous – it was horrendous but thankfully I've improved over the years. Receiving the award was a huge honour and a privilege but I do prefer to be back in the workrooms creating collections rather than up on stage or in the public eye.

However, hiding wasn't and still isn't an option for the founder of one of Australia's fastest growing fashion brands. That growth was clearly evident when plans for Morrison's fourth store in the leafy Perth suburb of Booragoon got underway. This store, in the hugely patronised Garden City Shopping Centre, was the ideal location for the launch of their strategic plan – to position themselves in large shopping centres.

Craig Steere was engaged as architect and together with a clever and perceptive creative team, completed a fit-out that took the brand to the next level. The Garden City store looked amazing and was immediately embraced by a growing clientele. A few years on Peter Alexander, the 'Pyjama King', opened one of his stores right next door to Morrison. The significance of that would not have been lost on Kylie and would no doubt have prompted a moment of proud reflection – after all it was the Peter Alexander concept that fuelled her vision to build her own brand.

Just as Kylie felt it was all coming together, there was yet another change on the horizon; one that would really impact on her life and business. They would soon be a family of five – Kylie, Richard, Morrison, Baxter and…Louis.

[Kylie] I was heavily pregnant with Louis as we prepared to open Garden City. Thankfully, he didn't arrive before the opening night which was an amazing but incredibly busy time for us. When he did arrive, I was more relaxed than I had been with Baxter, but because I was still covering design and some production, everything was a constant juggle. We took extra people on board to cover production and a couple of girls to help me design. It was really rewarding to see our staff grow into their own roles without me having to micro-manage or oversee that progression. It made it a lot easier but it also made us more of a family as everyone took ownership and responsibility for their own position in the company. That's something you only hope happens in your own business although you have a far greater likelihood of it happening if you build a team that is aligned with your vision and your brand.

You can only ever hope your staff will take ownership and responsibility for their own position in your company... and you have a far greater likelihood of it happening if you build a team that is aligned with your vision and your brand.

By 2007 the stores were thriving but not Paddington – it was a constant struggle. Finally, when the end of the lease drew near the decision was made to close the doors. The release from a highly stressful situation together with the joys of a newborn and the triumph of the Booragoon opening signalled another remarkable year, but then October arrived and with it came great sadness. Morrison, or Morri as he was known to his family of 12 years, slipped away to pet heaven, leaving behind an unforgettable legacy – his memory and his name.

[Kylie] When Morri died, I think it was a big turning point for me. I just kept going, but that's when the business got REAL and I do think that happy-go-lucky girl changed a bit. The loss of Morri was probably made worse for me because I was struggling with the children and the business and then Morri...it was then that I realised a lot of the enjoyment I once got from the business was gone.

For any woman in business who has young children I would advise them to be careful of getting too caught up in it all. You get so tired, you don't think clearly, you don't take care of your health because you're too busy looking after everybody else. The stress snowballs and resentment can set in – and that can be self-defeating, so you have to be aware and learn to say no and take time out for yourself. It took me a long while to learn this, but once you identify what you are feeling you can manage it and that can make all the difference – not just to your business but to your longevity within your business as well.

By 2008 we knew we needed a store in Melbourne because our brand was really aligned with the Melbourne customer. Every shopping centre will give you their performance information but we also spoke to people in the industry about area performance, and with all that information we decided on Chadstone. Chadstone is one of the largest shopping centres in the Southern Hemisphere and it had always been a dream to open there. The shop fit-out was the next level. By this time, we knew how we wanted the store to look and so worked with the shop fit out company. We engaged a PR group and then did a massive opening – it was spectacular, we had models on swings in the store and everything looked just amazing. One of the girls who worked for us in Perth moved to Melbourne to head it up so we took the entire team over for the opening and we all celebrated together. It was an incredible night.

There were more celebrations when they won Ernst & Young's, Entrepreneur Of The Year in the category of young West Australian. For Kylie it was a huge honour.

[Kylie] We were nominated for the award but I had no idea we were going to win. The media opportunities, the accolades, the recognition you receive as an Ernst and Young Entrepreneur Of The Year is amazing. It gave us the confidence to believe we must know what we are doing, as well as the great opportunities to learn from the people we met – people we still call on for advice. Entering the award program was a time intensive exercise but if you are in business it's definitely worth getting involved.

November arrived with yet another award, the auspicious Ragtraders Women's Fashion Retailer of the Year. This was a highly significant acknowledgement of Morrison, as the recipients of the awards were traditionally the best of the best of Australia's fashion retailing elite. Kylie and Richard were among the guests when the winner was announced at a glittering cocktail reception in Sydney. For a comparatively unknown west coast brand to take out the top gong was a defining moment for them both, the night when the fashion industry couldn't help but sit up and take notice. Triumph!

So, 2008 started and 'almost' finished with spectacular success but, as many of us remember, it was also the year that would end with the beginning of the Global Financial Crisis (GFC) – the tipping-point. Before it hit Morrison had moved again - from upstairs in High Street down to the street level below. The move gave them far greater floor space, but it came at a cost – a massive increase in rent and the need for yet another fit-out. It was a fit-out that Kylie described as 'horrendously expensive', but with Morrison still undergoing expansion the additional space and fit out was necessary.

It was at that time the suggestion was made to bring in extra senior management. Kylie was unsure but her state of mind, at the time, made her doubt her instincts and led her to believe it was the best thing for the company. It wasn't long before she realised that her acceptance to step somewhat aside was, in fact, a cry for help. It had come from a state of critically low energy and, despite a year of significant acknowledgment, bottom of the barrel confidence.

[Kylie] At the time I believed I should relinquish my responsibility, not all of it, but I'd lost so much confidence after having children so I went with the suggestion that other people would know how to run my business better than I did. But ours was and still is a business built on emotion and a connection with our product, our staff and our customers, and without those relationships we would not have had such enduring success. I understand better now that when you have a team that works well together, like ours, it's vital that whoever you take on board is also able to work as part of that team. If they can't it can have a significant negative impact on everyone.

Although I didn't agree with every decision, I still said nothing. In some ways my silence cost us, but experience teaches you and so I know I will never let that happen again. I am an emotional person but I no longer agree with the suggestion made at the time that my emotions hindered the business – I now know they make it. Now I trust myself more, and often say to others just starting out, if you know your business as I did and you feel something isn't right – trust in those instincts, don't just go along with it, find the courage to speak out.

The end of the year was fast approaching. Now with more people on the payroll, larger premises, much higher rent and continuing expansion, Morrison was pushing itself to the limit. They were aware of a shift in the financial climate, but they never expected it would impact them with any great significance. They were wrong. The GFC struck suddenly with an almighty blow and just as suddenly people stopped spending.

> *I am an emotional person but I no longer agree with the suggestion made at the time that my emotions hindered the business - I now know they make it.*

[Kylie] It was horrendous, frightening, I'd never experienced anything like it. Right from the start our business had only ever been fantastic. We'd had so many years of people just buying our product and loving it and then almost overnight – to just stop buying – it was diabolical. This happened at a time when our team wasn't happy, morale was down, people didn't feel like working and so when sales became really tough it got really bad.

We were in strife and knew we had to cut back somewhere. Senior management was the first to go. Three or four redundancies in head office and a cut-back on casual hours in our retail stores was next. But the best and most significant decision came from us not wanting to cut staff. Instead we put our main team, around 20 people, on nine-day fortnights and that move probably saved us.

One of the biggest mistakes we made was moving into the building in High Street and paying huge rent – it was absolutely ridiculous. You must watch those expenses, particularly when you first start out. Don't pay astronomical rents if you don't need to. Again, because of the state I was in with the children I didn't bother to look at the simple things – like how much it was going to cost us. I allowed others to make those decisions for me. It was an expensive lesson but a good one and now I always ask myself if I'm not sure about something, 'How much do I need to sell just to pay the rent?' and then, 'Is it really worth it?' It's a good habit to get into.

Don't pay astronomical rents if you don't need to. I always ask myself now, 'How much do I need to sell just to pay the rent?' and then, 'Is it really worth it?'

One of our old landlords was aware we were in trouble and knew about a place that might suit us. It was an old warehouse on Marine Terrace in South Fremantle. It was derelict but there was so much space and scope we decided to take it on. We had no money so Richard did the move with big vans and we got backpackers in to help us paint it all out in white. The stress was huge. I don't know how we got through it, but that move was the best thing we could have done. From the day we moved in everyone loved it. The atmosphere is great, we've got space, we've got a great outlook over the ocean – but the most noticeable thing at the time was the stress – it was released almost immediately.

It took us a couple of years after the GFC to recover, although retail itself still hasn't recovered so we have to work very hard for every dollar. In fashion, you must have the best product, you must have the best representation of that product, you must be across social media, online marketing and you must have constant contact with your customers.

Going through the hard times taught me so much. I now know things can turn overnight – overnight everything can just go. So, we've reduced our debt and I no longer take our sales for granted. I take my decision-making very seriously and I am more cautious. If a store isn't performing now, I act very quickly to find out where the problem is and deal with it immediately. I listen more closely to other people in the industry. I now read industry-based information every day and without fail take the time to read our weekly management report. I've also learned to speak up and I'm happy to say I've come out the other side of the GFC with greater knowledge and far more strength and confidence.

Business can turn overnight - overnight everything can just go.

The GFC also taught me how important it is to control your growth and your expenses. I now ask myself, 'Will the business survive if sales halve tomorrow and be prepared for it if they do?' Part of that is the understanding that you have to be across everything. I read an article on Richard Pratt of Visy Industries in Melbourne. He had a massive business, and every day when he got to work he would walk through the factory area. He knew every bit of it and exactly what was going on right to the end of his life. It was a large organisation – it wasn't BHP but it was still big enough to make him, in the year before his death, Australia's fourth-richest person. My business is very small but it's still important to be across everything. Some people say you need to work on the business, not in it – I disagree. I totally believe you need to do both.

I've been able to do both because I have built an amazing team and it's that team that continues to carry Morrison forward. One of the most important things you can do for your business is to have a team that is trustworthy, honest, passionate, hard-working and who respect you and your brand values. They must also share your vision and goals. Our short-term goals – to maintain our quality, to do the best range we have ever done, to get the best sales we have ever got and to offer the best customer service possible – need to be lived every day and everyone at Morrison understands this is a whole of company approach. Our long-term goal doesn't change – we simply want to be the best there is, the best clothing brand in Australia.

The GFC taught me how important it is to control your growth and your expenses. I now ask myself, 'Will the business survive if sales halve tomorrow, and am I prepared for it if they do?'

I'm talking a lot about me but Richard has been instrumental in the growth of the business. He is a great networker and the eternal optimist – everything is going to be great, we need to build, build, build – flat out. He always wants to open new stores and grow and he's very good at negotiating. In fact, he's negotiated some deals that I don't think even many larger brands could have pulled off. So that push to grow has been good, but not always. Paddington was a disaster for us. Not enough research was done and when we closed Richard decided we should open further down Oxford Street to where he thought there would be more walking traffic – but everyone had deserted Paddington when Bondi Junction opened. Again, we should have done more research and again we had to close that store. So there have been decisions made that were detrimental to the business, but on the flip side, if it wasn't for the way Richard was and is, if it wasn't for him ringing people, talking to them, then who knows. I see myself as a worker and I will stay in the office with the team and just work and not get out there and do all the things Richard does. So, whilst we frustrate each other we do understand that the business needs our different strengths.

As we've grown and evolved, our customer base has grown with us for a number of reasons: the quality of our clothing has always been consistent and the vision for our brand has never changed – we simply want to design beautiful clothes for real women. We put an enormous amount of energy and care into every garment and that is reflected in every collection. That's what are our customers have come to expect and trust. The integrity of your brand is everything.

Success in this industry comes from understanding your customers. It's very easy to get caught up in running the office and growing the business but spending time in the stores gives you the opportunity to keep up with what is happening, to talk to customers and listen to feedback from your retail teams. There is nothing like being on the floor – it's gold. Quite often I'll walk into one of the stores and I'll say to the girls, let me see how well I know our customer – what would I pick for that customer walking through the door right now? I usually get it right.

> *Some people say you need to work on the business, not in it – I disagree. I totally believe you need to do both.*

There is very calculated decision-making in our design process...it comes 100 per cent from a business perspective. I'm not interested in designing clothes that only look good on a hanger, or something only a blogger would look amazing in. That process and knowledge didn't happen overnight and I've certainly made mistakes along the way. I remember when our wholesale ranges were selling really well. I got a bit too confident and so looked outside our marketplace. I found a drapey jersey fabric that was very popular at the time and so bought it in six different colours and made a lot of the collection from it. It was so off-mark, it didn't suit our market, it didn't sell, so it was a real stuff up – an expensive mistake. But as a result, I now have an even greater understanding of what our customer base really wants and needs in their wardrobe.

Within two years Morrison had recovered sufficiently from the GFC to open more stores, one in Adelaide's Rundall Street and then another in Sydney's beautiful Strand Arcade. This was a small store surrounded by other high-end designers, and whilst turnover was acceptable Kylie and Richard decided not to renew the lease. Instead, their focus had turned to larger shopping centres and higher turnovers.

[Kylie]   We had researched Westfield Sydney in the Pitt Street Mall where a lot of the luxury brands were located and attracting a large Asian market. No one can just go in and lease a space in there; you actually have to be offered a position. So, when we were offered that opportunity, we took it. The store has been amazing for us but it was a really big step because the rents are just so huge. It's still our highest rent store although when our lease came up recently, we were thinking it would be disastrous not to be invited back – we were, but many others haven't been so fortunate.

The journey continued. Baxter was now six and at school, and Diz the nanny was still at home with Louis. Robyn Radford still checked on her daughter every day, who, like her brand, continued to strengthen.

[Kylie]   I've had to learn to be tough but in a nice way. It's not a bad thing even though women are often judged for being tough, but at times it's necessary. It shows resilience, strength, determination and loyalty. I will be tough if I have to be to look after my girls. If I have to make tough decisions so we are all OK, then that's what I'll do. We all have mortgages, responsibilities and kids; the reality is that this business has to earn an income for all of us.

That style of management gave Morrison the capacity to grow at extraordinary speed, and in doing so earned Kylie a position on BRW's young rich list. Most would be happy, but not Kylie. She was mortified when it was published.

[Kylie]   I don't know where they got their information – perhaps it was calculated on what they thought the business was worth, but I didn't like it. I had a team of people working so hard, cash flow was tough, we were trying to build a business and we just didn't have what they suggested. It's a list based purely on money and I don't consider that as positive – it just isn't that important.

When I was growing up, even though we didn't have a lot, I don't ever remember discussing money and I actually don't care too much about it. Yes, I like to have enough to buy groceries and pay the bills but I don't think it's the most important thing in life or that your happiness depends on how much you make or what you can buy. Too many people put themselves under enormous pressure just to have more money because they think by having it, they are successful. That's just sad.

If you want to be the best in any industry you have to understand it's all hard work, you have to put the effort in, there is no other way.

For me success is about having a business I love and great pride in the amazing team I have created. If you surround yourself with people who are not passionate, who are not connected to you and are there just to earn an income you won't get the same result – or satisfaction. I want Morrison to be the best clothing brand and so does my team.

The fashion world is an interesting mix of many different personalities. You've got those who are just energy out – they are seen at every event; they wear all the brands and perception is the most important thing to them. But what you see is not always a true indication of the way things really are. Instagram and social media play a huge part. You see some designers travelling the world, looking amazing and here am I still living in Hammy Hill, trying to pay a mortgage, looking after a family and there they are spending all of summer on some sensational yacht. You have to wonder how they do that – I mean, who is working on next season's collection? Then you get those behind the scenes companies like Cue or the family owned Sea Folly; they have been around for years and are so successful but you don't see them out there – they are the ones working away, concentrating on the business, rather than just the PR surrounding it. We are a bit like that – probably because I don't really enjoy going out that much (laughter). I don't enjoy all the events and the fanfare – but it's about balance and knowing when you really need to attend events to show respect and fulfil your commitments. But if you want to be the best in this industry you have to understand it's all hard work, you have to put the effort in, there is no other way.

It was that dedication and relentless determination that opened the doors for Morrison to one of Australia's biggest department stores.

[Kylie]   Richard contacted Bernie Brookes (CEO, Myer) to ask if he would come to our head office in High Street to have a look at what we were doing. Bernie agreed. I'll never forget the day he came to see us. He wandered up and down the street. He couldn't find us but he didn't stop looking until he did which I thought was remarkable because he is such a busy man. Myer then offered us a contract which was so exciting. It wasn't an easy path and it took us a long time to get that contract. You only get in if you are good, although if you're a young, trendy 'everyone wants you' brand, they usually come to you. We were and still are the opposite. We are stable, not a fast fashion brand but we have a strong following, we are efficient and have a strong sense of brand.

Myer are very good to deal with but at the start it was all very new to us and came with a lot of changes to the way we dispatch – different barcodes, different processes and on-time deliveries. When the Myer stock comes in everything else stops for the girls. It's a huge effort but it's worth it. It's a big contract so it's a big deal to us.

With the Myer contract came even more reward – Myer Designer of the Year.

[Kylie]   When they announced our name, I sat there for a moment and thought – wow. Because as a child Myer was the only department store in Launceston, so it was a big deal. I remember I rushed to the toilet at this huge gala event so I could ring Mum as I always do. She just cried and said, "Oh darlin' I'm so proud..."

I never underestimated Kylie. It didn't matter what she undertook, I always knew she would be successful. From a very early age she took control of her destiny; she was strong-willed and determined to the point of being stubborn. She was always a leader and has never stopped believing in herself or her ability to achieve her dream. She has never doubted that she could do anything as long as she gave it her best.

Robyn Radford, Kylie's Mother

[Kylie]   The Myer Designer of the Year award is based on the entire brand – the deliveries, product, quality, reliability, response time, marketing, everything – not just on the designs and sell through. Until we won that award, I didn't realise our efficiencies, I thought we were doing what everyone else does because that's the way we work – everything has to be perfect, perfectly hung and labelled properly. But apparently not everyone is as efficient. But we take it very, very seriously so it was great to get the award and that feedback from Myer that we were doing it well.

When we win these kinds of awards it makes me look back at my life and I can't help but think, how on earth did someone from Tassie end up here, so I do honestly believe that part of your life is mapped out for you. I don't like to gloat or talk about it too much but I'm incredibly proud of what we've achieved. I have to admit though, there have been times when I've been on the floor, it hasn't been easy and I have thought I could just walk away from it all. But you can't, there's the debt, staff who rely on you, the need to earn a living and to be honest – I do want to succeed.

My family has always come first. If my kids, for whatever reason, needed me to be there full time, I'd give it all up tomorrow – but I've created a team around me that has enabled me to put my family first. If I hadn't had kids – oh my god, I would be travelling most of the time, I would live and breathe the business, this would be 'my everything'. I would have built it faster, taken it further. But I did have kids and I wouldn't want it any other way. So, the business was sacrificed somewhat but I'm okay with that.

I do want to be successful, although for a woman to admit that she's often seen as selfish and tough, but for a man – oh wow that's great. But times are changing. In saying that I'm sure some men feel they would rather sacrifice the business for the family but can't because there's real pressure on them to succeed, and that must be tough at times.

By 2014 Morrison had seven stores around the country but nothing in Melbourne. The Emporium was a new and luxurious shopping centre in the heart of the city. As the largest Australian designer precinct in the country, it was time for Morrison to take another big step.

[Kylie]   It's been a really good store for us but it was a big decision, because like Westfield in Sydney, it's expensive. But it all comes down to negotiation and how much contribution you can get towards your fit-out. This is really important because what you don't have to spend on your fit-out you can put into your stock. Rich did the negotiating and our financial controller, Michelle, who has been with us forever, gave us the go ahead. Michelle is amazing – she's so across our business and if she had said no, even though we are the owners, we wouldn't have gone ahead – end of story.

If I'm unsure about anything in the business I just ask Michelle. But when I get the monthly figures, I know exactly where we are at and know when something doesn't look right. I can do the store orders now, which is millions of dollars of stock, and before I've even looked at the budget Michelle allows me, more often than not I am within a hundred to a thousand dollars of it. There is something like a sixth sense that grows over time – you need that in business.

I remember talking to a fabric agent and I must have looked a bit upset because he asked if I was okay. When I told him I had just looked at the monthly figures, he suggested it was better not to know. That baffled me and I thought, oh my god, can you imagine not knowing. There was a time, because I was just too stressed with the kids, that I didn't want to know. But that's when things go wrong and did go wrong – so that was another lesson for me. It takes effort and looking at the figures can be confronting but in the long run it's so important and it's also empowering.

Her resolve to be across everything compelled Kylie to step out of her own store and look at what others, not just her competition, were doing. It was whilst walking around the massive Chadstone Shopping Centre in Melbourne that Kylie noticed a series of eye-catching posters of different brands and stores located within the centre. She wondered why her own brand hadn't been offered the opportunity to do the same. Kylie quickly realised it was because Morrison didn't have a marketing person to look out for those opportunities. It was in that moment she made the decision to invest in a marketing manager; a move that would prove highly beneficial to the company.

[Kylie]   A girl had phoned me a few years earlier about a marketing position, but at that time we couldn't afford to make such an investment. She had incredible experience. She had been with Sea Folly and it was with her understanding of that business that enabled her to turn it into an international brand. So, when I saw those posters, I remembered her and set up a time for us to meet when I returned to Perth.

As soon as we met, I could tell she would be great for the business. If you're in an interview and have to try to work someone out, then they are probably not the right person for you. So, I go on my gut instinct when I hire someone; they need to fit because I do believe cultural fit and connection is far much more important than experience.

Go on your gut instinct when you hire someone.

Simone totally got the vision of the business; she totally got the brand. She picked up all the social media, all the direct marketing and communication with our customers and brought with her that bigger business vision and experience. She knows what she's doing. She is inspirational, passionate and incredibly particular, and hiring her was the best thing I could have done for our team.

It was also really important to have someone like Simone handle our social media. We don't use print media a great deal because these days it's far more powerful to have your clothes on a blogger in a street – someone who has a million followers. Bloggers are the powerhouses, the most influential people in fashion. Fashion editors are still powerful but it's the blogger or someone famous who looks amazing and is photographed wearing your designs – that can make or break a brand. It's as simple as that. Initially, when Instagram started people were putting stuff up because they loved it but now, they are paid for it. It sounds a bit shallow but at the end of the day you pay to advertise – it's just a different way of doing it, although because bloggers don't have to say so, most people don't realise they are paid posts.

So, with Simone on board Kylie's team grew stronger and so did the brand as more locations were added to their rapidly growing stable of stores.

[Kylie]   We needed a presence in all key locations so we opened our first Queensland store in Indooroopilly, and then in August 2016 a second in Pacific Fare on the Gold Coast. We then launched two more stores in Victoria, one in Eastland and the other in Hawksburn, which is a really good shopping hub and where you can always get a carpark (lesson learned). We really wanted to be there – it's strip shopping, not a shopping centre and so gives the brand a sense of relevance in that market – the lower overheads also make a difference.

People in the industry are often surprised by our business – our growth, the amount we sell, the product and our efficiencies. Because we are not out there all the time, they don't know our story. Some companies take on a marketing manager to get their story out there before they even begin – it took me 12 years. So, we've done it the other way around and hopefully now we'll see the benefit of getting an incredible business model in place, getting incredible people together, getting the product right and everything else right and be able to say – hey, here we are, we've got a great brand and we are doing really well.

It did work. The brand was making an impact and gaining even more attention, not just from customers but from those in lofty positions in the world of fashion. In March 2016 Morrison once again took the spotlight when it received, for the second time, WA Designer of the Year.

[Kylie]   Again, I had no idea we were going to win but this time, to be honest, I felt our team deserved to win unlike the first time when I felt very uncomfortable. I still often think though, how did this all happen? But then I look at the energy I have to keep moving forward, how I want everything to be done yesterday, and always with the belief that whatever I decide to do is going to work. I came to Perth with $40 – most people would think, what if I starve? What if I end up homeless? I didn't even think about that.

I have worked hard, but I feel so fortunate because not only do I have a successful business I am also now in a position where I can make a difference to other peoples' lives. There is such a reward in knowing that women feel beautiful when they wear our clothes. I remember a woman came up to me several months after we did a styling session in Kalgoorlie. She said it had changed her life because although she was a bigger woman, we had shown her how she should best dress for her size – to hear that was gold. We also get involved in Breast Cancer Care WA pamper days – where we donate outfits and accessories to those dealing with breast cancer. I know the women love it and it makes them feel good – so it's great to be able to do that.

Clothing is powerful! It can change how you feel. If you feel good about yourself you can achieve so much more. It doesn't have to be designer. The 'carefree hippie' can look and feel great in a beautiful, embroidered and free flowing maxi skirt. Clothes just identify who you are. I remember when I put on a suit for the first time when I worked in the city – I felt pretty good, powerful and strong. Clothes can give you that confidence but if you don't get it right it can work the other way too – both women and men should take that on board.

> *Clothes give you confidence but if you don't get it right it can work the other way - both women and men should take that on board.*

Morrison soon grew to ten stores but with that growth came an ever-expanding mass of surplus or out of season stock – a major problem for any retailer. Fortunately, a resolution of what to do with the stock was found on Melbourne's South Wharf.

[Kylie] We opened a store at Direct Factory Outlet (DFO) South Wharf in Melbourne which is a collection of stores, national and international brands, in the one centre. It's really important to turn your stock over particularly when it's older seasons – you can't keep it, it's money – so it has to go. At DFO it's done in a way that is brand aligned (not just selling out of an old warehouse) because it's so very, very important to maintain your branding. Even your discounted stock still needs to look good.

Again, it was that professionalism and dedication to doing it right, along with their commitment to Myer, that led to the opening of three concession stores (a miniature store operated by Morrison but within a Myer Department store). The granting of the concession stores located in Sydney, Melbourne and Perth was a demonstration of the national chain's continuing confidence in the brand and the team behind it.

[Kylie]   Opening the Myer concession stores was really exciting for me, possibly because years ago Mum and Dad bought me a pair of Country Road pyjamas for Christmas. They were one of the best presents I'd ever received – I couldn't believe I actually owned a pair. Country Road was such a huge designer back then and at that time they were one of the only companies to have a concession store within Myer. Now to think I have my own Morrison store within Myer – wow – that's amazing and exciting. (Kylie smiles as she tells that story.)

With experience on their side, Kylie and Richard learned to respond quickly when stores struggled. Therefore, when they realised the Pacific Fare Store on the Gold Coast in Queensland wasn't performing, they made the decision to close. It was disappointing but they accepted it had to be done. Small business has been a struggle in Australia since 2016, particularly for the fashion industry. However, Morrison has not only endured through the struggles, it has gone from strength to strength.

Sadly, not everything was destined to be as enduring. With the start of 2017 came the end of Kylie's marriage to Richard. For the benefit of the business and their sons, the two have remained business partners and are both involved and equally committed to raising their boys. While Kylie acknowledges that remaining business partners is not without its challenges, for now it works.

[Kylie] Richard and I have had to work at it and admittedly it hasn't been easy but fortunately we're both really happy about the way the business is going.

Since 2017 we've absolutely 100 per cent topped our growth. That hasn't happened without challenges. Retail hasn't really improved; we still have to work 110 times harder than we used to but I think we've become better at what we do.

One of the things we did was employ a merchandise planner to really closely monitor and work on our stock control. We'd previously done it ourselves but having someone with far more experience and expertise in that area made a massive difference to our business.

Some might not think about it, but stock control is really, really important. When you start out it's easy to keep designing and developing, but at the end of the day, it doesn't matter how much product you sell, if you have too much stock it has to go. You have to discount it, which reduces your margin and damages your brand.

By employing a merchandise planner, we were able to find an amazing balance. So now all of our design, our ordering, our stock control between the stores and the warehouse is so closely monitored, and that means greater efficiency.

So, 2017 had its challenges and triumphs but nothing quite compared to the salubrious international attention Morrison received on Tuesday the 7th of November 2017 – the day when a race stops the nation.

Article by Claire Davies
PerthNow – WA News – 12 November 2017

THE Fremantle designer of a $600 dress worn by Paris Jackson at the Melbourne Cup says pre-orders have almost sold out before the outfit has even hit stores.

WA label Morrison has received a flurry of international interest after the 19-year-old daughter of pop icon Michael Jackson appeared at Flemington in the russet-hued Clementine dress.

After providing a selection of dresses for consideration, Morrison founder Kylie Radford was told Jackson loved the collection.

"Stylist Trevor Stones said she was a dream, with the fitting only taking a few minutes.

Ms Radford said the response had been "insane" with international orders coming from the US, Spain, Dubai and Iceland.

"She looked incredible and the dress fit her like a glove," Ms Radford said.

"I have received messages of congratulations from far and wide — some people I haven't spoken to in over 15 years.

"Social media has gone crazy; the phones are nuts and we've had people going into our stores and Myer concessions to congratulate us."

It's yet to hit stores but pre-orders have almost sold out.

"We are running around like crazy at the moment trying to secure more velvet so that we can make more," said Ms Radford.

Jackson described the dress as "the most like me out of the options I was given".

"It's one of my favourite colours. It's comfortable, it's soft and don't feel like I want to die in it," the teenage model told Elle magazine.

[Kylie]   It was just so exciting! We had been asked to provide a selection of dresses for Paris Jackson to consider for her appearance at the Melbourne Cup. On its own that was a big thing for us but then to have her select it because she loved it, apparently because it was soft, was in her favourite colour and was more her style, was amazing.

It created a lot of interest and online orders from overseas. It's been great not just from a sales perspective but for the brand as well, because we've been introduced to a whole world of people who hadn't previously known about us. It's all been incredible but at the end of the day what's important is that it did really suit her.

It was an amazing and valued acknowledgement of the brand, a welcome relief from the challenges Morrison was facing – the same challenges every other Australian clothing designer was encountering.

It was expected that by 2018 the economy would show some signs of recovery but even a year later, Australia and much of the world was still waiting. The massive impact on small business was horrendous. Morrison didn't escape unscathed; however, Kylie and her team came to realise that a swift response and adjustment to any change in the marketplace was crucial to their survival. It was their preparedness to take action quickly that contributed to their ability to withstand what was a catastrophic downturn across all sectors of industry.

Like everyone in business we've had to adjust to reduce our risk. High rents in Sydney made it necessary for us to close our city store. Also, we closed the store we had in Chadstone but only because the Australian Designer section underwent a relocation within the centre. Chadstone has always been a great centre for us so once a suitable position becomes available in the new location we plan to reopen there.

In January this year [2019] we felt it was time for a change in approach and so made the big decision to move from Myer across to David Jones. I very much wanted to go back to the wholesale model rather than concession like we had in Myer. Myer was amazing to deal with and I really appreciated their support during our time together, but we felt our brand aligned more closely with Australian designer brands at David Jones. It's still early days but we have been performing well and so we are looking forward to a long, fruitful and mutually beneficial relationship with them.

Unfortunately, but again because of the economic climate, we had to make our merchandise planner redundant this year. It wasn't an easy decision. She was great, and she got us organised, and because of her knowledge and input we now get the right stock through and people are buying it straight away rather than waiting for it to go on sale – we now literally sell out of things.

Customers have so much to choose from out there so if they walk into one of our stores and there's nothing for them, they're not going to buy, even if they think that Morrison is an awesome brand and want to support it. At the end of the day, they will only buy something they like.

So, for us it's about being really proactive. We make sure that every garment that goes into a store ticks the boxes for our customers and we work very, very hard at that. Now, we shut the door and criticise and critique every garment to work out if it belongs in the range or not, even down to the colour. Sometimes it takes us half a day to choose the colour for one silk — everything is now very considered.

A lot of brands have closed down over the last 12 months so the fact that we've continued to survive is a massive reward for me — a big pat on the back to my team because we're still here and people are loving it. The feedback I've had from this season's range is the best we've ever received and that's incredible to hear.

At the end of May [2019] we opened another store in Church Street Brighton, Victoria. It's a gorgeous store in an area that has a real village feel which works really well for us. There's also a good mix of other brands that we align with which we now understand is so important in this business. So when the opportunity came up we grabbed it, plus it was great timing because we are still waiting for the right position in Chadstone.

Our online store has also grown really rapidly. It's doing so well, which is once again thanks to the great team we have who control the online store. But all our people interconnect. The merchandise team feed information through to the design team; the specifics of what we need, what our customers want, what sells well and what's relevant to the market — all that kind of stuff. That feeds through to the retail stores, through to wholesale, through to online.

Three to four years ago, and the whole period before that, we used to drop stock into the stores, let's say in July. Then come December, there's no new stock, you go on sale, you sell through that stock until January and then you drop in winter. We don't do that anymore, we now drop in new, well-considered styles continuously, so there's freshness every week.

It's so important because everything is so instant these days. It's, I see it, I like it, I'll take it. No longer can you send out a look and expect that people will wait for it to arrive into the stores. If they have something on like a wedding, they go out and they get what they want to wear there and then — they won't wait for it. So, buying behaviour has changed and we've changed with that.

Basically, we're now like a little fine-tuned machine. It feels like everybody's just connected, all working in the same direction and it's really good.

When Kylie started out in business there was very little help out there. Today there are literally thousands of online sites that can guide you through the process of starting a business, any business. But even with all the guidance and help available you are the only one who can make it happen.

[Kylie] I grew up in a very small town and came to Perth looking for opportunities because I actually do believe you can do whatever you put your mind to. I believed I would find something, I believed it would be successful and it was that belief that drove it and enabled it to happen. I am now creating an environment where my children will be given many opportunities but whether they take them or not — who knows? There's opportunity everywhere, you just have to go out and look, don't just sit around waiting for them to come to you because if you do that life will just pass you by — that's when you live with regret.

I think a lot of people, particularly women, are in situations where they don't want to be and are living from day to day – they just exist. I was fortunate to have the support of my husband which enabled me to grow a successful business. That has allowed me to live the life I want, to make decisions for myself, and so now I have a certain level of control over my life. I've been able to travel with my kids, be there for them, teach them about compassion, respect and loyalty, go to their assemblies and get involved in their schooling life – not every mum has that opportunity.

It won't be long before I'm 50 (2023) and I don't want to look back and think I've missed out on seeing my children grow up. It's been really hard work to manage both and I do hope it won't always be this frantic. I'd like to think that I won't always be so on edge and dictated to by daily sales – although that's retail – but I still want to be working like I am, and I will always want to be busy.

I have an energy that some people don't have and I think that's what makes me different. I want everything done yesterday – there's a sense of urgency, an adrenaline and fire within me which I think is so important to have in business. You can't run a business if you're complacent – you can't just sit back – you have to drive it.

I've never been one to sit back but one of the things that I've really had to take on board is that every team needs a leader. I'm not talking about someone who leads from above but someone a team can look up to, respect, be inspired by and can lead with confidence. Time and experience have allowed me to identify that a business is far more powerful when the team has a strong leader.

Some of my team have been working with me for years and years. Actually, I used to buy coffee on my way to work every morning from one of our girls, Tanya Vidovich. We just connected so she started wrapping gifts for us at Christmas time. She then worked her way up to becoming an integral member of our design team and has now been with us for 16 years. I've also been dealing with some of my suppliers since the start. I think it's because I keep it real and allow everyone the space to be honest and say it like it is. If I do a design and the girls don't like it, they say, 'What is THAT?' I do the same. It's emotional but it's detached. It's about whatever is best for the brand – we all know that – although as much as we love it and feel passionate about it, it is just work.

Obviously, we are serious and passionate about what we do but you can't be serious all the time or you would go crazy. My aunt taught me that – she's hilarious and once said to me, 'Darlin' relax, don't take life so seriously.' I often think about that comment and now understand that you can't and don't need to control everything, and sometimes laughter is the best way.

I can honestly say I'm now pretty relaxed and happy with everything in my life, although I would really love to spend more time with Mum and Dad as they are getting older. But other than that, I don't want much more. I don't live with regrets, I like who I am, I'm a nice person like my Mum – and my kids are proud of me. I even have a girlfriend who says really nice things to others about me, in front of me. One day she said, 'Kylie is proof that you can achieve a lot in life and in business and still be a really nice person.' Someone else in a magazine called me the nicest person in the fashion industry – those comments are really lovely to hear. Ooh, do I sound shallow telling you that?

Enthusiasm is the genius of sincerity, and truth accomplishes no victories without it.

Edward G. Bulwer-Lytton

Morrison is a very successful business, but it has taken far more than just being nice to get it there. She may have grown tougher over the years and there may have been many changes and challenges along the way, but from the outset this woman was prepared to give whatever it took to become the best – the alternative was simply unacceptable. Kylie had no idea where she was going when she arrived in Western Australia at the age of 21, she just knew she had to keep moving forward. If there was ever doubt it was fleeting, as was her tolerance of negative input. Risks were taken only to maintain that forward momentum but as always, she was, and is, ever true to herself, her brand and the extraordinary team she has developed.

The success Kylie has achieved over her business life should be proof enough of why it is so important to just begin your own journey – even when you are not entirely sure of which direction you are headed, just so long as you begin. As Kylie says, If you don't start somewhere you may never get an opportunity. Equal in value is to follow your gut instinct, to learn and grow from every step you take, to work relentlessly hard with honesty and integrity, and to believe, without question, in your own ability to reach your chosen destination. By doing so you too may ultimately declare, like Kylie – I am proud of how and where I have arrived.

Kylie and the brand she created have come a long way from where it all began. From the small, but very well-run Fremantle store to having over 60 staff, 11 flagship stores and showcased in more than 100 retailers nationally including 14 David Jones stores, it would be fair to say that Kylie has achieved a staggering amount.

She is still as down to earth as when her journey started but, equally, she has come a long way. Kylie believes if she had a tail it would wag a lot; she is still 'over the moon' every time she see's someone dressed in one of her designs. But today Kylie acknowledges that she doesn't get quite so 'beside herself' as she did when she saw her first white shirt in InStyle magazine. On that day she remembers her invisible tail did wag a lot.

Kylie is a woman driven. That burning excitement within her goes on and her love for her business and 'her girls' never diminishes. The pride her parents and her children have in her continues to drive Kylie to be the best in her field. But it goes even deeper. Her success will always be shaped by integrity, decency, honesty and respect for her team, her suppliers and her customers – and that is what makes her one of the fashion industry's enduring and shining lights.

So, what next…

> [Kylie] I love it that we are still moving forward, still growing, which you have to do if you want to survive in business. But what's even more important to me is that I always feel satisfied that I am the person I am meant to be and want to be. I want my life to sit right; to always feel good about the things I do – to have balance, less stress and to be less frantic. I have my boys and they are beautiful. I have this business and it's amazing. So, to think about what's next – what more do I want to achieve? Well, that's hard to answer because I don't really want anything else – I am really happy with what I have. I already have it all.

How many of us can say that! Yes, it's taken her years of hard work, but they do say the harder you work the luckier you get and the greater the reward – Morrison is a great reward and becoming greater. So, congratulations Kylie Radford!

"Coming together is the beginning.
Keeping together is progress.
Working together is success."

Henry Ford

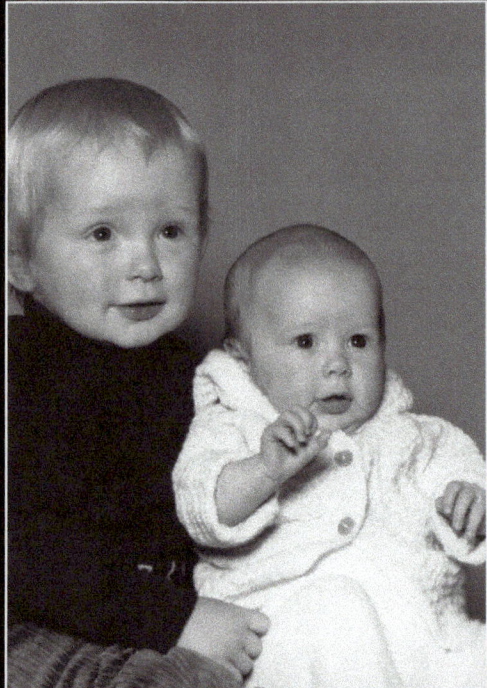

David and Kylie

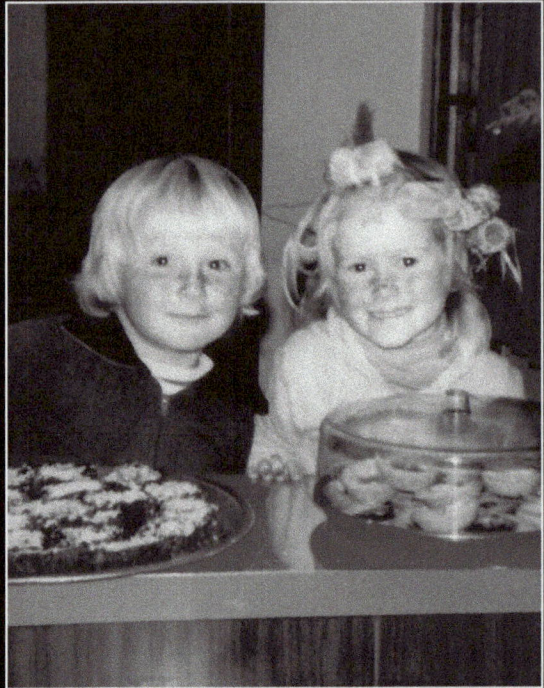

David with his style conscious sister, Kylie

Kylie with her mother
Robyn Radford

The Radford family home.
Launceston, Tasmania

Kylie Graduates.
With her parents

Kylie in the car she bought
when she arrived in Perth WA

Morrison Garden City

Morrison Garden City - Designed by Craig Steere

Morrison - Chadstone

Morrison - Fremantle

Morrison - Fremantle

Morrison very much at home
in a fashion shoot

Morrison

Paris the fashion hub of the world

Premiere Vision - Paris

Kylie surrounded
by paperwork

Kylie talking to STM Fashion Editor
Damien Woolnough at Garden City
Fashion 2019

Kylie with business partner
Richard Poulson

Kylie at WA Designer of the Year
with Richard Poulson and Mariella
Harvey-Hanrahan

Kylie Radford

Kylie with her sons, Baxter and Louis

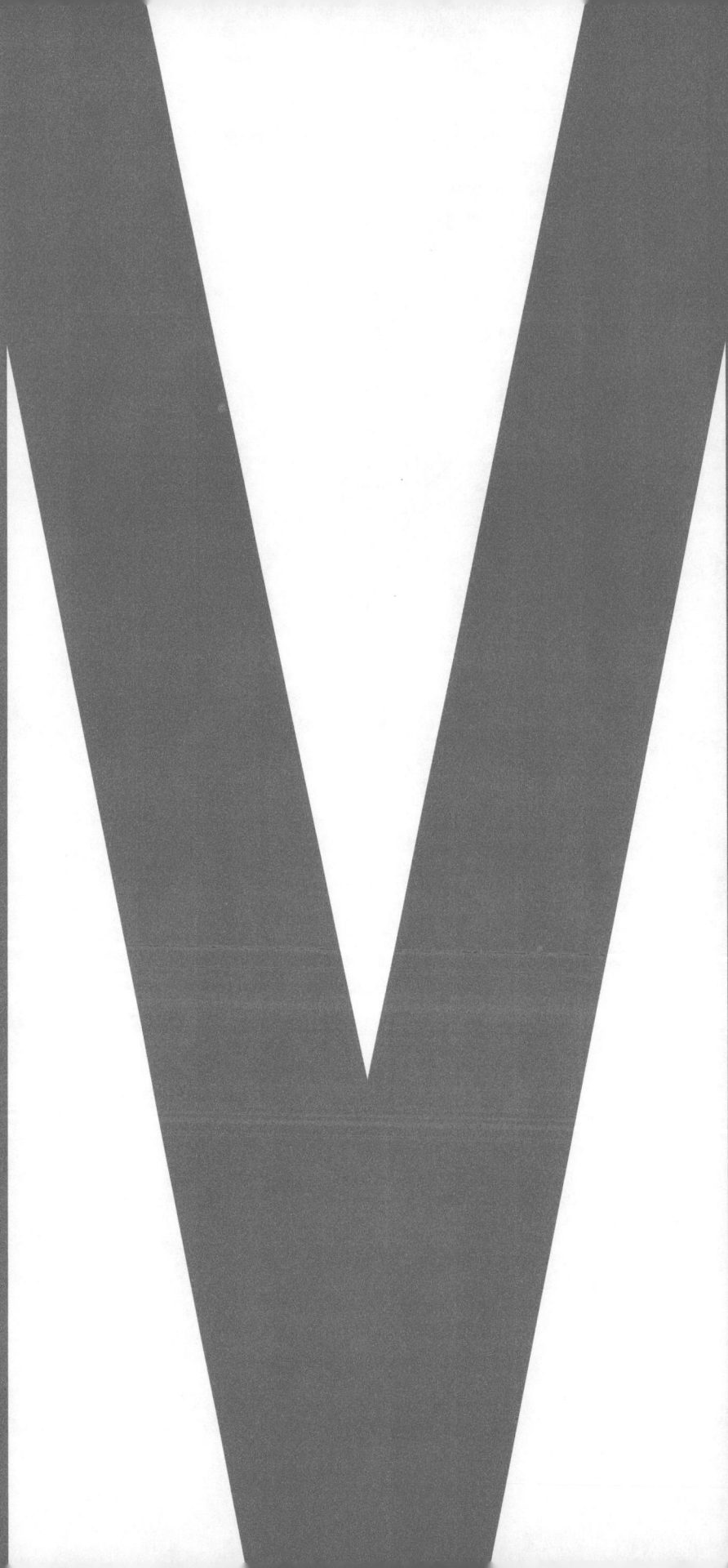

3

Taking a Risk,
Reshaping an Industry

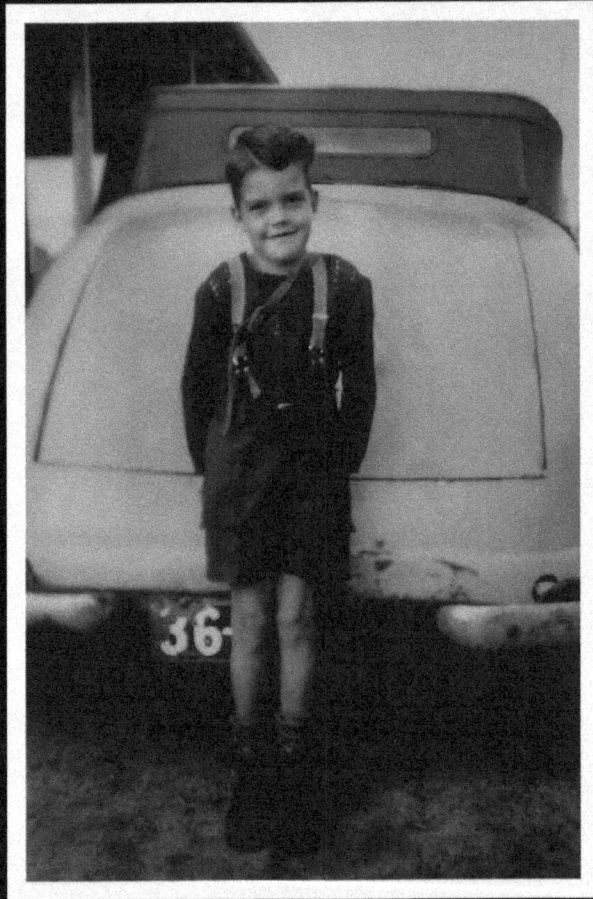

"Cash is king - it's an old saying but nothing could be truer. Know your cash position everyday - don't be in business if you don't."

He left the country life more than half a century ago but still calls himself a country boy. He became one of the State's largest retailers of electrical appliances but still calls himself a fridge salesman. His determination to develop exceptional and distinctive enterprises was born from a desire to not only be the best but to be different. This took him on a journey from the ordinary to the extraordinary.

His love of retail and his thirst for industry-knowledge saw him start and build unique businesses. In each, he attained a level of excellence which attracted the buying attention of national and international retailers. Over time he sold to them what he had created. He gave his name, his face and his distinctive voice to grow his business and it worked; it did grow, and it continued to grow.

His retail success became well known around the State as did his passion for football. It was when those worlds collided that any lingering, but closely guarded, anonymity vanished. But a growing public profile together with significant business acumen enabled him to take a struggling football team and turn it into a success story both on and off the field.

He is a man passionate about many things, from racehorses and punting to football and golf, but business is what really makes this man's pulse race. Even now, after more than 40 years of commercial success – along with his share of the tough times – his enthusiasm and appetite for business continues. He is a visionary, he is an iconic retailer and businessman, he is the man behind the Rick Hart chain of stores – Rick Hart Fans, Rick Hart Classic Appliances and Kitchen Headquarters, he is…

Rick Hart

Richard John Hart (Rick) was proudly named after his father, Richard Thomas Hart (Dick), a farmer's son from Nukarni in Western Australia's Wheatbelt. Dick worked on the family wheat and sheep farm until the Second World War drew him into the air force. His horizons were somewhat broadened when posted to Darwin and so life as a farmer didn't hold quite the same attraction on his return home. During his absence a young woman had moved to nearby Merredin to work as the local telephonist for the PMG now known as Telstra. Rosalie Isabella Stewart, a confident and capable woman, caught the young airman's eye. After a relatively brief courtship the two said "I do". With those words spoken Mr and Mrs Hart set about building a life for themselves and the children they would one day have. A life that would come to influence and take one of their children on a vibrant, entrepreneurial journey.

Still in the air force, the newly married couple moved to Bullsbrook so Dick could take up his station at Pearce Airbase. It wasn't long before their first child was born. Rick made his entrance on the 19th of December, just in time for Christmas. It was 1943. Within a year the little family had returned to the Wheatbelt but this time to Merredin. Rick enjoyed two years of 'only child attention' before his sister, Sue, was born in 1946. With the arrival of Tony in 1947 the Hart family was complete. Life was wonderful.

> [Rick] As kids, we didn't have any great demands, but Mum and Dad tried very hard to look after us and made sure we had everything we wanted and did everything we wanted. I was spoilt but no more than the other two although they probably had a different view on that. In those days, all I wanted was a tennis racquet, a cricket bat and a bike and that made me pretty self-sufficient.
>
> There were always plenty of things for us bush kids to do. The Railway Dam was a beautiful place and we spent a lot of time there. We also spent a lot of time at my grandparents' farm in Nukarni. My Granddad, Alf, was a pioneer of the area and he developed the property from scratch – very hard work in those days. He was sort of my hero.
>
> He used to call me Richie; I think I was probably his favourite. He used to look after me pretty much. He taught me to drive and even let me drive his car into Merredin on a Saturday afternoon where he'd shout me to the pictures while he'd go off and do his thing. I didn't know what his thing was but I found out later that he enjoyed the races so he would go off to the local

club where he could have a bet and a drink or two. Quite often when he came to pick me up after the pictures he'd say, "Oh Richie, it's a bit cold to drive home so I think we'll stay in the car and go home in the morning." I'd say, "Okay Grandpa." I didn't know at the time but that was obviously because he'd drunk a little too much.

He was chairman of the road board, which is now known as the shire council, and was always patron of the football club and all that sort of stuff. He was a great man.

From about the time I was nine or 10 up to when I left school at 17 we used to do shifts on the tractor and other work around the farm so the farm and my Granddad had a big influence on my life.

My Dad had a much lesser profile. He didn't want to be a farmer like Grandpa, so he did building and repair work in and around the place. But he was a big sporting man, very good footballer, very good cricketer; he spent his life playing cricket. I didn't see much of him playing football because his career was probably over by the time I was born, but he played cricket until he was quite an age.

As a kid, I loved going to the cricket and to the wonderful afternoon teas that the ladies put on for the cricketers. The sponge cake with jam, cream and strawberries on top was my favourite but I also loved the lamingtons with cream and the curried egg sandwiches. The farmers' wives made them and they were amazing.

Rick was 10 when his parents bought the Post Office and General Store in Korbel, a 20-minute drive from Merredin. It was in that general store where Rick had his first real taste of retail. He, Sue and Tony all worked in the shop on weekends, after school and when on holidays. Rick loved it although that was more likely because it gave him endless opportunities to raid the biscuit barrels – unless, of course, his mother was watching.

[Rick] Mills & Wares made these Coconut Ring biscuits that came in big tin cases so we had to bag them up; they were my favourite. Then there was the chocolate that came in big slabs in wooden boxes. We had to take those slabs of beautiful peanut rough and break them up and then put the pieces in the chocolate jars that were on the counter. We ate more than we put into the jars.

Everything came in bulk, like potatoes, which came in big hessian sacks that we had to re-bag into 14-pound brown paper bags to make it quicker to serve customers. In those days people didn't come in and pick out their vegetables, weigh them, put them in plastic bags and then take them to the checkout; they had to actually ask over the counter, "I'll have a bag of potatoes".

The general store also had a telephone exchange. Mum ran the switchboard but we kids were all trained to do it. People would ring the exchange and ask, "Can I have Korbel 24," so you'd put a plug into Korbel 24, you'd ring the phone and they'd answer at the other end. As kids we were a bit nosey, and sometimes we'd listen in to their telephone conversations. Occasionally we'd hear some juicy gossip. We also had petrol bowsers, a petrol depot with drums out the back and a post office with mail sorting facilities. There was a little railway siding across the road and every morning we would go there to collect the parcels and mailbags for the post office. We got a lot of experience and training as kids, and so for a time, my whole life revolved around that store.

Mum pretty much ran the store because Dad was a builder and he did renovations for post offices around the State so he was away a lot. But we got on really well and he taught me a lot.

He used to talk to me about how important it was that when you make a commitment you always stick to it; that your teammates are the most important people around you because if you let them down then you've let the whole team down.

He taught me things about honouring your promises, your word is your bond and that you never, never welch on a bet – if you bet someone something, you stick to it and you better pay them or else.

Mum instilled different principles in us. She taught us good values and good manners, which cutlery to use, which glass to use; we also learned how to lay a table because Mum always set the dinner table beautifully.

It was Dad who introduced me to horse racing, which has become a big part of my life. He took me to the races for the first time when I was about 15, although I followed racing as a kid because of the sporting magazines I used to read in the store. Those magazines always had a lot about racehorses.

I was absolutely mad about sport as a kid, it didn't matter what sport it was, because in the country you can do any sport you want; I was a full bottle on them all. I never knew about betting but I used to listen to the races. One day Dad took me to Ascot racecourse and as he was placing a bet I said, "Dad, I'd like to have a bet too," and he said, "What would you like to do?" I said, "I don't know, how do you do it?"

He told me it would be better if I just picked a quinella, which is first and second in a row, and then gave me five shillings to have a go.

I picked these two horses and blow me down if they didn't come in. If that bet had lost, then my five shillings would have gone with it and maybe I would have been turned off racing for evermore. But because of the excitement of that win I have maintained an interest in horses all the way through.

Rick's interest in sport, horses and punting greatly influenced him over the years, so much so, that he eventually purchased a farm in the hills of Serpentine. The farm gave him the opportunity to keep, at times, more than 30 racehorses; all well-loved, well fed and content. He still has his farm where his dreams are kept alive with a few unraced babies awaiting their shot at glory. Their paddock mate, Jacks or Better, Rick's prized gelding who had an amazing 19 victories (two Group Ones) including the Railway Stakes in 1995, is now a grand 28 years old, and deservedly has the pick of the paddocks where he will remain until his days come to an end.

Rick was and still is a happy, jovial man who rarely gives time to miserable memories. He's much happier telling jokes or reliving the good time stories, his days at school are especially recalled with a grin – how he looked forward to going every day; the hour on the bus going to and from school wasn't a problem for young Rick. He realised he was one of the lucky ones – he was second or top both in the classroom and out on the sports field; he had loads of interests and many friends.

[Rick]   I was a tall kid but I was a gentle giant. I never felt any real aggression other than on the basketball court or on the footy and hockey field until one day this little fella who was the boss of the school ground really riled me. He was my age, a little bit shorter than me but very tough. He was one of those rough, tough kids where any time there was a fight, he'd be in it and he'd always be the winner. People were scared of him. Anyway, on this one day he just got the best of me, I can't remember why but I'd had enough.

Back in those days there were a few kids around that if there was going to be a fight, they'd bring out the gymnasium mats and put them behind the recreation hall and then they'd tell all the kids there was a fight on. It was a pretty fair way to do it.

Anyway, because I'd lost my block and I didn't want there to be any doubt that he could get the better of me, I belted the crap out of him. I was hailed the winner and that was the last problem that I, or anyone else had with that bloke.

So, I loved school and learning but I never used to think much about what I wanted to do when I left. When I was a little kid all I wanted to be was an iceman, you know the iceman that used to come around with ice blocks on the back of the truck. As I got older, I wanted to be a journalist or a sports commentator. I don't think I gave it much thought other than I thought I'd be good at it.

I wrote to the ABC to get an interview about being a sports commentator and when I was next in Perth, I went to see them; I was 14 or 15. They talked to me about my knowledge of sport and all that sort of stuff. The bloke said, "Okay, that's good but your voice isn't good enough to be a commentator."

So, then I became fully focused on being a journalist. I knew I had to get a high mark in English, so I put all of my efforts into it. I was also pretty good in History, but you had to pass four subjects to get your leaving certificate. In the end I got a distinction in English and a high mark in History but I didn't get through the others and so I bombed out. I made a strategic error; I put all my eggs in one basket so to speak. Not that it's made any difference but the one regret I still have, if I have one at all, is that I didn't get that Leaving certificate.

Rick, still focused on a career in journalism, had submitted an application for a cadet journalist position with The West Australian Newspaper. He never gave a second thought to the possibility that his results might prevent him from pursuing his dream.

Whist waiting to hear if his application was successful Rick's parents decided to separate. His mother moved to Perth with the two younger children, Sue and Tony and once there bought a school tuck-shop, or delicatessen as they are better known today. Rick, with his mind on his career, soon followed them. It was 1961, Rick was 18 years old.

Victoria Park was a long way from Korbel, and having only ever known life in the country, he vowed to one day return. But for now, his address was to be the little house that adjoined the tuck-shop at 2A Cargill Street, Victoria Park, over the road from Cargill Street Primary School.

> [Rick] It was at that shop that I had my first taste of how trading laws can so adversely affect a retail business. Small shops in those days were only able to sell essential items like milk and bread after 6pm. By law, every night we had to put these chicken wire screens over the shelves – and then padlock them! That was to ensure customers couldn't be served with non-essential items like a can of baked beans or a packet of pasta. To make sure shop keepers complied with the law they sent inspectors around to police it. We took it as normal but when you look back you realise how ridiculous the retail laws were, although in saying that here we are 50 years later and, in many ways, they still are ridiculous!

When you look back you realise how ridiculous the retail laws were, although in saying that here we are 50 years later and, in many ways, they still are ridiculous!

Every day school lunch orders had to be filled, local customers had to be served, stock had to be ordered and delivered and then stacked on the shelves. From her country life experience Mrs Hart knew only too well how to run a business, but it was hard work. Her children, as they had always done, helped out when they weren't at school or, in Rick's instance, at work in his new job - not the one he had hoped for. Only days before leaving Korbel for Perth Rick had discovered his dream of journalism was over. His application for a cadetship was among 300 other applicants. There were a mere 10 cadetships available and sadly his was, all too quickly, lost in the system. Rick didn't even make it to the first interview. He was devastated…but only for a moment.

> [Rick] My second option, and one that I really wanted to do, was to join one of the big stock firms like Dalgety's, Wesfarmers or Elders and become a stock and station agent. I had applied for a job with all of them. The first one that came back was Dalgety's, so I went for an interview as soon as I arrived in Perth and got the job.
>
> Dalgety's was a conglomerate, a big company which was very diversified in what it sold. They were heavily involved with the farming community. Amongst other things, they sold shearing equipment, sheep dips, as well as wool for the farmers. They had facilities for sheep and cattle auctions, woolsheds in Fremantle and shipped to and from the stations in the North-West.
>
> The idea was that I would get trained in Perth, and after about six months, I'd be relocated to Merredin, Kellerberrin or Geraldton or wherever it might be.

As it turned out, I got allocated to a metropolitan job. It was in their wholesale company that distributed wine and spirits, tobacco and cigarettes. It was a bit like a poisoned chalice!

Rick and another young lad, John Chalmers, started work at Dalgety on the same day. Both loved a drink, racehorses and hockey. They soon became firm friends; today more than 50 years later that friendship continues.

[Rick]   I'd been invited to train with the WAFL club, East Perth, I think more as a companion for my mate who they were keen to get. I asked East Perth how often they trained and they said Tuesdays and Thursdays. I told them I could only train Thursdays because I worked on Tuesday – plus I was enjoying my city life. Having come from Merredin where I played sport every Saturday and Sunday, trained four days a week and played basketball, I just didn't want to get involved in full-time training.

That didn't sit well with East Perth. "Bad luck mate, you're no good to us." That's when I decided I'd play hockey with my good mate John Chalmers. That team was happy enough for me to train once a week although I regret not being more dedicated to footy because I probably could have done quite well.

Yes, there's always hindsight – but never as much foresight! It seems, more often than not, foresight is a gift for those with a life full of experiences, and Rick at 18 didn't have too many of them. Fortunately, he found he loved his work at Dalgety and also that he loved city living. Within six months the idea of returning to Merredin was abandoned. Was that foresight? Unlikely, but the extraordinary life he was destined to lead was dependent on him remaining in the 'big smoke'.

At Dalgety's one of his tasks was to reconcile the shipping account. The clerk given the job of teaching Rick would take a full day to do the reconciliation, a job that Rick found he could do in a matter of hours (before calculators). No wonder he calls himself a bush accountant. The big boss noticed. Soon he was moving up through the ranks and eventually landed a position in the highly desired liquor division.

In time the job took him all over the State and into many a country bar. At six foot three he was well able to look after himself and so was often found fighting alongside the publican in bar brawls that ended on dusty, country town streets.

[Rick]   While at Dalgety's I got very good training in business procedures, skills and systems and all those sorts of things. That really gave me a good grounding in the basics of running a business. Having been with the company for a dozen years or more I was thrilled to be appointed general manager of a division that was assigned to the purchase of eight or nine liquor stores in Perth. I think it was also around that point that I decided I wanted to get into a hotel or something like it but I didn't know quite how I was going to do that.

Not long after they'd bought these liquor stores, the government changed all the licensing regulations, allowing taverns, liquor stores and wine bars on every corner. The old company, which was based in London, became concerned about the changes and quickly made a decision to sell them all.

My job then was to disassemble this array of liquor stores that I'd just been involved in putting together and that's when I realised, shit, there's not going to be a job for me at the end of this.

Rick knew he was on shaky ground. There was nowhere to go at Dalgety, and that was the moment his thinking shifted, the moment he found the 'how' he'd been looking for. He would buy one of the Dalgety liquor stores. This was his opportunity to do something for himself. Full of enthusiasm, Rick, together with a long-time colleague from Dalgety, made an offer to purchase one of the best of them. Negotiations were in full swing when the boys' bank manager prompted them to question their judgement of it being such a great idea. "Boys, you don't want to take such big risks at your age." Naturally, as everyone knew back then, bank managers know best. Relieved to have received such knowledgeable advice and, just in the nick of time, the two withdrew their offer to purchase the $34,000 business. That relief turned to bitter disappointment when the following year the same liquor store resold for $150,000.

> *Whilst bank managers, friends, parents and men in dark suits generally have good intentions, they don't always give the best advice.*

All too soon, just as Rick predicted, with the demise of the liquor arm of the company there was no job for him. He was made redundant. His brief career at the helm of what had the potential to be a retail liquor empire, came to an abrupt end.

The upshot of the experience was a heightened awareness and respect for gut feeling. It was a vital tool that would come to play a significant role in all his future decision making.

It was now July 1973. Rick was 30; he was without a job; he had just bought a house and his wife was six months pregnant with their first child. They were worrying times.

[Rick]   I was nervous and I also felt betrayed. I'd been a loyal servant to Dalgety's for 13 years, and all I could think was Jesus, surely, they could find me a job somewhere. But there was nothing I could do so I went off into the wilderness, just knowing I'd think of something.

As Rick pondered his future, he took a few odd jobs. A good friend, Mal McGrath, the owner of a building company in Balcatta, gave him a job as a labourer. It provided just enough money to live. The experience also taught Rick something about himself – labouring was not for him and therefore he would only do it for as long as necessary.

Fortunately, he ran into another good friend, Oliver Drake-Brockman, a legendary football commentator and real estate agent. Oliver (Olly) and his real estate business partner, Warren Woolf, offered Rick a job in their agency at Woolf Drake Brockman. Their office was situated under the

Civic Clock Tower in Inglewood and where immediately Rick set to work on obtaining his real estate licence with Warren as his mentor.

A lack of finances gave Rick no option but to continue working as a labourer for three to four days a week, with weekends and any spare time spent focused on real estate and the racetrack.

Without any properties to sell Warren gave him a listing. It was a block of land in Quinns Rocks, an outer coastal suburb of Perth. Beggars can't be choosers, so Rick jumped at the opportunity. He drove the 34 miles out to where he hammered his 'For Sale' sign into the $5,000 site overlooking the Indian Ocean. On the first day he advertised he received a call from the owner of another Quinns Rocks block – she wanted Rick to sell it. He signed her up but, in the meantime, he received a cash offer on the first block. Once again, he made the long drive out but this time to remove the 'For Sale' sign and re-erect it on his new listing around the corner.

> [Rick]   So, there I was just banging the sign in on the second block when this couple drove up and parked their car behind mine. This bloke got out and asked if it was for sale. I said yep it's $5,000.
>
> He turned to his wife and said, "We'd like to buy it wouldn't we love, it's just what we're looking for. So, I signed them up on the boot of my car then and there – and that was my introduction to real estate.
>
> I went back to the office and in jest said to Warren, "How long has this been going on?" He just looked at me and said, "Well now you have nothing left to sell – you need to get out there and find some listings."
>
> Olly had some good contacts, could sell ice to an Eskimo and he liked having a good time but it was Warren who was the really switched on real estate person in the office. Not only was he a good salesman, he was a good at everything type of bloke.
>
> Warren recommended I take on Balga, a working-class area because in those days there were State Housing Commission loans with low interest rates for low-income families. A seller could transfer the loan to a buyer if they qualified so it made selling in the Balga area very easy.
>
> I'd read this book by a real estate guru in America and I developed a similar system to his. I started dropping letters into people's letterboxes, letting them know I was the area specialist, and if they ever needed an appraisal or help with selling, I was always in the neighbourhood. Here's my number, call me anytime. That's when I became the Balga specialist.
>
> I was doing quite well but I still wanted to have a crack at being in business for myself. Maybe it was because of my background of the store in Korbel, Mum's tuckshop in Vic Park and then being at Dalgety's and seeing business transacted. They all gave me a taste of how people could operate in business and make good money.

While not overly captivated by real estate, Rick recognised from his time in the industry that he had developed a flair for accounting, had an innate ability to build rapport with people and had a mighty grasp on the importance of buying in the right location for both commercial and residential property. While he acknowledged those attributes Rick may not have been as aware that he was open and ready for any opportunity should one pass his way. But that quickly changed when a casual conversation revealed a life changing opportunity. It was pure chance but from that conversation a lifelong passion for retail and ultimately an appliance empire was born.

> [Rick] Over a beer at the pub, a mate of mine just happened to mention a bunch of new but banged up refrigerators that were going up for grabs. It was an insurance write-off. The insurance company were trying to sell off the damaged goods but they weren't having any luck. We "wannabe" entrepreneurs thought we could sell them ourselves and so decided to have a crack with an offer. We made a pretty ridiculous bid, and much to our surprise they accepted it. So, we got them but then we thought – now what to do with a hundred refrigerators?

We made a pretty ridiculous bid, and much to our surprise they accepted it. So, we got them but then we thought – now what to do with a hundred refrigerators?

As luck would have it, the brother of Ricks new business partner had a panel beating business in the industrial area of Osborne Park. He ran the business at the back of the building but out the front was a very small and unused office – not ideal but still a retail space.

They soon had refrigerators crammed into every corner and up to the ceiling of their new, so-called showroom. More space was needed. Again, a family member of Rick's new business partner came to the rescue. His mother agreed to park her car on her front lawn; her garage became their storeroom.

It was mid-1975 and the boys were ready to start selling their wares. The Sunday Times Readers Mart was the best place to let customers know that 'Northern Discounts' located at number 95 Howe Street was open for business – but only on Sunday's. The rest of the week was spent working in their 'real' jobs.

Sundays became very busy as customers flocked to buy a refrigerator with a dent in the door at half the price of a dent-less one. Around 12 weeks later the stock was all but sold – but not before it became very apparent to the location-savvy Rick that customers were quite prepared, if not happy, to shop in the well-known industrial area.

Rick had an idea, it was risky, but it was an opportunity he didn't think they should miss. Soon Rambler box air conditioners and ultra-modern colour televisions joined a freshly delivered load of brand-new refrigerators in the front office. Their business was now officially on the move.

Rick is quick to admit his partner was a great salesman and he himself only average, although it didn't take him long to learn. But it was Rick's interest in accounting and business practices that drove the business in the right direction. Often, as he poured over their profit and loss sheets, memories of growing up in Merredin would flood his thoughts; how he put whatever he wanted, usually lollies, onto his mother's account at Mr Picks, the local grocer. Now himself a retailer, that memory became another lesson learned on his pathway of life.

> [Rick]   Don't let a day end without checking the day's figures, and always have some idea of where they are at. There is an old saying in business, Cash is king, and nothing could be truer. You must know what your cash position and what your expenses are even if you write them down on the back of an old envelope – just work them out daily. Then you will know what income you need to generate to meet those expenses. It's a simple formula that many business owners tend to overlook.

With that knowledge, this is probably a good place to introduce Rick's other occupation – as a bookmaker (bookie) with a love of racehorses. It had all started when he was 25 while still working at Dalgety. Ken Gray was the father of one of Ricks friend's; he was also a top Perth bookie. Rick pestered him time and again for a job at the races. Aware of Rick's passion for the horses and his desire to make some quick cash Ken reluctantly agreed to take him on as his penciller. He presumed Rick wouldn't be able to handle it; in his eyes not only was Rick far too big to be any good but even worse, he was left-handed! It took a mere 15 minutes for Ken to learn a big lesson – never presume; the young man was raw talent. Soon Rick's Saturday's were spent at the metro races with the task of keeping a running total on the money Ken held on each horse. It was hard work and at times frenzied but his time balancing worksheets at Dalgety made him a natural.

Rick was passionate about his pencilling position but he was now juggling many balls. His Dalgety days were behind him but his commitments to real estate and now his retailing business were spiralling – upwards! Then he accepted yet another role, as steward at the greyhounds (another interest). Something had to give. Not surprisingly, it was his short-lived but profitable real estate career that was put out to pasture.

By 1979 with a few wins under his belt and his retail business doing remarkably well, he was again ready for something new. Rick was ready to take the next step – up onto the bookie stand itself. A daunting aspiration!

If he thought pencilling was tough, being a 'rookie bookie' was brain chaos and pressure at its best. Constantly exercising care and judgement, he accepted bet after calculated bet from frantic, value-searching punters, whilst at the same time keeping a tight rein on his profit and loss. The pressure was relentless but not only did the big man love every minute of it, the financial rewards made it very worth his while.

With life's commitments now spread between a growing retail business, midweek race meetings, Saturday mornings on the retail floor and afternoons spent in the bookies ring, there was little time left for his young family. Sunday was all they had, and whilst it was never enough, Rick accepted this was a sacrifice that most in business have to make.

Northern Discounts continued to flourish, and it wasn't long before a second store was opened in Nollamara. Both stores provided a customer service that no competitor came close to offering. Vast product knowledge, going out to people's homes to check on space for air conditioners, try before you buy offers, trade-ins, picking up the old while delivering the new, even free Jelly Beans on the front counter – they tried anything just to be different, anything to make the act of buying an enjoyable and memorable experience. Rick read every piece of literature on the retail industry – newsletters, magazines and books. He became convinced that doing things differently to your competitor and offering great customer service was the key to success. More than 40 years later that conviction remains unchanged.

[Rick]   When we started our business, I identified that people in the whitegoods industry weren't doing it really well. I could see that people were being ripped off and that customer service was appalling; if you had a problem, basically, you were on your own.

> *I could see that people were being ripped off and that customer service was appalling; if you had a problem, basically, you were on your own.*

Some people can't see the wood for the trees. They just run their business and if it's ticking along okay, they're happy. Some business owners don't even consider how they could or why they should improve their business.

I used to subscribe to a series of training newsletters called, I think, 'The Success Business'. The guy who wrote it had some wonderful ideas and out of that, I thought, if we can run our business differently to everyone else, in terms of our product mix, then we'll do well.

If we were selling 20 TVs how could we be different to the bloke down the street who's selling the same 20 TVs? My answer to that was to find a brand or a size that wasn't in every other store and to be different –[to] sell video recorders as well.

I soon recognised that every electrical store appeared to stock every possible product just so they didn't miss any sales. But what happened then is that they became irrelevant to the suppliers, simply because they were selling a bit of this and a bit of that. Would have been a different story if they had massive buying power.

I decided then that we needed to specialise in areas that weren't being catered for like cooking, kitchen appliances, air conditioners and also colour TVs because they were such a big volume business.

We started offering extra services, like lending out TVs. People would come in and look at a TV but often they couldn't decide which one they wanted. So, we allowed them to take it home and use it over the weekend. If by Monday, they didn't want it we told them to ring us and we'd go and collect it.

Do you know how many we picked up? None!

Why? Because parents would put the TV on for the kids and then they'd all get into watching this new colour television. Dad couldn't then say, "I think we better take it back; we can't afford it, or whatever." So, they never called.

We also made sure that if customers had a problem, there was no hiding behind the door. If people came in and said, "I bought a washing machine but it's not working, I want my money back," we'd go the extra mile to make sure they were looked after. We'd say, "Okay, no problem at all, we'll give you your money back." No one had ever seen that in Perth.

No one had ever seen that kind of customer service in Perth.

So, while we accepted the problem, we then had to solve it – they still needed a washing machine. So, we would show them another brand. We'd tell them to take it home and if it wasn't any good to come back and we'd give them their money back. None ever came back.

That was called awesome customer service.

The business was thriving, and that together with Rick's success at the races made the late 70s exciting times. But trouble was brewing. Rick and his business partner could see that while they had a good business, as partners, they could no longer agree – ON ANYTHING!

A split was inevitable and that came in late 1979. At 36 years old, Rick was ready and keen to step out into the business world, alone. As there were two stores, they assumed it would be an easy split. Rick took the Nollamara store and his partner took Osborne Park, which was still located at the front of his brother's panel beating business.

Rick immediately renamed his store Rick Hart Discounts and that together with strong business practices – exceptional customer service and a continued effort to do things differently – the Nollamara store surpassed expectation. Regrettably, the Osborne Park store didn't do so well and after six months his ex-business partner succumbed to closure.

When he initially formed the partnership, Rick, like so many others before him and no doubt since, gave little or no thought to the ramifications of forming a partnership or if, down the track, it was to collapse. With the closure of the Osborne Park store came wisdom and lessons; but as is often the way, that wisdom and those lessons came at a hefty price.

[Rick] Because it was a partnership, we were still jointly liable for each other's debts. There were unpaid debts as a result of the closure, and so as his business partner they eventually came after me.

I had my own bills to pay and then I had a fair few of his as well. Trying to keep my business going at the same time was almost impossible. I was in my mid-30s with a young family and there were times I didn't know how we would get through. In saying that, throughout it all I never thought of throwing the towel in. Somehow or other with God and support from people around the place I managed to get through...but only just.

I had a great relationship with my suppliers and that helped, but I'd also learnt a valuable lesson about dealing with banks years before when I wanted to buy the Dalgety liquor store. From that time on I decided I would always take charge of any negotiation. I never again went cap in hand to the bank saying, "Please sir, will you lend me $10,000?" Instead it became, "I need $10,000, this is what I need it for, these are the terms, it will be paid back by this time and this is what it will do for our business." By giving a proper presentation, in writing, of every step of the way, the banks have more confidence in your credibility and ability to pay them back.

I got the loan from the bank and with that I was able to keep my head above water.

I never again went cap in hand to the bank saying, "Please sir, will you lend me $10,000?" Instead it became, "I need $10,000, this is what I need it for, these are the terms, it will be paid back by this time and this is what it will do for our business."

Rick was eventually free to look forward, and so with one eye on the business and the other on opportunity he decided it was time for some serious market research. Back in those days so-called research was done over a beer at the local pub. These days it's a little more sophisticated. There are times however that Rick still likes to do it the old way.

From his research, Rick came to understand what it meant for a business to be localised. In parochial Perth if a customer lived any more than five minutes from the store, they would consider it too far to travel. Rick recognised that Nollamara was always going to be just that – local and therefore, strong growth in that location was unlikely.

Rick needed and was ready to take a big step; he wanted to develop something sensational. Now with far greater knowledge, a trust in his gut instinct and an understanding that location was the priority, he sensed it was time to return to Osborne Park; a location that he saw as anything but local. Rick found the perfect site at 42 Guthrie Street, Osborne Park. He knew, as he signed the lease that he would have to close the Nollamara store – he couldn't manage the capital on both. But there lay yet another problem – the two years still remaining on the Nollamara lease.

[Rick] I went to see a solicitor, John Rando; he had long hair and played in a band, but he was a very, very prominent lawyer.

He read the lease and said, "There's no way you can get out of this. So, what's the worst thing that could happen here?"

I told him I'd go broke.

So, he said, "Alright, what if I can get it delayed in the courts for a couple of years?"

"Yeah, I reckon I'll be on my feet by that time," I said.

"Okay, then this is what you need to do…"

For some time, I had been asking the landlord for support because they had changed the whole face of the shopping centre. The shop was getting broken into twice a week and so when they told me they were going to open a roller-skate park right next door, I knew what that would do to the business. I voiced my concern but that fell on deaf ears.

So, I did as John Rando suggested. I loaded up the truck at midnight and took it all to 42 Guthrie Street.

A lot of our customers who said they were going to come over from Nollamara to Osborne Park didn't arrive – they were happy shopping in their own little area so we lost a lot of business. But by making the move to Osborne Park, by concentrating and trimming the business model further and by making sure we were real specialists in cooking and kitchen appliances it took off at a hundred miles an hour.

In the meantime, we got sued by the landlord and about two years later the lawyer rang up and said, "It's been to court and guess what, you lost the case. You have to pay $20,000."

I said, "That's okay, I can handle that. I'll get a cheque drawn out." And he said, "No, you're not going to give them $20,000, we're going to offer them $500 a month." And that's what we did.

Now with nothing to hold him back and 1980 at an end, a new era in white goods shopping was about to explode as RICK HART Genuine Discount Warehouse hit the Perth retail arena. Rick knew this business had to be different, otherwise it would be hard to compete with the already established retailers. With great thought and meticulous planning Rick drove his vision to reality. When the doors opened, the Rick Hart showroom had the largest range and presented like no other in Perth and, of course, all of this was coupled with amazing customer service. Curious about the location and the new concept, customers came from all over. They loved the warehouse-style showroom with its massive range of wall-to-wall ovens, cooktops and dishwashers – and they raved about the service.

If you want to beat the competition, be different.

[Rick] Around the same time as I opened Osborne Park, I came across an opportunity to purchase a bunch of seemingly old-fashioned ceiling fans from a wholesaler who couldn't move them. I never wanted to stock fans because they were such a low-priced item but customers would often come in looking for them. So, when this opportunity came up, I decided to give it a go. When the fans arrived in the store, we put a sign out on the roadside and suddenly we were inundated with customers wanting one. We couldn't keep up with the demand, so we sourced a range of different styles from overseas. That's when interest in them went from just being a cooling device to an interior design statement. Everyone wanted one. To cultivate that emerging market, we established Rick Hart Fans. We opened our first store in Fremantle followed by Victoria Park, Midland, Gosnells, Osborne Park and then Morley. The marketing campaign was driven with the tag line – "Join the Rick Hart Fan Club". That was the clincher that took the sale of fans, at the peak, to an incredible 25,000 units per annum.

So not only was his gut instinct paying off with ceiling fans but Rick's gut instinct about Osborne Park was also paying big dividends. Subsequently, and not surprisingly, he became hell-bent on buying the freehold of 42 Guthrie Street. That opportunity arose in the mid-80s. The property was owned by a veteran Osborne Park tradie who had relocated to Darwin. Rick made many an offer to purchase but all were rejected; the owner simply didn't want to sell. Until one day. Rick's incessant letters and phone calls finally saw the resolute tradie succumb to his offer. The purchase not only turned out to be a lucrative reward for Rick's perseverance, but it became the first of numerous property acquisitions in the area.

By 1990 with business booming and bookmaking continuing to be the source of some extra cash, Rick was on the lookout for another property to purchase. Soon his interest became focused on a commercial site just up the road. With confidence in the area, in the business and in his ability, Rick, at a serious stretch, purchased 52 Guthrie Street. Friends called him crazy, but he had a plan.

[Rick] Not everyone can, but everyone should want to buy the site they are doing business from. Not only does it provide stability and adds to your asset base but it's way better to pay off your own mortgage than renting and helping someone else pay off theirs.

Soon a magnificent, state of the art showroom appeared on the retail skyline. Wall-to-wall specialist upmarket, imported appliances – Miele, Bosch, Blanco – well-presented and knowledgeable staff and of course extraordinary customer service. He named it Rick Hart Classic Appliances, and it was an instant success.

[Rick] Bringing imported brands like those to the market was considered by many to be a risky strategy – but being a pioneer was something that appealed to me. It was a risk, but a calculated one which paid off – the luxury brands became really popular with our customers and today those brands and others like them are an integral part of the market.

If you want people to spend more, give them what they want; so, you need to know what they want... market research - just do it.

There was no doubt, no one else was doing it like Rick Hart Classic Appliances and there was no doubt the rise of an appliance empire was on track, not that Rick gave that a second thought – he was just a boy from li'l old Merredin.

Bookmaking was still keeping him busy, but his interest was dwindling as were the crowds at the races; it was getting harder to make a dollar. It was time for some honest deliberation. Where did the future lie and where was his time best spent? Bookmaking was a dying profession while his retail business was thriving.

He had to make a choice between the two. While he loved both, ultimately the decision was an easy one, but it was a sad day when he finally stepped off the bookies stand for the last time.

It was now 1992 and Rick was nearly 50. Some would think of slowing down but Rick was just warming up.

With the success of the Osborne Park store clearly evident, gut instinct told him it was time to expand. Before long there was a second store, Rockingham. In 1993, there was a third, Canning Vale. Never in his wildest dreams did Rick predict that the growth would spearhead an amazing chain of stores, and a position in the market as WA's largest independent electrical retailer. He was simply driven to keep moving forward thus motivating him to embark on a strategic, yet conservative path to open even more stores. Rick's strategy was inspired by his perception that the electrical retail industry needed an iconic retailer, doing what many others were failing to do – provide a point of difference for the consumer, and most importantly deliver amazing customer service. And so, in 1995, consequent to that thinking, Rick added Mandurah to the mix, in '96 he added Karrinyup then Claremont, O'Connor, Midland, Joondalup until there were 18 successful stores, all with Rick at the helm. The expansion was swift and frantic.

The development of the Rick Hart brand and its showcase stores provided the WA consumer with that 'something different'. However, despite becoming WA's number one kitchen appliance retailer, customers were still able to buy their television, or toaster from Rick Hart – and at Perth's most competitive price. This was a key to the future success of the business. The stores became a one-stop destination for Perth's home builders and renovators alike.

[Rick]   It was during the initial expansion that my two oldest children, Belinda and Michael, had reached the age where they were interested in joining the business. Belinda started first and then Michael. They both started at the bottom because A, they felt more comfortable with that and B, because I believe, like everybody else, they should work their way up. What was interesting is that it didn't take too many years before they both held executive roles.

At that time my youngest, Jeremy, was still at school but I always had great hopes that he would one day join me. That wish was fulfilled some years later. At one stage I had all three kids working in the business at the same time.

I have to say that one of the joys of owning a business is being able to work with your children in a business that you have created. I was very fortunate to be able to do that successfully for a long while.

Amidst the growth, Rick's interest in horse racing prompted him to stand for a committee position at the West Australian Turf Club (now known as Perth Racing). Not long after, he was elected vice-chairman; yet again he excelled.

Did this man ever sleep? The answer is yes, and it seems this is a very important point and one that science is only just beginning to understand. Rick is one of the lucky ones – sleep comes effortlessly. Perhaps this is why he so comfortably manages the demands of being a highly driven individual. When the business day is over Rick switches off; stress, what's stress? When he goes to sleep at night it might only be for five hours but it's a good five hours; although research does suggest two additional hours sleep a night would be even better.

Worry only about the things you can control - and sleep well.

With the business doing so well it wasn't all that surprising to learn that it was being closely scrutinised by local and national retailers. What was surprising was when Rick discovered that his business had also appeared on the radar of a vast South African publicly listed company.

The HiFi Corporation was part of a huge corporation with more than 700 stores throughout Africa. They were looking for retail expansion opportunities, and Australia, just across the Indian Ocean, was their target market. Their objective was to get their foot in the front door of a very successful retail enterprise and the Rick Hart operation in Western Australia stood out.

They made a significant offer to acquire a majority interest in Rick's business. It was tempting. But the big man took it all in his rather large stride, thanked them for their interest and went to close the door.

"Come and see what we do, before you make your final decision," they said. Rick, who loves to travel, more so for golf, thought hey, what the heck, Johannesburg looks nice. So off he flew to South Africa. He was instantly gobsmacked. The company had an almost identical business model, only in reverse order – mainly brown goods (eg TV's, audio equipment etc), very few whitegoods, warehouse-style outlet and big advertising and promotional spends. Their buying power was immense; Rick saw the potential and his mind was changed.

Never say no to an opportunity until you really understand what's on offer.

Today, as a result of that experience Rick always makes time to meet people who come to him with an idea or concept.

[Rick] By 1999 the South Africans and I had done the deal; they held a majority interest in the operation and that was when the excitement really began. With their colossal buying power and subsequent ability to place massive orders in Chinese factories I could clearly see we were on the threshold of an unprecedented shift in the TV and electronics market in Western Australia.

The company had also expanded into New South Wales as the HiFi Corporation. A man called Nick Kirby was sent across from South Africa to run it. Rick and Nick talked often and with deep mutual respect they soon became firm friends.

The company introduced a wave of brown goods imported from China at the lowest prices ever seen in the market. On a Saturday in 2000 after a massive marketing campaign, the likes of which Perth had never seen, the Rick Hart HiFi Corporation opened for its first day of trading. Queues of customers lined the streets surrounding the new Belmont store and by the end of that day they had taken an astounding $1 million.

The Rick Hart HiFi Corporation was an instant success.

Rick's business had been a member of the Retravision buying group for almost 20 years but now with the success of the Rick Hart brand he recognised the need for more independence. It therefore made sense to him to leave Retravision (taking around 30 per cent of their market share with him) and join the much larger national buying group NARTA.

[Rick]   Interestingly, my CEO, Ron Parmenter, and I went to see the Retravision CEO to advise him of our exit plan. Once we delivered the news his response was simply, "C'est la vie!" We found that reaction astonishing considering a fair amount of his business was about to walk out the door. I would have thought a simple, 'Can we do anything to change your mind', might have been more appropriate, bearing in mind the ultimate effect it would have on shareholders.

For Rick, gut instinct and taking action paid off yet again – the move across to NARTA was a turning point. The success of the overall business was exhilarating. It felt like nothing could go wrong and for the next two years it didn't. A sudden and dramatic downturn in the South African economy however, triggered the urgent need for counteractive action. A phone call explained that due to the financial decline of the South African economy the parent company was now in damage control and had no alternative but to extricate itself from its Australian operations. With that call the highly successful partnership came to a grinding halt.

As the business had been doing exceptionally well, they understandably wanted 'top dollar'. Rick was given the opportunity to buy back their share of the total Rick Hart business, but he decided against it. The business had changed significantly and so it was no longer of any interest to Rick... unless of course he could buy it at a discounted price. That was never going to happen – well not at that moment in time.

[Rick]   The South Africans then quickly identified a potential buyer for their shares. It was Strathfield, a publicly listed Australian company with a large profile in mobile phone and car audio, with about 140 stores around Australia. As a market leader in their own field they were looking to expand their business into home entertainment. A meeting was arranged between me, the South Africans and Strathfield. At that time, I believed they were a suitable partner who would add some value to the overall business; so, the deal was done.

However, it soon became apparent it wasn't going to be the partnership made in heaven as I'd expected – in fact, it was essentially a disaster, almost from the start. In those circumstances, as a minority shareholder, it wasn't ever going to work for me. Their business strategy was overly complicated, and their rigid viewpoint and refusal to consider alternative suggestions, in my view, is what eventually drove their side of the company into financial decline. After lengthy discussions with Nick, who had stayed on at Strathfield in New South Wales, the two of us structured a deal for me to buy back the WA side of the business. I had one condition; Nick would have to agree to move across to Perth and run the Rick Hart business – he agreed. Strathfield then accepted the proposal I put forward and so all seemed set for the buyback to proceed.

With that deal seemingly done, a more relaxed Rick accepted an invitation from a supplier to take a quick trip to South Africa to attend the Cricket World Cup.

It was while he was in Johannesburg that Rick received some alarming news. He heard that Strathfield was offering their share of the business around despite having agreed to sell to him. More disturbing - apparently, they had already received an offer from one of Rick's biggest competitors – Retravision.

[Rick]   I knew there would be many hoops Strathfield would have to jump through before a deal like this could be finalised. The process of completing the transaction with any outsider would be complicated, if not impossible; but I had to act quickly.

Now on a mission, Rick rushed back to Perth.

Aware that Strathfield needed money quickly because the banks were circling, Rick called the Strathfield hierarchy and set up a meeting. Armed with a cheque and a signed share certificate he met with the now very anxious management. His efforts to act quickly were rewarded. The Retravision offer was significantly higher, but time was of the essence. They weren't happy but were not in a position to argue. They accepted the cheque, signed it off and the deal was done. Rick owned his name once again and it was back to business – only this time he had Nick Kirby on the payroll.

Retail is an amazing industry; the opportunities go way beyond the monetary. In this industry anything is possible and it's fun.

[Rick]   Retail is an amazing industry. Admittedly over the years, it has lost some of its lustre as a career, however no one should ever underestimate the appeal it has for those that enter the industry. My view has always been that retail provides something new each and every day, without fail. A new set of customers, a new set of challenges; for me, every day in retail is an adrenaline rush. You never know what's about to unfold. The desire for a university education in youngsters of today often means that retail largely gets disregarded as a career, however, suffice to say, those who do find their way into the retail industry invariably find it a rewarding and invigorating role, and they rarely leave it! People often overlook or perhaps they are unaware of the opportunities that exist within. Opportunities that go way beyond the monetary; opportunities that are very real. Positions in management, the potential for business ownership, the amazing travel prospects that are created from the relationships that are formed with international companies. In this industry, anything is possible and it's fun.

The desire for a university education in youngsters of today often means that retail largely gets disregarded as a career. They don't know what they're missing!

Rick was now ready to move forward. He was 'crazy busy' – rebuilding and restructuring his re-acquired empire, providing for his young family, fulfilling his role as vice-chairman at Perth Racing, as an owner of racehorses and as a serious punter. So really there was no room for anything else – unless of course that 'anything' involved sport or a business opportunity. Then and only then would he move heaven and earth to make more room in his already jam-packed diary. That occasion arrived in 2002 with a request. A request that not only encompassed sport and business but also, two of his greatest passions – football and the colour purple – aka the Fremantle Dockers. His diary was put on immediate notice.

Rick's loyalty to Fremantle football began with his uncle, Jack Hart, who played for East Fremantle before the war. But it was the great Jack Sheedy, who also played for East Fremantle and became a legend of WA football, who truly captivated the young Rick. Jack was his boyhood hero.

While the port city had a great history of football dating back to the early 1880s, it was the West Coast Eagles that was the first West Australian team to join the AFL and hence why Rick had given them his initial AFL allegiance. However, Rick's loyalty to Jack Sheedy and Fremantle football never wavered. There was never a doubt – if a Fremantle team was to be admitted into the AFL, Rick would be right there behind them. That wish was fulfilled when in April 1995, donned in purple, red and green guernseys emblazoned with a white anchor, the Fremantle Football Club, nicknamed the Dockers, took to the AFL field. Rick's realigned allegiance was swift and irrevocable.

During those first few years the team worked hard and showed glimpses of promise, but sadly they had little success. According to Rick, it had also become apparent the Fremantle Football Club didn't have the local support one would have expected from a city steeped in football tradition. Disappointingly but perhaps unconsciously, the club had not embraced the Fremantle culture. Therefore, their moderate on-field success, combined with a lack of local support and poor attendances at games, triggered a decline in new memberships and sponsorship interest. This made those formative years difficult ones for the fledgling club.

In the season of 2001, club performance was at its lowest with just two wins from 22 games, with that second win not coming until the last round. It was a year of disappointments topped by a trading loss of around $2 million. That amount was in addition to the previous accumulated losses, compounded by a debt to the tune of around $8 million. The club was in a precarious financial position and looked set to go down with its anchor.

[Rick] Andrew Demetriou, the then general manager football at the AFL, a powerful figure in his own right, made a cruel but probably fair declaration to the media: "The Fremantle Football Club is a basket case on the brink of losing its AFL licence." For everyone involved with Fremantle Football Club, they were crushing words to hear at a time when morale was at its lowest ebb; undeniably there was an urgent need for swift action.

Bring in a man with a profile, a well-established and successful businessman; one who knows a bit about football. Mr Hart please step forward to be our chairman and please, get us out of this mess.

Rick accepted the position and the challenge, but it was blatantly clear it wasn't going to be a quick fix or an easy one, and he knew he couldn't do it alone.

So, first things first; recruit very good people. Cameron Schwab had been appointed to the role of CEO in 2001, however the football administrators had some reservations. Rick was given the task of assessing the suitability of Schwab as CEO as well as the entire management team. It didn't take long for Rick to identify the CEO's strengths and subsequently developed a healthy confidence in his ability to embrace and deliver the required outcomes demanded of the role. With deep mutual respect, the two became a formidable team. They proceeded to initiate structural changes to management that would result in the club gaining a robust and respected position within the AFL. An essential need for significant change that would enable forward movement necessitated an almost clean sweep of the management team. The result was the appointment of a group of exceptional personnel to the football club. Gary Walton came on as number cruncher (leaving some years later to become CEO of the WA Football Commission, a position he held for four years). Not long after Steve Rosich stepped into the marketing and sponsorship role, only later to become club CEO. Today, Steve is one of the most respected CEOs in the AFL.

[Rick] On and off the field the club was having little success, however we identified there was potential for strong revenue streams, particularly if on-field improvement could be developed. If the club appeared to be successful, the more people would want to be a part of it. It's almost a chicken and egg scenario – if you don't have money you don't have culture – and it's hard to win without a winning culture! Therefore, we needed to improve revenue first. So, with a strong management team in place and a renewed focus, Cameron and I were ready to embark on a strategy to significantly improve revenues.

Our number one focus was to increase members, sponsors and attendance. Chris Connolly was the head coach and even though he'd only been there for a couple of months he was passionate about doing whatever he could to help market the club. So, together with Cameron and Chris, we went to function after function to talk about the future potential of the club. With some exciting but cliff-hanging moments on the field it helped create the unique Fremantle Dockers ethos. It was full of promise one moment and disappointments the next but the supporters started to rally and understood that it wasn't all beer and skittles.

Slowly but surely people could see there was a new regime at the Fremantle Dockers and they were interested; memberships started to grow, new sponsors came on board and in 2003 the team, for the first time, made it to the finals. That was a momentous occasion for Fremantle, a dream come true.

Some exciting but cliff-hanging moments on the field helped create the unique Fremantle Dockers ethos... full of promise one moment and disappointments the next.

[Rick] Even though the team suffered a significant loss in that first final there were incredible scenes at Subiaco Oval after the game. Our fans, who had made their presence felt through the entire night, stayed on in their droves post game. They cheered their team almost as if they had won. The noise was unbelievable. There were also scarves, beanies and flags being waved all over the place. The atmosphere was amazing for everyone who was still there – not just the supporters – and for that moment in time everyone was united. So, it was a significant moment in the history of Fremantle Dockers. For me the emotion in the lead up and during the game was overwhelming. Even though we were probably never in the game the reaction from the supporters both during and after the game had all of us overcome with emotion. It's hard to describe how it felt but even to this day the memory of that night still makes every hair on my body stand on end.

That was the year that Fremantle turned the corner and started running as a football club must – as a business. But that success was not replicated on the field. Disappointingly, the exhilaration of the 2003 season was followed by defeat after defeat. It was an emotional roller coaster of a journey that took until 2006 before they would again experience the unforgettable finals feeling. The drought was broken by footballing brilliance, with players like Matthew Pavlich, Peter Bell, Paul Haselby, Shaun McManus and Troy Cook – but they didn't do it alone – the whole Fremantle Dockers team were on fire, determined to win. They made it through to the preliminary finals and even though they were defeated by the Sydney Swans it was an exhilarating season, nonetheless.

When Rick took the reins in 2002 there were about 23,000 members; within six years that number had risen to more than 43,000, demonstrating the growth of the club. In 2009, when he stepped down from his post, the club was in great shape with strong and sustainable growth potential and is still highly respected in the AFL. His dedication and hard work had a huge impact on the Fremantle Football Club which, at the end of his tenure, recognised his contribution with a coveted FFC life membership.

Surround yourself with good people, it doesn't guarantee success, but it gives you the very best chance of achieving it.

Rick loved purple, he loved the club, he loved the team and he loved the role, but it was a lot of work, particularly at a time when his attention was required elsewhere. The role of president in any football club is purely honorary but bills still need to be paid.

So, when Rick wasn't doing football business it was business as usual on the showroom floor.

Back in 2004, only a year after re-acquiring his business from Strathfield, an opportunity had presented itself. Park Discounts in Victoria Park was a very successful member of the buying group and retailer, Retravision (the same buying group Rick had left two years earlier to join NARTA). The business was up for sale; it was an opportunity too good to miss.

[Rick] Park Discounts was doing a significant turnover and was located in an area that I knew would be advantageous to the Rick Hart operation. It was a substantial investment and one that would require debt to fund the purchase. Our bankers at the time were Bankwest and they readily approved the funding so we were ready to go. However, the vendors were peeved at the time Bankwest was indicating the process would take and so threatened to withdraw from the sale. We needed to move quickly if we were to complete the deal.

I'd been to an Eagles concert at Subiaco Oval only a few nights before where I met a delightful chap who had just arrived in WA on appointment to the National Australia Bank (NAB). We got on really well and he suggested I contact him if I ever had any banking requirements. So shortly after, I called him and presented him with the scenario – particularly the need to move quickly. He, virtually on a handshake, undertook to do the funding immediately and worry about the paperwork later. Bankwest couldn't believe it could be completed but it was.

With the Park Discounts acquisition done we shifted our business to NAB and have subsequently become long-term NAB customers. I'm not sure if the banking process back then would meet the stringent policies of today but he got it done and the acquisition added significantly to the growth of Rick Hart in 2004.

I guess the moral to that story is that it's always important to have a very strong banking relationship. Even though we did have one at the time, they couldn't do the deal in the requisite time and as a result we shifted to another bank. NAB, has now been our main bank for many, many years, with a relationship that remains strong today.

So, with Park Discounts now added to the Rick Hart empire, business continued to flourish. However, as Rick had experienced, retail expenses don't stop, they keep going up. Therefore, he knew he had to grow or be swallowed up by inflation – so grow the business he did. (Rick points out many businesses fail because their owners don't understand this.)

[Rick]   When a business gets to a significant size, if it doesn't continue to grow exponentially it will wither on the vine. Invariably, expenses continue to escalate and therefore revenue growth is essential to keep pace with those expenses otherwise the business may eventually fail.

When a business gets to a significant size, if it doesn't continue to grow exponentially it will wither on the vine.

By 2004, there were a total of 18 Rick Hart outlets, all with strong cash flows. It was a very healthy business but as always continued growth was vital. However, with so much money tied up in re-investing in the business, with expansions and in stock, Rick didn't know where the next stage of growth was going to come from. He had taken the business as far as he could as a privately funded business. He'd come to the end of this particular journey; it was time to consider other options, maybe even sell.

2005 – Step in Clive Peeters.

Clive Peeters, a Victorian company, was keen to develop their brand and seek a public listing. Purchasing the Rick Hart chain and its name enabled the company to grow – almost overnight. The Clive Peeters board shrewdly chose to continue to trade as Rick Hart in Western Australia due to it being a significant and well recognised brand within the State.

Rick, stayed on as managing director and for the first three years growth was strong, particularly in Western Australia. Rick, always looking for a way to do things differently, took what he believed was a fresh and exciting concept to the Clive Peeters board; his idea was disregarded. Disappointed, Rick stored the idea and continued on.

By 2008 the business should have been booming at the now publicly listed company. On the west coast it was flourishing but on the east coast it was floundering. In private discussions with Nick Kirby, Rick expressed his concerns about the business and its inexplicable and regular cash flow problems. Having learnt a few lessons along the way Rick was on the ball with figures. On seeing a number of discrepancies, he was prompted to ask a few questions at board level however, no logical explanation was forthcoming. In retrospect, those questions should have been a wake-up call for head office.

On a Saturday morning, some months later, Rick was over in Melbourne in his role as chairman of the Dockers. He was doing his usual thing, enjoying a cappuccino and a ham and cheese toastie in the city's iconic Block Arcade when his mobile phone rang. The caller had some disturbing news. Rick was stunned into silence by the magnitude of the information he had just received. He realised it could well mean the end of the empire he had so proudly and painstakingly created.

The young bookkeeper at Clive Peeters had been caught stealing from the company; ultimately to the tune of a massive $19 million. It was an inconceivable amount and hence the news quickly hit the media. As Rick points out, it doesn't matter how big your business is, things can go wrong so you must have good business processes in place and you must keep your eye on the figures. If you don't someone else will.

A good idea if you are going into business, is to have some understanding of numbers. Do a basic accounting course and never rely on others to tell you where you are at financially.

The fallout from the embezzlement didn't greatly affect the Rick Hart business, they were the jewel in the crown, but on the other side of the country the shockwaves continued to hit. Clive Peeters battled on, but it wasn't business as usual. Rick, disappointed at the company's reaction to the whole affair and unable to see a way forward, wanted out. Finally, in 2009 he pulled the pin on his namesake, the empire he'd started 30 years earlier. It was a tough decision but already his mind had moved on. Rick's gut instinct about the concept he'd taken to the CEO a year earlier had been gnawing away at him. Now his plan had advanced to the point where he was ready to make it centre stage in the next chapter of his life.

His vision was to create an unprecedented retail experience; a vision that was becoming rapidly clearer. It took a massive year of research and planning, but he didn't do it alone. This time he had a business partner, Nick Kirby.

Nick was honest and reliable; a man of integrity and like Rick, had retail in his blood. The two men trusted in each other's instincts, so Nick was not about to ignore Rick's gut feeling that Perth was ready for this new retail experience.

The two identified a unique niche in the market and then set out to create Kitchen Headquarters (KHQ); a working showroom offering only the very best in kitchen and laundry appliances. In an extraordinarily short period of time, it would become one the best kitchen appliance showrooms in the country; but not before a few challenges were thrown in its way.

The premises had to be amazing and in the right location if they were to get this right. Rick and Nick found just that at 22 King Edward Road, Osborne Park, the suburb where business had started for Rick. He was returning to the suburb he took a risk on so many years before and which now was unquestionably, the best retail area in Perth.

Together they crunched the numbers and were comfortable to the point they felt it was relatively risk free – they had a concept that would survive and one that had potential for huge growth. But Rick and Nick failed to take one thing into consideration; and that one thing could well have proved fatal.

The lease was signed, the showroom was taking shape, the big-name brands were on board, advertisements for staff were bringing in the best – what could go wrong? The boys had thought of everything. Except one thing – the fear factor.

The competition, now well aware that Rick was about to launch a new brand into the industry, were worried, and with good reason. Rick had a reputation for being an outstanding and well-respected retailer with an exceptional track record. Nervous about their position in the market, the competition applied all the political pressure they could muster - the hard word went out to suppliers. Over the ensuing weeks, one by one each supplier capitulated. Some of the biggest names in the business withdrew their promise of support and supply just weeks before Kitchen Headquarters was due to open its doors.

Never underestimate your competition.

It was an incredibly difficult time, and Rick and Nick felt the pressure but they had no choice, they were in too far – it was full steam ahead. With a show of support from many long-time suppliers and some fabulous new brands, like the sensational Swiss brand V Zug, Kitchen Headquarters opened its doors.

Opening night came in June 2010 amid a flurry of advertising and media attention. A relentless advertising campaign followed. The recognisable face reappeared on TV, on radio and in newspapers – there was no doubt the local boy was back in business and Perth was ready to support him.

Sometimes the best money you can spend is on advertising - branding is paramount.

Meanwhile, Clive Peeters was hanging on precariously, but that $19 million hit was always going to be a bridge too far and by July 2010 they were in administration.

In that moment everything changed. Suddenly the big-name brands were back knocking at the KHQ door trying to secure their space on the showroom floor. It was a momentous turnaround. With that shift they now had what the experienced Rick and Nick believed was all they needed to dominate the market; the best sales team, all the best brands and the best retail space in the State. And it seems they were right – Kitchen Headquarters was very quickly a formidable competitor in the industry.

It was a great achievement, but the road Rick had taken to get there had shown him that obstacles can appear with every turn, even for the most seasoned traveller. Despite understanding this and despite his propensity to expect the unexpected, nothing could have prepared Rick for what lay around the next corner.

It was 5.30 am and Rick had just sat down to read the morning paper. There it was in bold print – the news he never expected to see. Harvey Norman, his biggest competitor, had 'swooped in' and purchased the remnants of the Rick Hart and Clive Peeters brand, including Rick's name!

[Rick]   It was difficult for me, but you move on. As it turned out, the Harvey Norman venture into Rick Hart territory was an abject failure. After a series of disastrous name changes, they couldn't replicate the business model and eventually closed in 2014. Now that hit home.

*As it turned out, the Harvey Norman venture into
Rick Hart territory was an abject failure.*

It was the end of an era. After 35 years as a retailing icon, the Rick Hart business was gone. It came as a great shock for Rick and his family but as disheartening as the takeover and eventual demise was, it didn't hinder the upward path of Kitchen Headquarters.

Ready for something new, the WA market had embraced the unique concept of KHQ. But it was also the familiar face behind the brand that gave confidence and created loyalty; a face that was local, well known and trusted. Rick had returned to television and radio promoting high-end products from a high-end showroom in that gravelly voice that had become so familiar to so many over the years.

Almost from the outset the business traded strongly, far exceeding initial expectations.

As so often happens, when a business is successful it captures the attention of customers, suppliers and of course competitors wanting a piece of the pie. Rick had seen it happen before with the businesses he had started.

They were just two years in, and business and potential were riding high. Rick and Nick were both enjoying the success of their creation when Winning Appliances, a large family business based on the east coast of Australia approached with an offer to purchase. KHQ was at an exciting phase of its development and so the two partners had no interest in selling. But a year and a half later (with the fledgling business only into its fourth year of trading) a second approach was made. This time the offer was too good to walk away from.

For Rick it meant an accelerated exit strategy and an end to the risks that came from being in business. He also quite liked the idea of taking life a little easier.

[Rick]   In business you can predict few things, and certainly you cannot predict what the future trading results are likely to be. WA was showing signs of entering a post boom slump, which meant the road ahead could possibly get bumpy. So, Nick and I felt the offer had probably come just at the right time. We also saw it as an opportunity for us to continue to be involved in developing the concept further while at the same time facilitating the introduction of a new name into the State. So, we agreed, and the sale went ahead. Nick became head of WA retail, and I took on a three-year role as brand ambassador.

However, almost immediately changes were implemented. The name was changed, the brilliant yellow of KHQ was replaced with the Winning pale grey and white; Rick and his well-known voice and face disappeared (returning eventually) from TV, radio and print media. Almost overnight, essentially all traces of the former business, apart from the staff, was gone. This was to be a game changer in the understanding between the parties, and both Rick and Nick struggled to connect with what they considered to be a strange strategy to adopt.

> [Rick]   When you buy a business that is doing well you would expect the new owners would want to give that growth the best opportunity to continue. Winning is very well known on the east coast but not here on the west, therefore whilst change was expected, in my opinion, it would have been better to introduce the company to the State in a more measured approach. It does take time for loyal customers to adjust to change and in this case the changes happened almost overnight.
>
> So, the sale transaction hasn't exactly been plain sailing and some of the cream has been taken out of the deal, due to missed targets along the way. But you go into these deals with your eyes wide open, you take the good with the bad, and you never look in the rear-vision mirror. Rather, you learn from the experience.
>
> My advice to business owners contemplating a sale – make sure it's a walk-in walk-out deal. Don't commit to contingency plans for the future – there's a new owner with different ideals, different culture and objectives that often have little to do with the previous owner. So, if you get involved in a sale let them do their due diligence – if they want your business – other than tax issues it would be wise not to commit to any future performance expectations. Caveat emptor!

Rick, always loyal to his customers and clients who have supported him over the years, continues to believe in the concept he launched and to do his best to help it thrive. But is that all there is left? Are there any other concepts, fresh ideas, a daring to be different, a desire to do it better? Maybe – because, he tells me the flame still flickers. So, unless it goes out, I don't think we've seen the last of Rick Hart, the country boy, the boy from Merredin.

Good luck Rick and thank you for sharing your highs and your lows. No doubt there will be more to come but may the highs far outweigh the lows.

Postscript

Only days before this book went to print Rick made a decision that will inevitably alter the course of his life once again - he resigned from Winning Appliances. Is history about to repeat itself? Stay tuned.

Born with retail in his bones

Sue, Rick and Tony

Rick with Sue and Tony at the family home in Merredin

A love of football begins

At Merredin High School

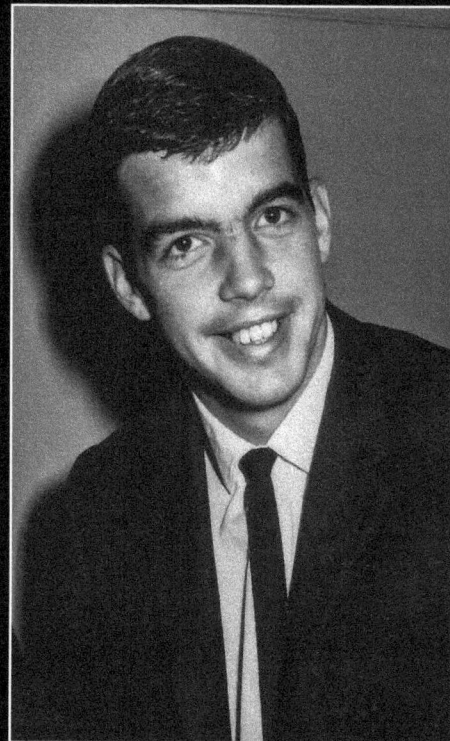

The delivery van

Rick Hart Warehouse Guthrie Street

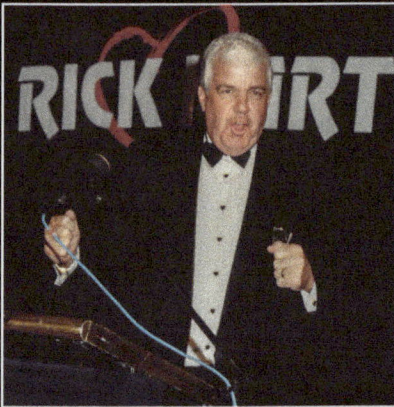
At the Rick Hart Annual Ball

Rick Hart Golf Day

Clive Savage, Rick Hart and Peter
Tsouras – Australian Retail Legends

At Miele in Germany

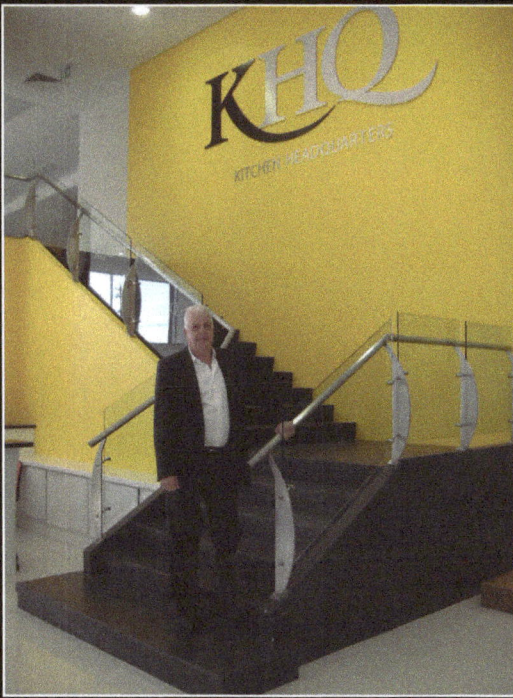

KHQ Osborne Park opens for business 2010

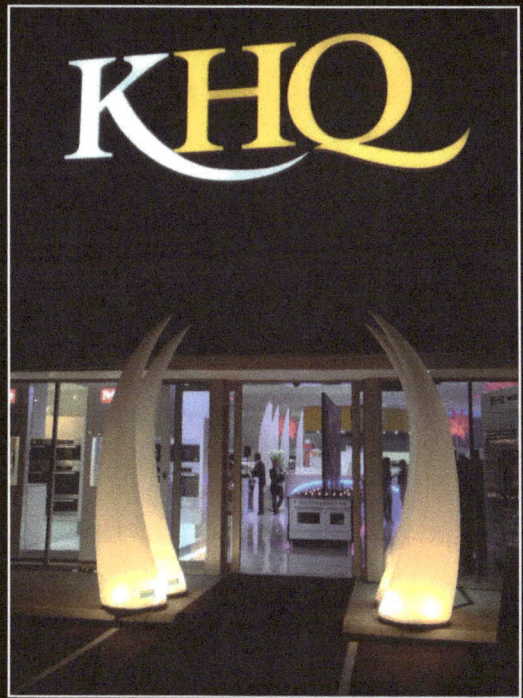

Opening night of KHQ O'Connor

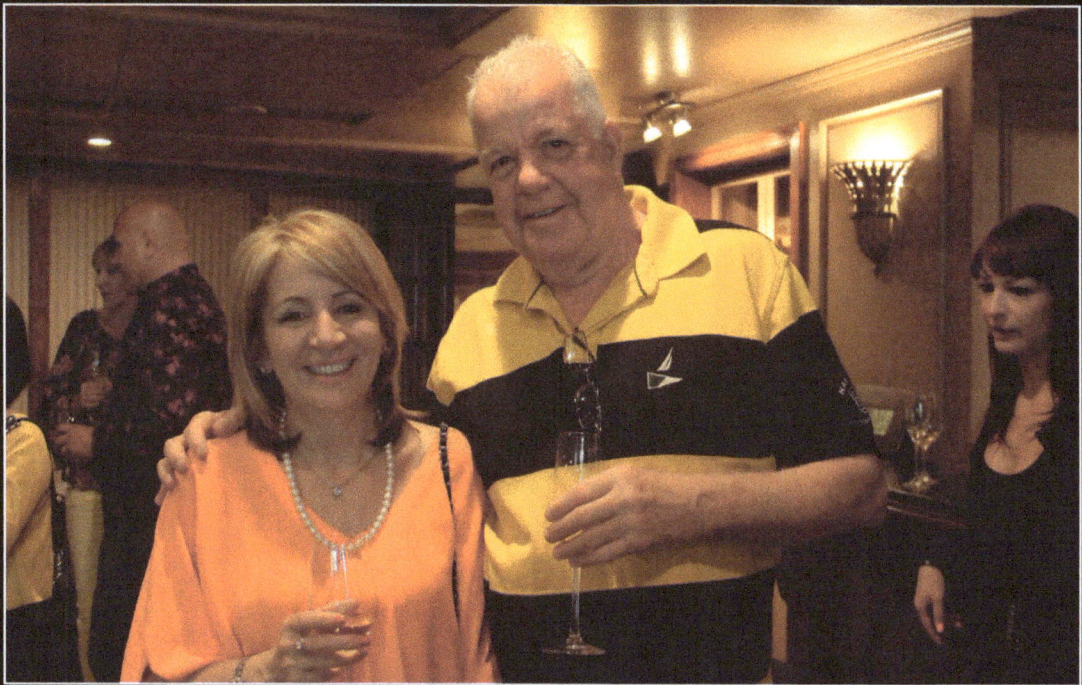

Rick with Kaye Spencer of NARTA

Vince Garreffa of Mondo's , Rick and
international chef Antonio Carluccio

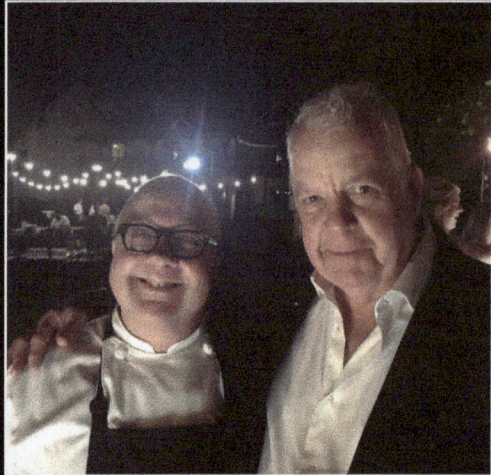

Rick with *The West Australian* Food Editor
Rob Broadfield

His prize racehorse - Jacks or Better

Another race won with jockey Pat
Carberry on Trade Down

Rick Hart and Nick Kirby
in Xmas spirit

Nick Kirby, Adam Connell from Miele, Rick
and Gavin Stewart

Rick with his children; Michael, Belinda and Jeremy

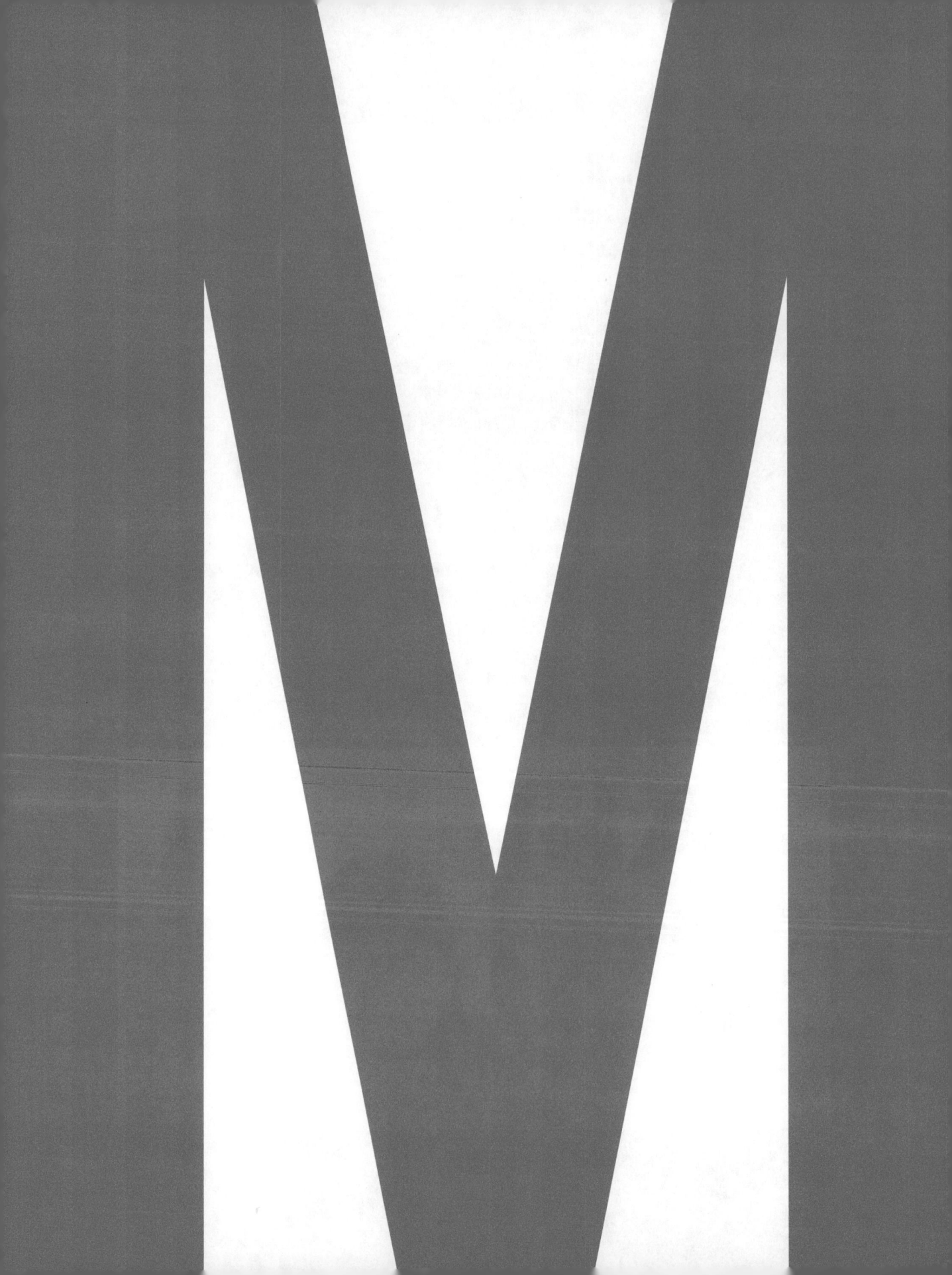

4 Thinking Big, Building Strong, Going Global

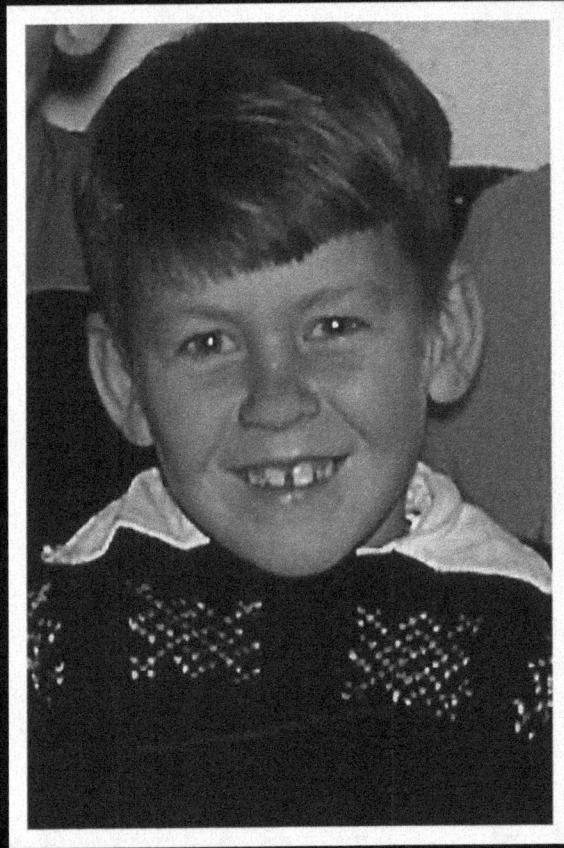

"To build an empire you must build on solid foundations, if not it will crumble in five to ten years. Have a clear idea at the beginning what you want to achieve and build it accordingly - never underestimate the significance of this."

Some might call him a pawnbroker and, in some ways, that label is correct. But it is a word that fails to portray the real man; he is so much more than that. If you should ever meet him, he won't be wearing the characteristic cap (unless he's on the golf course), have a jeweller's loupe around his neck, or indeed be sitting on a stool at a dusty glass counter filled with dubious diamond jewellery. No, he wears an impeccably tailored suit with the obligatory tie and has a fabulous corner office with an outlook over Perth's Swan River – the ultimate recognition of someone who has made it to the top. But this man's career started way down in the secure, but crowded, basement of a government department. With diligence, skill and great integrity, he worked his way up the public sector ladder to where life was still secure but far more comfortable and far less crowded.

Then, just before his 40th birthday, he arrived at one of those confronting forks in the road – as Robert Frost put it, 'One path was well worn while the other was overgrown in leaves no step had trodden black'. After only a brief hesitation, he made the life changing decision to veer off his predictable path and from that moment he never looked back.

He has now travelled the world, lived abroad, has exported intellectual property with greater success than most in Australia and turned a company of 21 local stores into more than 850 around the globe. With dignity and modesty, he admits he is proud of what he has achieved. Justifiably so; it wasn't an easy road, but with relentless determination he has made great inroads in changing public perception of an often loathed and misunderstood industry.

He has had a remarkable journey but what makes it so remarkable are the extraordinary relationships he forged with the police department, the government and his customers – unprecedented in the world of pawn broking. Deeply etched into every facet of this man's character are the company's five documented principles – respect, integrity, professionalism, collaboration and passion. It was those five principles that helped him navigate unchartered waters and upon which his empire was built.

He is a proud man, he is humble, he is an innovator and a pioneer, he is the man behind the internationally renowned Cash Converters, he is…

Peter Cumins

Peter Cumins was born into a very ordinary family. Mr and Mrs Cumins senior, like so many new Australians, were UK imports, direct from Hull – diehard rugby league country. The couple arrived in Perth in 1950 with their young son, Brian. Home was a small weatherboard and asbestos rental in Hilton Park, a state housing subdivision, not far from the port city of Fremantle.

They barely had time to bring out the Scott Bonner, before Tony was born and then soon after on the 2nd of July 1951, Peter made his debut into the Cumins family. All three brothers shared the one bedroom so there was the typical rivalry you expect between boys, but life was happy, busy and very noisy.

Perth in the 1950s was a very different place for children to grow up. It was small, safe, conservative and carefree. The Cumins boys, like most children of the era, were free to explore; they would roam the streets or jump on their bikes and head to Port Beach for a swim or ride to the river to fish. There was only one rule; they had to be home before nightfall. The boys never broke that rule. After busy days of adventuring the two younger brothers, Tony and Peter (Brian was already off doing his own thing) would return home. Mrs Cumins, despite working full time as a kindergarten teacher's aide, always had dinner ready. Together they would sit as a family at the kitchen table and talk. There was no eating in front of the TV and not just because TV was so new to Australia (introduced in September 1956) and very few were affluent enough to have it, but simply because, in the Cumins household, having dinner together was important. It was a time for talking, and after dinner they would stay seated, listening to the wireless, playing cards or board games; and always there was laughter. Theirs was a happy home where honesty and deep respect for each other was paramount. Not once did Peter hear his father raise his voice at his mother or use bad language in front of her. They taught their sons by example. Even when his parents were in their eighties, they would walk arm in arm. Never did his mother have to open her car door when her husband was around. It was an idyllic childhood, filled with wonderful moments in which wonderful memories were created.

Mr Cumins senior's first love was definitely his family but in a very close second place came rugby league. It hadn't taken him long after his arrival in Perth to find a rugby league club to support – from the sidelines of course – he was far too busy, not to mention exhausted from laying bricks under the hot Australian sun for any sporting commitments. Fremantle Rugby League Club was the lucky recipient of the Cumins family support. Initially the brothers watched with their father from the sidelines, but Peter and Tony soon joined the club as junior players. From that moment they too were forever hooked on the game. Peter played until he was 34. He still holds the club record for the most first-grade games played. He represented Western Australia 23 times; is deservedly a life member of the club and not surprisingly is in the West Australian Rugby League Hall of Fame. It seems, even at a young age, Peter was destined for great things.

The game dominated the Cumins family social calendar. Peter's parents taxied Peter, Tony and their teammates all over the metropolitan area to wherever the fixtures took them. From Wanneroo to Mandurah, a distance of more 100km (before the freeway went through), they would drive with a car full of excited children, no doubt all talking at the same time. It was time consuming but they were the kind of parents who just wanted to be involved. They were there for every game support-ing the team and their sons; never pushy, just encouraging. Peter's father sat on the club committee and his mother worked in the canteen. There were always at least 13 rugby jumpers hanging on the clothesline at home – Mrs Cumins volunteered for that as well. There was never any doubt that theirs was a rugby league family, but Peter also played Aussie Rules for Hilton Park. That was on Saturday because Sunday was irrefutably rugby league day. But no matter what the sport, his parents were always there cheering him on.

As parents they were proud of their sons and saw potential in each of them, although possibly not quite to the extent of the success their middle son would ultimately achieve. A success born from taking a small local business on a transformational journey and under his leadership see it emerge as a hugely successful, international, publicly listed company.

The level of his success could well be attributed to Peter's attitude. Whatever he did, he wanted to be the best at it. In his opinion, if you are not going to do your best, why bother at all, although that view didn't extend to his schooling – in that he simply wasn't interested. Fortunately, Hilton Park Primary School, to which he walked each day with Tony, had one redeeming factor – rugby league was part of the sporting curriculum.

While Peter may have been an unmotivated student, high grades came without effort – particularly maths, so much so he couldn't understand why Brian and Tony struggled with it. It was a 'doddle' for him, and that really 'bugged' his brothers – not that they weren't clever. Brian, the oldest of the three, was entrepreneurial from an early age.

[Peter] Every week the newspaper ran a crossword competition where the winner won $500. That was a huge amount back then and Brian wanted to win it. So, he used to send Tony and I off to buy dozens of copies of the Daily News and together we would cut out all the cross-words. Brian would then fill them in and send them off. It cost him about $40 every week but that was okay because he also won the competition every week – that was until the Daily News stopped him from entering.

I never would have thought about doing anything like that although afterwards I thought it was a bloody good idea. (Laughter)

Brian would later use his talents to become a highly successful and well-liked entrepreneur. Peter would use his talents in a completely different way – but the day would eventually arrive when the two would combine their talents to form a formidable partnership.

But that was a long way off. Peter was still a 'little tacker' blitzing his way through primary school without any effort. He even played the guitar well although he attributes that talent to Harry Barker, a teacher at the Fremantle Music School. Harry pushed his students to be their very best. They formed an orchestra and, because the school was close to the port, the young musicians would board the visiting ships and play for the passengers. They were also regulars on one of Channel Seven's children's programmes.

> [Peter] I still strum occasionally but without the practice it simply doesn't sound like it used to. But like anything in life, you get back what you put in.

So, Peter clearly had a very full childhood and a happy one. He never got into trouble, not that he did anything wrong, but Peter appreciates it was his upbringing that moulded his behaviour. Very early on his parents instilled in their sons the importance of taking responsibility for oneself, respecting teachers, the police, anyone in authority and that included them as parents. It also included respect for self. Peter is convinced that these attributes are vital if you are to succeed in life. He drummed it into his own children along with the importance of sport because he equally believes that sport keeps you busy, keeps you out of trouble and teaches you about commitment, determination and respect for others.

This may well be the thinking of someone born in the 50s but that doesn't make his line of thought out of date. It was those beliefs, together with sheer determination and effort that led to Peter being richly rewarded by life, despite such humble beginnings. When you compare the disparities between the world in which Peter grew up in, to the craziness and indulgences of the world today, those attributes that Peter considers so important should therefore, surely, warrant far greater attention.

Far better it is to dare mighty things, to win glorious triumphs, even though chequered by failure, than to take rank with those poor spirits who neither enjoy much nor suffer much, because they live in the grey twilight that knows not victory nor defeat.

Theodore Roosevelt

> [Peter] Kids today aren't permitted to experience disappointment. They've removed the competition out of everything – you get a participation certificate, no one wins the race, no one

loses it, you play a game, and no one keeps the score. Why bother doing your best or strive to achieve if everyone gets the same result. You have to learn at an early age how to win and lose because life is a competition – fair or unfair – and if we don't let our kids experience it how will they cope when that inevitable day arrives?

Maybe it's a contributing factor in the continual upward spiral of youth suicide in this country.

Peter was now at high school where he continued to breeze through. At Hamilton High School, or Hammy High as it was affectionately known, he remained at the top of his class. He was a leader, the captain of the team and had friends in abundance. His parents were very proud of their middle son and always looked forward to seeing what he would achieve when he eventually entered university. But, as Mr and Mrs Cumins discovered, your children don't always do what is best for them or, dare we admit, do what we think is best for them.

Peter had two driving passions in his life – to play rugby and get a job so he could buy a car. Therefore, by the time his third year of high school was over he'd made the decision to leave school. Not long after turning 16 he had a job and had purchased his first car – a 'gruesome' two-toned EH Holden. He was happy. His parents, on the other hand, were devastated.

Peter was and is the mirror image of his father; honest, hardworking and adoring of his family but when it came to work, his dad didn't want him to be anything like him. He was a bricklayer and although he continued working in the field until he was 60, it was backbreaking work. He would often warn Peter – it's too hot, it's too hard and you're smarter than the average bear – so get an office job where there's air-conditioning. Peter listened, not that he had any goals or great ambition other than owning a car, but he saw that working in an office was an opportunity to dress up in a suit and impress the girls. He admits, girls were definitely a motivating factor behind the job applications he sent off to the Commonwealth Bank (very prestigious), the public service and the Fremantle Port Authority. He was offered a job at all three but accepted the Port Authority position as junior office boy. He chose to take that job simply because it was close to home and that meant he could ride his bike to work.

Fremantle was a vibrant metropolis in those days. It was where P&O had its head office, as did all the big shipping firms. The port was alive with passenger ships, live cargo and the thousands of wharfies loading and unloading ships (shipping containers hadn't been invented at that stage). The Port Authority where Peter worked was one of the biggest employers in Fremantle. He loved the job but after just two years he was ready for something different.

Peter and his brother Tony decided to go together on a working holiday. However, before they could leave Peter had to make some real money. Tony, a wool classer, got him a job labouring at Western Livestock's wool stores – the 'big black sheds' on Leach Highway. In the late 60s there was a whole industry revolving around wool and as a labourer you could earn senior wages at 18.

Six months on, with enough money in their pockets the brothers were off. Firstly to Adelaide and then Melbourne but ultimately, they were headed for Sydney, the rugby league capital of Australia.

Upon arriving in Sydney, they moved into McClay Street, Potts Point – the infamous red-light district of Kings Cross. For two young Perth lads it was an eye-opening introduction to big city life. They found work in the wool warehousing suburb of Ultimo; Tony as a wool classer and Peter as a labourer. It was whilst working in the "stinking hot wool stores" of Ultimo that Peter realised there weren't too many girls that liked their men smelling of "greasy, dirty wool". But the money was good.

They stayed in Sydney for six months working, partying and of course playing rugby league for Coogee. It was then up to Queensland for a further four months of labouring before the pair finally decided to head back to Perth. They'd had fun. For Peter that working holiday experience ended with a life defining conclusion; labouring was not for him. His father's words finally getting through. "Use your noggin', it's a better way to go."

Back at home in Perth, Peter went out looking for work. Still not career focused he simply wanted a job that was close to home, paid reasonably well and would give him a start in an office. A few different jobs helped determine the path he would eventually take.

First there was the 'I like Swipe' job which came with an unexpected bonus that would impact his future and the path he would walk in life. His mate had bought the Fremantle rights to a pyramid styled scheme selling Swipe, a concentrated cleaning solution. When thousands of cartons of the product turned up on his mate's doorstep, Peter and a few other well-intentioned mates took on the selling role.

Peter had no intention of walking footpaths selling cleaning products for too long but on one particular Friday night in 1969 that's exactly what the 18 year old was doing.

> [Peter] I was out knocking on doors with the 'I like Swipe' badge fastened to my white shirt. I knocked on a door of a home in Hamilton Hill and this young girl answered so I asked if I could give a Swipe demonstration.
>
> "I live with my Gran – I'll get her."
>
> Gran (Doreen) came to the door. She looked me up and down and obviously satisfied I wasn't a bad sort, let me in. We went into the living room which had yellow walls but around the light switch it was grubby with fingerprints. I got out my cleaning cloth, sprayed the Swipe and started work. I kept thinking, how good is this, because I could see it was working.

The Swipe did remove the fingerprints but, to his horror, where Peter had wiped, the wall was now a patchy white – not a brighter, cleaner yellow as he'd expected. Doreen, he found out, was a smoker. For years, she along with her cigarette-puffing friends got together every week, in the living room, to play cards. So, beneath the smoke-stains the walls were in fact white; unfortunately for Peter that was now very obvious.

Doreen wasn't happy. "That's all very good young man but if you think you're leaving before you've cleaned the rest of the walls you'd better think again."

[Peter]   I was there for hours, cleaning that 'fricking' living room wall.

But all was not lost; Doreen's granddaughter, Darryl, chatted to Peter as he cleaned. Peter believes the attraction was the short shorts he was wearing but whatever it was by the time he left, he'd asked Darryl out. No more than a couple of years later they married and became the happily ever after couple.

After his wall cleaning debacle, Peter recognised that Swipe selling wasn't for him and was eager to try something different…sales repping at Cynthia Chinaware, in Cottesloe.

[Peter]   It was all souvenir stuff out of China – little ashtrays with black swans on the side or sticky tape dispensers covered in pictures of kangaroo paws.

But I got bored of trundling around the city or out to the airport trying to flog it all – so I threw in the towel. I then applied for an office job at Fremantle Hospital that I'd seen advertised.

I got the job just before my 20th birthday. It was in the payroll department. Don't let anyone tell you that maths isn't important in life, it is, so help your kids to master it.

It was in this job that Peter's mathematic competencies really came to the fore. He grasped the work quickly. It was also a job that came with opportunities and not only did Peter accept every opportunity, but he gave every one of them his best. That work ethic and attitude came to the attention of department bosses and consequently it wasn't long before he was rewarded with a promotion.

It was the 1970s, the time when computers were gaining prominence in the workplace. The government decided it was time to install a new payroll system into its teaching hospitals. Despite minimal experience Peter was put on a working party to implement the system and to train the staff of the top five teaching hospitals. He enjoyed the challenge and hence wanted more.

However, the Australian Public Service was and still is all about job titles, classifications and levels (Level 1 being the lowest). To move up through the levels and salary bandings, relevant qualifications are a prerequisite; Peter had none. He'd left school at 16. Now at 20 he was ready to do the study, however as a married man supporting his wife, he couldn't afford to study full-time. Undeterred by the situation, he enrolled as a part-time, mature age student in accountancy at Fremantle Technical College. It would take him a lot longer to complete but he was determined to get the qualifications he needed in order to get to the next level and beyond.

There were times when going to college after work was the last thing Peter felt like doing. It would often clash with rugby league training or catching up with his mates at the pub. In the middle of winter, when he would rather have been at home by the wood fire, he was there in class, having won yet another battle with his inner voice. Peter admits he might not have completed his diploma in accounting if it hadn't been for the public service 'level system'. It's a system that drives those ambitious enough to get out there and improve themselves, knowing there's a pathway to promotion at the end. For decision makers, the system is a powerful assessment tool for evaluating a candidate's level of dedication, performance and drive when determining who is most worthy of promotion. Peter clearly stood out as being a worthy one.

Not long after getting his diploma, the head of the payroll department, who'd been in the position for 30 years, retired. Peter, now 23 and qualified, was chosen to take over the role. The job came with a big jump in salary but also in responsibility. Fortunately, those years of captaining sports teams had unleashed the natural leader within him and he was confident and ready for the new role and the challenges it presented.

At 23 Peter was a good leader. Today, after years of experience, he is well qualified to define the qualities it takes to become one.

> [Peter] Strong leaders need to be honest. They need to have integrity, to be good communicators who set good examples and who would never ask another to do a job they weren't prepared to do themselves. They need to be clear and confident in their vision and how to deliver the requisites of proposed tasks. They also need to be sure that their employees have not only the skills, the support and the encouragement to complete the task at hand but also be able to recognise those who are not capable of doing so. Very importantly, if someone isn't up to the task, act quickly and reassign the role if necessary. Don't waste their time or yours if someone can't cut it.

Very importantly, if someone isn't up to the task, act quickly and reassign the role if necessary. Don't waste their time or yours if someone can't cut it.

The hospital was a huge organisation, made up of many different departments, each with a department head. In 1972, Peter, like every other head of department, was expected to recruit his own staff. Eventually, the CEO decided to create one department to manage all recruitment. Peter was given the role of personnel officer. The job required more training and development, courses on recruitment, on performance appraisals, personnel planning – anything that would assist him to deliver in his new human resources role.

Peter started the department from scratch. At first he only had caterers and cleaners and then tradesmen were added. Before long he was handling the recruitment of everyone employed by the hospital – professional staff, radiographers and the medical typing pool (a massive job in itself with 20 headset-wearing staff required to transcribe doctor's notes for medical records.)

Each recruitment process had to be developed and implemented – position description, selection criteria; whatever was required Peter delivered.

Peter's willingness to accept every opportunity and every challenge has clearly played a pivotal role in his journey. Over time, experience has only strengthened his belief that making the most of yourself has life shaping potential – no matter what path you take.

> [Peter] If you clean floors for a living, make them sparkle because doing what you do well can lead to rewards you might never have thought possible.

Most of us would probably apply Peter's line of thinking to significant tasks – but see no great point in giving a menial task the same level of effort. I remember as a young child, the task of making my bed was just a matter of pulling it up, it didn't matter that the sheets were crumpled underneath. I only made it because if I didn't my mother would get very upset. What I eventually learned – the reward of a well-made bed was a better night's sleep. I now see that same attitude in my own son. When it comes to his studies he does as little as possible despite knowing (deep down) that if he were to put in a little extra effort, he would achieve better results. As Peter said, "If you do even the most insignificant things well it can lead to rewards you never thought possible." So why don't we?

With every new job – labourer, door to door salesman, sales rep, payroll officer, HR manager, Peter's skill set grew. Fremantle Hospital was also growing, rapidly, and with that growth came the government's decision to decentralise it. To do so required a massive overhaul which included the establishment of a new industrial relations department. With over 30 different unions at Fremantle Hospital covering more than 3000 staff (plumbers, cleaners, caterers, nurses etc.) it was a mammoth undertaking. Peter stood out as the ideal candidate to implement and manage the new department.

Successes make you feel confident to believe that making it to the top is achievable. So, take every opportunity - it keeps you moving forward.

His communications skills were exceptional and fundamental to his success in the role. Peter was the person the secretaries of each of the unions turned to whenever there were issues, which was often. It became known that he would do his best to find a resolution before strike action became necessary. He admits there were still strikes but possibly not as many as there might have been. As a result of his work and growing reputation he was asked to take the role of Teaching Hospitals' Representative on the Industrial Relations Commission.

[Peter]   I was really chuffed when I was invited to take on the role not only because it was an acknowledgement of my capabilities, but it also came with a much broader responsibility, encompassing not only Fremantle but the entire State of WA.

I was required to sit with the Commissioner and listen to people's complaints – someone had to decide on the outcome. I could see there were some very poor management practices and so a lot of these people had legitimate complaints. Nepotism was huge; some guy fancied his secretary and so she would get a promotion; a manager would take a dislike to a staff member, which often led to unfair reclassification decisions. A whole lot of stuff like that went on. So, it struck me that not everyone applied the principles of management as fairly as they should, which I had always taken as something you would do naturally. So, my role in the Industrial Relations Commission was to put some justice back in, and that was something I really enjoyed doing.

By the early 80s, despite still being so young, Peter decided he had gone as far as he could at Fremantle Hospital and was looking to broaden his horizons. The CEO, who recognised Peter's value to the organisation, didn't want to lose him. He took it upon himself to mentor Peter. He also gave him every available opportunity, including the task of taking responsibility for all the allied health services of the hospital. It was in that role that Peter met Diana, the Princess of Wales.

[Peter] It sticks in my mind to this day. The hospital had built a new orthopaedic wing on South Terrace and named it the Princess of Wales Wing. The Princess herself came to Perth to open it. As a senior executive I was invited to morning tea in the boardroom and got to meet her. She was drop dead gorgeous, stunning and she had such an aura and charisma – it just made you melt.

She visited the patients in the new wing and spoke to everyone and was just so interested in everything we were doing at the hospital. She was incredible and when she looked at you, she engaged you.

Peter, like many of us, was gobsmacked by the people's princess. But even in his awe he recognised the trait that made her so amazing – the genuine interest she showed to whomever she was speaking. Peter believes that asset is an invaluable tool both in life and in business and one he feels everyone should work at developing within themselves.

Still at Fremantle Hospital, Peter was now looking towards the top job. He was happy to stay at Fremantle but just as happy to look at Sir Charles Gairdner or Royal Perth hospitals. There was no doubt ambition had well and truly set in.

[Peter] I'd had quite a few successes and it made me confident enough to believe making it to the top was actually achievable. When you are at the bottom of any organisation the top feels like such a long way away and getting there seems an almost impossible dream – so some don't even try.

That's why it's so important to take every opportunity even if you don't think you're up to it – it keeps you moving forward. A great way to start is to have smaller, achievable goals, and of course, whatever the job, do it to the best of your ability – you will get noticed.

My advice to anyone is: anything and everything is possible.

We have a girl on the front desk; every day I walk in and without thinking she asks if I would like a cup of tea and I always hear her ask that of all the staff. Although she has the worst job in the office, she does it so well and continually shows initiative. She also looks after the kitchen and every day it's immaculate. She's already worked out where she wants to go next in the organisation and I can say that realising that dream is not far away. Some people never work it out – they always hope they'll get a promotion but they just don't put in the effort.

One day Alice came to a fork in the road and saw a Cheshire cat in a tree. "Which road do I take?" she asked. "Where do you want to go?" was his response. "I don't know," Alice answered. "Then," said the cat, "it doesn't matter."

Lewis Carroll

[Peter] Admittedly not everyone wants the top job. Some people are happy and comfortable to stay in a job they enjoy and know how to do, in that way there's no stress or pressure. As a boss I need people like that because if everyone was overly ambitious you couldn't satisfy them. There are only limited top roles but there are many roles available for those who are less ambitious.

Peter's own ambition led him on a search for fresh opportunities and challenges out in the community. He found what he was looking for in Rotary and quickly undertook the role of the hospital's representative at Fremantle Rotary Club.

[Peter] I really enjoyed the role and became very active in the community and started to take a greater interest in what was happening in the Fremantle area.

I realised that as Fremantle was a safe Labor seat the Labor government didn't need to spend any money on the hospital as they knew it was next to impossible to lose the seat. When the Liberals got in, they knew it was next to impossible to win the seat so they didn't spend any money either. So, we (the senior executive team at the hospital) were constantly fighting about funding with whichever government was in power at the time. Equipment for Fremantle Hospital, as specialists in orthopaedic surgery with a strong oncology and nuclear medicine facility, was and still is horrifyingly expensive. So, I became heavily involved in fund raising through Rotary to buy equipment like MRI machines.

Peter still had his eye on the hospital's top job, and so when the CEO retired, Peter was hopeful he would take over. Disappointingly, someone else was appointed. He was naturally upset but only fleetingly. He quickly recognised the new boss's capabilities – he was highly qualified, very experienced, 'smart as' and a 'very nice bloke'. He was noticeably worthy of the position. However, after only 12 months in the role the WA premier recruited the CEO to head up the Health Department and so, once again, the CEO's position was vacant. Just as that happened a new premier for Western Australia was voted in. Peter remembers vividly how quick he was to introduce a 'senior executive service'.

[Peter] Without any advertising or calling for applications the premier brought in a fellow from the Education Department to take on the role of CEO of Fremantle Hospital. It was hard to accept because it was clear to everyone, he had no experience in running a hospital. He had no idea what he was doing and so it killed morale.

Fremantle Hospital became one of many organisations to reel from the blows of what would go down in history as the infamous political scandal known as WA Inc.

Peter was incensed. He was compelled to do something but felt there was only one solution – get Labor out. And with that he joined the Liberal Party!

He took long service leave and campaigned throughout the following year. It was during this time that he met an extraordinary man; an inspiration who would become Peter's mentor. He was the charismatic Sir Charles Court, the 21st Premier of Western Australia.

*If you have to tell someone you're the boss,
you don't have gravitas.*

[Peter] He was a statesman in the true sense of the word, an amazing man – he looked like a leader, and he had gravitas. Gravitas is what you gain from experience, success and power – it's not charisma, which is the charming, engaging vibe people send out and makes you feel immediately comfortable. Gravitas is very different. It's almost an aura – you know when you've never met the boss, but when he walks into the room you just know who he is. It's the way they carry themselves, the way they talk, the way they engage. If you have to tell someone you're the boss, you don't have gravitas. Sir Charles Court had both gravitas and charisma in abundance.

He took a liking to me, to where I'd come from (a working-class family), my track record and that I was a Fremantle local. He liked what motivated me to join the Party – being unhappy about what was happening but prepared to do something about it as distinct from someone whose decision to get into politics is ego driven.

Very early on we were having a discussion and he said, "Peter you've got a very difficult task at Fremantle, but you've got potential, so if you really want a career in politics don't give up, even if you get beaten – DON'T GIVE UP!

The best thing he told me, "Never promise anything you can't deliver, particularly in politics because it will always come back to bite you." He said, "Lead your life beyond reproach." To my knowledge I cannot think of anything that Charles Court did that ever brought him criticism – whether you liked his politics or not, he was still a decent bloke.

Sir Charles Court, as he became later addressed, organised a fundraiser for Peter and asked John Howard, the leader of the Liberal Party, to attend. It was a huge success. But the challenge was too great, and Peter lost at the ballot box. He quit politics and returned to work a disappointed but wiser man. The 'other guy' was still in charge and after everything Peter had been through, he knew he couldn't continue to work with him. Change had to happen.

It did – at a family barbecue on a Sunday afternoon in June 1990.

> [Peter] I was standing at the barbecue turning the snaggers and I remember my brother Brian coming up and saying, "Mate, this is the last time I'm going to ask you; I've started a business called Cash Converters and I think it's got real legs, but I need someone to manage it for me – what do you think?"
>
> Brian had asked me to work with him plenty of times before but I was never interested. I was happy where I was – but timing is everything. Things had changed and so had I.

Peter was 39. He and Darryl had three children who were growing up fast, his rugby playing days were over and they were living in a very comfortable home in Spearwood. As a well-paid senior executive, they could afford for Darryl to be a stay-at-home mother which was very important to them both. After 21 years in the public service and three lots of long service leave the family had been on some amazing holidays and more were on the horizon. As a public servant he was on flexitime so there was plenty of time for family and golf. He played golf every Thursday and Saturday at Royal Fremantle where he was a member. Life was just getting very comfortable.

Peter knew what was at risk if he did join Brian – the life he and his family had become accustomed to. But as US author, Neale Donald Walsch said, "Life begins at the end of your comfort zone."

> [Peter] I asked Darryl what she thought I should do and she said, "Peter just go for it!"

No doubt Darryl would have felt great apprehension as they drove home after the barbecue, but she had faith in her husband and so the decision was made. With that a new chapter in their lives began.

You must be the change you wish to see in the world.

Mahatma Gandhi

Brian, like Peter, belonged to Rotary. In 1984 Brian had met a fellow Rotarian who owned a pawn broking business in Maylands. It was just as you would imagine a pawn broking shop to be – bars on dusty windows; higgledy-piggledy piles of 'stuff' stacked high, a cabinet full of jewellery; and the pawnbroker, with his jeweller's loupe and cap, looked the part as well.

> [Peter] Brian is the entrepreneur of our family. He was looking to start another business and so went out to Maylands and spent some time with this guy (the pawnbroker). He couldn't believe the margin he was making and so was interested in seeing how the business worked. Brian made some suggestions such as opening up the store a bit more to make it a little less

crowded and to present everything more professionally. Brian was certain that with those changes he would get more people through the door and double his turnover.

The pawnbroker disagreed. "Brian, that's not the way it's done. Pawn broking customers are desperate, and they don't need any of that – they just come for the money 'cos they have nowhere else to go." He couldn't see the business in any other way.

So, Brian asked if he would mind if he had a go at opening a store himself. The guy had no problem with the idea and even offered to help and give him some training. He was good at valuing jewellery and knew all about diamonds and precious metals, so Brian took him up on his offer.

Brian was soon ready to open his first store – Victoria Park Pawnbrokers on Albany Highway in Victoria Park. He set it up like a retail store, and to give privacy to those who needed to pawn goods he made a side entry – that proved to be a very good idea. No more than twelve months later Brian was calling on his mates, including his younger brother Tony, to open stores in other areas – all with different names but all doing the same thing. Brian, ever the entrepreneur, was a partner in each store. He showed them how to work the business. Eventually, they decided to engage an advertising company to come up with a brand name that would bring all the stores under the one banner. Late on a Sunday night all the owners went out and removed their old signs. By Monday morning the new signs were up. Then in 1987 the TV ads started. They could only afford one advertisement and chose for it to air on Channel 7, after the evening news, five nights a week. With that ad, "We are the Cash Converters" was born. By the time Peter joined the business there were 21 stores, the majority in Perth.

Brian recognised the business had the potential to be franchised nationally and so just before the family barbecue he had set up a sub-franchise agreement with Peter Senior (the golfer) in Queensland. This was a good strategic move, but it meant big changes had to happen if the business was to grow and be sustainable. Training and processes would have to be implemented, and it would have to be done professionally. Brian knew there was no one better to handle the job than his middle brother and that is why, at that Sunday barbecue, Peter's life took a significant change in direction.

[Peter]   Whilst Brian was out expanding the company, I was back in the office building the business structure and organisation – it was a good combo!

To build an empire you have to build on solid foundations, if not it will crumble in five to ten years. History has proven this to be correct over and over. So, you must have a clear idea at the beginning what you want to achieve and build it accordingly – don't underestimate the significance of this.

Peter being Peter, meticulously researched the franchising potential. He recognised that trading, which is essentially pawn broking, had been around for thousands of years, and moneylenders, like the Medici family of Florence, had been around for almost as long.

Brian had a great track record and Peter believed in him, and once his research was complete, he also believed in the concept. And so, with belief and confidence he began to build.

[Peter] There was a lot involved in building the foundations – creating a professional image, a professional retail space, staff, uniforms, operating manuals for new franchisees, how to start a business, business plans, cash flows and the development of training programmes specific to the core skills of the business. You couldn't just walk into Office Works and buy an off-the-shelf pawnbroker training kit – not that Office Works was around back then. You had to be able to value jewellery; you had to be able to identify if the stone was a diamond, the cut and the clarity of the diamond or, if it was gold, how many carats.

It took Peter a number of years to complete and introduce the systems and processes but during those years the business grew – and rapidly at that.

[Peter] We were approached by this fellow, a pom, who was about to move back to his home in the UK. He'd seen the concept and thought it would work back there. So, in 1991 we sold him our first international licence. I went to the UK and got him established. He then sent people out to Australia and we taught them here.

Brian and I have always felt immense responsibility and obligation with the sale of every franchise. These people risk a significant amount of capital on a business we tell them is good – so if they fail, we take it personally, even if it's not our fault. We do our best to minimise that possibility, but it still happens.

A lot of people are entrepreneurial but it's pretty scary starting a business from scratch. With a franchise it's like having the safety net of a business partner who knows the business inside out and already has runs on the board. However, that entrepreneurial part of their personality sometimes takes over and they want to do it in their own way – but that's when they most often come unstuck.

One of our core processes is, "Treat the customer with respect and empathy", because generally, when someone is pawning an item they are doing so because they are in financial stress which is unpleasant for them. We developed an 11-step process and one of those steps is to put the customer at ease and to remove their embarrassment. This is where we see the common thread of failure – the franchisee is often only interested in trying to buy the goods from the customer for as little as possible. They give no thought to the next time or for the power of word of mouth – "Don't go down there, they made me feel small and tried to rip me off".

Obviously, that is no way to build a relationship with a customer. 'Respect' is one of the five core values of the Cash Converters brand – it's the 'why' behind our success. The old saying, "If it ain't broke don't fix it," is a wise maxim but perhaps some just feel they can do it better, and perhaps they can, but then why bother paying for the expense of a franchise if you don't want to follow a proven system?

When you buy a franchise, you get a lot of support and guidance. To help us help our franchisees, we send mystery shoppers out into the stores every month. We then mark the results on a table so they can see how they are performing. We reward those who get top marks. Not surprisingly, they are also the ones who are usually at the top of the tables when it comes to

KPIs (key performance indicators) and profit, and interestingly those at the bottom blame the mystery shopper – nearly every time.

The processes we have in place took a tremendous amount of work and time to perfect. We did that just so that we could see where our franchisees were going right or wrong and help them if needed. Quite often when we sit down with those who are struggling, we find they haven't followed the processes or they won't accept any responsibility – for them it's always someone else's fault – always.

Having good processes and systems in place is paramount to the longevity and robustness of a business...the foundations of a brand. All the best businesses have great brands – Nike, Apple, McDonald's, Coca Cola...

A brand must have its own personality and set of values, so we developed, with the help of stakeholders, franchisees and corporate staff, five core values; Professionalism, respect, collaboration, integrity and passion. Right from the start our staff have those brand values drummed into them so they totally understand what is expected of them and of any decisions they make around the business – there is no ambiguity. They are listed on our kitchen wall, so you can't ignore them, and they become a part of everything we do. As the person at the top, I live by them as well.

> *Having good processes and systems in place is paramount to the longevity and robustness of any business.*

Of all the lessons Peter acquired along the way, the one he feels is key to all good business is, surround yourself with a strong team. He firmly believes that you can't physically do everything yourself or even have the know-how, so it's vital to have quality people working with you.

[Peter]   Don't be afraid that someone is going to take your job because you think they are smarter than you are. In my view if they are that clever, they deserve it and will eventually take it anyway. However, I also learnt that when a plan goes wrong it is generally the weak link that lets the side down. The important point here is that if you are the one who selected that weak link, take responsibility for it – then act quickly to remove those people from the team. I didn't always do it that way because I felt sorry for the person – not anymore because the rest of the team suffers if you do. It's far better to be at the top of the tree and enjoy the rewards and recognition of being able to bring together a team that gets the job done quickly and done well.

Don't be afraid that someone is going to take your job because you think they are smarter than you are. If they are that clever, they deserve it and will eventually take it anyway.

Just as Brian predicted, Peter's vast experience, together with his perseverance and his 'give it your best' attitude enabled him to not only take Cash Converters to the next level but way beyond. By designing an all-encompassing business system and building a strong and cohesive team of people to implement and manage it, Cash Converters grew at a tremendous pace. At one point a new store was opening, somewhere in the world, every 36 hours. France, Belgium, Holland. Wherever they opened Peter was there to help establish the business. It was exhausting but exhilarating.

[Peter]   Brian owned 75 per cent of the business. In 1995 he wanted to take some money off the table. We were a private company, so the best option was to float Cash Converters. We approached a number of stockbrokers but because it was a pawn broking business a lot of people had a negative perception of it. That made it difficult to get people on board to support the idea.

I was aware of this possible reaction so in the lead up to the float we started a few programmes. One of the things that had struck me was that in our business you could buy or sell anything without ID — so you didn't have to prove you owned the goods. The whole industry had a really poor reputation, which was probably warranted, but we wanted to do things differently, legitimately. Our relationship with the police department wasn't good either; they considered all pawnbrokers to be a bit dodgy and treated them accordingly.

I came up with the idea of a 100-point ID check, the same as you need to open a bank account. So we developed this huge database and software program where we kept our customers' details on file. We kept a copy of their passport, driver's licence that sort of thing and then we issued the customer with a laminated ID card with their photo on it for future use. We then made the database available to the police department to crosscheck with their stolen property reports.

Ultimately, all the rules that we set in place became part of the statute for pawn broking in each state of Australia. I felt pretty chuffed about that.

An unintended consequence of this ID check and database collection was the demise of many pawn broking businesses around the country. Unlike Cash Converters they weren't out there spending millions on television advertising, developing a concept or creating a brand. A brand that was attracting people to their stores where they could make legitimate transactions. Many pawnbrokers still preferred doing business with the 'Dodgy Dave's'. But change in the industry was underway and with it came a strong competitive advantage for Cash Converters.

Despite the business now being a credible and hugely successful international chain, Cash Converters did not meet the listing rules of the ASX (Australian Stock Exchange). The managing partner of Price Waterhouse Coopers, Reg Webb, saw it differently. He liked the concept and the business, as did stockbroker Greg Hancock. However, regardless of their view, Peter and Brian were unable to generate enough support to float the company in Australia. After all their effort it was difficult not to be disappointed. However, Greg then made a suggestion that would change the course of Cash Converters and all those involved.

"You have stores in the UK and Europe, so there is a relevance on the London market – go and list on the London Stock Exchange."

By this time there were 110 stores in Australia and 60 in the UK. In 1995, seemingly without any great effort, Cash Converters was accepted and listed on the full board of the London Stock Exchange. It was a hugely successful float.

Most people fail because they aren't prepared to put in what's required to get the job done or to be ultimately successful. Find a way - never let anyone stop you.

Less than a year later, they received a long hoped for invitation – onto the ASX. It was a warm February day in 1997 when the entire staff walked out of their head office on St Georges Terrace and marched around the corner to the Australian Stock Exchange building.

[Peter] We just stood there and watched as the words "Cash Converters" rolled out onto that massive digital screen for our first day of trading – we all felt immense pride. It was a great day.

This was a case of us really wanting to do something, but obstacles just kept getting thrown in the way. We didn't give up. It was tough, but we found a way around the obstacles, and whilst it might have taken a while, we eventually got what we wanted.

It's amazing how, particularly in small business, people try to throw hurdles in front of you. Some in business stumble and don't get back up while others do. Pitifully, the more successful some become the more people want to pull them down – that's not unique to Australia – it happens everywhere. But one thing that is unique to Australia, and only because we don't have a strong class system, is that pretty much anyone can be successful if they are prepared to give it a go.

One thing that is unique to Australia, and only because we don't have a strong class system, is that pretty much anyone can be successful if they are prepared to give it a go.

Most people fail because they aren't prepared to put in what's required to get the job done or to be ultimately successful. Many want to be, but they just don't go that extra mile. All I can say is find a way – never let anyone stop you. But you really have to want to, you really need to have the desire.

Once we listed Cash Converters, we had access to the capital markets, providing the means to grow the company significantly. Previously, all profit generated was reinvested back into the company to build whatever was essential for rapid growth.

When you grow rapidly your revenue may grow but your overheads also have to grow to accommodate an expanding empire. Hence, we decided to concentrate our efforts primarily in Australia – let the international business continue to grow, but turn this market into a really solid, high profit generating, cash flow business. The business is still growing here and inter-nationally. We have over 800 stores in 21 countries – 227 of those are in the UK alone.

Admittedly there have been many copycats along the way because the enticement of reward is certainly there, but none have succeeded in quite the same way as us.

Cash Converters is a brand thirty years and millions of dollars in the making. It would be very difficult for anyone to compete against a company that most people recognise and which has such a strong presence in major cities and towns across the country. So, it is not surprising that others have had no great success in copying the concept.

When Cash Converters emerged on the pawn broking landscape it triggered significant change. For many that was unwanted change, however nothing could compare to the change the entire industry was about to confront. Two massive competitors were emerging on the horizon and no one, includ-ing Peter, could anticipate the impact this would have on any of them.

[Peter] Firstly – China arrived and brought with it DVD players, printers, movie cameras – you name it, they came in by the millions and all at prices never seen before. All of a sudden you could buy a DVD player for $49.99 – what did that make a second-hand one worth? It had a massive impact on our business and put a lot of pressure on the business model, so we knew we had to adjust it.

The franchisees naturally came to us with, "What's your solution? What are we going to do?"

I took it really personally because it was me who'd convinced them to join our network; to invest half a million dollars in the business. With the arrival of China, it became a real strug-gle, and so I took that responsibility personally and I still do. But we found the solution and survived.

I'd just got back from the US where I'd seen this unsecured lending. I took the idea to Brian with the thinking that we might be able to do 1000 transactions a month, but he goes – "NO, we could do 10,000". So, Brian invested his money and we changed the business model and added money lending to our business stable. It quickly became a really significant part of our business.

China was a massive hurdle but an even bigger one was looming. An online phenomenon was taking the world by storm and it was heading towards Australia. As the nation prepared for the millennium, eBay was unleashed onto our computer networks.

> [Peter] At the time of eBay's arrival, we all thought it would really damage our business and we were very concerned. But as I've said before – there are plenty of hurdles in business and you just have to manoeuvre your way around them. We have a great team and together we came up with a solution; our own online retail space called Webshop. It's been a great success.

A positive by-product of this new online sensation was one the Cash Converters team had not considered. It came in the form of buyer perception. Suddenly, the buying and selling of second-hand goods was, for the first time, an acceptable if not "savvy" thing to do. No longer would one try to hide their bargain buy; now it was, "I bought this Longines watch on eBay for $800 – it retails for $2,500."

Have no doubt – if you are not constantly aware of changes in your industry, you will get left behind.

> [Peter] We broke the barriers down even further because unlike eBay we would advertise a product online, but our customers were then able to drop into the store to have a closer look. On top of that was the added guarantee that if something went wrong, it's easy to go back to where you bought it.

> Our retail sales soared because of our online business. A lot of our customers started looking online but actually ended up buying in the stores. So, eBay actually helped us stay competitive. Whilst initially we thought it would be catastrophic it made us rethink and has turned into a positive. Have no doubt – if you are not constantly aware of changes in your industry, you will get left behind.

By 2002 Cash Converters was well and truly a successful public company. But Brian being the true entrepreneur felt it was time for him to move on, time to explore and conquer new territory and so in 2002 he left the company he had started nearly 20 years earlier.

> [Peter] In business you really need to know what kind of person you are. Brian is the entrepreneur, the thinker and has the balls to give his ideas a go, whereas I'm the builder. While I look at the risks associated, he only looks at the upside. He'd say we could sell 10,000 of them and make a million and I'd say, gee I think we'd struggle to sell a 1,000 so we'll lose a million. So, he'd invest his own money to make it happen – he's amazing. But we have a great balance. We both know that I wouldn't have come up with Cash Converters, but he knows, without me, he couldn't have built it to where it is today.

> A good entrepreneur knows when it's time to get out of the business, which for Brian was in

2002 – but a lot of entrepreneurs don't know when to move on. They build a business and then stay on and try and manage it – but if it's not their skill set the business goes pear shaped. We've all seen it happen.

His brother Tony had left the company in 1997 to pursue his love of cooking and so with both brothers out of the business Peter was now alone at the helm. It was business as usual but that meant more stress and more obstacles – fortunately, nothing new to Peter.

[Peter]   Challenges and stresses greet me on a daily basis, but I manage them by staying in the moment. If there's a problem I confront it head on – always have done. Stressing about a problem doesn't solve it. You need to find out the cause then you can fix it. Stress comes when you don't know where you're going or how you're going to fix it – that's when you lose clarity. But if you have clarity of thought you can identify the problem, find the solution and then it's just about taking the necessary action to resolve the issue.

The will to win, the desire to succeed, the urge to reach your full potential...these are the keys that will unlock the door to personal excellence.

Confucius

One of the things I've learned over the years is to deal with the difficult things first thing in the morning. Make the hard calls early – don't leave them till the end of the day and then put them off till the next. Get them out of the way – it feels so much better. I think putting off till tomorrow is why a lot of people don't sleep well. They go to bed worrying about how they are going to solve the problem tomorrow. I say...NO, SOLVE IT TODAY!

As a company we've been through some great times and some tough times. But I've been lucky, I've had some great personal and business achievements along the way. Some of my proudest moments have come when the entire company has come together in unity to solve a problem and then go on to achieve some astounding outcomes. We won the industry awards for leading franchise exporter of intellectual property. That was pretty good too, particularly as we were up against some amazing high-tech exporters. There are very few Australian franchise companies that have been able to successfully export their business – many have tried, and many have failed – so I am very proud of what we have achieved.

I'm also very proud of what this business has done for our family and how it has helped our children on their journey through life. Not only has it given us all an amazing lifestyle, travel and some personal wealth, but my son Brodie, who joined the business after leaving school, has found his niche and an unexpected passion for the business.

Brodie finished his TEE year with pretty average grades because, like me at school, he didn't open a book. We told him he wasn't going to go surfing every day or lay around on the couch while he thought about what he wanted to do with his life. So, we put him to work at one of the stores we owned in Phoenix Shopping Centre. It totally changed his life. It became clear, very quickly, that he was good in the role, so I invested in some training for him and by 23 he was managing the store and ultimately became a partner.

We didn't give him ownership; he had to go off to the bank and borrow the money for his share of the equity. We then, together, bought another store, in Clarkson. When the company bought them back as part of our growth strategy, he came to work in the office as Corporate Store, Business Development Manager for WA. He later moved to Mexico City to set the stores up there – so he's done really well for himself.

Without the wins along the way or if we'd made it too easy for him, Brodie may never have had the confidence or courage to pursue the career he's made for himself. He now puts in 110 per cent, he's straightforward and honest – and when you live life like that, you get back.

Our staff like my son, are all treated with respect and honesty. If I know I can't deliver, I will never dangle the carrot just to get what I want.

I see honesty as a requirement of being successful, as is integrity and being self-motivated. Successful people are driven to get on with the job and have the confidence to make things happen – people will follow someone who is confident.

Leaders have to believe in their own ability – it's not for the faint-hearted. If you want to be the one leading the way you have to believe 100 per cent in the direction you are taking everyone, or you won't get there. You have to be able to excite people enough to get them to follow you across a tumultuous river even it looks like an impossible crossing.

Take a genuine interest in whomever you speak to. It is an invaluable tool both in life and in business and one everyone should work at developing within themselves.

Being at the top of the tree brings great reward although at times it can be a solitary road. It would be nice to just be like everybody else and go down to the pub. But you can't do that. I think as a leader, as a boss, you have to keep a distance. It gets down to respect. You can't respect your boss if you saw him pissed as a parrot down at the pub last Friday night, so you don't do it. I'm happy for it to be that way; it's been worth it. It's been a joy to be in the position to lead my staff through many challenges and to watch them grow, take bolder steps and with encouragement be confident enough to think and step outside the box. What's important is to create the right environment so your staff feel comfortable enough to speak out and be applauded, even if their idea doesn't come to anything. It's like taking risks; you have to be prepared to do so, they don't always work out, but at least you gave it a try.

I look back now at some of the projects I've taken on that were not overly successful, but I learned so much along the way it was worth every disappointment. I learned to recognise when it's time to call it a day. That was an important lesson because you can get really caught up in an idea. You can spend so much money and time trying to make a concept work, so you just want to keep going. Then emotion gets in the way of making good decisions. This is when you really need good processes and KPI benchmarks – if we don't get to this point by March, we will pull the pin – you must have those markers.

Having a formal education has also enabled me to achieve the success I have. I'm not saying you can't be successful without one, but for me it was a cornerstone of being able to run a large organisation because it's all about financing and balance sheets. In saying that, all the training programmes I did made a massive difference too. But I strongly recommend a formal education because there's no doubt, in most circumstances, it's tougher without one.

But no matter how much education or how much experience you have there will always be another obstacle just waiting around the corner. That's business, that's life. A couple of years ago we went through a pretty rough patch. There where changes in legislation for banks and finance companies where the introduction of greater regulation and compliance procedures added a huge cost to providing finance. It had a huge impact on us and we saw a big drop in our share price. It was a very stressful period. We've now, finally come out the other side and our business profit is increasing again, and the company is surging forward. I'd like the share price to be higher, but we are doing okay and we're heading in the right direction.

It was during this period of legislative change that Peter went to the Cash Converters board and advised he was ready to move towards retirement. In his mind, June 2018 was to be the month he would finish. With that, a new CEO with a financial services background was appointed. Peter needed to stay for a while to help with his transition into the role.

[Peter] I thought I was ready for retirement, but the board offered me a project in Europe for 12 months and I jumped at it. The objective was to consolidate our European businesses, including the UK, into one company and then list that on the London Stock Exchange. We have businesses in France, Belgium, Spain, Switzerland and England which are all owned by different people. We knew if we could buy the licences back to consolidate all of their earnings, we would create a much bigger company, crystallise the value and raise some capital at the same time and so grow the business at a greater rate. The board wanted me to pull it together because over many years I had developed strong personal relationships with all the owners of the business in these countries.

There's a photo of me with two gentlemen at the opening of a store in Amsterdam in 1995. They wanted to celebrate the occasion with me by eating raw herring which is a delicacy in Holland. I had to eat the whole fish. The head is cut off, the insides are cut out but it still has the tail and skin on and you just munch all the way down to the tail. It was revolting. I couldn't eat fish for about three years after that. So clearly, I'm prepared to put my body on the line for the company (laughter) but that is how great relationships are forged.

The two guys in that photo own the licence for Holland and so all the franchisees in Holland pay them the franchise fee and then we get a royalty from that. Those are the guys we are buying the licence off.

That's the project I've been working on since 2017 but we have now realised it's going to take a little bit longer than first thought; it looks like it could be at least another 12 months.

It requires spending a lot of time in Europe, but Darryl and I are great travellers, so it's been good fun.

I'm still a director of the company – my official title now is Executive Deputy-Chairman but I'm no longer responsible for the day-to-day business so that pressure's off, and because this is a project-based thing it's a nice way to go.

I'm very lucky, I still love the business. I love going to work each day, it's exciting, challenging and stimulating – in fact I can't wait to get there in the mornings. With this new project I've finally got the balance between work, family and hobbies right. It wasn't always that way and my family has suffered because of it. I used to be away for weeks on end. If it hadn't been for Darryl who managed three children, the house and helped and supported me, I wouldn't have achieved the success I have, and still had a happy marriage and great kids. It's definitely been a team thing. Without that kind of support, I don't know how you would cope with the level of commitment that is required to be successful.

I do have a great group of friends and people that I turn to regularly for advice, like my brother Brian who always has a great perspective on things, Reg Webb who is chairman of our board and Michael Cook who was a senior partner of a big law firm before going out on his own. He does our franchise agreements and has provided some very wise counsel over the years. Admittedly, you have to be really comfortable in your own skin to seek counsel. Some people think it's a failing if they ask questions or advice, but no one knows everything – I certainly don't and don't pretend to.

That's why I made the commitment to the new CEO that I'm here to give him all the support and any advice he requires, and it's my pleasure to share my knowledge with him if he should need it. But I won't get in his way, although when you've been running the show for a long time it's sometimes hard to stand back.

So, with many battles won, challenges overcome and stores continuing to open around the globe, one would ask, if once this project is complete will Peter then sit back and enjoy the fruits of his achievements…or will he consider doing the same in the USA as he is currently doing in Europe?

[Peter]   That's what the board would probably like but I think I would have retired by then. For now, I've got my little spot here whilst I'm working on this project and I can come and go as I please. I look at what I've achieved and how far I've come and people often say – Oh Peter, how long are you going to keep doing this for? When are you going to retire? But if I wasn't working, I think I'd struggle. I couldn't imagine playing golf every day, maybe once a week would be pretty good though. To be honest when I considered retiring completely it scared the hell out of me. Now as a director of the company I love, it's not as onerous. I have board meetings and I add value where I can; I just don't want to be the man that does it every day, I've had enough of that. More golf, more fun, more travel! Life is good and I'm very pleased that I've moved on in a way that has allowed that to happen.

If and when I retire, I'd like to think that with my experience of running a public company, I could add some value as a board member in a not for profit organisation – I think I'd enjoy that.

Before he took on the consolidation project, before he stepped down as CEO and before he became a director on the Cash Converters' Board, Peter had thought that when the time came to hang up his cap and jeweller's loupe (tongue in cheek) he would likely sell his share of the company. He believed, like all great leaders, he would not make a great passenger. For Peter, if he wasn't in the driver's seat, he wouldn't be in the car. How things can change when you decide to take on new challenges and conquer new territory.

So, for now Peter is very happy to continue as a director on the board, consolidating the Cash Converters' brand in Europe, to play the occasional game of golf and travel the world with Darryl.

[Peter]   I'm happy with who I am, I have a great life and enjoy all the good times and all the challenges, but if they put Pete Cumins in a box tomorrow and all my mates came around and said, "He was a good bloke" – I'd be happy with that to be honest.

Thanks Peter.

Peter at kindy. Back row L-R Mrs Cumins (kindy aide), Tony, third along, Peter, fourth along

Mr and Mrs Cumins Snr with their three sons

Peter's first place of employment - Fremantle Port Authority

Peter in his Rugby days

Help Peter Help You

If you believe like Peter, that we should get a lot more service from our Legislative Members and that they be more accountable to the voters, then cast your vote for PETER CUMINS.

He is dedicated to serve you, to serve Fremantle and to make Western Australia a fairer and better place for us all.

Help Peter to HELP YOU by letting him know your areas of concern NOW.

Hotline
335 7498

Postal Address
P.O. Box 440, W.A.
Fremantle 6160

VOTE
CUMINS
FOR THE NEXT STATE ELECTION

LIBERAL

YOUR LIBERAL TEAM FOR THE UPPER HOUSE

GRIFFITHS   PENDAL   AIREY

HARSTE   HARDWICK

IN THE SOUTH METROPOLITAN REGION

YOUR LIBERAL VOTE IS IMPORTANT FOR A STRONG HOUSE OF REVIEW

LIBERAL

Authorised by TAA Hertford, 640 Murray Street, West Perth
Printed by All Media Direct, 84/8 Murray Hwy East Victoria Inc.

FOR THE NEXT ELECTION
Join the Age of Reason

With PETER CUMINS
...NOW CANDIDATE FOR THE SEAT OF **FREMANTLE**

Running for the Liberal Party

Peter Cumins' Home & Heart are in Fremantle

Peter Cumins knows and understands Fremantle as only someone who has lived and worked here all his life can ever do.

He met his wife Darryl whilst they were both at Hamilton Hill Senior High School.

With a daughter and two sons, Katie, Brodie and Peter aged 9, 7 and 3, they are every inch a Fremantle family and aware first hand of the worries and rising costs that we face as citizens. Peter answered the call to serve because he believes the very base of our society is under threat by the undermining of the family unit in a society where law and order and education standards have fallen badly in recent years.

Peter Cumins is active in Fremantle

Peter is the Manager of Industrial and General Services at Fremantle Hospital, where he has worked for seventeen years; before that he worked at Fremantle Port Authority. He is a qualified Accountant and a member of the National Institute of Accountants and the Australian Institute of Management.

As well as being professionally successful, Peter is an outstanding sportsman who has represented Fremantle with distinction. A former President of the Fremantle Rugby League Club and W.A. State Player on 13 occasions, Peter played a record 260 First Grade Games for Fremantle. He is currently Vice President of the Fremantle City Golf Club and was last year's Club Champion.

Peter Cumins shares your problems

Peter is dedicated to stopping the rot that has set in over recent years of Labor neglect. As we count the rising costs, we witness the progressive erosion of so much West Australians have long regarded as fundamental to our way of life.

● IT IS NO LONGER SAFE TO WALK THE STREETS OF FREMANTLE.

The cost of Justice is too high. The leaders of the forces of law and order are on record as being badly understaffed.

No lesser person than the Chief Justice believes the legal system is rapidly pricing itself beyond the means of the broad mass of our society. Above all Peter believes that the protection of individual rights starts with MORE EFFECTIVE LAW AND ORDER.

● ALL IS NOT WELL WITH OUR EDUCATION SYSTEM.

Peter's position is clear. He stands for a MORE RATIONAL AND RELEVANT EDUCATIONAL SYSTEM to better equip students to become productive and responsible adults.

● MORE JOB OPPORTUNITIES FOR SCHOOL LEAVERS and a return to a better work ethic.

● THERE IS TOO MUCH GOVERNMENT INVOLVEMENT IN BUSINESS

Peter is committed to a free enterprise system, to employ on merit, not "Jobs for the Boys."

● WESTERN AUSTRALIA NEEDS TO GET BACK ON AN EVEN KEEL, to restore the integrity of its once proud institutions. This process starts at the roots of our democracy by the way you cast your vote on ELECTION DAY.

Peter's election brochure

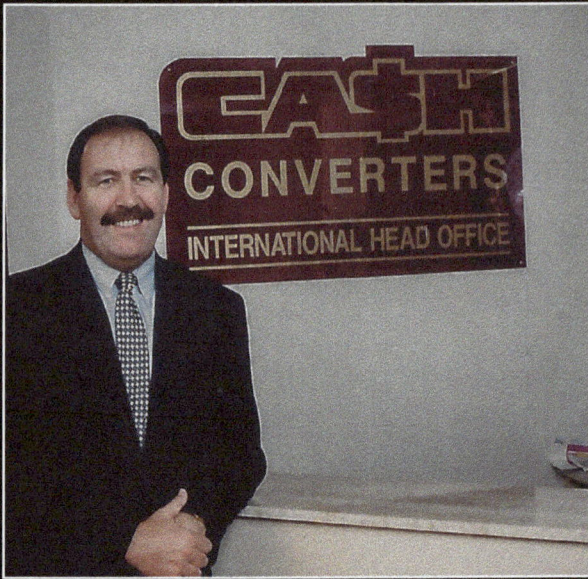
Early days at Cash Converters

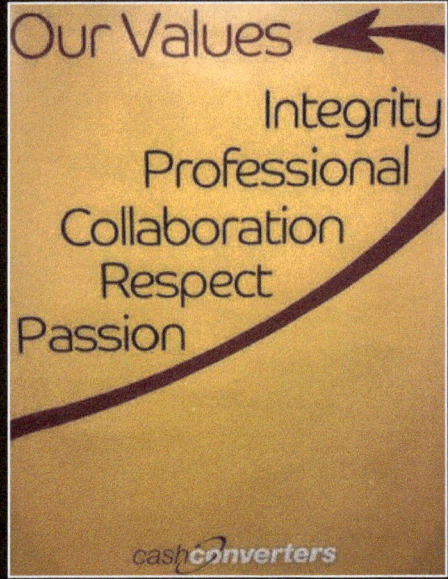
Cash Converters 5 Core Values

Our Values

Integrity
Professional
Collaboration
Respect
Passion

cash converters

First Cash Converters store in New Zealand

Cash Converters UK

Cash Converters Canada

Spruiking for business Burwood NSW

Cash Converters South Africa

Eating whole raw herring to celebrate the opening of Cash Converters Amstersdam 1995

Father and son

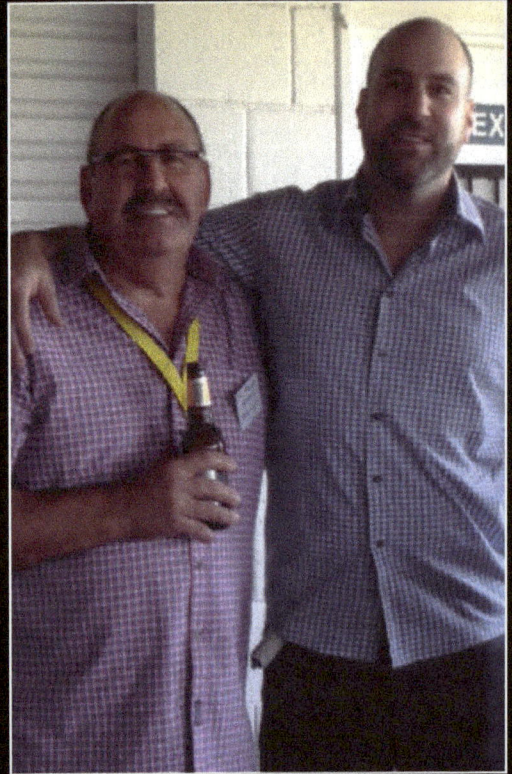

Peter with his son Brodie

The Cumins family

Brothers - Peter, Brian and Tony

Peter and Darryl

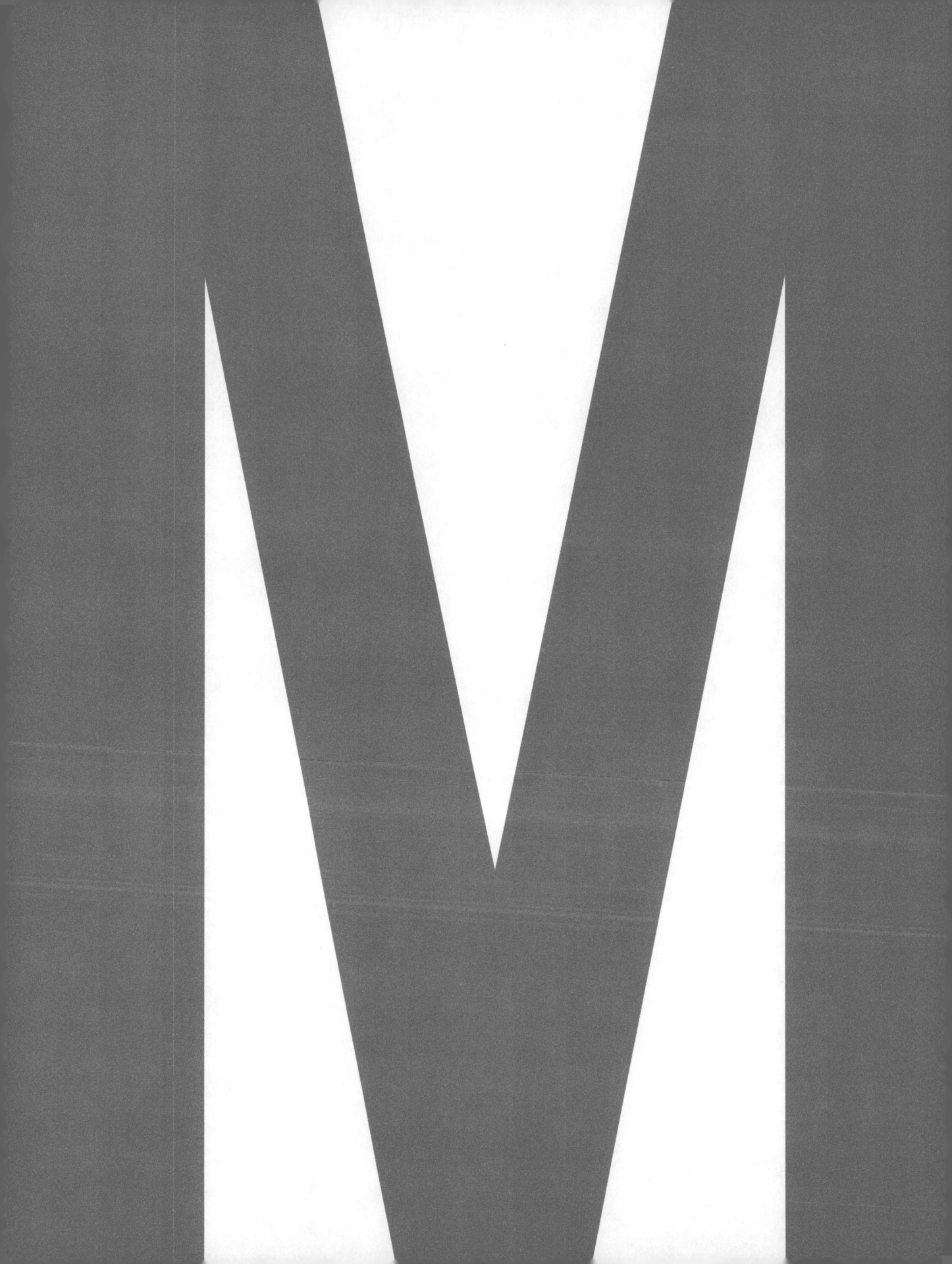

5

Navigating the Roller-Coaster Ride of Business

"Challenges and obstacles are there to teach you. Embrace them, resolve them or overcome them and then move forward with greater strength and wisdom."

She thinks, talks and moves at a million miles a minute. She dreams big dreams but hers don't stay dreams for long. With a determination so relentless, a passion so intense and a self-belief so dynamic, she swiftly converts her dreams into a striking reality.

She's a regular on TV but it's not her feminine and petite appearance that has led her to our screens – it is her knowledge and significant achievements in an industry where feminine is – to say the least, uncommon – if not unwelcome. The industry where the presumption was, "She won't have what it takes to make it", is a lesson in itself – never presume! She's highly perceptive and sensitive and when blended with the tough, ballsy and courageous elements of her personality she gains an unexpected edge.

The industry she decided to take on and conquer is undoubtedly "A man's world" but she made her mark in a few short years – albeit having built the intellectual foundation over many. She's read every rulebook, acted on every ounce of intuition and built her brand and unique business from the ground up, brick by brick. She brought together a strong, supportive, near all-female team and in the process earned great respect as she fearlessly broke through the glass ceiling.

Breaking through that ceiling was no easy feat. It took relentless courage and risk but with each new venture she embarked upon, she prospered. Her greatest dream, to create an unparalleled new business, was all-consuming and she was driven to see it through to reality. She expected to encounter obstacle after obstacle, and she did, that's business. But when her greatest challenge emerged, never did she expect it would be cultivated from her own strongly held business philosophies.

She is a concept to completion, rapid renovations specialist; she was the creator of Million Dollar Makeovers and The Renovation Company; she was the founder of World of Renovation, she is…

Sasha deBretton

It was clear from the outset that Sasha was going to be anything but 'an ordinary girl' – and that is in part thanks to an unusual mix of genes, life experiences and frozen peas.

Manuel Nunez was a chilled and passionate Spaniard. He was born in Morocco after his parents fled to Casablanca to escape the Spanish Civil War of 1936-39. He was somewhat of a band playing beach bum with little drive, unlike the daughter he would eventually have. In no great hurry to make a peseta, he moved back to Spain to chill a little further. As fortune would have it, he was doing his usual thing, relaxing in a Spanish bar on a night way back in '65 when a gorgeous young English girl walked in. Alison Baker was quite the opposite to the young Spaniard. She was a passionate artist, carefree but feisty. Their eyes met and the rest, as they say, is history. Their love affair continues to this day albeit a long way from that little Spanish bar.

Manuel Nunez and his wife Alison Nunez were overjoyed in 1967 when their first child, Scott, arrived on their carefree scene. They loved their life however they now had a child to care for. With work hard to find in Spain they decided to cross the Channel and settle in Alison's hometown of London.

Mr and Mrs Baker, Alison's parents, were fabulously humble people despite being "rather posh". They drove Bentleys, lived in beautiful homes and enjoyed life to the full – but there were no silver spoons in this family. Mr Baker was an army colonel. When he returned from the war, he had joined his father-in-law's fruit and vegetable wholesaling company, GJ Wright Ltd. He took on the role of managing director and put in long, hard hours, but as is always the way in business, problems arose every day. However, it was one particular problem that gave the entrepreneur in the colonel the opportunity to emerge.

The wholesaling of fruit and vegetables was a tough business and Mr Baker needed to find a way to maintain GJ Wright's competitive position in the industry. After much research and debate he decided to diversify into frozen foods; a very new concept in the UK. He installed cool rooms into each of the six branches that were scattered from one end of the country to the other. But a problem remained – how to transport the frozen produce between the branches without the goods spoiling. Further research led him to a new invention – refrigerator/freezer trucks. Such trucks had never been used in England so Mr Baker, who could see their potential, decided to import them. With the perishable food problem solved he did a deal with Sweden's Findus Foods, and once the TV advertisements started to appear, frozen peas and fish fingers became a common sight on dinner tables throughout the country. You can imagine what that did for the business, not to mention Mr and Mrs Baker's bank balance.

He didn't stop there. He dabbled in stocks and shares, and then property, enjoying healthy success all the way. This is where the wonders of DNA come into play. Well before she was even a twinkle in her parents' eyes, the wheels were in motion for Sasha to, one day, inherit her grandfather's strong and successful, entrepreneurial spirit. But that was still a long way off. For now, it was just good for Mr and Mrs Baker to have their daughter, her Spanish husband and their grandson with them in England.

Alison too loved being back in London and close to her parents but her sun loving husband struggled with the cold climate. They both agreed it was time to find a new home. It was 1970 when the 'Land Down Under' appeared on their radar. All their friends were talking about Australia and the "Ten Pound ticket".

In 1945 Australia's Chifley Government had introduced the Assisted Passage Migration Scheme to entice immigrants to its shores. The subsidised fare between England and Australia was only £10, hence the nickname (Ten Pound Pom), and children travelled free. The new migrants were promised a brighter future, employment and housing. The scheme was followed up by the very successful Bring out a Briton campaign. By 1972 more than a million migrants had moved from the British Isles to Australia, including the Nunezes who chose Perth, Western Australia as their new home.

Mr and Mrs Baker were deeply saddened to see their daughter and her family set sail for Australia. They knew Alison was a free spirit and so if they wanted to stay close there was only one thing to do – follow them out.

Manuel Nunez had always been the laidback, watch the world go by kind of guy, but once in Australia he changed – he wanted to make something of his life. He got a job in a local Perth bank. Soon after, with help from his father-in-law, he bought a block of land on Kempenfeldt Avenue in Sorrento. It was on top of a hill with sweeping views over the sparkling Indian Ocean. With a love of European architecture and the influences from a childhood spent in Morocco and Spain, a standard 4x2 spec home emerged as a white-washed Spanish hacienda. Manuel and Alison worked tirelessly on the land to create a spectacular tiered landscape and pool area. It was the ideal home for what was now a family of four. Sasha Nunez had entered the world on the 17th of August 1972, two years after their arrival in Perth. Her parents, her brother Scott and her grandparents showered Sasha with love and instilled in her a confidence that has remained ever since.

[Sasha]   I had a lovely childhood, growing up in Sorrento overlooking the Indian Ocean. It was a house that stood out from the rest with its European flavours and fabulous gardens. Every morning when I woke up, I would look out and see this beautiful view. That view had a huge influence on me and because of it, I've always loved open spaces and aspired to have nice things.

Sasha's grandfather, Tom Baker, who she absolutely adored, was another major influence in her life. When she talks of him Sasha's eyes mist over as she remembers the man who died when she was 20.

[Sasha]   Grandpa was a well-dressed, good-looking man, with neat handwriting – very particular; everything had to be in order. He was posh and plumy and yet he had this amazing heart, so generous, and he loved to cook. I'm like him in so many ways – I like systems and routine, I'm super organised, particular and methodical – and I love to cook too.

When he arrived in Australia, he continued to buy properties. He bought these big commercial sites in Balcatta and rented them out to Target – so he really was quite the entrepreneur.

My brother Scott and I would watch him, and he would always say to us, "Buy a house when you're young, you will be ten steps ahead."

Scott, who is five years older than me, built his first house when he was 21. Grandpa helped him out, he always did. When we were growing up, he would give us money or invest in shares for us and we'd get the dividends.

Grandpa was just so generous, but he also wanted us to achieve and do well for ourselves. I remember once driving over to his house in my little VW when I was about 17. I had no money, so I asked him for 20 bucks for petrol. He didn't hesitate but the way he looked at me I could almost hear him say – Oh, Sash is going to be the one to fail. I felt so ashamed and embarrassed because all of my cousins were doing accountancy degrees and here I was the uni dropout. He wouldn't have cared but I just wanted him to be proud of me. He had such a big influence on my life, and because of him I never stopped thinking how I could get ahead.

I always knew I wanted a career. I never thought about having my own business because I only really wanted to be a news reporter or a movie star like Julia Roberts.

I was good at school, but I had to apply myself, I wasn't a straight-A brainiac, I had to work hard and study hard. I'm a terrible mathematician and I hate formulas. I'm a creative. I was good at drama and loved subjects like economics, human biology and history – probably because my parents are European, and we travelled a lot when I was young.

I've always been organised and efficient – I discovered very early that it was laborious to work long hours. So, I was like, how can I get this done in the fastest possible way so that I can have more free time to watch TV and chill out? I'm still like that and I believe it's been a key to my success.

I am so much like my Grandfather, but I've also got a fair bit of both my parents. They are quite hilarious, a little like Basil and Sybil off 'Faulty Towers'. They're very humble. Even though my Grandfather helped them out, my Mum never had a silver spoon in her mouth, nor does she care about money, she's not materialistic at all. My Dad's a complete comedian, really funny, very chilled out and very relaxed...he's the, "Oh I'll get around to it tomorrow" – not like me at all. But he loves to spend money, so that's where he and I are alike because I love spending money too.

Dad winged it when he got a job as an ANZ bank teller but he must have been pretty good at it because he quickly became a bank manager. He then learnt all about borrowing off equity and mortgages and all that sort of stuff. He was only at the ANZ for about five years – but in that time he learnt a lot. When he left the bank, he started his own rubbish business. That doesn't sound very glamorous but, in those days people only had little tiny bins. So, he introduced those garden relief bags where people would fill them with their garden refuse and then he'd collect them. He started building up area rounds and selling them off to other people – a bit like franchises today but without the rules, and it was very successful.

So, Manuel may have been a laid-back Spaniard, but he did have an entrepreneurial streak and it was silently impacting on his young daughter. Young Sasha's future was growing brighter and brighter under the influence of the colourful illustrations that surrounded her in life.

[Sasha]   Dad did really well with his garden refuse business but he retired at 40 so that he could take us on a big holiday. He took us to Europe where the four of us travelled around in a motor home. It was on that holiday that I first met the Spanish side of our family.

We went to see my Aunt Isabella (Dad's sister) in the south of Spain. She was very poor. In those days there was no such thing as contraception, and so she and her husband had seven kids, but he left her and took off for America. If you had no money in Spain back then life was really difficult because there was no social security. She then met a drunk who used to busk for money. Aunt Isabella had another two kids with him.

One morning she found a baby in a basket that had been left on her doorstep and took that child in as well. But with all those children, no money and no social security they had to live in this tiny ramshackle house. There was just a lounge room and a makeshift kitchen out the back. They had four folding beds which they all slept in – two or three crammed into a bed. They couldn't afford to go to the dentist so they all had dodgy teeth. Aunt Isabella took them out of school when they were seven or eight because she needed help around the house – it was a tough life for them all.

When we arrived, they were so happy to see us and had prepared this big lunch. We all crowded into that tiny house. As I looked around, I suddenly thought about what we had in Australia. We had a lovely house on the beach, a beautiful childhood, a good education, travel and freedom...and here were 11 kids, my cousins, all with rotten teeth and no education. They lived in a part of Spain that's on the rock of Gibraltar, where all the drugs from Morocco come in and because they had no money the kids got into selling drugs to survive.

I was only 13 but that lunch was a pivotal moment in my life. Dad's other family, who we also visited while were in Spain, were all doing quite well.

When we left Spain, we travelled through Turkey and Greece. We were away for a whole year and it was in that time Mum taught me how to cook amazing dishes – she made me the cook I am today. That whole trip changed my horizons completely, I'd caught the travel bug. There was a big wide world out there and I decided that one day I would see it all.

Her Spanish experience was an eye opener but as I sat and listened to Sasha recount her meeting with her cousins, I couldn't help but think about her own father, Manuel. He had been living a relaxed and carefree life with little thought of his future, when a chance meeting with an English girl changed everything. She bought out in him the desire to make change – to do something with his life. He could have stayed in Spain and had an easy time of it, but instead he took a chance. By taking what probably seemed like a risk at the time his life was so positively changed on every level. Life is about opportunities and missed opportunities, what is and what might have been, continuing to dream or living the dream. The choice of taking an opportunity or not is ours alone to make, albeit at times great courage is required.

*A ship in harbor is safe, but that is not
what ships are built for.*

John A Shedd 1928

[Sasha]   After selling off the rubbish rounds Dad built a number of houses. He's a true perfectionist and does everything himself, with his own hands, so it takes time but Mum is always there to help. Now we joke that I renovate whole houses in two weeks and he does them in 12 years – and that's his average! Some have taken him years longer, but he always finished them.

I'm also a perfectionist as were my Father and Grandfather. But there are two types of perfectionists, some perfectionists never launch because they are so worried about getting every detail right.

I'm the other kind of perfectionist. I'm very particular about my vision and the results I want to achieve but it doesn't have to be perfect, I just map it out, launch it and then I tweak it as I go – but first I take action.

Maybe there is something innate in me but when I was little, everything I did, I did fast. Whenever I got assignments they were done way ahead of time, I was never a last-minute girl. I hate having my to-do list with things on it, so when I've got a task, it's done and then it's, delete, delete, delete and my to-do list is empty again.

After our trip to Europe I really started to think more and more about my career because I knew I wanted to have nice houses, nice cars and nice things, especially after meeting my cousins in Spain. I knew I would have to work for it but I was driven – just like my Grandpa was.

I was quite entrepreneurial from a young age. I was always trying to sell stuff, always making chocolate cakes or putting on concerts for the local kids – anything to make some money because I wanted money to buy lollies. At 14 I got my first real job in a cafe at Hillarys marina near to where I lived in Sorrento. At 16, when I was in Year 11, I started working in Myer at the Max Factor counter and then as a counter manager at Lancôme where they taught me about beauty therapy and make-up. I was doing some photographic modelling and when the photographer found out I did my own hair and make-up, he asked if I would do the make-up for his photographic shoots. I then did weddings and balls and was making quite good money. It was at that point that I realised how good it was to have the flexibility of having your own business.

From high school I went straight to university. I wanted to be a news reporter and so should have done journalism, but the career counsellor suggested media studies. I really didn't like it – too much on the technical side for me.

I did psychology as a minor which I enjoyed more than media studies, but I just didn't feel like any of it was really me. I decided to drop out after the first semester, work for a bit and then re-establish what I really wanted to do.

No matter what I did I always managed my time. I was always thinking how I could do it smarter not harder. Remembering my cousins in Spain and how they lived and then watching my brother build houses and getting ahead in his life, I instinctively knew I needed and wanted to do the same. Then suddenly my Grandfather died – I was devastated.

I could hear his words, "Buy a house when you're young and you'll be ten steps ahead." He had left me a small inheritance, $20,000, enough to put a deposit on a house, so I started looking. I had just turned 20.

I could hear his words, "Buy a house when you're young and you'll be ten steps ahead."

I'd always known that it had to be more than just a house with four walls – a box with no outlook. I found what I was looking for; it had high vaulted ceilings and a feeling of space, but most importantly to me – it had a view to the ocean.

I had to take a risk and up my price. It was almost double my budget but I instinctively knew, from a resale perspective, that in time that sea view would be worth something – but I'd have to stretch myself to get there.

My Dad, with his bank experience, said just buy the house, rent it out and let someone else pay off your mortgage.

Sasha bought the house with the sea view. Then on her father's advice, she rented it out. By doing so Sasha achieved her first major goal and now she wanted to achieve another – one that she had set at the age of 13 – to see more of the world.

[Sasha] When I was leaving my Mum hugged and whispered to me, "Spread your wings and fly my darling". They were powerful words to hear and made me believe in myself even more – they gave me the freedom to feel I could do what I wanted to do. I now say those same words to my own daughter.

"Spread your wings and fly my darling."

Sasha travelled with a girlfriend for six months before heading to Spain. On her own she returned to the home of her Aunt Isabella and her cousins. As she relayed the story of this visit, she became deeply distressed. So much had changed in the seven years since her last visit and none of it was good. We are often so sheltered that little can prepare us when faced with the realities of what life delivers to some – and for what she was about to face Sasha was certainly not prepared.

[Sasha] One of my cousins Louie, who I'd met when I was 13, had died of AIDS. He'd been selling and using drugs, but he was also sharing needles. I remember when all that stuff came out about AIDS, it scared me – but bloody hell, you never think it's going to happen to someone you know.

Then Marco, another cousin, also contracted AIDS from sharing needles. When I got to my aunt's he was lying on the couch in that same little house where we'd all had lunch together. He looked like a skeleton because he couldn't eat. The whole family was there just wailing. As I stood in front of the couch, they all had their arms around me, sobbing. I had to use all my strength just to stand straight without collapsing under their weight. Then he died – in front of us. I still remember his face and his body. It was terrible, just awful, devastating.

Then Aunt Isabella's daughter died of a heart attack bought on by years of overdosing on drugs which weakened her heart. Now one of her other sons, Favier, has also got AIDS. He hasn't died from it because he's on medication, but I saw him again a couple of years ago – he was walking around like a skeleton. He hugged me and said, "I can't have a relationship, I can't have children, I don't want to give anybody this disease."

Then there is the baby that had been left in the bassinet on aunty's doorstep. He was a drug addict's baby and so was born with brain damage. Her other kids, when they were still really young, started having babies of their own, and so Aunty had to look after her grandchildren as well – she was only 35 or 40 – far out! She's now 80 and still looking after her grandkids and great grandkids. I feel so sad for her; she's had such a hard life.

The thing is, they're such beautiful people, but they had no education. They only sold drugs to make money to put food on the table, that's how poor they were. Now half of them are dead which is just fucking awful.

I left there completely shaken and devastated but continued to travel around. I went to see my Dad's brother and another sister who lived in Marbella and the Costa del Sol. From there I headed to the beautiful island of Menorca to stay with my god mum, Beverley. She's fabulous and a lot of fun, and taught me something that has had a huge impact on my life.

After going through a terrible divorce, she started her own business in Menorca. She is doing really well for herself and is strong and independent. One day she said to me, "Sash, just make sure you can stand on your own two feet because you can't always rely on a man." After seeing what had happened to Aunt Isabella, that comment really sank in and I sort of went ka-ching, yeah, I agree with you, I get it.

"Sash, just make sure you can stand on your own two feet because you can't always rely on a man."

I turned 21 while I was in Europe and just after my birthday I really started thinking about my cousins and my aunt and how they lived. It was then I decided that I really wanted to do something with my own life and be successful, because I didn't want to struggle or ever worry about money. I'd always had 'drive' but after that it just got stronger. I wanted nice things but I knew to get them I'd have to work hard.

I decided I was going to stay in Europe. I had just got a job and had only done one shift when my Mother rang. "It's Christmas, you have to come home." So, I did – but the whole way home I was thinking I'll stay for the summer but then I'm going straight back.

As determined as she was to return to Europe it wasn't to be – well not at that moment in time.

[Sasha] I'd returned from Europe and got a job managing the bar at The Good, The Bad and The Ugly Mexican restaurant. I was enjoying it and then I met Matt. He was 29. He was lovely but he wanted to settle down and have babies. That scared the pants off me. I was only 22 and so it was the last thing I wanted to do. I wanted to have a career, buy more houses and travel the world.

Despite her fears, her doubts and her desire to see more of the world Sasha chose instead to become Mrs deBretton. If she had chosen the alternative path Sasha might now be living on the other side of the world, where no doubt, with her drive and determination, she would have achieved the success she yearned. Living in Perth however, was not going to stand in her way of striving for what she wanted.

[Sasha] A friend of mine was working at Yellow Pages, a great marketing company where you could win trips around the world, have a company car and earn good money. It sounded good, so I got a job there and learnt about advertising, building brands and discipline – huge discipline.

They were very clever at what they did – they would dangle carrots but you had to work bloody hard to get those carrots. The carrots were world trips. I knew that if I was good at it I'd get to travel, which was what I really wanted to do.

We would each be given a box filled with 200 advertising contracts and we had a six-month deadline to get through them all. It was a huge task because we had to do everything, including designing the ads. But I'm a person who doesn't like anything on my to-do list so I went on a mission to just plough through that box, get that work done and get rid of the next contract and then the next. It's funny, I'll never forget those boxes.

I was determined so I'd always finish way before everybody else, but then they'd give me another box and so I'd start all over again.

Everybody in the office would do all the customers that would increase their sales numbers first. So, they would track along quite nicely and the managers would only see good results. But right at the end of the deadline they'd dump all the bad accounts and end up with a lousy result. I did the reverse.

I would spend the first two weeks ringing every single client, introduce myself and ask questions – how their business was travelling, what they wanted to do, if they intended to increase their marketing portfolio, repeat it, or decrease it.

I'd make separate piles. For anybody that was going to cancel, I'd get them out of the way first, so I would know my bottom line – I knew I could rework them later. Then it was onto the decrease pile – how could I get them to a repeat? Then onto my repeat pile; I'd work with them on a 'redesign ad' to try to get them to increase. Finally, I'd get to my increase pile…all good there.

So, my little strategy to work on all my shitty contracts first was good but by doing it that way my figures initially fell. When my manager saw that happening, he came and told me I was going to fail.

That was like a red rag to a bull for me, it really pissed me off. Don't tell me that I'm going to fail, just don't ever tell me that because I've got my strategy – you just watch me!

> *Don't tell me that I'm going to fail,*
> *just don't ever tell me that because I've got my strategy –*
> *you just watch me!*

I had to go out and prove him wrong! If anybody ever tells me I'm going to fail, I always need to prove them wrong!

So, I just carried on with what I was doing, thinking, I'll show you. Then on the deadline my figures, which had all gone down, suddenly jumped up while everyone else's figures, which had gone up initially, fell. I won the trip in my first year. I was the first one who had tracked that way at Yellow Pages, so when I won it changed the way they did things.

I remember the manager came up to me and said, "I got you that trip, if it wasn't for me you wouldn't have got there". And I said to him, "I would have got there anyway, but you know what, thanks for telling me I was going to fail because you did probably push me a little bit harder so I do have to acknowledge you for that – but you need to learn how to be a better manager."

From then on, I won the trip every year. They then introduced the CEO Club which was only for the top one per cent of the company – I was in that top one per cent. The 'carrots' in the CEO Club were all seven-star trips, incredibly luxurious. I've done the Orient Express, Tahitian cruises and the palaces in India, they were all amazing.

I'd grown up camping with Mum and Dad where nothing was glamorous but, on those luxury trips, we were spoilt rotten. You would never spend that kind of money on yourself unless you were infinitely wealthy and could afford to go to that extreme. When you're exposed to that kind of experience it's hard to settle for less.

I knew that if I worked hard the trips would be my reward, so I worked hard. I didn't chitchat, it was head down bum up and I worked smart. All the other reps stayed in the office until late every night trying to win the trips. I never worked that way. Basically, I looked at them as if they were buying those trips with their time.

Most of us know that the only way to succeed is to work hard, and yet despite good intentions we don't push ourselves, instead we look for an easier way. Sasha is not that kind of person. Working hard was something that came naturally to her, as was working smart. However, it was her grandfather's words about buying property that gave Sasha her greatest direction. She knew where she was going.

[Sasha] I had renovated that first house I bought when I was 20 and within two years it had gone up in value by $109,000, which was a lot in 1994. My Dad then said, "Borrow against the equity."

From his work at the bank my Dad knew what he was talking about, so I went OK and found a house on a duplex block in Karrinyup, right by the lake. It was cute, and I could see the renovation potential. I thought, I'll subdivide but just sell off the back block because it would take two years to build and I felt it wasn't worth the hassle.

I quickly renovated the front house and sold off the back block. It was easy cash that went straight back into the pocket; I then sold the front house. It was money for jam.

I bought another one on the lake, did a ten-day reno and flipped it. Then it was onto the next one in Sorrento, close to the first house I'd bought. Again, it had ocean views perched on top of the hill, so I subdivided the front block, sold it, then did another one.

By this time, I was making good money. At first it was $80,000 to $135,000 a property, but once I start subdividing, I was selling the front blocks for $250,000 and then selling the back house for the same or more than the cost of the whole lot. I was making about $250-$500K per house and at 25 or 26 years old that was good money.

That was a while ago now, but it's still possible to make good money although it's a lot tougher in this market. Back then there were peaks and troughs, but they weren't substantial and there was always growth, so I used to pick areas. I always bought something with a view, location, something I could subdivide, the worst house, the best street, the ugly duckling, renovate, add value... I stuck to those core principals and never bought anything that needed massive structural work, only cosmetic, then I could get in and out in a few weeks – pretty it up, sell it off and make a bomb.

Again, it was, how can I do it the smart way not the hard way? I'm not going to go build on a block that's going to take three years, because I'm impatient. So, I thought better to just sell the block, put the money straight in my pocket and roll that money quickly into something else – that was my strategy.

At the age of 25, while still at the yellow pages and buying and selling property Sasha decided to return to university to do a marketing degree, part-time.

[Sasha] I wanted to enhance my career and I felt a marketing degree would make me a better sales rep or marketing executive. I loved it all – economics, marketing, the creativity of designing ads, the different media and business units, managing people, the core values of running a business, cash flow and brand building. I learnt so much.

To find the time and the energy to work as a top salesperson at Yellow Pages, to buy, subdivide, renovate and sell real estate and to study part-time at university is an indication of the intensity of Sasha's determination. A lessening of that drive would have been expected when she added something extra to the mix – a major something extra – the birth of her daughter. Georgia deBretton was born in December 1999. Two years later at the age of 29 Sasha graduated from university with Honours in Marketing.

[Sasha] I just loved having a daughter but I also wanted to be a millionaire by the time I was 30 and I wanted to buy a house on West Coast Drive. I achieved both. The house on West Coast Drive was a million dollars and so Matt and I had to have a big mortgage, but I knew I could renovate it and make money. My Mum was so worried about me, but my Dad said some words that have stuck with me ever since.

"There're three types of people in this world Sash; there're those that make it happen, there're those that watch it happen and there're those that wonder what happened – which one are you?"

That was Dad's way of giving me the courage to say to myself, put your balls on the line Sash and go for it.

"There're three types of people in this world Sash; there're those that make it happen, there're those that watch it happen and there're those that wonder what happened – which one are you?"

Buying the house on West Coast Drive allowed Sasha to tick off on another major goal. Then, with her innate flare and style she transformed it. Her confidence grew. However, life and its lessons were again standing at Sasha's front door, demanding attention. This time she listened to her inner voice.

[Sasha]   My husband Matt was a lovely support. He used to say, "I trust you," because I was the driving force, the instigator, I was the mover and shaker. So, whilst it was great because he never held me back and was so gentle, he never challenged me – I did whatever I wanted.

After Georgia came things changed, and I felt Matt was just like a flat mate and a friend. As lovely as he was and is, I got bored with that. I needed someone to challenge me mentally.

Anyway, I made the choice to leave him when Georgia was three. I didn't want to be one of those people that you hear saying that they stayed for the kids then 20 years later they leave but are still miserable because they regret they didn't do it sooner. That wasn't for me. I look at life as if you've got one chance and you're never coming back.

For me to leave my husband, sell my dream house on West Coast Drive and start all over again was massive. But then another huge driving force to rebuild just kicked in and I started buying more property. I was 30.

I never doubted what I was doing but Dad was saying, "Be careful about the market, stop buying stuff, the market's going to crash".

Dad has very good foresight with that stuff because he listens to the news – I don't. I have my blinkers on because I can't stand the negativity and all the bullshit and dramas you hear in the news.

If I've got a gut instinct, I know something's going to work and so I just follow that. If you listen to everybody else talk about how bad the market is, you'd never do anything.

I was still at the Yellow Pages and back buying and selling properties when I met a guy. He was working for one of the big builders. We got together and after a while he suggested we should build a spec home. In the boom people were building little spec homes and selling them off and making a couple of hundred grand so I thought OK, we'll do a couple of those.

But my hunch was always to renovate, subdivide, flip houses and blocks; for me building was just too slow. But I wanted to make him happy so I thought – oh well, let's mix up the portfolio.

My hunch was always to renovate; for me building was just too slow. But I wanted to make him happy so I thought - oh well, let's mix up the portfolio.

He had no money, so I built the two display homes with these builders. They took three years to build a shell on a sandpit, no customer service, no carpets, no blinds. I had to fit it all out, do the landscaping – all of it, and just at that time the GFC hit. Property prices fell so the projected profit was nothing. We made nothing out of one and 45 or 50K on the other.

For three years' work, it wasn't worth it. That's when my gut instinct really went into overdrive. Why build for three years when I can renovate a whole house in two or four weeks? The market can't shift on you that quickly.

> *We made nothing out of one and 45 or 50K on the other. For three years' work; it wasn't worth it. That's when my gut instinct really went into overdrive.*

From that experience emerged a business idea but when I told my boyfriend about it, he said, "No, you don't need to do that, just stay at home and be with the kids."

I was disappointed, but I thought he needed to shine as he'd been bankrupt and was just starting to get back on his feet. I'd been working my arse off for so long, so I agreed to work part-time for a while and just be there for my daughter and his son – but I stored the business idea because in my heart I knew it could fly.

So, I became a full-time Mum and I enjoyed it, but the enjoyment only lasted a year; I found out my boyfriend was cheating on me in more ways than one – so I left him.

During the boom I'd bought a few houses and renovated them. I also bought a penthouse off the plan in the new Fini Burswood development. I needed to get finance to settle on it but when the boom ended prices had fallen, so the valuation on the penthouse dropped below my cash offer. Normally, I could work it by moving money around but with the GFC the banks had stopped lending and finance was hard to get.

I was still working at the Yellow Pages but things were changing there too – the corporate market had started to shift when the GFC hit in Perth.

I needed money and fast. The income I was earning at the Yellow Pages whilst still high, was not enough and now the money in buying, renovating and selling for a profit wasn't there either – everything had gone down.

I made the decision to keep Burswood but sell off the other four or five properties I had left. I bought and renovated in the boom so when I sold them it was at a bit of a loss. But I chose to do it – that's what I call an 'opportunity cost'. I knew that if I got rid of them, even though I was dropping a bit of money, I could take those funds and put them into another property where I could make money. You can't get rich on a one-sided coin. You win when you chose to accept a loss to pick up a bigger win and play the market. It's like playing chess.

When Sasha made those comments, I was reminded of my days selling real estate. I remember some Vendors, who were really struggling, were unable to even consider that it might have been advantageous to sell their property at a loss. By doing so they would then have been able to move forward instead of backwards. But all they could focus on was what they would lose, not what they might gain as a result of being able to put those funds into a better investment. Unlike Sasha.

With the Burswood settlement looming Sasha needed finance but her back was to the wall. Things were serious, and she needed to act quickly. She searched for an answer and in doing so, just like her grandfather so many years before, found a solution that would change the course of her life. The only difference was Sasha's solution had been sitting idle within her for years.

[Sasha]   When I broke up with that guy, I went on a mission to rebuild. I then found myself in this situation where I had millions of dollars in finance but with an income that was falling way short. It was pretty scary, but it started me thinking about the idea I'd spoken to him a few years earlier.

Perth property prices had dumped 30 per cent but I had developed this rapid renovation system while doing my own renovations where I would go in, buy a property, gut it, renovate it and sell it in a very short time frame, two to four weeks.

I'd already done a business plan, the brochures and the marketing background – so I was ready. I'm always amazed when I hear someone who is starting a business but doesn't have a business plan or doesn't think they need one – WHAT? That's crazy! You can't not do one. Mine is about 82 pages long and sets out the concept, the product or the service, the price point, the demographic, marketing, everything. That's essential stuff to know. I worked on mine for about three months and I've still got it today.

I'm always amazed when I hear someone who is starting a business but doesn't have a business plan or doesn't think they need one – WHAT? That's crazy! You can't not do one.

From my experience with builders being really slow, and having my own rapid renovation system, having learnt discipline and sales skills at Yellow Pages, marketing and branding, I knew from putting my business plan together with my skill set and experience that I had a concept I could take to the market. I also had a hunch that I'd make it a very successful business.

I also instinctively knew that I would need to build my brand really hard and really fast because I would be up against the big boys. I didn't have all of the experience or the skills, so it was a little scary, but I knew how to do my own renovations. Then I had to fight my inner doubting voice – Yes Sasha it's easy doing it for yourself because if you make a mistake you just go in and fix it, it doesn't matter. But how are you going to do that with clients? What do you really know Sasha?

Sasha may not have known everything, but she did know how to silence her inner voice. She called on that extraordinary self-belief and determination and got on with the tasks on her ever-expanding to-do list. Building licence, business name, bank managers… However, despite the many voices of doubt, including her own, Sasha went head-on and launched – there was no turning back, not that she ever thought of doing so.

[Sasha] I felt anxious like anyone would when launching something new. Then my Dad said, "Well, I hope it doesn't fail." That put the fire in me, I said to him, "Well Dad, my belief in this business is far greater than your doubt. So, if my belief is far greater than your doubt then this business will be successful – so you just watch me." I was pretty upset with him, but I knew he was just worried about me. I mean, I'd gone through a divorce, I'd gone through a second separation, I was a single mum Georgia was eight, I had bought all these properties during the boom, my mortgages were huge, my back was to the wall but there I was about to launch a new business built on a hunch.

My back was to the wall but there I was about to launch a new business built on a hunch.

I wasn't sure how I would manage because I couldn't leave Yellow Pages as I was still trying to get the finance for the penthouse that was due to settle in March 2010. But I had no choice. I was either going to lose some of my properties or I was going to save them, but there were two things I was sure of – I had to do something and there was no way I was going to fail – I just knew it.

It was at that point that I finally acknowledged that whenever I didn't follow my gut, I made the wrong decision. I vowed never to let that happen again.

It was at that point that I finally acknowledged that whenever I didn't follow my gut, I made the wrong decision. I vowed never to let that happen again.

It was at a trade show in June 2009 with a trestle table and a few before and after photographs, that Sasha, on a hunch and wing and a prayer, launched Million Dollar Makeovers.

[Sasha] I booked three renovations in that first month, two in the second month and five in the third. At first, I was a little nervous about my design skills. To give me a bit of extra confidence I paid a very good interior designer to come with me on a couple of consults. On the first consult I knew I didn't need her. By then any doubt was gone.

The GFC had hit hard and property prices had dropped significantly so I had decided I would target the resale market. I knew I could help people sell their homes quicker and for way more if we did it up for a sale. But as it turned out people were apprehensive about spending to sell. Because of the state of the economy they believed they would have to drop their price plus pay stamp duty on a new home and so decided it was better to stay put and use that few hundred grand it would cost them to move, into a renovation. So, I altered my target market soon after we launched at the trade show. You need to be open to what the market is asking for and then change, tweak, improve or whatever is called for.

My days got pretty crazy, pretty quickly. I'd get up at five to fit in a run. Then I'd get Georgia up, get her ready for school, drag her to site by seven o'clock so I could sort out the tradies, drop her to school, visit my Yellow Pages clients, pick Georgia up from school, go back on site to check on the tradies, get on the phone to organise the following day, get Georgia home, homework, dinner and put her to bed. Often after she was in bed my clients would come over to do all their designs and selections on my kitchen bench. After they'd gone, I could finally sit and do my marketing brochures, printing and pay my tradies.

Because of the credit crunch the banks wouldn't lend me any money for the business but in that first month of Million Dollar Makeovers I made a $40,000 profit. I was working from home and my margins were tiny, so I knew if I could make that much money on three renos in the first month then this was going to be huge. I still had the other seven renovations booked for the next two months.

I could see the light at the end of the tunnel, but I was completely exhausted because I wasn't going to bed until one or two in the morning. There was just so much to do, and as the business was so new, every document, every template, every operations manual and procedure had to be developed. It had to be done but I had to do it all myself.

Although the money was starting to roll in, I still couldn't afford to get staff but with so many renovations booked I was swamped and overwhelmed. I'd met Renae Hunt, a school mum, who at the time was selling land. I'd bought a few blocks through her and in that process saw how organised and diligent she was and thought she'd make a great project manager. So, in September I asked her to cover for me whilst I was seeing my Yellow Pages clients – she's been with me ever since. I think she's a legend – and so do all of our clients.

By March the following year with Million Dollar Makeovers making its mark on Perth property, Sasha had finally been able to secure finance for the penthouse. On the day of settlement, the 10th of March 2010, she and Georgia moved into their new home up on the 18th floor. On that same day another friend, Dina, joined the business as financial controller. But there was still one more thing to do before Sasha could really start to fly.

[Sasha]   At 9 am on the morning of settlement I went to see my boss at the Yellow Pages and resigned – there and then. They didn't want me to leave but there were no employment agreements and there was strong mutual respect, so they let me go. They knew about Million Dollar Makeovers but they had no idea how big it was getting or going to get.

Neither did Sasha. Nevertheless, after 13 years at the Yellow Pages, armed only with mammoth self-belief, sheer determination and a whole load of courage, Sasha walked out one door and into the next – the front door of the penthouse. For the next two years the 18th floor would not only be hers and Georgia's home, it would be the home of Million Dollar Makeovers.

They knew about Million Dollar Makeovers but they had no idea how big it was getting or going to get.

[Sasha]   By that time, I was feeling confident about the business, but I had no idea it would go to where it's gone. Soon I had eleven staff operating out of the penthouse, working off the dining table and the kitchen bench – it was a lot of fun and we all loved the space. Even though it was brand new I gutted it and did a Sasha spec reno, so it was pretty cool. The view was amazing and when our clients came to do their design selections they were blown away. It worked really well, and the business just kept on expanding.

In the first year, 2009-10 we turned over $2.5 million and in the second year we went to five million plus. At that point I went, "Okay, we're onto something here – and the growth just continued.

I realised after the second year when the turnover and my staff doubled that we needed to have a more professional front – we needed a showroom.

I felt we should be in the western suburbs and on a busy road. In 2012 I found the ideal space to lease on Stirling Highway, Claremont. The showroom needed to look really specky and glamourous, so I designed it in a way that when you entered you had to walk down a central runway lined with all these columns and beautiful white sheers to create 'vignettes' – French for little rooms. We made our design room look amazing as well with a huge chandelier in the centre and our admin department went upstairs.

Sasha's experience at Yellow Pages together with a marketing degree was instrumental in how she ran her new business. Sasha's philosophy is – you must have a strategy then stick to it, tweak it, evolve it, make it better, watch what everyone else is doing but run your own race.

I've never worried about my competition, but I always like to know what they're doing.

[Sasha]   I've never worried about my competition, but I always like to know what they're doing. I think there's enough in the market for everyone, even in a tough market. You just have to be different to the average bear, deliver something niche, unique, better than the others, faster than the others.

The upshot of that spec home building experience, where I had to finish everything myself, was that I recognised there was a massive gap in the market. An empty room has no soul, it's just an empty room, so to hand back an empty shell to clients is just wrong. I was gifted with an innate interior design flare but what about those who aren't. What do they do when they are handed the keys to a brick and concrete shell, supposedly their brand-new dream home, and try to pull it all together? It's so easy and disappointing, not to mention expensive, to get your interior design wrong. So, I filled the gap by doing all the frilly bits, which is the interior design. We do it really well and when it's done right it adds significant value.

Doing renovations for myself was rewarding. To see an ugly duckling, a red brick, run down and overgrown thing turn into something beautiful in six weeks is unbelievably satisfying. But with Million Dollar Makeovers I get to do it for other people. To change your client's life in a really short time frame; to see them so happy with what you have done – there's no greater satisfaction.

I also get huge pleasure and satisfaction from watching my team grow; a team that I brought together. They are a mostly female, talented, multitasking and communicative team. Half are friends or people I worked with at the Yellow Pages. I brought them in specifically because I knew their work ethic and that strategy has worked really well for me. I also use a really good recruitment agent (she was once a client) who really understands my business and the company culture. Getting the right team together is fundamental to any successful business.

When I started Million Dollar Makeovers, I had to do everything myself because I was on my own. I'm not afraid of hard work but now that I have a team, I'm a queen delegator. What that does is give me time to focus, grow, evolve and tweak the business. I inspire and lead my team, but I don't get bogged down in day-to-day stuff like admin. No one is allowed to email me unless it's top priority and my PA organises my diary and vets phone calls and emails.

I don't micromanage. I give the girls full freedom to step up and be their own manager, to own their job, and because of that I've watched them evolve, blossom and grow, and that has been incredibly satisfying. Their input and work ethic have also had a hugely positive impact on my business.

I had to be very strategic in my marketing strategy but with no money to advertise I had to find another way to get my name out there. I had to find free publicity.

With thirteen years' experience at the Yellow Pages, and from my marketing background, I knew that to be number one and to have equity in your business you must have brand equity – you must create a brand that people know and trust.

When I started out the banks weren't lending, so I had to be very strategic in my marketing strategy and come up with a way to build my brand. But with no money to advertise I had to find another way to get my name out there. I had to find free publicity. I went to the newspapers with, "I've just renovated this house in two weeks, here's the before and afters, do you want the story on how I did it?" They jumped at the chance and some put a full or half page in. We also placed sign boards out the front of the properties we were renovating. They were like a real estate agent's sign, saying, "We are renovating now, ready in six weeks". We also wrapped our on-site skips bins with our Million Dollar Makeover signs. All these ideas built our profile hugely and at relatively no cost. But I was aware that people would be sceptical about what we could do in two weeks, so I got a freelance company to film the renos as proof. I would get in front of the camera and just wing it and then I put them on our website and with that the clients just kept coming.

For the first two years we only did cosmetic renovations – new kitchens, bathrooms, flooring, painting, blinds – quick and easy. I didn't want to do structural work, double storeys or additions because it takes longer and is fraught with problems. But after a while people started asking, will you build my house; will you do an extension? When you get asked often enough you start to question – can we? We had all the trades, the architects, everything, so we decided to just wing it...and that's when we started getting million dollar contracts.

We did a $2 million property in Mt Claremont in 16 weeks, fully finished and stunning. Both Channel 7 and FOXTEL filmed it. We are bloody good at what we do, and I don't mind saying it.

To be honest, at the start with everything I was doing I expected the building companies to copy me, but they didn't. It took me a while to realise why – they had a different business model and economies of scale. They build multiples of cookie cutter approach houses and they weren't interested in the frilly bits, the interior design.

When I started, no one was really doing renovation, but now that the building industry has been down for a few years all the big builders are jumping in and new people have popped up as well. I wanted to be the renovation queen, and believing people would copycat me I built my brand quickly. Now they are copying, but do they do it as well as us? Nup. Will they ever do it as well us? Nup, because I won't let them – I'll always stay one step ahead.

I made millions over the years doing my own renovations and so the original concept behind the name Million Dollar Makeovers was to help other people make millions of dollars through their own renovations. I then launched a second brand, The Renovation Company, because Million Dollar Makeovers had a stigma. Whilst the brand was huge in the marketplace, a lot of people thought because of the name that we only did high-end renovations with million-dollar budgets. So, The Renovation Company does exactly what the name says – renovations, cosmetic interior and exterior fit outs. We also have Sasha deBretton Interiors which does commercial renovations and fit outs for restaurants, hotels, bars, pubs and clubs.

Across those three companies we get about 800 leads a year but we only do 20 to 30 renovations. Initially we were doing way more than that but I pulled it back. I'd rather do the bigger renos, than lots of smaller ones where everyone is busy and you need more staff and there's greater chance of mistakes being made. It all gets back to my philosophy of working smarter not harder.

Throughout our interviews Sasha repeatedly reiterated that in business you should never try to do everything yourself. When a business owner struggles to delegate or pay for something to be done, her belief is that the business will struggle. Better to find the funds to pay others to do the jobs that take your eyes off the bigger picture. Some of that fiercely held belief was to come back to haunt Sasha, but more on that later.

[Sasha]   I control the business now. I have operations manuals, procedures, systems, I have reports, I do audits, I have checks in place – so everyone in the company knows what needs to be done and how it needs to be done. The building industry is the second toughest industry in the world next to finance. More builders go bankrupt than any other business. So, I was just determined I was going to do things differently – and I have.

I never consciously thought, I want to be an interior designer – I was just around unique buildings that my Dad built. When I started buying my own houses, I became interested because I needed a new kitchen, new flooring and a new bathroom. When I started putting all of it together, I realised I had a natural talent. I loved it and when you love what you do the money rolls in. When I initially launched, I needed the money but for a long time now it hasn't been important.

> *What I love about business, any business, is you go into it quite naively. Thank god because if you knew what you were in for you would probably think twice.*

What I love about business, any business, is you go into it quite naively. Thank god because if you knew what you were in for you would probably think twice. But it's exciting when you go in with just a wish and a dream and a hunch, not knowing where it may actually go and then suddenly you see the light ahead. But that's when you really have to start pushing it, really keep your finger on the pulse, be really strategic.

The stats say only 4 per cent of businesses across Australia turn over more than a million dollars a year, which is staggering, but it's that 4 per cent that turn over the millions and the hundreds of millions.

Perth is so different to Sydney and Melbourne. They have triple the population and are more stable. We're boom or bust here. So, you have to be more savvy if you want to be really successful but you don't need to reinvent the wheel. I found a gap in the market, I found a niche, I gave it a go, I had no fear, I just made sure I stayed on top because you can't be complacent in business, you must keep your finger on the pulse.

When you have a vision or a goal, and you want something to come together, you must have a plan and then you have to action the plan. I write my goals down, not as much as I used to, because now I use vision boards. I remember one night I was at my computer and I had just written down that I wanted to go to the Caribbean and suddenly – and I'll never forget this – I got this random email from Yellow Pages saying I'd won a cruise to the Caribbean. BANG, within moments, I was like, I've just written that goal down.

I then thought, oh my god that's amazing, so I went and did a course on goal setting. They told us to write down 101 goals. I don't know how they decided on that number, but I started doing it and things really started to happen. I was loving the journey, and once I saw the potential, I wanted to take over the world. But I started putting myself under a huge amount of pressure and stress – I was killing myself.

I started having anxiety and panic attacks which I'd never had in my life, then palpitations, dizzy spells and, collapsing a few times, I ended up in hospital. I had all sorts of tests, CAT scans, ECGs and finally after two years of no answers and going, 'what the frick is this thing?' Then a doctor said to me, Sasha this is a classic stress induced anxiety; you're just way too stressed.

Step in Anne McKevitt.

Sasha decided she needed a business coach. She'd heard about a woman who had a similar background to her own. She too had started as a property developer and interior designer. She was a regular on the BBC, a global celebrity and an interior designer to the stars. Her name was Anne McKevitt. You can read about Anne on the net where she is listed among the world's most admired and powerful business leaders by publications like Time Magazine, Forbes and The New York Times. Drive and vision led Anne, among other ventures, to develop a range of paint colours that she potted in clear tins.

[Sasha] They were flying off the shelves and giving well-known brands a run for their money when Walmart stepped in and bought the company. That wasn't luck – you don't become a billionaire through sheer luck – it takes a whole lot more than that.

Anne was globally recognised. She was leading an extraordinary life, with achievements spread across the continents and was considered to be the UK's answer to Martha Stewart. She spent her time between Los Angeles, New York and London but, fortunately for Sasha, Anne had decided to make Sydney, Australia her home.

She told me she charged $US10,000 an hour or $US40,000 a month. I responded with, "That's frigging ridiculous, who charges fees like that?"

[Sasha]   An ex of mine had been at a convention that Anne was speaking at. I'd never heard of her but when he told me that she was a renovator, a TV celebrity and a business coach I thought, oh that's interesting, she'd understand my business. I had no idea about her journey – so there I was, this naive new businesswoman emailing her my TV footage that I had produced freelance.

I had to email her for a year because when she told me she charged $US10,000 an hour or $US40,000 a month, I responded with: "That's frigging ridiculous, who charges fees like that? I'm not paying $10,000 an hour to speak to you, I just want to have a talk to you to decide if you're going to be my coach." I think she quite enjoyed my cheekiness and later said it was my sheer persistence that made her decide to meet me. I'd sent her an email: "I'm coming to Sydney for a conference. I want to meet up with you for an hour, no $10,000, let's have a chat and see if we can do something." So, I met her – she was not what I expected. I expected this billionaire to walk in, all blinged and glammed up but she was just normal, unassuming and humble – I mean she drives a Ford Captiva (she'd probably hate me saying that, but it just shows how down to earth she is). When she spoke, she kind of floored me – she had a strong Scottish accent. I definitely didn't expect that.

She's a business coach to so many stars around the world, some amazing people plus loads of high-profile companies. Obviously, once you've run a business and developed remarkable concepts and business principles people really want your help.

Anyway, we worked out a few things and she became my mentor – she's awesome, an incredible woman.

I believe everyone should have a mentor in business, a second set of eyes looking in, but you have to get the right mentor. Anne was amazing. She had already walked down my path which was awesome because I wanted to minimise my mistakes and fast track my success. I couldn't have found anybody better.

At the time I was going nuts setting my 101 goals. I laugh now but I was so motivated, I was a maniac. In those early days I was on fire, but I was also getting sick. Anne came along and told me to "settle down petal", and "who sets 101 goals – three is enough". She taught me how to pare things back, less is more and how to make considered decisions – she slowed me down.

I could bounce ideas off her, she was my sounding board. She showed me how to create a high-end brand that was more subtle. I came from the Yellow Pages where it was all very salesy, big headlines, lots of text. She said, "Sash you've got yellow blood; you need a blood transfusion. Just create Million Dollar Makeovers, luxury renovations and that's it." So, we built the brand together.

She was always telling me off because I'd wear all this bling. I remember once wearing this full-on diamante Swarovski crystal belt that I paid $700 for and she said, "Sasha, I'm a billionaire and I wouldn't even pay $700 for a belt, so if you keep spending like that, you'll only ever be a multi-millionaire".

I thought, well OK, multi-millionaire isn't bad, and what can you really do with a billion dollars anyway? I'd rather not be a billionaire if that's how I've got to be to get there, it's not fun. I'd rather be able to buy a $700 belt if I feel like it because if you work hard you should reward yourself a little.

The business just grew; Anne was instrumental in that. I will always remember when she came out on a sales call with me. The client's budget was $300K and I was happy to sign because it was a lot of money, but Anne stepped in and said, hang on a minute. She made a few suggestions. She stopped me going in for the quick deal and so instead of $300,000 we ended signing a $1 million contract. That really opened my eyes.

Because I was so motivated and energetic, I wanted to do everything. I started designing furniture and had it manufactured offshore and then imported it. I hooked up with this company that promised to deliver, they seemed really awesome and promised good quality control but when it arrived the quality was really poor. Then I had to find the room to store it. So it was a whole new business and I ended up selling it all off at a garage sale – I lost money on that idea.

All the time Anne was in the background saying, "Just concentrate on doing what you do really, really well," which is renovations. "You don't need to be a furniture designer." She taught me to focus, to just concentrate on what I do best.

She taught me to focus, to just concentrate on what I do best.

I'd never had any TV presentation training, I just winged it, but Anne had worked in it so she came over from Sydney with a cameraman and she trained me. She slowed me down, restyled me, de-blinged me and taught me how to be on camera.

I can really see why she has done so well – she's strong and determined and doesn't put up with shit but she's calm and centred. I'm such a bull at a gate and get so frustrated when anyone around me moves too slowly.

One day Anne said, "Sash, you've got to understand you're like an Olympic athlete and your staff and trades are just runners and they are happy to be runners." Well I wasn't happy with that and thought if I'm an Olympic athlete then I want all my staff in training for the Olympics, because I don't want average staff, I want phenomenal staff.

Anne believed that staff just go to work and are happy to do an average job and so didn't believe in incentivising; but I'd come from the Yellow Pages' culture where they dangled carrots like trips and rewards and everyone was driven because of the carrots.

So, I decided that if my staff did an awesome job, I'd reward them with an experience they'd never forget. Like fully paid trips with husbands and kids. I also introduced 'tradie of the month' and the year. My staff all became Olympians, so recognition and appreciation is important.

When I told Anne, we'd increased our sales by $4 million since putting incentives in place, she went "Okay...maybe it does work", so I've taught her a few things as well.

So, I run my businesses with that mentality. I open all my meetings with, "Welcome Olympians." I have lots of mantras – we play an A game, not a B game; we are a jumbo jet in the sky, but we only have first and business class, there's no premium economy or economy. We want our clients to expect and receive the best.

When I interview prospective employees, I look for attitude; mindset. I always say, I don't employ anybody average so if you're average there's the door. You will need to be an Olympian and you need to win gold medals for our clients – you will be working hard, you will be challenged, but you will be rewarded and you're going to have a ball.

Anne once said to me, "Sasha I see qualities in you that I don't see in my Fortune 500s – I believe you could turn this into a billion-dollar company." Far out! Coming from Anne that was huge for me!

Another time she said, "Sash, you were successful when I met you, you were always going to be successful, I just wanted to minimise your mistakes along the way." I think she's done that.

"Anne was instrumental in my growth as a businesswoman and in my brand but there came a time when I knew I no longer needed her. We're great friends but my partner at the time, Mal, was a great businessman and so I was able to turn to him for the support I needed. No doubt there will come a time when I do need her again because I do believe in standing on the shoulders of giants.

Mal, being a country boy, was such a different bear. We had this amazing connection on a business and emotional level and at the time he was exactly what I needed and what I wanted. Mal didn't chase me; he didn't call me every minute of the day and didn't act like a sooky puppy around me like some of the others had. But I think I had become conditioned to think that if a man doesn't behave like a sooky puppy then he isn't really interested. I misread Mal totally and that brought out this vulnerable side in me, so I tried to change him to be what I thought he should be.

When I realised why and what I was doing it was like an epiphany. I thought, oh my god...and the relief of not having to worry or to try to change him was amazing, and for the first time I felt utter freedom, total freedom to be me. As a woman I found that so empowering and it has had a huge impact on both my personal and business life.

I only mention Sasha's personal relationship here because often we make judgements based on preconceived ideas of how something should be. This can severely limit our capacity to reach our full potential – be it in our personal or in our business lives. For Sasha that realisation bought the wheels of her life into alignment, possibly for the first time.

[Sasha] I feel so much more balanced now – if you're imbalanced in any way, in relationships or in business, I think you struggle to evolve. So, I've worked hard to have a good balance between work and home. At the end of the day you need to be able to clear your mind and not think about business. I used to go to bed thinking about all the things I had to do tomorrow, other people, my relationships, everything...but I haven't done that for years, I sleep like a baby now. I've learned to switch off.

There must be something in Sasha's work-life philosophy. In 2009 she launched Million Dollar Makeovers and by 2011 she had won the Telstra Businesswoman of the Year Award for Innovation. In that same year she was one of WA Business News' 40 under 40. The following year she was awarded Ernst & Young Entrepreneur Of The Year – in the category of emerging business. These awards are considered to be among some of the world's most prestigious business awards. The judges said, "Sasha's energy and enthusiasm are remarkably high, even by entrepreneurial standards, and the way she builds brand equity gives the business every chance of being highly successful in many markets."

It was a remarkable acknowledgment for someone who'd been in business barely four years, but that wasn't the end of it. Sasha was then sent to Monte Carlo in 2013 for the Ernst & Young World Entrepreneur Of The Year awards – one of the most prized awards of them all. She didn't win but just being there was life changing. The opportunity to mingle and learn from some of the world's most outstanding businesspeople was an extraordinary and empowering experience for Sasha.

I think some women don't succeed in business - or in fact go into business for themselves - for many reasons... fear, lack of belief, families, lack of support.

[Sasha] I feel very grateful, very empowered and inspired to be a woman in business, able to stand on my own two feet; to show and teach my staff and other women, particularly my daughter, that we are capable, that we can do it. I think some women don't succeed in business – or in fact go into business for themselves – for many reasons...fear, lack of belief, families, lack of support. But I actually think it's easier for women to succeed in business. We're a niche, there are a lot of gaps in the market and I think fundamentally we are much better organisers and multitaskers. I do think it's really easy for us to make a difference and make a splash. I've reached the point where I'm proud to be able to say I've become the woman I wanted to be, more than I hoped I would be, and I've achieved more than I thought I could achieve.

I have worked my butt off. I've had long and sleepless nights but now with an awesome team I'm in a position where I can work two hours a day if that's all I want to do, or I can travel for three months which is what I've just done. I'm so grateful for the journey.

But to get to that point I had to make sacrifices like time with my daughter. I think any business owner would probably say the biggest sacrifice when building a business is time with their children. I used to feel guilty about it, but I've moved beyond that guilt because I know everything I've done has been for us and for her future. She'll have her own journey, but I just hope with what I've learned along the way I can teach her to do it the smart way.

Sasha spent three months travelling through Europe in 2016. Like many parents, leaving her child wasn't easy. She wrote Georgia a letter before she left so that if anything did happen whilst she was away Georgia would always have it to read and remember. It's a very private letter but Sasha was happy to share a few excerpts because they clearly define some of the lessons Sasha has learned along the way.

My darling I cannot put into words the depth of love, emotion and adoration I have for you... Having you to look after drives the determination in me to work hard and achieve amazing success because I want you always to be looked after, safe and I need to know that if anything ever happened to me, you would be in a financial position to live a very comfortable life because I don't want you to go without. I want you to have the best and that is the driving force behind everything I do in the businesses to make sure you are set up and to show you how to be a role model so one day you can achieve great things for yourself, your heart and for your own children...

Success comes in many ways. Being financially stable and capable gives you a lifestyle for yourself and those you love, to see the amazing world we live in, to travel, to create experiences and memories. You can help yourself and then you can help the ones you love.

Success comes in being a good person...with having a big heart. When someone hurts you and your heart hurts, know it's not always intentional – some things just hurt because you care.

Challenges and obstacles are there to teach you. Embrace them, resolve them or overcome them and then move forward with greater strength and wisdom.

Without life's lessons and you learning from them, you cannot evolve as a better, bigger, wiser, more experienced person unless you go through this journey. The key is to embrace the journey and go through it with strength, resilience and an understanding that whatever is happening is meant to happen to teach you something. It's not always easy to see the lesson but it's always there and eventually you will see it, even if it's years later. Sometimes when time passes, and experience is with you, the lesson comes...

You have been given the best of me so move forward with that faith...so, whatever happens, if you get knocked down, you get back up. You keep moving forward. Don't ever give up...

'Never give up' is a legacy Sasha clearly wants her daughter to inherit. It is that quality that has given her own life such depth, diversity, great triumphs and an appreciation of those triumphs. Over her journey Sasha has conquered many obstacles and as a result of those experiences has realised that whilst she is driven to be independent both financially and emotionally, she is also driven to make a difference.

[Sasha]   At the start the money was important. I value money, if you don't, you'll never have it. John Demartini (one of the world's leading authorities on human behaviour and personal development, business consultant and author) will tell you that if you don't value yourself, you'll never have great relationships, and if you don't value money, you'll never be successful in business. In order to have a certain lifestyle, to be able to educate your children, support your staff, give back to the economy, be charitable, you need to value money to bring it into your life. But eventually you move past the money journey and then you watch people grow and you help people grow, that's what I really love.

I want to be able to help other women in business. I will never do something that's just going to help me, it has to benefit the clients, my staff, the business, the broader community. We get so many leads and we cannot manage every single one, so we feed them through to other women in the same business. I'd rather do that than go...they're my competition so I'm not going to help them. There's plenty of business out there for us all and I believe if you're really good at what you do, no one's going to beat you anyway – but you have to stay on top of your game.

I'm also a great believer in having multiple income streams across your business so when you have quiet patches you're covered. Generally, over the year we do really well and we're really busy, but we do have quiet spells in January and February. By having a second or third income stream diversifies our risk.

It was during one of those 'quiet patches' that Sasha started thinking about how she could better handle those periods when business was slow and cash flow was tight. The idea came. She would open a design centre. A centre where Sasha and all of her suppliers could have their own displays, together, under the one roof, where everything from flooring, painting and blinds to curtains and kitchens would be on display. Where not only could clients do all of their selections but where anyone off the street could walk in and place an order. It was an idea born in very, very tough economic times but Sasha felt certain it would be successful and be a win-win solution for her, her clients, suppliers and off-the-street customers.

[Sasha]   We launched Million Dollar Makeovers as a high-end brand to do the full house renovation with structural, large job values. The Renovation Company was born to target the generic mass market but it was still full-on renovations so we still had quiet patches. Due to the economic downturn, I knew we had to do something, to diversify. We were getting those 800 odd leads and enquiries from people just wanting kitchens and bathrooms done; the small stuff, flooring, blinds and so on. We didn't want the little stuff; we loved the big stuff because it was a challenge, but then I thought about the extra revenue stream that was sitting there in those leads. What if we took on the smaller stuff and worked on volume?

If we were in a booming industry, if the economy was in good shape and my existing strategies were all working perfectly, I probably wouldn't think about other concepts. It's when you are in a tough market, that you're forced to think outside the box, to create and innovate.

So out of tough times World of Renovation was born. It came from a business insight that if all those 800 leads spent $5,000 to $10,000, or $15,000 or even $50,000, it would be quite a viable business. Plus, potentially those people who just came in for a kitchen or bathroom might convert to a bigger renovation.

I was leasing the building in Claremont, which was a great location, but we didn't have the space to expand and my lease was up. I didn't want to lease a property and fit it all out and spend a couple of million on the fit out of somebody else's building so I started to look for buildings to purchase. I couldn't find anything in Perth or along the highways of the Western Suburbs that were beautiful and would lend themselves to the idea behind World of Renovation.

I decided to launch in Fremantle because it's a hotspot to live and work and has beautiful and majestic heritage buildings. I found a property at 86 High Street and made an offer. It was literally an empty shell with pigeons and pigeon poo. It didn't stand out on the street because it was so rundown, but it was majestic, like a lot of the buildings in Fremantle.

I went to see my bank and as I do every time, I put a business plan together. I showed them the cash flow projections, the design inspirations and images of what I was trying to create – something unique in Perth. Generally, commercial banks only lend 65 per cent, but because they knew me and my trading history and because I'm in the building industry, they actually lent me 100 per cent of the building. That's almost unheard of in this market.

I got the building and did a 12-week fit out of what was a concrete shell. All the floors were cracked, the windows were rotting, and all the lintels had to come out and be replaced with ones from the eastern states. It's also a heritage building so we had a few hurdles to get over but nothing major and the council was very supportive.

Within the fit out and at the back of the building I included a gorgeous café, a French Brasserie. Because I love cooking it was something I always wanted to do. I also thought it would be a good idea to give customers and clients another reason to come in.

We launched World of Renovation on May 13, 2017 but before we opened, we did a huge amount of marketing. Now that I'm here I'm even more passionate about Fremantle and the community.

It was a good move not only because it was revalued and has gone up quite a bit, but local government is also in the midst of spending $1.3 billion on Fremantle. It hasn't been touched since the America's Cup in 1987 which is more than 30 years ago, so this was a very big up-grade with a lot of residential and that's good for my kind of business.

With our expansion and growth came the need for more financial investment and financial debt. Debt is good debt when it's used to get you to the next stage, however, when you expand like we did, it's not just buying a building and doing a fit out, it's the whole back end; all the new staff, all the new training, new systems, new processes, new technology. A lot had to happen and that was exhausting but I just kept going in every day because I believed so much in the concept and in my team.

> *A lot had to happen and that was exhausting but I just kept going in every day because I believed so much in the concept and in my team.*

I predicted it would go bang straight away and while we certainly got the numbers through the door, the transition to sales was slow to come. One, because the market is shit, and two, because people are fascinated and interested in what we have but they take three months to six months, even twelve months, to actually take action. So, I had to manoeuvre and manage my way through the infancy of the business while still supporting the other businesses.

It wasn't easy taking on the extra debt and waiting for the business to take off. But again because of the tough market I changed a few strategies. We'd never really pushed the commercial side of our business but once people could see what I did with the High Street building they absolutely loved it and so we started getting way more commercial leads.

I then purchased a majestic, old heritage hotel in Fremantle with the intention to convert it into luxury apartments – I'm very excited about it. My future will see me doing more of my own property developments but also doing more of the large commercial historic buildings because I feel so inspired to transform them.

When Sasha launched Million Dollar Makeovers in 2009 it was amid the GFC. Nobody, including Sasha, ever believed the recession would continue but it did and it's not over yet. To then launch World of Renovation in what is considered to be the worst economic climate that Western Australia has ever endured was courageous – but it has taken its toll.

[Sasha]   I have taken a massive but calculated risk. Sales have dropped but my debts have all gone up, so the cash flow is tough. I've had to sell properties and put my house on the line so I could inject more money into the businesses and to expand my brand. All this at a time when the industry is really feeling the pinch; not that it's just building, it's mining, it's all of my suppliers, everyone across the board has had a bad time of it. They're now saying it's going to go for another five to six years, that it's a 15-year recession not a seven year.

I launched all four of my businesses in tough markets. I've never known a boom and yet I built four successful brands. It's taken absolute tenacity, a driving force, strength and resilience, a never-give-up attitude, but it's fucking tough and stressful at times. I've learned to handle stress well because you have to be able to suck it up to survive in the fragile and volatile Perth economy. I think Perth entrepreneurs must be some of the best and strongest – if not the most resilient – in the world.

So, 2017 was especially tough. Today, I can honestly admit that...I'm going to get emotional now, although only very fleetingly...I sometimes asked myself, was it worth all the stress? The answer is yes. I love helping others. The work we do helps actualise people's dreams and that is too amazing to give up. So, I keep going; I keep believing in my team and believing in what we do, I keep innovating, I keep changing – I must, I have to.

Business is never easy, but I have learned through the tough times that the success of any business is simply sheer determination and the absolute WILL to succeed even when faced with great adversity.

Business is never easy, but I have learned through the tough times that the success of any business is simply sheer determination and the absolute WILL to succeed even when faced with great adversity. I have discovered I do my best work when I am forced to be more creative and when my back is to the wall, which it has been on a few occasions. I've learned you have to constantly change, adapt and innovate to take the business in a new direction because you can't move forward standing still. It's all strategy, strategy and strategy. Watch every part of your business, particularly cash flow and accounting. It's tough to admit but I learnt that the hard way! Now, I don't think there is anything I couldn't handle from a stress point of view, an experience point of view, a resilience point of view. I've grown such a thick, resilient skin and that is very empowering in itself.

I look at the pivotal things that have come out of this – out of having the balls to do something different; to go against the grain. I have gained great respect within the industry, and the support that I have received from suppliers and trades has been phenomenal.

I never realised how many people actually believed in me as a businesswoman until I presented this concept and now, I have all this amazing support from big companies. I feel very humbled, but now that it's open and tracking a little slower than what I would like it to be, I feel very accountable to make this be what it is supposed to be.

Our company perception is big. I built big brands through TV because when your brand is big, you get the awareness and the recognition which from my marketing experience is very, very important. But, in reality, we run a small and efficient team for what we actually deliver.

I don't have the big cash reserves like some people think I do because I am always reinvesting in my own homes or commercial property developments. What I have are the skills to know how to work with what I have; I'm creative, I'm aware so I re-juggle and re-calculate my position constantly; I manoeuvre or roll cash in a different way, or if the banks say no, I sell or move assets and cash around – I do whatever I have to do to make it work.

I've re-engaged Anne McKevitt as my business coach. She loves World of Renovation but she saw straight away that because we have built so many brands it was all getting too complicated.

As part of that thinking I've re-engaged Anne McKevitt as my business coach. She loves World of Renovation but she saw straight away that because we have built so many brands it was all getting too complicated. So, she is back on board to help me simplify things, to still expand but to scale back where we need to. She will also help build our brands stature through Instagram and Facebook as well as get another new brand – Sasha – out to the public face. I always stayed away from social media – I employed others to do that for me. Now I recognise the power it has when building a brand so I've had to learn and get up to speed with the technology-side of social media.

I've also been doing a home and garden TV series which has allowed me to really work Instagram and Facebook. It's a lot of fun but it was a two-pronged strategic marketing decision: one, to build the TV media personality, Sasha deBretton, the renovation queen which then flows on to the brand Sasha. It has given us traction – you know, through recognition when people walk in the store. So, it's been really good for business.

We now have a general manager in place, who has the systems and technical skills that I need to sort the back end out. So, with a general manager who has eased the pressure on me, Anne and the TV series, I now have what we need to make the changes to make this thing work.

We've had solid growth year on year with Million Dollar Makeovers and The Renovation Company which is incredible in these tough times. But the last two years have been tough, hence my expansion in a tight market. If all four businesses can survive and have growth through the tough years, then I really look forward to when the market returns.

Being in a male dominated industry has been good because most men in this industry just want to do the construction, they don't want to do the frilly bits, or if they do, not at the level or the quality of finish or interior design that we do. I went in and offered everything they didn't offer, and while some builders laughed and poo-pooed me when I started, they don't laugh anymore.

I've had a lot of clients come and say, "We've come to you because you're an all-female team and we want that female touch, that eye for detail." They want a different level of service, quality and communication.

That's why I choose to employ mostly women, because as women we're great communicators and multitaskers, we're wives, we're mothers, we're career women and we've learned how to juggle lots of balls – at the same time.

I remember a boyfriend's mum who was a businesswoman. She'd raised her boys on her own and it wasn't easy, but she was always very glamorous and dressed up, she painted her nails and was beautiful. I aspired to be that beautiful older woman who always looked after herself. I believe that in business you have to dress for success. We may be in the building industry but that doesn't mean we have to dress like the archetypal builder. We have a brand to uphold and all of my girls have to be on brand. If any of them look scruffy I always tell them – you're not on brand and if you can't dress properly and make yourself look pleasant and decent, how will anyone believe you can style their house? The way we present ourselves is part of our niche, our unique selling point.

I've always believed, you need to find a niche to succeed in business. You don't have to rein-vent the wheel, but you have to find a way to differentiate from all the other businesses –you do it better, you do it faster, with better customer service or with a unique selling point. I was a female in a man's world, I was passionate, and I offered the missing something.

Find the gap, find the problem, find something that's missing or something you can add value to.

So, I say to aspiring entrepreneurs, develop a product or a service around what you are pas-sionate about – if you find something frustrating within that, it will be frustrating other people too. Find the gap, find the problem, find something that's missing or something you can add value to. My success has come from my experience with builders – not liking that experience and seeing how bad the service was, seeing the gaps in the market and working out how I could do it better.

There are a lot of people who will do things they are passionate about but make no money – they could, but they just don't have that business mind which you need to succeed, so go and do a business course or study marketing – anything that will fast track your passion into a business that makes money.

I think the one thing that stops everybody is fear, lack of confidence, lack of belief and not having that drive and determination to give things a go.

I often hear people say, "Oh, I had an idea and then this obstacle came up, so it was obviously the universe telling me that I shouldn't do it." What an absolute mind limiting blockage.

I often hear people say, "Oh, I had an idea and then this obstacle came up, so it was obviously the universe telling me that I shouldn't do it." What an absolute mind limiting blockage. If you have an obstacle in the way, find a way to get around it, there's always a way. I relate it to being like a marathon runner jumping hurdles – they're all obstacles, and if they stop at the first hurdle, they'd never make it to the finish line. Every hurdle teaches you how to jump higher, stronger, smarter, how to get around it, under it, you just find a way to get to that finish line.

My Mum says nothing ever stopped me; I was always climbing up onto things – I had no fear. I still don't have any fear. I never doubted myself, but I wasn't always confident. It wasn't until I started winning the world trips at the Yellow Pages that my confidence just grew, and from then on, I always knew I would be successful.

But I also knew if I wanted to be successful and have a good life I'd have to work hard. I wasn't going to wait for somebody else to do it for me; I wasn't going to marry a rich guy; I had decided from very early on that I didn't want to work for somebody else for the rest of my life just earning an average wage – I knew I had to do it myself. I now feel incredibly capable on so many different levels and so many different tangents, but I never would have felt that if I had just worked for someone else.

So, if you are thinking about starting a business just do it. Don't do the hard slog for somebody else all your life. Do your business plan, take a calculated risk and just go for it. But be prepared to accept that you will have failures and it's a tough gig but the reward... It's like trading shares, there's high risk but if you are prepared there's high reward.

I've spent a lot of time renovating, restoring, going through divorces and relationship break-ups, building the business, being overwhelmed, I've done the long hours, had the stress and the health problems. Right now, I have my goals – to do my own property development again and the hotel conversion. But also slow down and cherry pick on the client side so I can have the best of both worlds. Yes okay, one day I will quit it all and just chill out but until I have achieved those goals, I will keep reinventing and testing myself. Nothing is ever set in concrete; all I know for sure is that I'm never going to get a second chance at this life, this is it, so now it's just about enjoying every minute of the journey.

After meeting with Sasha and talking about her journey I have learned so much myself and hope others reading her story will have that same experience. She is a giver, and whilst she is very confident and totally believes in who she is and how good she is at what she does, I have come to realise it is that belief that got her there. That in itself is a lesson for all of us who want to achieve in life and reach our fullest potential. Believe in yourself – without question. And never judge others!

[Sasha]   I believe you are responsible for your own happiness and when you're happy you can help others although you're not responsible for their happiness, that's up to them. But if I can make someone's journey a little more enjoyable then I will. I can do that now. With every renovation we do we donate funds to a company in Melbourne that builds charity homes and schools in Africa. Over the last few years I haven't been able to do as much but I intend to. If I can enhance the lives of people in Perth, people around Australia and in other countries, enhance the lives of my staff, my daughter, my family and friends nothing would make me happier.

And when I go to my grave, I'd like to think that I will be remembered as an ethical, inspiring, loving, caring, giving, motivational person that has touched lives and helped others. Being that person is what matters the most to me now.

Postscript

I finished writing Sasha's story in February 2018 but by April her world had turned upside down. Almost overnight she went from having a hugely successful business to liquidation.

It is during our darkest moments that we must focus to see the light.

Aristotle

Sasha was in Europe taking a three-month break at the end of what had been a hugely demanding 18 months. She was with her daughter Georgia, when the call came from Perth. Nothing could have been more unexpected than the news she was about to receive. "Sasha, we can't pay the bills. There's no money." Stunned into momentary silence, her almost inaudible whisper said it all: "NO, that can't be right." But it was and with that, the world she had so successfully built began to crumble around her.

[Sasha]   I'd been so happy in my little world. I was loving my little cafe (The French Brasserie within World of Renovation), our clients, the new store, I was loving everything. I had no idea the business was in trouble, nor did I think I had anything to worry about; we'd never had a problem in the past, so I never had reason to believe we'd have a problem in the future.

I knew our expenses were up, I knew the cafe was running at a loss, I knew the sales were low, but we had buffers in there, the backups from the year before, so I thought we were fine. I had asked questions, show me the cash flow, how are we going, that kind of thing but I was getting fed, "No, no, Sash everything's okay". I'm not a finance girl so off I went training my staff, dealing with clients, trying to focus on the sales because without sales you haven't got a business. I was just focusing on the front end but I should have watched the back end too.

When I got the call, I felt sick; I couldn't believe it could be true. I got on the first available flight back to Perth and went straight in to see the administrators and my solicitor, who's a good friend of mine. We didn't have all the financials at that point, so we didn't know the full picture, but we soon found out. There was no cash flow. There were 250-300 invoices that had not been input into the MYOB system but also, the way the input was being done was incorrect. I realised then there were serious bookkeeping errors, debts were up and the sales were low; we were in serious trouble.

By the time I found out the actual loses, instead of the positives that were supposed to be coming in, the beast was too big for me to turn around on my own – I needed a capital injection.

I went to see the bank that I'd been with for 25 years and they turned their back on me. I then went to see some external lenders who wanted a ridiculously high 24 per cent-plus interest rate, but they wouldn't support me either. It was the worst time in the WA economy and I just couldn't get finance.

My solicitor and the liquidators said, "Look Sash, it's okay if you want to trade through on one business name but that will cost another 200K to do that (I didn't have 200K because we'd run out of cash). However, if you liquidate it's only 50K and you just have to start again. If not, you'll have to find $1.5 million to put in and be sure you can do the sales."

I believed I could do the sales because we'd always been able to do that. We actually had all these quotes in the pipeline but because of the economy, clients were slower to make decisions. We also had loads of jobs stuck in council. If I could have bought those jobs forward, we may have been able to get through – but then I also had to find the $1.5 million.

I had to make a quick decision, but under pressure I deliberated – okay put this other $1.5 million in and trade through; wait a couple of extra months; get the sales in, save the building, save the brand, save my staff, save my livelihood, just spend another few months Sash.

Then there was my pride... I believed I could turn it around. I had amazing staff, the clients were there, the quotes were there, so I wanted to try. I didn't want to shut it down without me giving it a 100 per cent final push. For two months after I found out I worked seven days a week solid. I fought tooth and nail to save the business but in the end I couldn't.

To build up a business brand that was worth millions to have it suddenly be worth nothing was traumatic. It was my daughter's inheritance. I'd spent all those years working my arse off, I'd just bought that beautiful building, I'd just opened it, I had all my suppliers on board and had great support from everybody. So, I was very emotional. That's when my solicitor and the liquidators said something that had a real impact on how I was feeling. They said, "Remove the emotion, if this was just a business strategy, would you want to risk another $1.5 million of your personal funds, do you want to lose all your properties? Do you want the bank to foreclose on you? Or do you want to save your bacon now and still come out? You could try Sash, but we really don't think you should."

I had to listen to their advice. In hindsight it was the right advice from day one and I probably should have cut it a couple of months earlier. By trying to get through, trying to stay open, cost me an extra $650K not to mention the stress and anguish. So, I had no choice but to liquidate; I had to just swallow that bitter pill and cut my losses. It took me two months to make the decision but once I did it all happened very quickly.

I was told on the Wednesday, 3rd of April I should liquidate; on Friday the 5th of April the liquidators came in at lunchtime to tell the staff.

That was so hard; we were all so close, we were like a family. They were absolutely devastated, particularly my PA, Renee Paparone, because we started together, Sasha Jade, my head interior designer and Renee Hunt my project manager. But they all have such great skills levels, so opportunity will come out of this adversity.

At the same time as telling the staff the liquidators agreed to tell my trades and suppliers. I had this fear that they were going to hate me. They had thrown so much support behind me; how was I going to explain to them what had gone on? I hadn't been allowed to disclose but I wanted to tell them, face to face. So, I sent a quick text message to everyone calling an urgent meeting on that Friday. Those that could make it came in.

They'd only ever seen me looking glamorous but, on that day, I looked like this Chinese blowfish, my face was so puffy and red, you couldn't see my eyes.

I just said, "I'm really sorry guys, I tried everything within my power to turn this."

They were amazing and supportive. So many of them came up and said, Sash, you'll be back in the saddle. You'll be bigger and better and build bigger and better. Getting that support has been amazing.

Things happen for a reason and you have to look at those reasons logically and go, okay, that happened. I probably should have watched this or done that. It could have changed the outcome, but it is what it is and I have to accept that and just make the best decisions to move forward and never make those same mistakes again.

I think part of the reason for what happened is about location. Where we were before, in Claremont, was a great location but it wasn't a big building and I wanted to expand. My lease was up so I decided I didn't want to spend a couple of million on the fit out of somebody else's property so I started to look for buildings to purchase. That's when I found High Street. The building was gorgeous, and it fitted the style of what I wanted for World of Renovation. As to what I was anticipating with the move, well...

I think World of Renovation was a bit ahead of its time for the Perth market.

I had the full support of my bank due to the cash flow, the concept and the business plan. It was supposed to be hugely successful, turn over millions and millions and so the building suited that purpose. But Fremantle has a different clientele and we didn't get the traffic we expected. I expected our existing clientele to follow us because they had always come to us by appointment anyway, so I didn't think that moving from Claremont would be an issue; It was, they didn't come to Fremantle. I've always known location was a really important part, but I didn't think this location move would affect us.

Then there was the downturn in the economy, clients looking for cheaper deals because the high end had dropped out, all my expenses had gone up, debts had gone up, sales were slow to come and then there were the bookkeeping errors – and maybe it just wasn't a great time to expand.

I did that because I wanted to build more generic brands. I had Million Dollar Makeovers and I was on television, so my face had become connected with the brand; I was the brand. It happened naturally and very quickly. I don't think it's bad to have that connection, but you need some brands that are generic because then you have something you can sell or at least are easier to sell. That's why I started The Renovation Company and World of Renovation; to build generic brands. The Renovation Company along with the tagline, four-week renovations – awesome. They renovate, and they renovate fast, that's all you need to say, then you get the calls. World of Renovations – that name didn't even need a tagline.

I wouldn't change anything in terms of the branding, but when you do become a personal media brand – Sasha deBretton – there's a limit to that. It does reflect credibility and expertise which is why people come to you and give you their business, which is great if you want to stay in the business. But it's not good if you want to sell.

I had a couple of buyers who had wanted to buy me out before all of this, but it was too much brand Sasha – so it wasn't saleable. Not that I was ready to sell. I was happy in my own little world.

I used to read all of those business books that said, "All entrepreneurs go down and go bankrupt and bounce back up." But I always went, "I'll never be that girl, I'll never be one of those entrepreneurs that goes down. That's never going to happen to me."

When you're successful and you're flying high, it's easy to go, "I'm successful," and people ask you, How do you become successful? I'd say well, you delegate and give up control. That was the advice I used to give out. I do believe in delegating, I do trust people; I'm not a control freak, I believe in giving people the chance to grow and to shine. But, one of the biggest things I've learnt from this is that I delegate too much, I am too trusting; I gave up too much control but I know I will never, never, do that again.

I don't think this happened because I took my eye off the ball but because I was stretched too thin. I was so busy with sales, training new staff on the frontline, trying to help in the café; there was just so much going on with the expansion, and when I physically couldn't do everything, I gave away control.

I now know that was wrong. I also know I should have put more checks in place, more stringent checks. Our systems were outdated from when we expanded and grew, our back of house was outdated for what we needed. I should have got bookkeepers in earlier, I shouldn't have listened to anybody else, I should have listened to my gut; I should have made those calls earlier.

I could've, would've, should've done lots of things earlier – I didn't. But you can't cry over spilt milk, you just have to move on...

> *One of the biggest things I've learnt from this is that I delegate too much, I am too trusting; I gave up too much control but I know I will never, never, do that again.*

[Sasha]   Obviously, there's life lessons and business lessons that come out of this and I know I would be a much better mentor now – these are the reasons that made me successful and these are the reasons why I came unstuck, so watch that.

I would also now say to anyone going through a tough time, or if they have to face liquidation or shut down a business, don't let your pride get in the way, remove the emotion. Take it out and just look at the real figures, act quickly and don't flog a dead horse.

Try and find the positives and look after your emotional state. A lot of people go into severe depression, have nervous breakdowns, I probably turned into an alcoholic for three months.

> *I would also now say to anyone going through a tough time, if they have to face liquidation, or shut down a business, don't let your pride get in the way, remove the emotion...look at the real figures and act quickly.*

What helped me get through was the support I received from so many people. I also received a phone call from one of the biggest builders in Perth offering to do a partnership with me. The following week I got a call from an international property developer who flew me up to Kuala Lumpur to discuss working with them. After everything that had happened it was really nice to know that I was still wanted and there are still great opportunities. So those calls really gave me a pep up, but right now, I'm not ready to do anything – not just yet. I need to take time out although not too much time. I will start to rebuild soon!

I was proud to be a single mum; I was proud to be a woman in business that could stand on her own two feet and I was proud of what I had built. I loved it all but I was on adrenaline all the time and while I handled it, there were times I was extremely stressed. Now I look back and I go, "Why the fuck did you do that to yourself Sash? Why did you push? For what?" It was money at the end of the day because I like the lifestyle that having money affords.

But all of this has made me realise that money isn't everything. What does it matter, if at the end of the day you don't have your health, or worse, because of all the stress and anguish you put yourself under to build a business? So, I've made the decision to simplify everything, I've got out of my big house, I've gone to a cute little cottage where I feel like I'm in Europe. I now have time to spend with my daughter so we're more connected. We've had to learn to budget for the first time but that's been a good lesson for Georgia.

So, I don't look at what has happened as a failure because I know my business was hugely successful over the years. But I was getting flippant, complacent, I was playing the high roller, having extravagant trips because the money was rolling in. Without me going through this I wouldn't have learned all these lessons and for that I feel sincerely blessed.

I do have to start making some money. I have Sasha deBretton Developments, so I'm going back into doing my own property developments; buying, renovating and selling commercial and residential. There is still money to be made out of flipping property, but in this market you have to be very careful with what you buy. I'll be looking at stuff like little old houses where I will change the design and give it a lick of paint. I'll also be looking at old commercial buildings in Fremantle where I can change the zoning. I'll put apartments at the top, then sell them off but keep the bottom floor; that would still give me a rental income and I'd still own half a property, but I would have covered my entire costs.

That's the kind of stuff I'm ready and want to do now. I guess in a way I'm getting back in touch with my grass roots.

I've just gone through my roughest patch in my life, but I've come out of it feeling more balanced, more humble, pared back, calmer and wiser, and I have time to catch up with friends. But the best part is I'm happier now than I've been in years.

Thank you, Sasha, you are an inspiration!

"While they were saying among themselves
it cannot be done, it was done."

Helen Keller

Sasha's uncle Greg Baker, her parents Manuel and Alison, brother Scott and grandparents

Sasha's brother, grandfather and father

The Nunez Family

Ready for their family
adventure on the continent

Manuel with his sisters -
Antonia and Isabella

Sasha with her cousins
by the Rock of Gibraltar

Sasha

Million Dollar Makeovers' first office -
The Penthouse - Burswood

Pool area - before and after renovation

Dining room - before and after renovation

Kitchen - before and after renovation

Sasha - 2012 EY Entrepreneur Of The Year Award

Sasha with her business coach – International business-woman Ann McKevitt

Inside the Million Dollar Makeovers showroom

Million Dollar Makeovers 2nd home

Inside World of Renovation

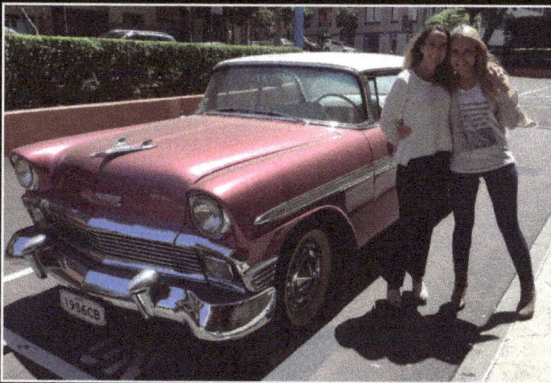
World of Renovation - High Street Fremantle

Sasha with Cherie Barber

Georgia and Sasha

Sasha with her daughter Georgia

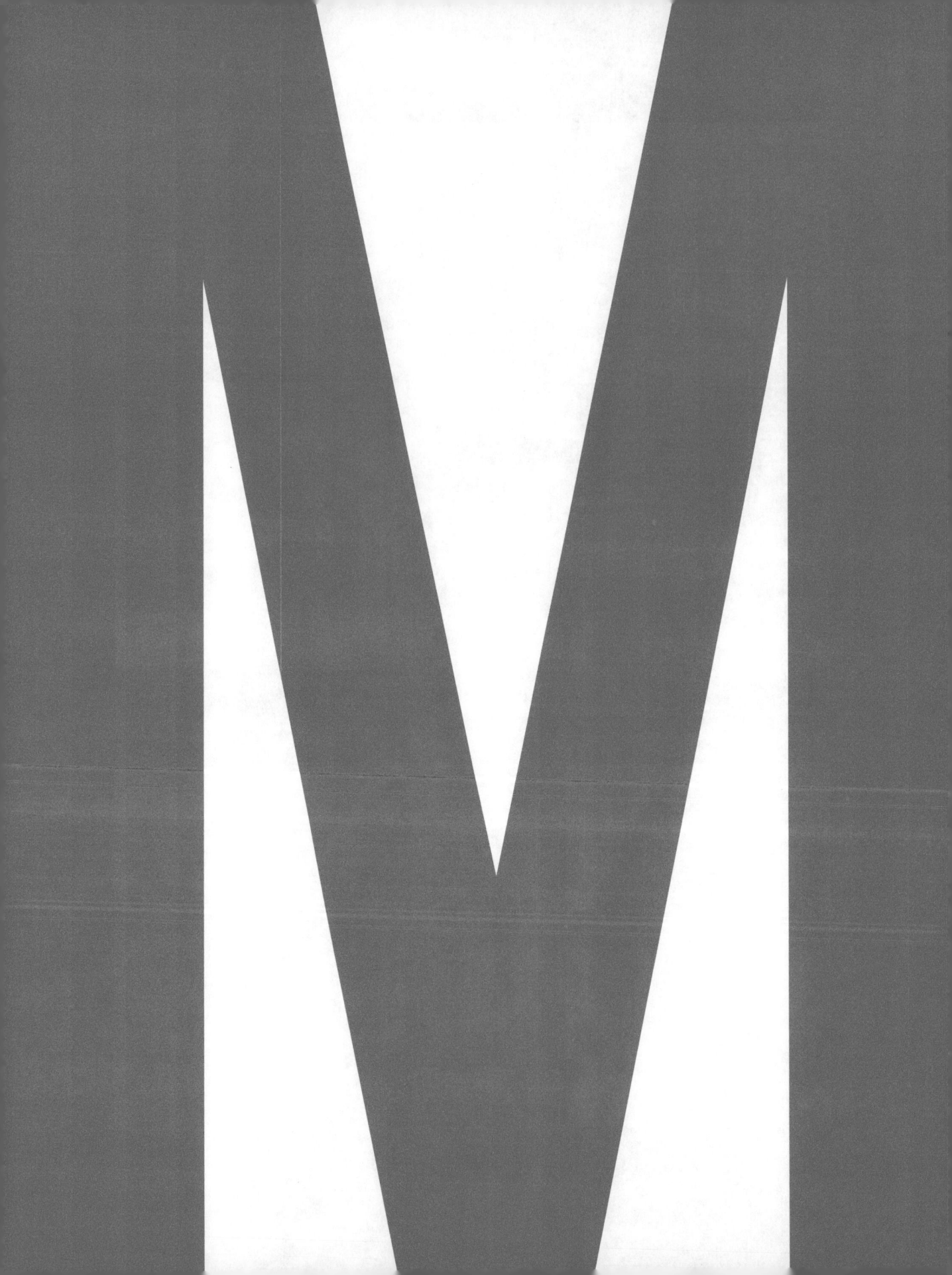

6 Mastering Collaboration and Partnerships

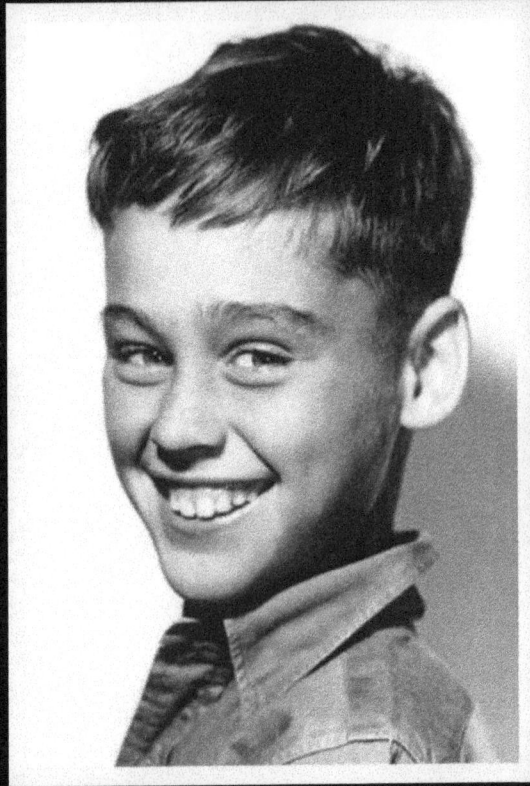

"Someone said to me winning's not everything and I said "Excuse me, of course winning is everything, but you have to know how to lose!" Don't go in without wanting to win but if you're not successful then dust yourself off and move on. That's more important than anything."

They say the first five years of a child's life are the formative years, the foun
dation that shapes the future development, performance and success of a
person. If that statement is true then it is not surprising to learn that a young
Nedlands lad, whose world from the 'get go' was surrounded by water, beer,
wine and spirits, would eventually have those liquids play a major role in his
life. But there was more to add to the mix. There was a free spirit, a love of
sport and horses, but more significant was a hugely traumatic, early life experience. It was an unusual combination that could easily have shaped the child
into being the kind of fellow who would spend his time at the local pub with
one hand on a beer, one eye watching the football and one ear tuned to the
bar radio, listening to the race caller's voice follow the horses down the home
straight. But no, this man chose a different road; the road less travelled – and
that choice has made all the difference.

Yes, he may well enjoy a beer at the bar and watching the football, but he
chose to stand behind the bar, to don his own footy boots, kick his own goals;
he chose to climb onto the horse itself and steer his life from an in the saddle
perspective. This seemingly quiet and unassuming chap, despite his 6 foot
2 frame and good looks, has achieved more than most. Perhaps that can be
attributed to his ability to take considerably more than one step at a time,
preferring to pack in all the opportunities and experiences that came and continue to come his way.

He has bought and sold islands, developed wineries and created football teams.
Many know him from an icon on the Swan and a school on a river, others for
his speed in and on the water, or his ability on a horse. Others still, for his
full bodied red or oak ripened white; less know him for his pots and pans or
cooking for the masses. Oh yes, this man has many strings to his bow, way too
many to mention here – that is for the story to come. Still, there is no time
or desire for this man of great humility to look back over a life of exceptional
achievements and admit a job well done. This self-confessed red wine junkie
has his eyes on the road ahead and with so many paths still to follow who
knows how many more strings he will add to his already full bow.

The owner of the bow is a highly successful publican, a collector of pubs and
bars, restaurants and bottle shops, he is a leader of the West Australian football
fraternity, he is a developer of property and of wine, he is an extraordinary
entrepreneur, he is…

Murray McHenry

So, where did the makings of such a man begin? It actually did start with liquor, well the mixing of liquor. As we all know Australia has always had a thirst for alcohol. Hence, long, long ago, barrels upon barrels of concentrated spirits were transported from England all the way to Australia. It was then precisely mixed according to industry regulations, which at the time varied from one state to the next. One for you, two for me wasn't good enough – mixing spirits was a serious business – serious enough to bring a chemist all the way from Ireland to Perth to get it right. For that sole purpose Thomas McHenry left Dublin and travelled to Western Australia with his wife and their seven children. It was 1919 when they settled into the ocean-side suburb of Cottesloe, and from that day forward liquor and water became indelibly entwined in all their lives.

Liquor strength laws were eventually made uniform around the country and with that change came the opportunity for Mr McHenry to move to Sydney to take on a similar role at a national level. Three of his sons remained on the west coast. With their knowledge of the liquor industry it was an almost natural progression for each to take out a lease on a public house (pub). In the late 1920s Alex, the oldest son, took on the Subiaco Hotel; Stephen, the second oldest, travelled 300km to start his life as a publican at the Mukinbudin Hotel while the youngest Joe, headed 200km north-east of Perth to the Moora pub.

But it is the story of Stephen that requires a more in-depth account as it was his life that would greatly influence the path his yet unborn son, Murray, would take some 25 years down the track.

Stephen Comnee McHenry at 27 years old, was immediately comfortable in the role of publican and in his new position on the Mucka footy team. It was a significant adjustment changing from Gaelic football to Aussie Rules, nevertheless Stephen embraced the game and the oddly shaped ball and helped his team take out the 1930 premiership. Despite making the most of his time in Mukinbudin it was a little far from the ocean and maybe a little quiet for the life loving Irishman. After a relatively short time behind the country bar he headed back to Perth and found another pub to lease. This time it was the Shaftsbury Hotel in Beaufort Street, Perth – a majestic building that later fell victim to Perth's thirst for modern architecture. From the Shaftsbury he went to the Clarendon in Fitzgerald Street, Northbridge, and then to the stately Palace Hotel. The Palace, set on the corner of William Street and St Georges Terrace in the centre of the city, was the site of the first licensed premises in Perth.

The opulent Palace Hotel had opened its doors in 1897 to meet the demands of the gold rush. Glamorous parties and celebrity sightings saw 108 St Georges Terrace quickly become the place to be seen.

By the time Stephen McHenry took over the lease in the early 1930s, a vibrant history had been well and truly established. The popularity, the fun and the laughter continued, although now with Stephen behind the beautifully hand carved bar, entertaining Irish tales added yet another dimension to the hotel's character.

Today, the chink of glasses and laughter has been replaced with the more sombre tones of office employees. The grand dining room and guest suites have long gone to make way for an adjoining 50-storey office tower. Whilst this distinctive concrete, steel and glass skyscraper now dominates the Perth skyline, at street level it pales into insignificance behind the beauty and graceful facade of what will always be remembered to the people of Perth as the Palace Hotel.

I jumped way ahead there and that will happen a lot in this story because of the way Murray lives his life – at a frenetic pace – he fits a lot in to a day. But right now I need to go back to 1935. It was the year that Stephen McHenry decided he was ready to leave the Palace and take on a new challenge; a challenge that came in the form of a publican's lease on the Nedlands Park Hotel. And it is this hotel, set on the banks of the Swan River that forms the backdrop for this story.

The Nedlands Park Hotel was built in 1908 and designed by architect Harold Boas as a residential hotel for farmers and country folk. But it was also a very popular watering hole for the locals, visitors to the nearby Nedlands Baths and students from around the corner at the State's only university, the University of Western Australia. A tram-stop out the front of the hotel provided easy access to and from the city and was just another element that added to the promise of ongoing success.

The Swan Brewery, a beer brewing company founded in 1857, was trying to purchase the Nedlands Park Hotel from its owners – a family who only wanted to sell to Stephen. Not in a position to do so Stephen made a deal with the Swan Brewery; they buy the hotel on the basis that he would have the tenancy. It was agreed and a simple week-to-week lease was set informally in place.

Stephen was in his element. He was a publican of a hotel that was set on a river's edge, which meant he was able to indulge his love of boats. (It was Stephen, his brother Alex, a four-time King's Cup rower, Gra Rosser also a King's Cup rower and a few other mates who pretty much put the initial wind in the sails of the Royal Perth Yacht Club down the road from the hotel.) Stephen was also happily married to Kitty Dix; they had two daughters, Joy and Julie, and an abundance of friends and acquaintances who all loved dropping into 'Steve's' for a drink on their way home. Life was good in Nedlands, Western Australia, but 1939 was looming and change was afoot.

By early 1941, Lieutenant Stephen McHenry was a long way from the Nedlands Park Hotel. He was at the coal face of war in North Africa with the 2/28th Battalion. His platoon was part of the Australian garrison that held the Libyan port of Tobruk. It was critical for the allied forces to secure North Africa as a base, but the conditions were horrendous. To enable them to carry out counter-attacks and to survive the extreme regional conditions, the Australian soldiers dug a network of linking tunnels and shelters below the ground. It was from those trenches they fought an unrelenting German and Italian offensive. Their ingenuity and determination to both survive and triumph, challenged the enemy who labelled them the Rats of Tobruk. The title was delivered with contempt, but it was received with pride and honour because the Rats of Tobruk became known as men of courage and inspiration throughout and well beyond World War II.

It was a courageous fight but with no way to replenish their ammunition or resources, it was soon apparent victory was impossible. With only one way to save his troops from what would have been a brutal and bloody end, Lieutenant McHenry made the agonising decision to raise the white flag. As soon as he and his men were taken behind enemy lines the German troops moved forward into the trenches. As they entered a massive explosion tore through them. Retribution was immediate. The German commander, convinced the prisoners had laid the trap, ordered they be shot. Archival photos show the blindfolded soldiers lined up in front of a German firing squad, Lieutenant McHenry among them.

But as history shows they were not destined for such an end. Extraordinarily, moments before the call to fire was issued, one of the German soldiers who had been held captive in the trenches, rushed to the commander, pleading their innocence. He insisted the Australian soldiers were not responsible for the explosion; for, if they had laid the trap, he would have seen them doing so. If not for that German soldier's bravery and strength of conviction Lieutenant McHenry and his men would most certainly have been shot. Instead, they were sent to Italy and imprisoned.

In 1945, after 3½ years as a prisoner of war, an almost skeletal Lieutenant Stephen Comnee McHenry returned home to Western Australia where he was later made a captain.

Getting back behind the bar at the Nedlands Park Hotel was a welcome distraction from the memories of war – but life had changed. Stephen's wife, Kitty, had died of cancer during his imprisonment. Their daughters, Joy and Julie, were growing up fast and were at school at Methodist Ladies College. They also had a home tutor, a bright and educated Anglo-Indian woman, Hazel Joyce Dallywater. Hazel hailed from India where her father ran British Rail. When he retired, in search of greater opportunities for his children, he moved his family to Perth, Western Australia. His son Sam Dallywater went into the Air Force and Hazel to UWA where she completed her diploma in education. To earn additional income, she tutored Joy and Julie after their mother died.

The girls adored Hazel, so when Stephen had to attend one of the many balls that were so common back in the late '40s, it seemed only natural to suggest their father take Hazel. It turned out to be a great match. It wasn't long before the two were married and welcoming a daughter – Sandra. Fifteen months later, on the 15th of March 1950, Murray Stephen McHenry, was born – and with his birth this story can really begin.

Almost from the moment he drew his first breath Murray was full on. He loved his sport, he loved the water, he loved horses, truth be, he couldn't and wouldn't sit still – from the start life was an adventure to be seized.

He spent his days at home at the hotel or with his dad and Murray Church (his namesake and King's Cup rower) at the Royal Perth Yacht Club. When he wasn't with them, Murray was swimming in the river, kicking a football or riding his beloved gelding, Silver.

Silver was a gift from his father's cousin Rex Roper, a farmer from Nukarni. Rex who had four daughters and was divorced, stayed often with the McHenrys when he was visiting Perth – probably to go to the races. He loved racehorses. His own Sparkling Blue ran in the 1959 Melbourne Cup but sadly he never made it into the history books. If he had, this story might have taken a very different path because Rex had a huge impact on Murray's life. Murray was the son Rex never had. Often Murray would travel back with his uncle to Nukarni, stopping at every hotel on the way for a couple of beers here and a couple of beers there. But once they reached the farm Rex would get straight to work – he took his farming very seriously. It was always a long trip, but young Murray loved every moment of it. He would sit and listen intently to his uncle's stories about life, about how to cook, how to be independent and the importance of working hard.

Murray was five when Uncle Rex gave him Silver. He lived in the stables behind the hotel, next to the laundry room overlooking Broadway. It's where the local policeman kept his horse too. Every day Murray would jump on Silver's back and with just a halter and a rope he'd ride around the local streets or up and down the foreshore in front of the hotel.

Horses were a common sight back in the '50s because most things were still delivered by horse and cart – bread, milk and even ice which was always in high demand at the hotel. When the ice arrived, it was Murray's job to chip off pieces from the huge blocks kept under hessian bags in the cool room. He'd then put the chipped ice into a calico bag and smash it up with a mallet ready for use in the bar. No doubt Murray would never have thought that instant ice machines would one day take over his job but if he had, he would have wished it would happen sooner – chipping ice in the middle of winter wasn't his idea of fun. So, the arrival of the ice cart brought him no joy, but the milk cart was a totally different story.

Murray loved milk, especially the creamy bit on top. So, he would get up very early and jump up into the horse drawn cart next to the milkman and together they would ride around Nedlands and up to Dalkeith delivering milk. Murray was up and down from the cart – running into every house, carefully placing the milk bottles on the doorsteps. The milkman was very happy for the young lad to do the running and Murray was equally happy, because not only was it a challenge but he was also paid for his work – in cream. A third of a pint to be exact.

Early one morning Hazel, still asleep after yet another late night working in the bar, didn't hear her energetic six year old return from his milk round. The independent Murray didn't wake his mother. Instead after downing his creamy pay packet for breakfast, he decided to ride Silver to kindy – why not, he rode him everywhere else. The two made their way down Broadway and on arriving at Nedlands Kindergarten Murray tied his beloved pony to the playground equipment. The kindergarten teacher was furious to see Silver in the playground. She immediately rang Hazel. "Your son has brought a horse to school." The bar manager was quickly sent to collect Silver who never again made that particular journey with his young owner.

Murray was always up to something; he was a fearless child, apparently not much has changed over the years. His constant antics were exhausting and at times frightening for his parents. A little too often they'd find him hanging precariously from the second storey roof gutters of the hotel. Daringly, he would place hand over hand on the seemingly flimsy gutters to make his way around the metal roof line, which no doubt was sharp in parts. Thankfully, the gutters never gave way or at least not before Murray, tired of his mother's anxious protests, gave up on that particular, perilous amusement.

Murray was a busy child but it was expected that he help around the hotel doing odd jobs. Impactful jobs like counting the money in the tills and then placing the notes and coins into separate calico bags. In the years to come that job had a hugely beneficial influence on his ability to handle money and figures. He was paid a few coins for the work he did but he'd always find a few extra in that 'special room' under the stairs. It was a private room between the bars – which for some reason was called The Killing Pen. It was his mother and father's office during the day but at night friends or business acquaintances would meet and share a bottle of something. It was considered a privilege to be invited into that room for a drink. For Murray, the best part of it was the pearl shell kept up high on a bench – it was always filled with coins. The height was never a deterrent. Murray would simply drag in a bar stool and climb up. He could just reach into the pearl shell, after which he would triumphantly climb down with a fist full of coins. Stephen and Hazel didn't object – they understood their son had expenses like milkshakes or sweet flavoured ice blocks. There was also the regular threepence entry fee into the Nedlands Baths – the jetty and buildings over the water where many children of the day learnt to swim.

Murray was always at the baths with his mates. On one of their daily visits they devised a plan – a contest that would ultimately become a regular but treacherous ritual. It began early one morning while the boys were waiting impatiently for Mr and Mrs Petersen to open the baths. Typically, none wanted to sit still, so, to kill time, they decided to race each other to the other side of the river – a distance of around 5 KM across and back. That is no easy feat – it's a seriously long way for anyone but when you are barely eight it's like swimming the English Channel. That didn't stop any of them. For a bunch of competitive young boys, the word risk or consequence didn't exist. Most of the time they made it there and back without mishap but not every time – there were a few very close calls – not that it was mentioned to anyone outside of their group.

How different life was back then, when children were free to be adventurous, when taking risks was almost expected – almost a rite of passage to manhood. There were no such things as iPads or computers, not to mention mobile phones. Back then life was for living and exploring. Experiences were real, not in cyber space accessed through virtual reality goggles or on a computer screen, where creativity and imaginations are often stifled.

Murray was an adventurous child. He was always respectful and most of the time well behaved – particularly when his father was around. Stephen was a fair man but he commanded respect and so when his father spoke, Murray listened.

Stephen had returned from war where he had seen things no man should ever have to see. Instead of allowing the memories to darken his days he decided to work hard but live life to the absolute fullest.

He loved his wine and his beer. When he ate steak, it was always with an inch of fat on it; when he smoked it was cigarettes with no filters, and if he didn't have any of those, he'd smoke a cigar. Every second weekend he'd take off with the boys to Rottnest – no wives or children allowed! As Murray remembers it, They'd get full of grog on the Friday afternoon and then leave for the island at 8 or 9pm, hours later than planned. After a weekend of more grog, hours upon hours of fishing and constant jokes and hearty laughter they'd all make the 29.5km crossing back to Royal Perth Yacht Club on the Monday morning.

There was no doubt Stephen McHenry enjoyed life, he was a vibrant and fun-loving man, but there was also no denying he didn't look after himself. Murray was eight years old when the consequences of his father's love of the good life had a life changing impact on his young son's world.

It was a Sunday, which meant the hotel wasn't open, so it was a quiet day. The family had just finished lunch, and as usual Stephen had left the table to read his Reader's Digest; Hazel was left to clear the lunch dishes and the children had been excused. Sandra took off for the squash courts on Broadway and Murray raced off to find his mates.

It was a very normal Sunday.

But Murray remembers the moment it changed to anything but normal.

> [Murray] I came back home and there was just grief everywhere. Everybody was trying to comfort my Mother and I was just left standing there like a cartoon character with a question mark over my head asking, "What's going on here?" Then I suddenly realised it was my Father – he'd died. I was told later it was a heart attack.
>
> The first thing I thought about was my sister. I jumped on my bike and took off to the squash courts. I ran in and told her she had to come home with me, but she rebelled and said she wouldn't. So, I had to say, "Look, something has gone seriously wrong." I didn't tell her what it was – I don't know why I didn't tell her, I just felt that I needed to get her back there.
>
> She sat on the seat and I stood up and we made it home. The rest of that day was almost a blur, with people coming and going well into the night.
>
> A few days later, they had the funeral but we weren't allowed to go; these days kids are up front and centre of them, but back then it wasn't seen fit that kids should see that sort of thing. So, we didn't go, but immediately post the funeral we were put on the ferry to Rottnest where Dad's good mate, Kevin O'Keefe, had the Rottnest Hotel.
>
> We stayed over there for a month, living upstairs at the Rottnest Pub. I became the best at the penny arcade and all the rest of it. When we came back, life had sort of returned to normal.

Perhaps normal in the eyes of an eight year old, but maybe not so much for Hazel. Almost immediately after her husband's death the Swan Brewery called an end to the informal lease on the hotel that the McHenrys had held for the last 23 years. With two children, Hazel needed an income. With the help from accountants and friends she managed to hold on and keep the lease going. It wasn't easy, Hazel was still mourning the loss of Stephen but there were children to care for and a hotel to run – so she just steeled herself to keep going. Hazel had been helping Stephen for years anyway, so she knew what needed to be done.

Murray's half-sisters, Joy and Julie, had moved to America a year earlier and after their father's death never returned to Australia, despite still being close to Hazel, Sandra and Murray. So, it was only Sandra and Murray that Hazel had to worry about – but her youngest was up to his usual antics – he just wouldn't sit still. Under enormous stress Hazel announced to Murray that he was going to boarding school. So off he went to Christ Church Grammar in Claremont – a school not too far from Nedlands.

> [Murray] I turned nine in my first term at Christ Church. I was generally good at sport, whether it was cricket, football, it didn't matter, I tried everything. I was also a good swimmer; in my first term at Christ Church I won a few swimming races, so I was immediately accepted.

> Boarding school was mostly full of country boys who in those days were pretty strong blokes. If you were good at sport like I was, they would respect you which was very handy for a nine year old where everyone was bigger and older – up to the 17 year olds.

While the sport side of school was Murray's thing, the academic side certainly wasn't. Fortunately, the years of handling money at the hotel gave him a skill that over the years became extremely beneficial to him in business and continues to be so.

> [Murray] To be honest, doing subjects like physics and chemistry were boring to me – really, I just wanted to get out and play sport. If something didn't come naturally, I just didn't put the extra effort in.

> I don't know why I didn't have that drive to say I had to do it. In comparison kids today seem to be more driven to achieve. Not me, I just couldn't wait for the bell to ring so I could get back out and kick that footy.

> We were also left to our own devices. Back then you never used to see parents screaming and cheering from the sidelines at their child's sports game. Kids are supported in everything they do now; they are driven everywhere and anywhere – if we wanted to do something we had to walk or ride our bikes.

At 13 Murray was given a great opportunity; to be coached in swimming at the brand-new Beatty Park swimming pool in West Perth. It had been purpose built for the Empire Games held in Perth in 1962. However, Beatty Park was a long way from his home, and with no other way to get there Murray had to ride his bike. It was uphill all the way and so Murray would leave the hotel at 5 am and furiously pedal the whole 10km to make it to the pool on time. Often arriving early, he would take a nap on the front steps while waiting for the gates to open. But it was worth it – the swimming coach was Harry Kelly, a legend of the sport. Whilst Murray enjoyed the challenge and the pressure, he was not used to the demands or the style of a professional coach.

> [Murray] I really wanted to train with Harry but every session he made me do ten laps just kicking with a board in front. I found that type of training boring. I just wanted to swim; I didn't want to kick. So, I didn't last long and eventually stopped swimming training altogether, although I still swam for the school. I always got beaten in freestyle but won in breaststroke along with another guy, Keith Bower. He was a school cricketer and didn't train either, but for whatever reason we were both good at breaststroke. I should have kept going with Harry Kelly, but that's history.

Football had also grabbed Murray's attention – it was another sport he loved and so again he put in the effort. But as so often happens in football, injuries see you play one week but not the next. That slowed him down, but it never stopped him loving the game; as would be seen in the years ahead. Then there was cricket – a sport that grabbed his time but not his passion. It was during the cricket season that one of the school's rowers tapped him on the shoulder.

"Why don't you come down to the boat club and give rowing a go?" Why not Murray thought. Little did he know the decision to give it a go would be the start of a passion that would stay with him for life.

> [Murray] I'm not sure if I found rowing or rowing found me. My Uncle Alex, who had the Subiaco Hotel, had won four King's Cup races, and Dad's mates, Gra Rosser and Murray Church, were both King's Cup rowers. Every year I would be at the Head of the River on Murray's boat, Mountain Lass, which was the "official/unofficial" boat that raised the letters when the boats crossed the finish line. So, I was surrounded by rowing from an early age but for whatever reason I was never that interested in getting involved myself.

It was 1966, Murray had just turned 15. It was part way through the season, leading into the Head of the River when he decided to give rowing a go. He was selected for the second eight and while they didn't win the Head of the River, Murray had proven he was a valuable member of the team.

The following season no other sport got a look in; the river and the rowing shed was all Murray was interested in. His return was rewarded with not only a place in the first eight, but he was also made Captain of Boats. On the first training session of the season the crew were back out on the water. They had just finished racing against Aquinas College and had turned their boat toward home when the coach called out to Murray telling him to change sides. That was the last thing Murray expected or wanted to hear. He didn't believe he was up to it and was concerned it would bring an end to his rowing; but you don't argue with your coach.

As it turned out he needn't have worried. He was a natural; an ambidextrous rower. By the time the training session was over Murray was able to row anywhere in the boat – position 1, 2, 7, 8 – every position came easily to him. Little did he know that a few years down the track that skill would give him a totally unexpected opportunity that would change the direction of all things to come.

[Murray] We had a really good bunch of guys in our crew and as Captain of Boats I remember saying to them, "Come on, we're going to win this year. We're not doing this to come second."

Everyone was motivated so we started a rowing camp. We decided we'd go to Mandurah to train. Mark Hohnen was in our crew and he was friends with the Manford family who owned Manfords Transport company. They put our boats on the back of one of their flat top trucks – trailers hadn't been invented. A couple of our crew already had their driver's licence so they drove us down there and we stayed at a beach house that belonged to the family of one of the other boys in our boat, John Meyer.

Over that 10 days we trained solidly, twice a day. We had fun and we really bonded but at the same time we were totally driven. It was great.

I was technically the captain of boats but the important thing about any team sport is the ability to work together. Having one person with the drive doesn't work – luckily, we had eight.

By the time our coach Don Fraser got back with us, we'd done a lot of work and there was an enormous team spirit. We ended up dead heating with Scotch College winning the Head of the River; in fact, we broke the record by 15 seconds. That record has never been broken – mainly because it used to be a mile but now it's 2,000m.

It's amazing the bond that came out of that success and it's still there today. A few of us still see each other on a regular basis and in 2017 all eight of us met up for our 50-year reunion. We spent it having lunch out on the river – there wasn't an oar in sight, but there was plenty of beer and wine.

As he was as a child, he was as a teen - energetic. He needed to be constantly occupied, to have fun and to be challenged. Christ Church provided that opportunity, enabling him to grow and develop as a person; but it was the passion and commitment of two remarkable teachers that had the greatest influence on his life at school and life beyond.

[Murray] As a boarder your teachers can have a real impact on you. One in particular was a fellow called Dean Bowker. He had been a student and captain at the school and returned as a teacher. To earn extra income, he lived on the school grounds. Whenever we had 'Father Sunday', without a dad I'd go, "Well what am I going to do?" And every year he'd say, "I'm coming with you." That made me feel so much better. He became a close mate right through my whole school life. He also did a lot for the school and for the community. I saw that and the way everyone respected him and I guess in a way I wanted to be like that too.

Another fantastic teacher was Akos Kovacs. It was because of him that I did gymnastics for a while. He was Hungarian with a very dry sense of humour and was always telling us these very colourful stories – I can only assume they were all true.

As boarders, we were at school all weekend, so we'd all go to the gym and do vaulting and climbing up ropes. It was wonderful to have that kind of an activity and a guy like him who was so dedicated to teaching.

At times he was tough on the kids who were a bit fat, which today you wouldn't get away with, but he taught us to watch what we ate and how to get our bodies in shape. Everyone took on board what he had to say and made changes to how we actually did look after ourselves. He was way before his time.

He passed away a few years ago but a lot of his stuff is still on the wall at Christ Church. He was really good at drawing and so he would draw up these sets of exercises and put them up on the boards in the gym so we could follow them. He was amazing – an extraordinary man; even now people remember and talk highly of him.

It just goes to show the influence teachers can have on young minds. A child is so much more capable of achieving if they are engaged, if they feel they belong, if they are guided by good values and actions, taught to set goals and encouraged to make a positive contribution and commitment to the broader community. I'm sure most would agree that every child should have that opportunity and every teacher should be encouraged and supported to provide that opportunity.

So, while weekends were spent at school, come school holidays it was back to the hotel to see his mother and sister and where life would return somewhat to normal. A change to that routine came in the school holidays of 1958 when Murray and Sandra accepted an invitation from their Uncle Rex's daughter Judy. She was working for the Bennit family at their Springfield Riding school in Bassendean (one of the biggest and most well-known riding schools in Western Australia). Judy wanted Sandra and Murray to go out and stay for a week. Little did either realise that what started as a mere school holiday activity would come to play a significant role in both their lives.

[Murray] We got infatuated with that week; mucking out stalls, feeding horses and riding. We didn't have our own horses so we just rode the school horses. It was amazing.

Over the journey, I did a couple of school holiday stays and one day they asked me to come back and work part-time. We got free accommodation and meals but you worked your butt off for that whole period. When we had time, we'd ride out through Midland to the back of Herne Hill where it was all low-lying land and in winter it would turn into lakes. We'd ride the horses through the water – it would be up to their chests but it was great fun.

I eventually did my instructor's certificate in equestrian, by which time I had my own horses. A group of us would travel around in this nine-horse float – sort of a prime mover, with living quarters and horse float. Off we would go to the Merredin Show, we'd go down south and out to Serpentine. Some were small trips, like to Kalamunda – then we'd just ride up there from Bassendean. It was quite a trek up the hill with the horses; when we got there, we'd compete all day and then ride home. We spent a huge amount of time outside and that suited all of us.

In 1959 Sandra and Murray started competing at the Royal Show. So, Murray's time was spent between boarding school, competing in equestrian events, rowing at school and in Saturday regattas. When he wasn't at a regatta, he was kicking a football or watching his favourite football team, East Fremantle, play against other West Australian Football League (WAFL) sides.

As his involvement and skill in equestrian events grew, so too did the time he needed to spend in the saddle. That meant he often had to leave school early to give him enough time to catch the train all the way out to Bassendean, do his riding and then back again. By the time he was on the train heading back to school it was dark. Hazel, concerned for her son's welfare decided that if he wanted to keep riding, he would have to do so as a day boy. While Murray loved being a boarder, he wanted to ride and so accepted her decision. Life soon became even busier, and within what seemed like a few moments in time, his days at Christ Church came to an end.

So, with school now behind him, Murray had finished with rowing for Christ Church but, as it turned out, rowing wasn't finished with Murray. With the camaraderie and success of winning the Head of the River, having an oar in hand had become a natural part of his life. The West Australian Rowing Club, based out of the sheds that still stand at the bottom of Barrack Street in Perth, was where Murray next showed his dedication to the sport. Within months he was racing with the club in Perth and over in Melbourne. It was his enthusiasm and his readiness to assist that made Murray a popular club member and probably the reason he received a phone call that would lead to a far greater involvement in the sport.

[Murray] They were calling for nominations for the King's Cup of 1969, which is the State Eight and the only interstate rowing competition at the time. There was only ever one race a year and each club had to put an eight-man crew out and those who'd nominated for the King's Cup would be selected out of that.

I was doing pre-season football training with Claremont Colts when I got a phone call asking if I could go and help out at the rowing club. The club hadn't nominated me but I went down anyway and rowed at the back of the boat. At the end someone said, "Has everyone had a fair go?" I'd been talking to this guy from Fremantle Rowing Club and although I didn't know him, he shouted out pointing at me and said, this guy can row both sides of the boat. So, they took another boat out and got me to row in different positions. Because I could row both sides (not many people used to do it back then) they selected me as the reserve on the team.

I was only 18 when the average age of the crew that year was 34 but every night at training someone was missing so I'd always get a row — which was all great.

I took training very seriously but I remember when I'd just bought my first car, a tan ute, I wanted to take a few days off to drive up to a friend's sheep station at Quobba, just north of Carnarvon and then on to the Winning Pool Races. It was a good drive up but, on the way home I had two English blokes with me and all we wanted to do was get back to Quobba to see the sunset and eat oysters off the rocks. I was speeding because the sun was already starting to set. I could see something ahead but I just thought it was haze on the road. As I got closer this thing stood up — it was cow and I went, "Oh shit, everyone, brace yourselves!" I was going 140 km an hour. I had a roo bar so I just gripped the wheel shouting at the other two, "I've got to go straight! I can't go off the road or we'll roll."

We hit the animal dead centre. It came up over the bonnet and ripped the cab off the ute, turning it into a coupé.

I was covered in cow shit and our luggage was strewn all over the road. I looked across at the two guys sitting there on the bench seat next to me and just burst out laughing. The guy in the middle had hit his head on the dash and the radio button was stuck on his forehead – it hadn't gone through or anything but it looked so funny. We couldn't get the car started and it started to get really cold so we started a fire of sorts. Then we saw headlights coming towards us; it was Mark and David Hohnen, my sister and a few others; they'd been following us back from the races. They towed us into Carnarvon. The next day I went into Wesfarmers, bought some goggles and drove back to Perth on my own; no one wanted to drive with me in the coupé. Let me tell you, that was a pretty hard and tiring drive but I had to get back for training.

It was a good lesson and we were very lucky. I think the experiences that you get away from unscathed in life teach you a lot. I'd spent time on the farm with my Uncle Rex and I think I knew not to slam on my brakes and just keep the wheel straight. If I hadn't, we would have rolled and that probably would have killed us. But it didn't, and I made it back and went straight to training.

Australia had won silver in rowing at the Mexico Olympics and so the Australian coach came over to Perth to look at the talent that was around. It was a Saturday morning. We took the boat all the way from Wesley College right up to the back of Clontarf. Of course, everybody had turned up, so as the reserve I was in the speedboat with my old rowing coach from Christ Church, Don Fraser, who also happened to be the King's Cup Chairman of Selectors.

So, there I was sitting in the boat getting bored shitless and just watching and listening. We got to the Canning River and the Australian Coach said, "What about the bloke in the boat there, I haven't seen him yet." It was like I had big 'R' for Reserve on my forehead. I remember he swore and said, "Surely I'm going to see him row."

So, they pulled the boat up on the beach and I got in. I was shitting myself, I thought hang on a minute, I'm on display here, so I was concentrating like buggery. Then they pulled the boat up and the coach said, "I want you to move up to another seat." They'd started me at the tail end and I worked my way up the boat until finally I was in the seven seat – and that's where I rowed in the 1969 King's Cup in Bundaberg, Queensland.

Being the youngest rower in the race was daunting in some ways but exciting so I wasn't particularly fazed and even less so after the race started.

I learnt a lot about what it takes to reach the top of the sport from that regatta. Firstly, we hadn't done the work required to win as rowing in WA, being a winter sport unlike on the east coast, meant we didn't have any racing before the King's Cup so we didn't have the fresh racing experience or conditioning. You can't be up there if you haven't put the work in.

You can't be up there if you haven't put the work in.

I came back to Perth immediately after my first King's Cup as I had to compete at the Royal Show. Not only had I not been in a saddle for nearly six months and so was all over the place, but I was also heavier. When I started rowing all I did was lift a couple of barbells but as it got more serious, I had to do more weight training and so was bulking up. I realised it was the time to make a choice between the two sports. Whilst I continued to ride for enjoyment, I was far more absorbed in my rowing – so I gave it everything, or at least at the time I thought I did. Now when I look back, I do think I could have done better.

The Australian coach then asked me to move to Sydney to row at Sydney Rowing Club and be a part of his quest for the Australian team, but I was unable to leave WA because I had to support my Mother at the hotel.

By 1970 Murray was back rowing for WA but a disagreement with his coach brought an end to that years King's Cup competition.

The following year Murray's sister, Sandra, escaped the confines of the hotel. She married winemaker David Hohnen and moved down to his family farm in Margaret River. David's brother, Mark Hohnen, had rowed with Murray at Christ Church and it was their friendship that had brought the two families together. David, after graduating in viticulture and oenology, returned to Margaret River where he was keen to use and further his knowledge.

Back then Vasse Felix and Cullen Wines were the only wineries in the region, and so David, Mark and Giles – the third Hohnen brother – established a small vineyard on the outskirts of Margaret River. They named it Cape Mentelle. Murray, with Steve's as a premium outlet for good wine, stepped on board as retail support.

Within six years they had their first commercial release and with that came an indication of what was to come. In 1983 and 1984 Cape Mentelle won the coveted Jimmy Watson Memorial Award for the best one-year-old dry red wine, cementing its position as a premium winemaker.

[Murray] My interest and passion for wine and the industry started well before my connection with Cape Mentelle. While my Dad was a prisoner of war in Italy he fell in love with wine. So, every Sunday night at home, he would open a bottle and ask us to taste it and give our opinion. Consequently, at a very early age, Sandra and I learned to understand and appreciate wine. She and I then set about establishing one of Perth's first drive-through liquor stores at the hotel and together we selected the wines we sold. Eventually, having a winemaker like David Hohnen as my brother-in-law took my interest in wine to another level. Then of course the hotel and the wine store within became an exceptional outlet to sell Cape Mentelle wine.

While both David and Mark ran the business side of Cape Mentelle, David also had the role of winemaker and wine marketer. Meanwhile, Murray was still working with his mother at the hotel and in his words, it was driving him nuts. As a person who couldn't sit still, he was always on the lookout for new opportunities and challenges. When Murray heard the Bassendean Hotel was up for sale his interest was positively piqued – only problem, where would he find the $300,000 he needed to buy it. He turned to his mother for advice and a loan and in that discussion convinced her they should buy it together. Murray was now well and truly stepping out from behind his parents' shadow as he became owner and publican of his own hotel.

[Murray] I was back into rowing so I moved into one of the upstairs guest rooms out at Bassendean. It worked well because training for the '71 King's Cup was on the river at Ashfield which was only a few minutes down the road. I'd get up in the morning to train then back to the hotel; on busy nights I'd head back down to the Nedlands Park Hotel to help out there. I had a manager of sorts so I floated between the two. It was pretty hard work because they were long days but for a bloke in his early 20s it was good, strong discipline, and all in all it was a lot of fun.

Murray had grown up watching his parents work hard, so he did the same. By doing so he managed to pay his mother out within 15 months of borrowing from her and renovate the hotel – not bad for a boy of 22. Looking back Murray believes that while it was very tough to lose his father when so young, it made him independent, taught him how to think and fend for himself and to take every opportunity that came his way.

[Murray] I think when kids are pushed out of their comfort zones, they excel. I think when kids are mollycoddled, they take a long time to get out of that cocoon. Let people have their way, let them get out and if they make a mistake, they will learn from it. I mean you're going to make mistakes, everyone does, there's no such thing as perfect but when you make a blue, just accept it, correct it and get on with it.

> *We all make mistakes, there's no such thing as perfect but when you make a blue, accept it, learn from it, correct it and get on with it.*

In 1972, only a year after buying the Bassendean Hotel, Murray's so-called marble was selected from the "call-up hat" of the National Service. This could so easily have meant disaster for both hotels because not having him there to help his mother in Nedlands or at the Bassendean there was every likelihood they would run into serious decline. Never one to let an obstacle get in his way, Murray went straight to the brigadier to explain what it would mean to his mother's and his own business if he had to drop everything and go away for two years.

You don't get if you don't ask.

[Murray] The brigadier was really understanding and organised for me to stay in WA to do all the training that was required. I had to move between different units but I had my nights off for work and weekends off for training. The only time I wasn't able to work was when we went away on camps; attendance at those was compulsory.

It was a full-on life and I was working seven days a week, but other than trying to be an athlete at the same time (which was a real challenge) and the food was crap, I really enjoyed my time in the Army. After my two-year stint I was back at Bassendean. It was running well and so I really wanted to sell it at that time but there were other pubs up for sale so I decided to lease it out instead.

In 1976 with the pub leased, Murray was back rowing a double skull with John Vos (his pair oared partner of eight years) focussing on the Montreal Olympics. He was determined and worked hard to make it happen; but it wasn't to be. Perhaps destiny raised its hand. If he hadn't been pipped at the post on the Nepean River and lost the opportunity to represent Australia, the pages of this next metamorphic chapter may never have been written.

[Murray] I was pretty disappointed when I missed out on the Olympics. I rowed in another King's Cup and also started coaching Christ Church Grammar for the Head of the River in 1977, but I started thinking, do I try for the next Olympics and go on for another four years? I thought I should but it was really hard in WA because we didn't have enough here – the isolation made it a very tough path to selection so the only choice I had was to move to Sydney – and that wasn't an option.

Despite making the decision to remain in Perth, Murray, now 27, was determined to row in the XXII Olympiad in Moscow. He just happened to be over in Sydney rowing, when he received a life changing phone call from friend and CEO of the Swan Brewery, Lloyd Zampatti. The Swan Brewery was about to move from their old site in Mounts Bay Road to their new purpose-built brewery in Canning Vale but had overspent in the development and now something had to give.

[Murray] Lloyd said to me, "Murray, I don't know if this is good news or bad news, but we're going to sell the hotel (the Nedlands Park Hotel)."

My initial reaction was, "Yeah, great. Do your best work – and no we're not interested because I'm more interested in my rowing."

I rang my Mother and she told me Dennis Marshall and Alan Bond (Bondy) had been all over the place that afternoon. Dennis is a good mate of mine today and later in life I got on well with Bondy but, I'd only just got the call. So, to have those dudes running around the place saying they were going to buy it on the same day I'd been told, really angered me.

The next morning, I was on the plane heading back home. I'd had a sleepless night of thinking and had decided, no, I've got to go back and do something about this – those guys are not going to get it.

Back in those days the Bondys of the world seemed to get whatever they wanted in Perth, and that fired me up – determination not to allow that to happen drove me to go back and tell Lloyd I was interested – how much?

I was told 30 Swan Brewery hotels were going to auction on the same day but they were giving their long-standing tenants the right to make a pre-auction bid. They didn't give me a price and I didn't know where to start, so I went in at half a million. Over 10 days I went in and out of their office at the old Emu Brewery to drop in yet another offer, only to keep getting it rejected by phone. So back in I'd go with another offer. I went up $50,000 with every bid and then on the tenth day I got to the million and that's when they finally said yes.

I was over the moon but then I thought, shit, now I've got to find the million, so that was the first problem. Second problem was nobody would give me the money. I was literally standing out the front of a bank on St Georges Terrace, probably looking a little overwhelmed, when this guy tapped me on the shoulder and said, "G'day Murray." It was Peter Lucas who'd grown up down the road from us in Nedlands. He asked what I was doing.

"Trying to borrow money off a bloody bank, they're a mob of wankers."

"That's why they're called bankers," he said. He could see I was pretty upset.

After I explained what was going on, he asked me to come over the road to his office. I had no idea what he did. I walked in and on the door were the letters CIBC – Canadian Imperial Banking Company. I later learned that the infamous Laurie Connell had been running it and had just exited to run Rothwell's; Peter had taken his place as the new head.

He said, "Look, I reckon the story's great, Canada's not awake yet but give me the rest of the day and I'll let you know."

So, I waited. In my view, things happen because they should happen, you create your own destiny and opportunities. Things go wrong; GFCs don't help, mining collapses and stock market collapses don't help and big organisations that affect the whole world with their conduct don't help. It's very hard to plan for these events but if you fly by the seat a little, stay focussed, believe in what you're doing and you're reasonably sensible about it, things usually work out alright.

Things go wrong. It's very hard to plan for these events but if you fly by the seat a little, stay focussed, believe in what you're doing and you're reasonably sensible, things usually work out alright.

Later that evening I got a phone call from Peter to say CIBC were going to back me in. So, all of a sudden I had a Canadian bank lending me a million dollars to buy the property my family had leased and lived in since 1935. It felt great to actually own it. As it was, our leasehold interests would have been worth nothing if I hadn't purchased the freehold.

But then I had this huge mortgage and needed to focus on paying it off – that's when I gave up on my dream of rowing for Australia. Someone said to me winning's not everything and I said, excuse me, of course winning is everything, but you have to know how to lose. You don't go into anything without wanting to win but if you're not successful then dust yourself off and move on. That's more important than anything. So that's what I did. I was still coaching Christ Church in the Head of the River and rowing with a mate, Peter Shakespeare, who was coaching us for the WA '78 King's Cup. As I hadn't won one, I was really putting in, but I was burning the candle at both ends. I was working late nights, every night, and I knew my heart wasn't in it as much as it needed to be.

I was totally exhausted and pretty worried that I'd borrowed too much money. So, I made the decision to stop rowing altogether and just concentrated on running the hotel and getting rid of that mortgage as fast as I could.

As an investment for my half-sisters, Dad had bought them the old tearoom site across the road from the hotel. When they moved to America, Hazel, to help them out financially, organised for our family trust to buy it from them. Then in 1966 the trust built Comnee flats on the site. When I took out my million-dollar loan we decided to sell the flats and pour the funds into the mortgage. Armstrong Jones bought them and converted the purple titled block into strata units and sold them off individually; you can still see the old name, Comnee Flats, although I think some of the letters have fallen off over the years.

Having grown up in a hotel, running one came relatively easy to Murray, but having a massive mortgage on top of all the other responsibilities was a whole new ball game. Action and some out-there thinking was needed, and Murray delivered. But it was the ease and his fresh and gutsy approach to taking that action that took him from the ordinary to extraordinary. To succeed, he knew changes had to be made and gut instinct told him exactly where to start.

[Murray] The Nedlands Park Hotel was a terrible name, just too cumbersome, so I changed it simply to Steve's — everyone called it that anyway. That was the start of the new era.

Sunday trading in the city was the next change. Country pubs had been serving alcohol on Sundays for years — it was the reason why so many people would make the drive out to places like the Mundaring Weir Hotel or down to Waikiki on a Sunday — just so they could get a drink. But in 1971 drinking in a pub on a Sunday was introduced in the city — the same year the drinking age dropped from 21 to 18. Initially, it was just for an hour on a Sunday morning and two hours in the afternoon from 4 pm but soon the hours were increased to two hours in the morning and three in the afternoon.

When it started in the city it was quite exciting; no one in the industry had any idea what it was going to be like. I decided that I wanted to make Steve's popular — the place to come to have fun. I love live music, so I introduced it to Steve's and that really brought people in. When we had our first Sunday morning opening it was good; we had a great turnout and I thought shit, but then the afternoon came and it just went crazy. We had 2,000 people trying to get in.

I introduced live music to Steve's. When we had our first Sunday morning opening it was good; but then the afternoon came and it just went crazy.

From then on, we did as much trade in those three hours every Sunday afternoon as we did for the rest of the week. It was huge and so was the preparation. At that point I was still rowing; if I wasn't out rowing on the Sunday morning, I was out coaching. I'd come back and sometimes I'd lie on the floor and have a short kip and then get ready for the afternoon session. That was a massive exercise. A lot of my rowing mates came in and worked, they were all strong guys and able to heave things around. We had to put temporary bars outside because it was an old building and wasn't set up to achieve what it had to achieve on those nights. Then it was getting the quantity of stock behind the bar that we knew we were going to need; from potato chips to dare I say it, cigarettes, which back in those days, represented a massive amount in sales. Moving the kegs was a big job on its own. They were 18-gallon kegs, which is about 80 litres, and   we had to line them up in the cellar and then every hour I'd go down and add another one into the line. The easy part was, there was only one beer, Swan Lager, and nothing else, not like today where there's thirty different beers on tap. Our record in one night was 42 kegs. Some pubs only do five to eight kegs a week, and we did 42 in three hours.

My role was mainly coordinating. Mobile phones didn't exist back then, so I had to continually move between the bars, checking everything was running smoothly and that stock levels were okay. I had to make sure we had the right mix of people working together. Good people behind the bar are those that hear each other's orders. Even if it's an order of four different types of drinks, they have it half in their head, so they know where the other person is about to move to. If someone doesn't have that sixth sense, they bump into everyone and that slows everything down; they are a pain in the backside to work with.

There was always something going on somewhere. We had more people inside than we could fit but there was the same amount lined up on the street outside, trying to get in. It would stay electric right through the whole three hours and when we finally stopped serving, we'd feel this sense of relief – we'd made it through another night – but then it was clean up. That took anywhere up to an hour and a half and then once everything was put away the group would sit around and have a beer together. In those days we'd only have one or two beers and that was it. Then you would just collapse and go to bed.

While it was exhausting it was a lot of fun. But pubs were different back then, people went out to have a good time. We didn't have security; we didn't need security. If there ever was an issue, you'd go and sort it out yourself. If somebody was being a little bit stupid, you'd go and tap them on the shoulder and they'd take one look at you and go, okay. You were respected.

But then we moved into an era where licensed premises had to have crowd control and that's when everything changed.

The crowd controllers would come dressed in black. During the day, they'd always have the dark sunglasses on, all pumped up from their gym workouts; they looked like blokes wanting to have a fight. That, in my opinion, changed some people's mentality, it incited people to misbehave in front of them, particularly after a few drinks.

But then we moved into an era where licensed premises had to have crowd control and that's when everything changed.

I might have been wrong, but I was totally opposed to it. I thought it was unnecessary to inflict them on us because up until then the amount of trouble we'd had was minimal – but it increased with crowd controllers. I had no say in who was sent out and I wasn't happy about that although if I thought the crowd controller was someone who would cause problems I'd phone and ask them not to send them again.

It was also incredibly expensive. You had to have two security workers just to open your doors and then an extra one per hundred people or whatever it was. So all of a sudden before we knew it, we had 12, 14, 15 crowd controllers floating around. The bill for the night could be in the thousands of dollars just for crowd controllers so then you had to up your margins to pick that up.

Today there's even more security in busy pubs and clubs but it's warranted these days because there's no respect; you go and tap somebody on the shoulder, and it's likely someone will push you or worse.

Nights out are also much longer than they used to be. If you go back to the '70s, people went to nightclubs or they went to hotels, they didn't do both. Pubs started out with a 10 pm closing, then it went to 11 o'clock, then midnight until the 1 am closing that we have now. People would come and have a drink and have fun, yes, they'd get a bit merry but then they'd head home, so it wasn't a problem. Now nightclubs are open until 6 am and so binge-type drinking goes on into the wee hours of the morning. Often, it's the lolly drinks because they are easier to keep drinking than beer which just bloats you – and that's when you have problems.

Things have really changed around the place, but Steve's was and probably still is very much a community pub. The core group of people that came here were a regular mix from young ones to older ones, and although it's slowly changing, a lot of those people have fond memories of Steve's. But it was the live music that really made Steve's different and why I believe people kept coming back.

I was a huge live music fan, so I'd go out and listen to bands practising in their garages. The first thing I'd look for was if the music made me feel happy. Then, if I thought they were good I'd get them to come and play at Steve's. The bands always wanted to play their original stuff, so I'd say that's great, I like what you're doing but you can't just play that. The music has to make the crowd happy, so you'll have to mix in covers with your original stuff. People are at a pub, not a concert where they pay to hear your originals. You have to play to the crowd.

I remember one of the bands I went to have a look at was three brothers – Andrew, Tim and Jon. They lived around the corner; I think it was on Mountjoy Road in Nedlands where they practised in their garage. They called themselves The Farriss Brothers. They were really good, so I asked them to come and play at the hotel.

Many years later on Australia Day I was at a function on the rooftop of Fraser's Restaurant in Kings Park. The Farriss Brothers had changed their name to INXS and they had a new lead vocalist, Michael Hutchence. They were the feature band for the Australia Day fireworks and so they were all over the radio which of course was booming out at the function. During an interview one of them said, "We got our start here in Perth at Steve's in Nedlands."

That was pretty amazing to hear.

We also had Brett Townsend and Tracy Caspersz who had the Boogie Street Band. There was Dave Hole, Loaded Dice, Fingerprint, Jim Fisher and the Outlaws – all really good bands.

They were great days and I'd like to say I made it all happen with no mistakes, but to be honest I went with the flow and gut feeling and it just worked, but it was never easy – it was a lot of hard slog.

I have to say hard work has never bothered me – I got that from my Mother who had a really hard work ethic. She followed through on everything and was incredibly accurate – almost over-accurate! She'd spend hours upon hours doing the bookkeeping making sure it was right – nothing ever escaped her. She had this second sense. If she thought something was missing she was generally right and pretty much knew where to look for it, or who was likely to have misplaced or stolen it, and if it was the latter, she'd move them on immediately. No second chances.

I guess I picked up on a lot of what she did – I'm fanatical on stock; if it's missing, why is it missing? I too have that second sense when something's not right. You have to have trust in your people in hospitality but unfortunately that trust is often abused, so the important thing is to be constantly aware of what's going on. If you do find an issue you have to stop it – get rid of the problem quickly. Back in Mum's day if she wasn't happy with someone, she just got rid of them no questions asked. These days, if you move people on there are repercussions, so you must find ways to manage them out of your business. I don't run that side of the business anymore as I have managers to take care of those day-to-day issues, but I still watch over. If I see something I'll talk to the manager and say, "Hey, this is my feel on this person – have a look and if you can see it, I suggest you find a way to move them on."

If you've got someone who's just in the job to take your money and not look after your customers, then there's no point having them - you need to get rid of them, quickly.

The problems aren't always about stealing, it could be a bad work ethic; an inability to service the customers; are they there for the right reasons? Business is about making money, so if you've got someone who's just in the job to take your money and not look after your customers, then there's no point having them – you need to get rid of them, quickly. I tell every staff member that the person they are serving is paying their wages, so treat them right, and if they don't – they're out the door.

When I travel, particularly in Europe, that's when I generally receive great customer service. They just know how to treat people, but they are also proud of what they do; delivering great customer service is just part of that. When I'm away I'm always watching and for that reason often pick up fresh ideas and new ways of doing things. I don't go out of my way to look for them but when you're open to opportunities and ideas you just seem to notice things more. So, my advice – be open.

I don't go out of my way to look for them but when you're open to opportunities and ideas you just seem to notice things more. So, my advice - be open.

I think it was after one of my trips away that I realised that the guest rooms upstairs at Steve's were well past their use-by date – there was plenty of superior accommodation around Perth, so I felt those rooms could be put to better use.

With my enjoyment of wine and food I felt we could really use the space to do something very different to what others were doing in Perth. I also felt a portion of our clients who had moved on in life from the youth market and were now young professionals, wanted something different. So, my plan for upstairs was to create the kind of place they would want to come to.

The walls upstairs were like the concrete tilt up panels you see today, and the floorboards ran straight underneath. So, we removed every second wall between the rooms to create a number of large, private dining rooms. We started wine dinners and established Stephenie's restaurant – Stephenie's being the feminine of Steve's. Again, trying to do something different I brought a chef over from Melbourne, David Braim, who I'd met, and liked his food. So downstairs it was still counter meals like every other suburban pub in Perth but upstairs we took dining to another level, almost fine dining but not quite.

The team running Stephenie's did an amazing job. I lost count of the number of Gold Plate awards we won for quality of food and service, as well as the wine list. As owners we set the goals and help achieve them but it's the staff who really win those awards

We then put in another bar and closed off the front driveway, so we had room to put more tables and chairs. We did it all quietly without council approval because we knew if we asked, they would knock us back. When they eventually came in to look at what we were up to we said the changes had been made way back – they accepted that and nothing more was ever said.

Another initiative in an attempt to capture more of the market was the creation of Steve's Fine Dining and Food Club. People would join to get special prices on their food and wine that they either consumed at the hotel or they could take home. It was hugely successful.

We've always been driven by wine sales and as such we made sure we had the best selection of any outlet in Perth to attract the wine consumers. We also had Steve's drive-through bottle shop which gave us a competitive edge despite the fact that wine sales represented only 20 per cent of our business, the other 80 per cent was food and beverage. As liquor stores evolved and became extremely good with their selections we had to compete even more strongly.

Finding new ways to compete keeps business interesting, which is good for me because I get bored doing the same thing day after day. So, one day I was analysing the diversity of our business; knowing that selling wine was a very strong part of what we did I decided we needed to control the market a bit more. I found the way to do that when Broadway Fair Liquor Store, up the road from the hotel, came up for sale. An old colleague, Jeff Dunstan, owned it with his in-laws. Jeff later left his brother-in-law to run it, so he could move to the Old Bridge Cellars liquor store in North Fremantle. However, many of the Nedlands clients followed him and that caused a family squabble to erupt so the Nedlands store was put on the market.

I jumped in and bought it a month or so before Christmas 1981 thinking – right, now I have Broadway covered. But then I needed someone really sharp to run it.

I rang Jeff who suggested a fellow called Laurie Hurley. Laurie was a great marketer not necessarily of wine but certainly of liquor. I enjoyed his style and so offered him a percentage of the store for free, on the basis that he would come and run it. He agreed but couldn't start until well after Christmas.

A couple of weeks later Laurie rang me and asked if I knew San Remo in Wembley and Como. I had no idea what he was talking about; I thought San Remo was spaghetti. It turned out they were liquor stores owned by Myer and were up for sale. So, I asked the agent to meet and have a talk about them and before I knew it, I'd bought both stores.

I thought San Remo was spaghetti. It turned out they were liquor stores owned by Myer and were up for sale.

I took them over between Christmas and New Year; Laurie still hadn't joined me, so all of a sudden, I was up to my armpits trying to organise them, do a stocktake and deal with the Christmas trade. It was a huge job but it was well worth it. Over the following two or three years, we bought the freeholds and built them up, particularly the Wembley store. Tony Saddler was right next door. Tony was a charismatic character and a huge marketer, so we fed off each other. That, together with Laurie as the driving force, turned them into fantastic liquor stores for us.

Jeff Dunstan came and joined us, and we branded the group McHenry, Dunstan and Hurley. We kept buying more and at one point had eight stores; Kalgoorlie, Geraldton, Broadway Fair, Dalkeith, Como, Wembley, Steve's and also Jeff's own store in Mount Lawley which was included in the rebrand. Eventually, some years later, we bought the Mt Lawley store and the freehold from Jeff.

Jeff fell out of the group after about six months and Laurie and I continued in a 20-80 per cent ownership respectively. We worked well together and built all the stores up to a level that attracted investor interest.

I'm a person who loves an asset, which isn't smart; I never buy anything with the intention of rolling it over - taking the money and running. But an opportunity came up at a time when I had realised, we were turning over massive amounts of money but not making a lot of profit and Steve's was propping it up all the time. Laurie was a great marketer and he knew how to shift stock but watching the bottom line was not his strongest point. So, at the end of '87 when I had an offer to do something different, I chose to sell all the stores – they all sold to the one buyer.

Back then there were a few sly operators in the industry who would advertise and undercut everyone else – even if they didn't have the stock. That kind of destroyed the marketplace, so it was good that we got out when we did. By that time, I had invested with a friend and started Hisco - a hospitality industry equipment supply business.

One of the assets my Father had was a 20 per cent share in a restaurant supply company called Gibsons & Paterson. It was a Sydney based firm which came to Perth in 1956 but when they couldn't make it work here, they decided to get out. The Teasdales who were managing it at the time thought the business was about to cross into profit, so they got three hoteliers to back them. My Father, a fellow called Dolph Clowes, who had the Rivervale Hotel, and the Quinlivans from the Ocean Beach Hotel – each took a 20 per cent share.

Eventually it came time for the Teasdales to retire so they offered Gibsons & Paterson to the three shareholders. I was still rowing and had no time and no interest in the business, neither did Dolph, so the Quinlivans bought the whole lot. A friend of mine, Bryan Greatrex who was working in an opposition company said, "Murray, why didn't you buy it, I would have run it for you!"

Twelve months later, in 1985, I agreed to back Bryan and together with Graeme Fitzsimmons we started Hisco. With good connections and associations already in the industry we had instant growth and that underpinned our future success.

I realised at that point Murray was quite different in his approach. Like most successful business-people Murray believes that to succeed in business you must surround yourself with good people. But Murray takes it one step further. He doesn't just employ good people he backs them; he goes into business with them. By doing so he is then able to continue with his own interests whilst leaving his business partner to run a business they are passionate about, have a solid knowledge of and have a highly vested interest in making it work.

Throughout our interview Murray kept reiterating, "It's all about people", and that was certainly proving to be true with Hisco.

> [Murray] Bryan Greatrex had the gift of the gab, he was everyone's mate in a pub, he had an ability to sell and had the confidence of the clients – basically he commanded the market. We overtook Gibsons and Paterson very quickly; today we are by far the dominant player even though there are now two multinationals in the market, and two or three smaller ones.
>
> But it hasn't all been smooth sailing, and you do make mistakes that in this business can prove costly. When you have a nice long lead-time, like a year, you can bring in container loads but then it's all yours and so you have to be sure that no matter when you release the product it is going to be saleable. Initially, when we got a company order, if they wanted their name on everything, we'd get it organised and then they'd draw down on it. But over the journey we've learned that's the worst thing you can do. If the company goes out of business, you're left with all this product that you can't sell. For instance, if a coffee chain wants their name on everything, we'll happily store it for them, but they have to buy it all outright.
>
> So, it has been a terrific success for us but over the past few years, like so many other businesses, it's been through tough times due to the very sudden downturn in the mining sector which flowed onto the hospitality industry – both vital sectors in our market.
>
> We've also had Bryan Greatrex suddenly retire which left a massive hole in the heart of the business. Fortunately, we have an amazing and dedicated staff and management team led by Brett Thompson and Alex England and so we are still the number one supplier in Western Australia.

Hisco was initially located on Stirling Highway in Nedlands under Golf Box and it was there that Murray met a man named Brian Leyden. Brian worked in Melbourne for Peter Rowland Catering whose clients included the likes of Flemington Racecourse.

When Perth business tycoon Alan Bond wanted a Melbourne company to cater for his daughter's wedding, Peter Rowland Catering was the natural choice to handle what would become the social calendar event of 1985.

As senior caterer, Brian got the job and was sent to Perth to set up a temporary kitchen to handle the wedding extravaganza. It just happened to be right next door to Hisco. But not only did Brian need to fit out his new kitchen he also needed to buy the very best French Champagne and wines that money could buy. He didn't have to travel far; Steve's was just down the road.

As the wedding drew closer Murray got to see the way Brian worked, and was greatly impressed. So, by the time the 3m-high wedding cake had been cut, after the fireworks had lit up the skies over the Swan River and after copious bottles of French Champagne had been consumed, Murray was left with no doubt that Brian Leyden was an extraordinarily gifted caterer.

With the wedding over Peter Rowland rang Brian to say it was time to pack up the kitchen and get back to Melbourne. But Brian didn't want to go; Perth, he had decided, was the place he wanted to be. As we now know, Murray likes to back good people so when he received a call from Brian to discuss a business proposition, he was open, ready and eager to listen.

> [Murray] Brian came to me and said, Peter Rowland wants to pull out of WA, to just shut it down. But Brian felt there were some great opportunities ahead with the America's Cup coming up. Brian was having a ball in Perth, he was a good operator and we got on well, so I said okay, what's involved?
>
> It looked promising, so I rang Peter Rowland. I didn't tell him about Brian, but I made him an offer based on the fact that as he was pulling out and would have to sell everything off and he probably wouldn't get much for it. So, I gave him some cash and got all the gear from him.
>
> Brian became my partner in what we called Southern Cross Catering. We then pitched for all the America's Cup work in Fremantle in the old wool stores building. Another catering company, Mustard Catering, was also in town and we were competing directly with each other. Mustard's accountant and advisor had gone to school with me, so one day I caught up with him and asked a few questions. I wanted to know if they were turning a profit. On hearing the answer, it made sense to meet with the owners of Mustard, Garry Rishworth and his business partner Phil Cogan (who later sold his share). We all agreed that if we put the businesses together, we could command the Perth market and that's what happened – in effect we merged with Mustard Catering.

By now Murray's fingers were well and truly immersed in many pies, supported by the people he had backed and partnered. He was seriously busy but that had little impact on the endlessly restless Murray, particularly when the next opportunity to emerge was laced with his passion for a game – the game of football.

> [Murray] Back in early 1987 the West Australian Football League's board of management was made up of a bunch of entrepreneurial guys including Richard Colless, a shareholder of property group, Armstrong Jones. They had succeeded in obtaining a licence from the VFL to enable them to enter a West Australian team (which was to become West Coast Eagles) into the competition. The idea was the team would be part of a multisport company that was not only going to run a team in the VFL, it was going to run basketball and netball – everything.

Rightly or wrongly the board decided there should be a public float, it should be owned by the public and no one should own more than X number of shares – less than 5 per cent I would guess – so shortly after that a prospectus was issued.

As a footy follower, on day one I went out and bought five or six notes (each note gave you the right to buy a seat and membership) and thought nothing of it until I got a phone call from Neil Hamilton, the Executive Chairman of Armstrong Jones.

He said, "Look Murray, something interesting has happened with this float with the Eagles. As of this morning it's only 24 per cent subscribed and it's going to fold – so I wouldn't mind bouncing it around with you."

> *"Look Murray, something interesting has happened with this float with the Eagles. It's going to fold - so I wouldn't mind bouncing it around with you."*

So, he came to my office at about five o'clock that afternoon and as Neil and I do, we opened a couple of Crownies, got the whiteboard out and started talking. Timing was the issue; the football season was about to start, the team was already up and running, ready to play game one – everything was in place except they were short 75 per cent of the required funding which included an upfront payment of $4 million to the VFL for the licence to play.

A few hours later and a few Crownies down, we both came to the conclusion that the only way we could quickly raise the $5 million needed to enter and run the team was to get five people with a million each rather than 100 people at whatever. It also meant the rules contained within the prospectus would need to be changed and urgently because we were out of time. At that point the multi-sport idea went out the door.

It was already 7 or 8 pm when Neil rang Richard Colless, but he managed to call an emergency board meeting for eight o'clock the next morning.

Then it was up to Neil and me. Who was going to put the money in? We started ringing around. Neil and I both agreed to put one mil in each, we got Mark Hohnen in London to put in one, although he couldn't even draw a football, Richard Colless put in another million and Ray Jones and Rob Armstrong, being Armstrong Jones, put in half a million each – We had our five million. The company was named Indian Pacific Ltd (IPL).

We were able to get it secured within 24 hours. Thankfully, it was at a time when there was a friendly banker in Perth; his name was Leon Ivory and he ran Broadlands Finance, a division of Bank of New Zealand.

We were then in the position to move forward but there were so many problems with the float that a shareholder could have, at any time, taken action against the board which had made some decisions that had put the company into serious risk before it had even started.

There was no blame but Neil Hamilton took a very strong corporate position and said that all inaugural board members should resign. They all stepped down and a new board was then set up. Neil took over as chairman from Richard Colless, and as a shareholder I immediately joined the board as did Mark Hohnen.

Some months later we recruited William (Bill) Kerr as the CEO and added Malcolm Atwell and Bill Mitchell as directors.

It was a risk for us all. The inaugural board had been so desperate to get the licence they had agreed to a load of unreasonable rules and so in the first three years we kept losing money. The VFL had 'tooled' them up. Both Brisbane and West Coast paid $4 million for a licence to bail out Melbourne clubs. Also, when West Coast flew to Melbourne, they had to pay their own airfares and accommodation but when Melbourne flew to Perth, the VFL would cover the expenses. We were also restricted because we had only one league side – we had a very small squad and so for the first two years there were times we didn't even have eighteen players to put on the field. Subsequently, people with long-term injuries had to be named in the side. We were up against some real challenges with the VFL; we knew something had to be done; changes had to be made if the West Coast Eagles were to survive.

> *We were up against some real challenges with the VFL; we knew something had to be done; changes had to be made if the West Coast Eagles were to survive.*

In the mid-1980s, a fellow called John Adams was contracted by then VFL Chairman Jack Hamilton to prepare a report on expanding the VFL competition which brought into the VFL the Brisbane Bears and West Coast Eagles. During that time, he registered the name Australian Football League (AFL) believing that if the competition did expand it would need a more nationally inclusive title.

We saw John as someone who could become a great ally for us and he did; we became friends and from then on wherever we went with John within the walls of the VFL, the doors would open.

Because of him we were able to get in front of the VFL people who had set up the rules for West Coast. We asked them, "Do you actually want the expanded clubs to fail, because the rules you've put in place are a guarantee that will happen." To their credit, the VFL's Ross Oakley and Allan Schwab understood there was a problem and said, "Right, we need to help you engineer change because when we go to the vote, you know you're not going to win, so we have to help you win the vote of the clubs."

We then got a young cadet journalist over to Perth – Eddie McGuire. Eddie would write columns in the newspaper supporting the changes we were seeking. One was the pre-draft picks. Consequently, we got to pick players like Peter Matera before the VFL clubs had a shot, giving us a higher inventory of players. Further changes came about when the VFL wanted to expand into South Australia. Max Basheer, President of the SANFL, was cautious and so he and I spent a lot of time working out everything that needed to be put right so that all clubs would get a fair deal. Basically, we rode on Max's back whilst he fought with the VFL for fairness – which by the way was all done with the support of Ross Oakley. It was Ross who then got the Melbourne clubs to understand why they really needed South Australia in the competition and why they then agreed to do whatever it would take to get South Australia on board. That included meeting our request to change the name of the Victorian Football League to Australian Football League so that it would be identified as a national competition. We came in on the flipside of all of that and consequently, all airfares, accommodation etc. were then paid for by the AFL and we went from making substantial losses to profits.

In the meantime, back at home, after three years of losses, we were running out of money, out of shareholder funds and we were desperate to get a better deal at Subiaco Oval.

History will tell you that WAFL supporters didn't move across to VFL. They just hated us and wouldn't come to any games. I understand that their hearts were very much with the WA clubs and accepting change was extremely difficult for them; but the fact is the WAFL was struggling financially. We always had four or five of the eight clubs owing us money because they couldn't pay their bills for suites (boxes) that they had for their sponsors. So it became a 'them and us' type of thing.

In the meantime, back at home, after three years of losses, we were running out of money, out of shareholder funds and we were desperate to get a better deal at Subiaco Oval.

Still we had no ground of our own, so throughout '87, '88 and '89 there was West Coast running around on borrowed grounds, training at various ovals on varying nights literally out of the back of a car. East Perth was the first club to give us a home in that they gave us full use of their oval and change room facilities; West Coast was very thankful for that.

It was at that point we (Indian Pacific Ltd (IPL), the company that owns West Coast) got together with the State government to form the WA Football Commission (WAFC). By the end of '89, they had pushed through legislation granting the WAFC a 99-year lease at Subiaco Oval. With that, we as a VFL team adopted the WAFC instead of the WAFL board. WAFL agreed to sign their powers over to the commission but as part of getting the deal through we had to agree for them to move into new premises while we would move into their old offices at Subiaco Oval. The offices were in the old wooden wing of the original members stand - uncomfortable but at least we had a home base for the first time since we'd started. The WAFC then moved into the old Freemasons building across the road, on the corner of Coghlan and Roberts roads.

Then in late 1989 IPL agreed for the commission to take 75¢ in every dollar of profit as a royalty. So basically, the shareholders' equity shrunk overnight to 25 per cent but by doing so the West Coast Eagles would finally become financially sustainable.

Up next was dealing with the rules around how the commission would administer its position on West Coast. We believed West Coast should be independent. Our financial deal was locked in by the end of 1989 into '90, but it would take until 1998 to come to agreement on the rules.

Throughout that time, I, on behalf of a number of shareholders, had to fight with people like the commission's inaugural chairman, Peter Tannock, and one-time CEO Jeff Ovens, purely to get independence for West Coast. Eventually we got it and at the same time got them to apply the same rules of independence to the Fremantle Dockers, who didn't enter the competition until 1995.

In achieving this agreement, the shareholders sold 100 per cent of Indian Pacific to the WAFC so today the club is a fully owned club of the WAFC as Fremantle has been from its beginning.

There was no way either club was ever going to be able to attract strong board members to drive them while the commission was standing over them telling them what to do. So, we basically told them they should stick to running the football commission and let other people run the football clubs. It wasn't easy but finally we got it all through, although the rules are slightly different between the two clubs.

Even when I became a commissioner, years later, and then chairman, I remained of the same opinion; the clubs must be run as a business independently but with a duty towards the game in Western Australia.

In 1990 with all that sorted, CEO Bill Kerr stepped down and Brian Cook took the role as chief executive of West Coast Eagles. Brian had come from being CEO of the WAFL and was the inaugural CEO of the Football Commission, so he knew what he was doing.

Bill and I stayed on the board but all the other directors stepped down. The commission then appointed Terry O'Connor and Dwayne Buckland while the fifth member had to be mutually decided. John Adams, who had been such an enormous support to us at the very start, was elected to that role.

In 1989, when John was acting CEO of West Coast Eagles/IPL he identified Trevor Nisbett, the Football Manager of Subiaco Football Club, as the ideal person to take on the role of football manager of West Coast.

Trevor took up those duties in September 1989 just as we were about to appoint a new coach, Michael Malthouse.

In his role at Subiaco, Trevor had identified some young talent (in those days it was possible to go unnoticed) and those players went on to become legends of West Coast.

It was Trevor's skill in identifying those initial players along with the appointment of Malthouse, that underpinned the 1990s success of the club.

His eventual appointment to CEO in 1999 was seen by many as a bad move by West Coast. However, with great support from my successor Michael Smith as chairman, and then successive chairmen right up until now (2018), Trevor is the second longest serving club CEO in the AFL; second only to Brian Cook who he replaced in 1999.

So Trevor, the boy from Bunbury, with whom I have had many "One more for no apparent", set the standard for the club. He is a fierce supporter of Western Australian football and that is very much appreciated by the football family in WA.

How opinions change when success comes along. I remember when we were recruiting Mick Malthouse as coach and we advised the commission, simply as a matter of courtesy, about our new recruit. They slammed the idea because they thought West Australians wouldn't accept a coach from Victoria.

We said to them, "What do you want to do? Do you want to win football games or not?"

To Peter Tannock's credit, he rang Neil back two hours later and said, "I was out of order, do what you think fits."

Another comment was, "I can't walk down St Georges Terrace if we do this." To which we replied, "We don't care how you walk down St Georges Terrace; everything will change when we start winning." And that's what we did.

On his arrival Mick didn't think we had a squad; he didn't know about the quality of the few blokes Trevor had tucked away, including Dean Kemp and Brett Heady.

On his arrival Mick didn't think we had a squad; he didn't know about the quality of the few blokes Trevor had tucked away, including Dean Kemp and Brett Heady.

By the way, neither did we think we had a squad to make the 1990 finals. But we had trust in Trevor that he knew those boys; he also knew that no one else was going to look at them. In the draft today, there isn't one kid in the country who's not known about, but back in 1990, there were plenty of unknowns.

Kempy was one of those kids. He came out as a legend of the game and yet he was this scrawny little kid, like a matchstick – you could have blown him away. To turn around after being a late additional draft pick in 1990 and become the player he became, was amazing. In my opinion he was the standout.

While everything was effectively falling into place in Perth the same could not be said for the east coast – trouble was brewing.

Throughout the period of transitioning to a national competition, the VFL Board, which was still in control, was having problems of its own. They had hoped that by expanding the competition and with the injection of $4 million from both the West Coast Eagles and the newly formed Brisbane Bears (bankrolled by controversial businessman Christopher Skase) their problems would be over. But, as Murray explains, it was only a temporary fix; a band aid, because the issues were inherent in the structure of the VFL and hence it didn't take long for the same problems to re-emerge.

AFL was now a national competition and it was clear the sport needed an independent and professional national body to steer it into the future. The AFL Commission, which had been formed in 1985 (initially to administer policy only), finally stepped in and took full administrative control of the AFL, eventually becoming the national governing body of the sport in 1993.

> [Murray] When you look at the AFL Commission today, chaired by Richard Goyder, we truly are a national body, with a healthy national competition – teams from NSW, SA, WA, Qld as well as the 10 Victorian teams – where everyone plays by the same rules. But it's taken from 1987 – more than 30 years – to get there, so it's been quite a journey.

The whole WAFL, WAFC, VFL, AFL journey was full on and Murray played a big part in making it all happen, but he did so at the same time while running Steve's Hotel, the wineries, vineyards, restaurants, numerous bottle shops, catering companies and the hotel suppliers. Admittedly he did have good people running some of those businesses, but Murray wasn't and still isn't the type of person to put his feet up, let others do the work and hope for the best. He is very hands-on, he gets involved – but even with the understanding that he can manage many things at once, you would think he wouldn't want to keep adding to what would already have been a lengthy to-do list.

Perhaps most wouldn't, but that it seems is the Murray McHenry style; but was buying an island his style?

It was 1987. Murray had just injected a million dollars into the Eagles, his catering business and Hisco were bubbling away and Steve's was going gangbusters. Murray felt he could do no wrong. Perhaps it was this sense of invincibility that led him to making an out of left field decision, one that wasn't influenced by his usual prerequisite – gut instinct.

> [Murray] I'd heard about some people who had entered into a contract with BHP to buy a 99-year lease on Cockatoo Island off the State's North-West coast. As it turned out they couldn't fulfil the contract, so the silly thing I did was to go and have a look at it with a mate, David Williams. In hindsight I should have gone alone. David is a lawyer but as soon as you put an ocean, a beach and a bit of land in the middle of nowhere, he just loves it. He was like a wound-up spring. I kept saying, "This is crazy, we shouldn't be doing this," but David found every reason to do it. At the time things were going really well for me and so I thought well there's no harm in this.
>
> So, the next I knew was we had taken over the existing contract with BHP – it cost us one dollar.

There are two leases on the island – one for mining and one for the town site and that's the one we bought.

The next I knew was we had taken over the existing contract with BHP – it cost us one dollar.

The mine site was right on the edge of the island. The town site itself had around 40 houses, including six dormitory style buildings where the miners lived. But two or three years earlier BHP had moved them all off Cockatoo to Koolan Island – I don't know why because you can literally pee from Koolan Island to Cockatoo – it's that close. Once they'd moved them across, BHP stopped spending money on the town and things were starting to get a bit loose. It was up to us to get everything into shape.

Cockatoo had a small jetty with a crane on it and so I became the crane driver. I remember the union guy yelling out to me, "Have you got a licence," and I just pulled something out of my pocket and said, yep. It wasn't difficult to operate because all it had was an up and down lever and things went up and down – so I did okay.

Then there was the power plant on the island which had to run the mine site, the conveyor belts, the houses – all that sort of thing. If you can imagine BHP on Cockatoo Island, their generator was 3000kva, which may not mean much to most people but that's big enough to run almost half of Nedlands in terms of power... it guzzled fuel. As soon as we took over the lease, the first thing we needed was a ship full of diesel. So, we decided to turn it all off.

The town generator was smaller but it still guzzled fuel, so we didn't want to use that either. We then found all these 3 and 5kva generators under the houses, in the old supermarket and in the clubhouse on top of the hill. The island is in cyclone territory and they were used as backups.

A friend of mine, Gary Prendiville, an engineer, knew how to keep costs down in remote locations because he'd grown up in isolated towns along the Nullarbor. His father had owned service stations at places like Balladonia and Norseman. By using the smaller gensets Gary was able to re-design the town generator, making it just large enough to handle the town site and put the streetlights on.

It was all a lot of fun; we got a group of friends up, got our hands dirty, got the whole place tied down and then thought, let's get ten blokes to put in $10,000 a year each and make it a getaway for friends – it was never intended to be a profit centre.

We then hired a couple, both cooks, and made them 'island managers' of sorts. If anyone wanted to go there, we'd say, "Yeah go on up, our island managers will organise all your food, just pay them for what you use and everybody's happy." We decked out ten of the houses with decent linen and all that sort of stuff and bought a tri-hulled boat so we could go from the island to the mainland and up into all the creeks.

When we bought the boat, a friend, Brian Coppin (Coppo), who had a house in Broome, said to us, "What are you guys doing? If the tide doesn't get you the sharks will and if the sharks don't get you the crocodiles will. You're all mad."

Of course, we all were! We knew he was right and we did see plenty of crocodiles – but we were having fun.

We loved going up there and everybody that went loved it. I never regretted buying it but by 1991 a lot had changed for me so when I got an early morning phone call from Alan Bond, it was a bit of a relief.

It was at about 4 am and Alan goes, "That island."

And I said, "Yeah."

"Are you ready to sell it? I've got a mate in Singapore who wants to buy it."

I said, "Oh...it's not really for sale. If he wants, he can join the syndicate."

"No, no, no, can you catch up later today?"

So, I went to Alan's office at four o'clock that afternoon and he said, "I'll pay you a million dollars for it."

I said, "No, that's not enough."

He said, "What do you want?"

I said, "Well, we'll only sell it for two million."

He goes, "Oh bugger you then, okay. You get a million up front and the rest of it is on the tick."

We insisted we hang onto one of the houses – we called it, a chalet agreement to make it look good. We kept it and decked it out on the basis that David and I could each use it for a month a year – Alan would then have use of it for the rest of the time.

In saying that, have we ever used it? NO!

Bondy of course went mad and spent a lot of money on the place. He built up the club on top of the hill, looking out over the archipelago of islands. He had a photographer go in and take these amazing photos at sunset of a girl in this pool looking out over the islands. He then had this big opening where he took a 747 that landed in Derby filled with guests that were somehow ferried across to the island – I don't know where they were all housed but apparently it was a fantastic show.

Only thing was we didn't get invited – we were really pissed off. We would have paid our own way just to go – but no, we didn't get invited; never got over that one!

As it turned out, we never got the second million. But I guess the moral of the story is, one million was fine.

Technically we still have the house but I don't even know who's got the town lease these days or the mining lease. It's one of the richest ore deposits in the world and over the years they've removed most of it. Apparently, there's still ore there but it's all under water. They could dig down through the water and pull it up, but whilst there's cheaper ore around they'll get that first.

While Murray kept his island in the sun for five years, it was only a year after purchasing it, that the gold in his Midas touch seemed to suddenly turn to stone. Black Monday – or Black Tuesday, depending on where you lived in the world – had hit in October 1987. However, it took until 1988 for Murray and many others to arrive at the precarious edge of a financial precipice, where the fingers of fear of how far they might fall clawed at those who stepped too close. Sadly for some, the abyss below became a place of surrender.

[Murray] It happened so quickly. At the time Steve's was going really well with the new restaurant and the wine and food club. I felt almost invincible, thinking, shit, I can't go wrong here, and then suddenly the stock market collapsed. Just as suddenly no one had any money, and if they did, they never showed it. People just stopped spending – gone were our sales of expensive wines with lunch – the best we could do were $15 bottles. That really hurt our bottom line.

On top of that we were being attacked by a local council in terms of our liquor licence, which back then, needed to be renewed annually. Although I didn't pay rates to Subiaco Council, I found myself up against them in the Liquor Licensing Court defending the licence. People were always getting into council's ear with complaints – someone threw up on my lawn, someone urinated on my lawn, somebody fornicated on my lawn. I may have seen someone pee on a lawn, but I certainly didn't see any fornicating – but all these people built their cases on that crap.

For years lawyer Richard Utting defended me and the licence. Richard became the Mayor of Fremantle; in fact, he's been the mayor of everything; he's a very colourful character – should have been an actor. The court sessions were always quite humorous, because he loved to expose the lies being told. But there were some pretty low times, sitting in court, listening to rhetoric that wasn't true but knowing there was nothing I could do about it; they had the floor and could say whatever they wanted. Eventually, licences became continuous, not annual, but not before we went through our fair share of problems.

Another challenge came when ex-politician Herb Graham was appointed chairman of the State Licensing Court. He'd been on a trip to Italy where he saw you could drink on every street corner, so he decided to create what was called the tavern; and granted licences to liquor stores.

That licence brought more competition into the market; Broadway Tavern opened, Minsky's opened, suddenly everyone was jumping in on our patch, and it really started to erode sections of our trade.

If Murray thought these issues had taken him to the stony bottom of the abyss he was mistaken – there was still further room to fall…but how far, was the question.

[Murray] In 1988 the Liquor Licensing Court was run by a single judge, Peter Sharkey. As in previous years we were again in front of the court to secure the licence of Steve's renewal. Some four days of listening to the same stories and complaints was exhausting but not unusual until the judge handed down his decision; then it was bewildering.

He refused the renewal.

The whole hospitality industry went into a spin of disbelief. I was also in disbelief and shock, however there was no time for emotions, I had to be proactive; I had a mortgage and had entered into a 20-year lease of the business with a public company. So, the long fight to restore the licence began.

People often ask why did we lose the licence? But that was the problem, I never had one. There was a technicality; I had the licence in my name and yet I traded as a company. When I bought the freehold, we put it into a company but the licence stayed initially in my Mother's name and then mine. We did everything right, we weren't morally trading illegally, it was inadvertently trading illegally. We were the same people, it's just that we had moved from being a trader in our own name to trading in our company's name, that's all that happened. Notwithstanding this, I wrote countless times to liquor licensing asking about it and they kept saying it wasn't a problem, that I could hold the licence in that way – but they were wrong.

On the day they closed us down, it was like bang, you're closed, but we had chefs, staff, what do you do about them? I tried to retain as many staff as I could, I kept all the full-timers going, I had them painting, cleaning, anything to try to keep them on. I kept the restaurant running. When people ordered wine, theoretically we'd have it delivered from the Waratah Wine Bin down the road and the paperwork showed as much, but I had $2 million worth of liquor stock locked up in the building. To be honest I was being a smart arse because it was a loss-making exercise anyway.

I'll never forget the support we had from our regulars; it was unbelievable. I ran four Sunday sessions because in those days we were huge. So, I kept the band playing and 800 people came in with their eskies; they thought it was wonderful – and it was. It was great fun, but we were haemorrhaging money. Again, being a smart arse, I just kept thinking, I'm going to keep it going, one way or the other, I'm going to keep it going. But there was no business to be made because we couldn't sell anything. We could sell food, so we sold hotdogs and hamburgers and kept it simple – but one by one the staff left.

It came as a real shock for me but I don't think I ever believed Steve's wasn't going to re-open, I kept thinking it was only a matter of when. I had the support of Pam Beggs, the Minister for Racing, Gaming and Liquor, who believed we'd had a bad deal and so she set about changing the Liquor Act.

I don't think I ever believed Steve's wasn't going to re-open, I kept thinking it was only a matter of when.

Meanwhile I was preparing to take the fight to court.

David Malcolm, who later became the Chief Justice, was acting for me in the months leading up to the court case. He was an old friend of the family and he said, "Murray, you can't win this." So, I had that reality before the court case started. There was massive expense; full on QCs and all that sort of stuff for something I knew I couldn't win but had to be seen fighting it in the interim of waiting for the new Act.

We timed the court case for late January 1989 because Pam said she'd be finished writing the new Act in the first two weeks of that month. I'd received the pages and read it back to front – I knew more about the new Act than the new Act knew about itself and our court case argument was based on it. The public service had just gone back to work after the Christmas break but then typically something went wrong at the printing office. So, the court case started without the new act. I rang Pam every day, I rang the state printers every day.

Even though I knew the new Act would eventually be introduced, the length of time it went on made it very hard, and those days of sitting in the court room were pretty low times and it was driving me nuts – let's just bring the guillotine down today because I knew it was going to happen eventually.

Fortunately, I had two barrister friends in Allan Fenbury, a part-time actor, and Richard Utting, one of the most theatrical people in a courtroom; they turned it into somewhat of a comedy show. They would take the opposition witness in the stand on these journeys so the lawyer on the other side kept asking, "Please sir, may I ask, where is this taking us?" and the judge would say, "I'm interested, let's keep going".

It seemed like everybody was helping me and that felt really good. Then one day this person walked into the court room; the judge looked up and said, "We'll stop for a moment, we have a visitor."

The person went up to the judge who then announced – "We have a new Act."

Phewwww!

It took a few days for the finding to come out – and when it did it was an amazing day. I think we got the message at 10:30 or 11 am. The brewery was all set, ready and waiting to get the call from us. Within minutes of getting our call their truck, loaded with kegs, arrived at Steve's. We had the bar open five minutes later. That night it was chockers. Everybody just came flying down to have a beer and celebrate with us – it felt like we'd been closed for an eternity.

We'd lost the licence in July '88 and we didn't get it back until St Patrick's Day 1989. Through that period, I tore up about $1.5 million and that was just losses – add loss of profit! I'd also just put a million dollars into West Coast, had bought Cockatoo Island, I had lawyers' fees coming out of my backside and a hotel that was losing money.

I had the support of my bank but they were wavering – it was at that point that Alan Bond rang me about buying Cockatoo Island and why I drove the sale of it – I needed some money to sort everything out.

There've been many times since that I've considered going back and suing the government – but there's no point. When things go bad, you get grounded very quickly; it's quite humbling. Once you've landed on the rocky bottom that's when you have to jump up and dust yourself off.

Funnily enough, I've found that if I go to bed at night and can't sleep, I just lie there wondering how I'm ever going to survive, but if I can get to sleep, I wake up feeling so much better and able to hit the next day running. A good night's sleep is just so important. In life, you have to learn how to cop it on the chin otherwise you may as well dig yourself a hole and stay in it. For me, I tend to look out and say, "It's a blue sky...let's go!"

If I go to bed at night and can't sleep, I just lie there wondering how I'm ever going to survive, but if I can get to sleep, I wake up feeling so much better and able to hit the next day running. A good night's sleep is just so important.

Right up until the day it closed, Steve's had enjoyed huge success. Every Sunday afternoon, summer or winter, the crowd was abuzz, the music was amazing and the line-up of patrons waiting to get inside was animated and long. Near two thousand people would come from the hills, the north, the south, the beaches, the country – from all over the place – just to hear the bands play and be caught up in what was one of the biggest and the best Sunday sessions in Perth.

[Murray] We used to be part of a circuit from the Raffles to the Windsor to the Albion, to Steve's, to the Shenton Park – where a band might play with you on a Wednesday and Thursday night and on the other nights, they'd be at one of the other venues. The band members weren't full-time musos, so two or three nights a week, was enough for them. I think anyone who grew up in the 70s and 80s, when we had great live music, was very lucky, it was just a wonderful period.

Whilst the loss of the liquor licence at Steve's was a difficult and humbling experience – not to mention costly – Murray retained his optimistic and 'always open to an opportunity' approach to life. As he says himself, if you can get a good night's sleep and look out for the blue sky then life's experiences are a little easier to deal with and learn from. Which is probably why yet another friend, airline pilot Gary Steel, approached him with a business proposition. Murray loved the idea, and why wouldn't he – it involved wine – Murray's greatest passion.

[Murray] Gary was a pilot with Ansett before the big pilot dispute of '89. He was based in Melbourne and was always on standby – in fact he was known as 'Seagull' because you had to throw a rock at him to make him fly, he just loved being on standby, and he also loved his wine.

I had known Gary for many years and so when I became involved with the West Coast Eagles, he joined the club in Melbourne. He was there at every function and always turned up with good bottles of wine, which was just fine with me, and we became good friends. In 1988 he wanted to open Domaine Wine Shippers, a wine distribution business, in every state. He asked me to partner him in WA, to which I agreed and so then I helped him set up here.

Gary became an agent, mostly for imported wines. He went around the world picking up agency lines like Billecart Salmon in Champagne. He and I then went through Burgundy before anybody else had really discovered it. He probably doesn't have an agreement with any of them but he's got a very strong and loyal bond with most of the top Burgundian houses – which is what you must have in this business.

Burgundian vineyards are tiny so there is a high demand around the world for their top-end wines. On a very small amount of land they make this fabulous wine but they only make 300 cases of it so, most of the wines, when you can get them, on-sell very quickly to other countries. Domaine has been and still is very successful with its allocation; there's no discounting or anything, you're just lucky if you can get it – and Gary always does. So, we had great success, and although the company continued to flourish and still does to this day, I sold my share to Gary and his family in 2013.

Domaine Wine Shippers was a welcome respite from all the challenges – just what Murray needed to boost his nosediving confidence in his business and in the economy. Then another success – on the football field West Coast Eagles were fast ascending the footy ladder. Murray, while spending a lot of time at Subiaco Oval recognised an area that needed some serious improvement and he knew just how to do it.

[Murray] Back in the late '80s the only catering at Subiaco Oval came out of red caravans – it was old fashioned food but it was all you could get. We knew from the Eagles' point of view we needed to have quality catering available to our sponsors and members – something my business partner at Mustard Catering, Brian Leyden, was fantastic at and could easily handle. So, when the catering tender came up for Subiaco Oval, Mustard Catering (Garry Rishworth, me and Brian Leyden) tendered for it. Peter Eakins, a hospitality person, former footballer and chairman of the Australian Hotels Association, was on the tender selection committee – he knew what we were capable of and ultimately, we got the job. We totally turned catering at Subiaco Oval around; we revolutionised it. Brian and I then bought Garry Rishworth out of Mustard and continued at Subiaco Oval.

In 1992 I agreed to do a joint venture with Ron Evans, the chairman of Essendon Football Club, who later became chairman of the AFL. Ron was also managing director and the second largest shareholder of the Spotless Group, a massive integrated services company. He kept talking to me about Spotless wanting to come to Perth to do a joint venture with us up at Kings Park Restaurant and Function Centre.

The head lease of the Kings Park complex was held by the O'Brien family who were also big shareholders of Spotless; so, Spotless did the deal with the O'Briens and we took on the operation. I wasn't happy to do the restaurant so I put chef Chris Taylor in touch with the O'Briens and we did the function centre. It was all very internal and so the fees were exorbitant which didn't really affect anyone but me. After a while I looked at it and thought there was no point being a part of a joint venture if I couldn't make any money. That's when Ron suggested Spotless take on 100 per cent of Mustard, which included the catering contract at Subiaco Oval. The deal went ahead in 1993 and I became a shareholder of Spotless which finished up being a very worthwhile transaction for me. In that same year Chris Taylor renamed the restaurant and function centre Fraser's, and Chris of course has become a local gastronomic legend.

Brian Leyden eventually left Spotless to return to Melbourne to work with Peter Rowland. He came back to Perth in that same year, 2009, to take on the role of managing director of Beaumonde Catering which he had just purchased. Then in 2016 he opened The Point Bar and Grill with Neil Irvine.

When Brian left Spotless, Paul Hopwood, or Hoppy as we all call him, who was working at Mustard, took over his role. Hoppy knew everything about the challenges of catering at Subiaco Oval. Some years after Mustard merged with Spotless, they transferred the Subiaco Oval contract to Delaware North but Hoppy, despite his knowledge, wasn't taken across. They were making a mistake; it's an old place and not an easy one to cater in, but Hoppy with his experience does it well. We kept telling them to employ him but for a long while they didn't. Eventually, they called him and he stepped back in. As you've heard me say, business success is all about good people and when you've got them you can't afford to lose them.

Football was changing in the West; Subiaco Oval was getting closer to its use-by date and as anyone who loves Aussie rules football knows, in 2017, Subiaco Oval ceased being the home to AFL in the West. A new era was about to begin, and Murray would be very much a part of it. But until then there were still a few goals to kick – and not all on the field. It was 1994 and Margaret River was calling.

[Murray] I've always been a farmer at heart; I love being on the land – it's where I'm at my happiest. I'd planted my first grape vines in 1984 on my sister Sandra's Burnside vineyard in Margaret River, selling the grapes to Cape Mentelle. But what I really wanted was my own vineyard. Twelve years later a good friend, Brian Sierakowski, and I purchased 100 hectares (250 acres) of land just south of Witchcliffe. We established Calgardup Brook Vineyard and because of its northerly aspect with less direct sunlight it's been a very good vineyard and produces some outstanding Shiraz and Chardonnay.

A couple of years after that I purchased 75 hectares on Rocky Road just outside Margaret River opposite Devil's Lair winery. As farmland, it had been fertilised with superphosphate, so it took some ten years to get rid of it. Now we have a really healthy soil environment that is probably the best it could possibly be. Everything we use is organic or bio-dynamic – no chemicals or artificial fertilisers, and to keep it all natural we use different animals for weed and pest control. We have areas of kikuyu grass which is a problem because it rips the water out of your soil and the only way to kill it is with Roundup. Roundup is a chemical and that's taboo for us so we put pigs into those areas. They rip out the runners and chew them up, although when they excrete it some of it's still alive, so it does keep coming back but they keep it to a minimum.

Another problem we have is with weevils which do a lot of damage to the vine and the fruit. They breed under what we call broadleaf which sits flat on the ground and from where a daisy grows. You can't see the weevils because not only are they smaller than fleas, but they eat from the inside out, so a plant or vine can look normal, but it's actually been hollowed out. A lot of vineyards put Dacron collars around the vine so when the weevil climbs up the trunk it gets trapped in the Dacron and it can't get out. But not only is this a labour-intensive exercise, it only lasts for a couple of years plus it can look pretty untidy after rain. So, we use chooks in the areas around the vineyard where weevils have broken out. The chooks eat the larvae and the live ones and, although we can't eradicate them completely, we can minimise the break-out...and we get fresh eggs!

Of course, by having chooks you then have the issue of feral cats, foxes and, dare I say it, hungry eagles. So again, to keep everything natural, we built these chook pens on old box trailers, so we can move them around. They are surrounded by a moveable electric fence which is powered by solar panels to keep the battery topped up and to open and close the coop. Sometimes if it's been raining the batteries will go and the cats will leap over the fence and the foxes will dig under. We know when it's a fox because they tend to go crazy and rip the chook apart while a cat will just kill them and maybe come back for it later.

Keeping everything organic and natural is the path we have chosen, and whilst it's taken a long time to get it there, the outcome has been worth it. As we say, a better environment gives you better wine.

Over those 10 years of developing Calgardup Brook Vineyard and Rocky Road, Murray spent a lot of time driving between Margaret River and Perth. Perhaps being able to get away onto the land at Margaret River gave him the energy and drive to keep going – knowing that by working hard, the opportunity to spend more time doing what he loved (farming) would one day arrive. But that dream would have to wait.

As usual Murray's commitments to so many projects and businesses continued to grow which left him little spare time. Rowing was one of his first passions to succumb to his time poor lifestyle. However, while many years had since passed, Murrays connection to the sport and his dedication to it had earnt him quite a reputation. He had won medals for Christ Church, broken records, become a prestigious King's Cup rower, been asked to coach a team in Germany (which naturally called for a German 'recce' before he declined the offer) and had coached the '77, '78 and '79 Christ Church Head of the River rowing teams.

Acknowledgement for that contribution ultimately came in 2002. A new boat had been named after him. Naturally, Murray was invited to the ceremonial boat christening of Murray McHenry. When it came time to break the sacrificial bottle of champagne over the bow, Murray, who was naturally comfortable with such a bottle in his hands, was ready. He swung, (slammed) the bottle against the newly crafted bow, but instead of the sound of breaking glass followed by applause and good wishes for safe passage there were gasps of horror. The champagne bottle, still in Murray's hands, was intact but where it had struck the new carbon-fibre bow there was a gaping hole. The maiden voyage for Murray McHenry was sadly but respectfully postponed.

Meanwhile Murray was still very involved with the West Coast Eagles, having become the chairman of the club in 1997 where his attention was required in many different areas and by many different people. As chairman, entrepreneur, wine retailer and owner of Steve's Hotel, he was the natural person for many of the players to turn to for advice, particularly so when the advice sought was all about a hotel.

[Murray] Peter Wilson and Karl Langdon came to me and said they had made an offer to take the lease on and manage the Wembley Hotel. The documents had been drawn up and everything was proceeding well; that was until the owners received another offer and tried to renege on the deal. The guys had already set themselves up and were ready to go so Peter Wilson and I stepped in and met up with the owners. They agreed to honour the deal if I got involved to provide support and experience for the boys.

Trevor Nisbett, myself and lawyer David Williams formed a syndicate with Peter and Karl simply to help them out and to ensure they had the right people on board. Peter went in to run it with Karl but then Karl dropped out so it was just Peter and the rest of us. We did that for a number of years until the owner of the connecting shopping centre, restructured the whole lease and took on the freehold – by that time we were happy to move on, so it worked out really well.

I can't say the same about another deal I got involved in. Just after we went into the Wembley Hotel, I was talked into buying a bar and food hall in Northbridge. We, the Wembley Hotel syndicate, bought 50 per cent of the building and the business. We completed extensive renovations and opened a new bar, Redheads, on the site and kept the food hall.

It was okay at first but then we started to run into all sorts of problems – so many problems. We had this huge New Year's Eve party organised – all the tickets had sold out. A few days before, on Christmas Eve, there was an incident and I was called in around midnight to run the bar. It was absolutely chaotic and at 4 am I was still there, standing in the middle of Lake Street looking up at the stars above, feeling pretty crushed and miserable and asking myself what the hell was I doing with a bar in the middle of Northbridge. I then had to pick my Mother up at 8 am and drive all the way to Margaret River for Christmas lunch with the family. There was no way I was going to let her down or the family because Christmas is a time we all try to get together – but I was shattered and pretty upset. After lunch I remember walking out amongst the vines questioning myself and just hoping that everything would be okay for New Year's

Eve – just so I wouldn't have to go back in and run it. I made up my mind then that I had to get out of it – it was really starting to affect me. A few weeks later I was talking to City of Perth councillor Rob Butler and he mentioned a fund the city had for developing open spaces within the city. I met with the CEO who agreed it was a good site for developing so they purchased it in 2003. After clearing the site, they built a cultural community space called Northbridge Piazza. It was officially opened in 2009.

So, Murray had another lucky escape – but, was that luck? Perhaps it was more about being aware and open to options and opportunities, not allowing fear to get in the way of finding a solution, being prepared to take a risk or to accept a loss to allow him to move forward. Perhaps it's knowing when something isn't working, knowing when it's time to walk away…what's that Kenny Rogers song?

You've got to know when to hold 'em
Know when to fold 'em
Know when to walk away
And know when to run.

It seems Murray does know when to walk away, when to run and when to stay.

His bar venture may not have turned out the way he had hoped, and it may have been the source of much stress and anxiety but he quickly recognised the impact it was having on him and made the decision to do something about it. He took a lesson from that episode – not to move too far from what he knew best, and a bar in the middle of nightclub land was just a little too far from the apple tree. But by refusing to dwell on what had been a challenging venture, his mind was clear and open to new opportunities. Although the sale of the property didn't go through until 2003, he didn't wait for it to settle or allow disappointment or fear of future failure to stop him looking for his next challenge.

After a 13-year stint as board member at West Coast Eagles Murray decided it was time to throw in the towel, though his involvement with the game continued. His private life was on shaky ground, so he retreated to his favourite place – Margaret River – and did what he did best; he set up another company. Again, it was all about the people (oh and wine) and for this company there was no question he had the right person to partner with - David Hohnen.

[Murray] In 2000 Verve Cliquot had already been a shareholder of Cape Mentelle for around nine years. David as managing director had had enough, he was sick and tired of all the travelling. The company had become huge and David was no longer doing what he loved to do so we suggested we split the two businesses; we would then buy back Cape Mentelle and the French could buy Cloudy Bay. We had always believed they only really wanted Cloudy Bay. As it turned out they didn't want to sell any part of Cape Mentelle but, if David wanted to go off to do his own family wine brand, then they would buy 100 per cent of the company.

So off we went and in that same year, with their knowledge and acceptance, we established McHenry Hohnen Vintners for the vintage of 2004. The ownership of Cape Mentelle passed to the French in 2001, with the understanding that David stay at the helm of both wineries until the end of 2003.

That worked well for us. I'm not a winemaker, so consequently I wouldn't have gone into the wine business if it wasn't for David. Freya, David's daughter, stepped on board as our wine-maker with her father watching over her shoulder, but because of his commitment to Cape Mentelle we didn't release our first vintage until 2004 – and that was with Cape Mentelle's ap-proval. We started building our own winery in 2005 on the Rocky Road site; we used another winery until it was finished – in time for the '07 vintage.

While I was developing the vineyard between 1999 and 2004, I would take a couple of beers and go and sit on the hill overlooking the property. As I watched the sunset I would mentally plan and visualise the winery building in that same position. Today, the wine building stands exactly where I pictured it would – in that high position.

I met my wife Chaise during that planning period, and so she would often come and sit there with me. She could see what I saw in the location which is why in March 2008 we chose to get married on that site. It will always be a very special place for me and no doubt for Chaise too.

My Mother Hazel, although with failing health, came and endorsed the planning. She passed away the year prior to finishing what is now a wonderful building and so it was a unanimous family decision to dedicate the property to her. We named it Hazel's Vineyard.

Our (three) privately owned vineyards were never included in the Cape Mentelle deal although we continued to grow for them and still do to this day.

David Hohnen had planted a new vineyard on Sebbs Road, further south, however in 2010 as a result of the 2008-09 GFC, an oversupply made it uneconomical to grow on all four vineyards so Sebbs Road was disbanded. Burnside, which is owned by David and my sister Sandra Hohnen, is now our cellar door and home to our Burnside Chardonnay. We continue to grow at both Calgardup Vineyard, which I own with Brian Sierakowski, and Rocky Road – now renamed Hazel's Vineyard and which is also home to our winery.

I was very happy spending most of my time down at Margaret River, playing farmer or viti-culturist or winemaker, and going backwards and forwards to Perth. I would have been very content just to stay on the farm but when you have a mortgage you have to constantly work out the best way to pay it off and how to be profitable at the same time – so I had no choice but to split my time between both places.

After I purchased the hotel in Nedlands, the land prices in the area started going crazy. Our land rates were exorbitant. Although the hotel was all on one lot, the state valuations office calculated it as if it was sub-divided into 10 housing blocks, and that's how they rated it. My argument back in those days was, if I have an ice-cream shop down at Cottesloe Beach and you rate it in the same way, ice creams are going to be $20 to $30 each; so, what you are doing to us?

But there was nothing we could do about it. As I understand it, land tax is one of those things where there is no formal appeal process; you can talk to someone but there's no adjudicator. The value and the decision are final and that's it.

So, there we were with half a million dollars in rates, half a million dollars in land tax rates and everything else on top – so just to open the doors we had to achieve a net profit of $15,000 every week.

The zoning on the hotel was just that – hotel – and that was all it could be, plus the zoning didn't allow anything to be above two storeys. But none of that was ever taken into account when they valued it. It is supposed to be based on GVR (gross rental value) but there is no way that actually occurs. In the end that type of rating pushed me to say, "I need to change this site."

Around the year 2000, the City of Nedlands elected a new mayor, John Paterson, who had been following our issues with the city. John and I met, and he suggested I apply for a re-development of our one-hectare site whilst retaining the 1908 building as a central building of significance.

I told him about the existing Town Planning Scheme and how the zoning would need to change from hotel to commercial/residential if we were to have any hope of moving forward whilst retaining the historical integrity of the site. John, a retired farmer, said let's just focus on the redevelopment application first. He then went about that very quickly. Unfortunately, he soon learned about the challenges of local politics. He only lasted one term – some just refused to accept his drive for change. However, during his appointment he did make progress including the engagement of Town Planner Daniel Arndt to specifically focus on the Nedlands area.

I realised the best thing I could do was to move forward and develop the site. I did a deal with John and Tim Roberts of Multiplex, a large construction company. We agreed that I would put in the land and they would do the building. I intended to convert the original hotel into four luxury apartments whilst they built four new apartment blocks. They were to build one on either side of the site, two across the front plus another block with ten apartments above a new restaurant, fine wine store and cellar, which once completed I would take back and do the fit-out myself.

To start the ball rolling I had to close Steve's but I didn't just want it to be open one day and closed the next. I wanted a proper going away party as it would be the last one at Steve's, so it had to be big. I thought let's go back over the journey and find, if I can, the bands people had always come to Steve's for. I got Loaded Dice, Fingerprint, The Boogie Street Band with Tracy Caspersz and Brett Townsend, and Dave Hole who I think played here for eight years straight on a Saturday night. He went on to become an international actor, although he continued to play and still does.

I decided to throw the party on New Year's Eve and close on January 1st, 2004. To get the night together we got somebody from the bands to coordinate the music. Then they sent tapes to each other so they could practice because they were all living in different parts of

Australia. We flew them all back to Perth for the event; when they got here, they virtually came in and played cold on the night.

We shut the whole place off. We had semitrailers drive into the car park and set the stage up in front of them. We set bars up everywhere; we didn't care because it was our last night. Upstairs in the restaurant I had a glazier come in and take out all the glass windows, so everyone up there could look down and hear the bands. I brought in different chefs and we set it up like a marketplace. I think we had about 1500 guests. They all came dressed up; it was very much an up-market night, not like it was in the '70s.

Fingerprint were the last ones on because they were the real covers band and they were full on; there were guys jumping into the trees playing guitar; it was just fantastic. We filmed it all.

It was an unforgettable night; everyone had such an amazing time. So, 2004 arrived and once everyone left, we closed the doors of Steve's for the last time.

So, for Murray 2004 started with an end and a beginning. But as Murray knows only too well, nothing happens without hard work and a clear mind – an awareness that has been a constant companion since his Christ Church days.

[Murray] I've always been very health and exercise aware. I've made sure that I stay in reasonable nick because you can cope with a whole lot more if you're healthy. So, I look after myself, I eat well and do enough exercise, I don't try to be an athlete anymore, those days are well past me. I've got a couple of false bits in my hips, so running is out; I use my rowing machine at home looking over the river so I can pretend I'm out there, I also walk a lot, pretty much every day. If it's out in the streets it's a good hour, if it's on a treadmill with inclines, it's thirty minutes. Then I do a small circuit, press-ups and those sorts of things and I do that pretty much every day, five to six days a week. I do all of this because I know that if I'm not fit and healthy, I'm just not as alert.

They say the brain is no different to the rest of the muscles in your body – you either use it or you lose it.

It's a well-known fact that exercise has a positive impact on the brain in that when the heart rate increases more oxygen is pumped into the brain, not to mention the release of hormones into the body that nourish the growth of brain cells. But what is even more interesting, particularly where Murray is concerned, is the exercises that involve different parts of the brain, like coordination, rhythm and strategy, have a higher impact on cognitive performance than mental tasks alone or exercises that don't include those elements. Rowing is one such exercise that involves all of the above, so no wonder Murray just keeps going.

Stay in reasonable nick because you can cope with a whole lot more if you're healthy.

Meanwhile back on the foreshore in Nedlands, Steve's had been sealed and the renovations and building works had begun. First to rise were two apartment blocks overlooking the foreshore and river – one six storeys and the other four – both with luxurious penthouse apartments. The location was ideal for such a development, but when you build so close to the river, problems with water often arise. The development at Number 35 The Esplanade was no exception. From the outset difficult soil conditions and the required removal of water and acid sulphate soils made this a time consuming and costly process. But this was to be a luxurious development so there was to be no cutting corners. To add to costs, an on-site water treatment system was installed during construction, to process groundwater before it was released into the storm water drains. Once construction was complete it would turn contaminated water into drinking water. They were the first clean water tanks to be used in Australia and they came at a price, but the result was worth it.

[Murray] When we finished the first two apartment blocks, we were then supposed to build on the back western block but Multiplex decided, as part of the joint venture with me, that we had too much product. So instead of building on the land, they sold the seven lots off individually. The individual purchasers then entered into a contract with us to have seven townhouses designed and built all at the same time.

I was already in the process of converting the old building into four luxury apartments and was happy with the way they were coming together. I have to admit it was such a humbling experience – the opportunity to restore the 1908 building, to protect and pay respect to its architectural heritage and yet still provide the future owners with a modern apartment. Of course, I didn't do it on my own, we had a great team. In particular, three people were vital to the success of the restoration project; Phillip Griffith who was the architect, builder Brendon Mainstone and all-round tradesman Gary Mottram; those guys were so dedicated, and I have massive respect for what they delivered.

Once that was done all we had left to do was build the restaurant and the ten apartments above it. The restaurant was to be handed back to me as an empty shell that I would fit-out and they would take the apartments. But somewhere along the line they decided there wasn't enough in the deal for them to continue and they pulled out of the joint venture. So, I thought – okay I'll do it on my own. And I did.

Only problem was when we finished, we fell straight into the middle of the GFC.

Throughout construction the real estate market had kept rising and everyone believed it would just keep going. There were a lot of opportunists putting down tiny deposits as they weren't required to pay anything further until the building was finished. I sold all ten apartments off the plans very quickly; but we were still in the throes of finishing the project off and consequently there were a lot of apartments yet to settle. Then the GFC hit and so when it came time to settle, the buyers went to the banks. By then the banks had clamped down and weren't lending any money, so the buyers rang me and said, "We can't settle".

What could I do? No one expected a GFC. If we thought the market was hot, yeah of course it was. Did we think it was going to go from hot to freezing cold? No, we didn't. We thought it might level out or not rise as much but we sure didn't expect what happened. Of the 10 apartments we sold off the plan only four settled. I took a hit anywhere between $300,000 and $500,000 per apartment, and then I had the holding costs and all the rest of it on top. Of course, my bank started calling me, "What's going on?" Overnight the property market had dropped 20 to 25 per cent. I was right in the middle and there was nothing I could do...other than have a lot of sleepless nights.

Chaise and I had just finished building a beautiful apartment in Cottesloe looking straight out at Rottnest. It was like a sea change for us – we were across the road from the surf club, and I was in the ocean pretty much every day. I was really enjoying the lifestyle. Then the GFC hit and we were left with all those apartments, with masses of debt and banks breathing down my neck. I just thought, I've got to be fair to the bank. So, we put everything on the market. The first thing to get an offer, of course, was our new apartment in Cottesloe. So, tear in my eye, we copped it sweet and left.

We rented for 18 months because I had leased out all the empty apartments to get an income. I initially had no intention of moving back there but when one of the tenants left, for financial reasons, we moved back in. We are still there today, in the now 120-year-old building where I began life, and I have to say it's a fantastic place to live.

Perth still hasn't recovered from the GFC. We also had the mining collapse, or at least a slow-down of infrastructure, and so the building of mines stopped. The people that had come flooding into Perth to build all those things, up and left, and so of course the rental market took a hit. Initially, we were getting $4,000 a week from some of the big international companies, but suddenly it was... "WHAT! You want $1,000 a week?" At that luxury end of the market rentals dropped almost 70 per cent.

At Steve's, the first tenants to leave were in the oil and gas sector – their company had decided to get out of WA. Under an international clause, a global company can revoke a lease. They can just say, "Business is finished, we have to go."

So, there was no point fighting that one. But we were lucky, we had some great tenants. They were very fair and paid for two months in advance but left straight away. So, when we moved back in, someone was paying our rent for about a month, which was a good feeling and brought us some relief.

As Murray talked about this time in his life, he was very frank – they were hard times, they were uncomfortable and there were great disappointments, but there is no sign of regret, no wondering what might have been and no resentment for the losses. There is no embellishment and certainly no self-pity; for Murray, that's life, it happens; close of chapter and onto the next.

How people react to stressful events is often indicative of what they achieve in life. Some can be so immobilised with distress at what has happened and filled with fear of what might lie ahead that they are unable, or refuse, to entertain any thought of taking further risks – just in case they fail again. Unfortunately, the belief they will fail again often overrides the belief they won't.

But not Murray. Perhaps his aptitude for staying busy and starting new projects doesn't allow him time to ponder or question. No doubt over the years there would have been moments of self-reflection, the gathering of thoughts and maybe a tinge of anxiety, but they were fleeting and rare.

And that seems to be where the successful differ – they continue to move forward, to look for opportunity and take risks even when things go wrong, albeit every risk receives thorough thought and assessment. Do these people ever doubt themselves? It appears not, or perhaps they just don't acknowledge it. They give no time to listen to their negative inner voice, or maybe they simply don't hear it and therefore, thoughts of failure struggle to exist within them. It seems the successful don't stop behind an obstacle and dwell on the unfairness of its presence; instead they get to work immediately on forging an obstacle bypass – and once back on track there's no looking back – it's always onward, it's always forward. Learning how to silence the negative voice is surely a step in the right direction.

It seems the successful don't stop behind an obstacle and dwell on the unfairness of its presence; instead they get to work immediately on forging an obstacle bypass and once past, there is no looking back.

Murray's commitment to the hospitality industry and the people within it, has, over the years, been acknowledged by the community, by the media and by the upper echelons of business. But for Murray personally, such recognition was never necessary, nor did it ever have any great impact on him – until one night in November 2009.

[Murray] I had to attend an industry function, the Lion Nathan Gala Ball and presentation of the AHA Aon Hotel Awards for Excellence. I flew in from Singapore and got changed into a dinner suit at the airport, kicking and screaming because I hate going to those kinds of functions. It was a big night with 1100 guests expected. When Chaise and I arrived, we were seated with two other couples at what was a table for ten. We thought it was a bit odd that the others hadn't turned up. Then, former editor of The West Australian Paul Murray, who was the MC, got up and started talking about someone's life and I'm going, "Hang on a minute, this is a bit familiar". I realised he was talking about me and that I was being bestowed with the Hospitality Industry Lifetime Achievement Award. I was completely taken by surprise. I then had to get up and talk and accept the award. When I got back to our table the other guests had arrived. There was my sister Sandra and David Hohnen, David and Noellene Williams and Brian and Wendy Sierakowski. They had all been waiting in the wings because they knew if I had seen my sister, who never comes to Perth for anything, I would have known something was going on.

But I had no idea – I don't go out seeking these things so when it happens it's a really nice surprise. Receiving that award at that time, after all that had occurred with the closure of Steve's, the redevelopment, the GFC and then the re-opening of Steve's probably made it particularly special.

So, with the GFC behind him, well not quite but certainly filed away in the tougher times folder, Steve's was finally open again, and life was returning somewhat to normal. Well normal for Murray that is – frantic is probably a better description if another was to walk a day in his shoes.

[Murray] Our first Sunday session after we re-opened, everyone came down, even my Mother was there sitting at the bar. We didn't change a thing but it wasn't the same; it just didn't have the vibe and it never came back. The mojo was gone.

Live music in WA – which had always been our big attraction – was changing and by the time we re-opened it had dropped off considerably. These days, the quality and how we listen to our music is totally different; back then you could only get a scratchy vinyl and that's why live music was so popular, but now you get great music everywhere – on your phone, in your car, while you're out jogging. With the quality being so much better, live music is now considered second rate – the only live music is in a studio where they can tidy it up and make it perfect, but by achieving perfection and expectations of that perfection, the fun of live music has gone.

However, in saying that it was a good feeling to get the new bar open and we were busy. What was interesting was that most of the people that came back in were those who had started coming to Steve's 30 or 40 years before. They'd moved on in their lives and didn't want to come back to what was here previously, so they were comfortable with the new Steve's. Now I see a lot of guys walk in with a young person and when they introduce me it's their son or daughter who they have brought in to have their first drink because it's where they'd had their first drink. So, it is still very much a community place and one that has developed naturally.

But you are only as good as your weakest link. At times we can have 20 staff working here, and it only takes one to let you down. A customer can have a bad experience, or they don't get the food quality that they expect, so consequently you lose trade. There's plenty of choice out there now so you need to be at the top of your game all the time, and that's hard.

It's also an emotional and creative business, particularly in food. So, if someone brings their shit to work, it's going to be shit for the customer. I remind the staff all the time – leave your problems at home. When you come into work you are here to look after your clients; if you think you are here to look after yourself then don't join us, go somewhere else.

So, Steve's Bar and Bistro was back up and running. It was very different to what it had been, but Murray's gut instinct drove that change. He managed to create a relaxed atmosphere. To this day it continues to attract a vibrant mix of clientele. The wine list is considered to be among the best, the underground cellar is filled with character and is a big drawcard as is the wine store; both are stocked with some incredibly rare wines, and of course there's always McHenry Hohnen on the shelves. Typically, Murray rejects any suggestion he could have achieved the results without great people around him.

[Murray] Look, it's all about your staff and great customer service. I'm always telling the managers, "You can't be here 24/7 – you open at seven or eight in the morning and close at midnight, seven days a week, so your number two person is just as important as you are; they are going to be here when you are not." So, it's really important to find a quality number two who may not be ready for the top position but aspires to it. Then it's about direction; giving staff something to look forward to. For me it's about making sure we have top-end management in place.

> *Your number two person is just as important as you are; they are going to be here when you are not. So, it's really important to find a quality number two who may not be ready for the top position but aspires to it.*

It's also about finding ways to do things differently. For that purpose, we have a resident sommelier who is here to talk and help customers select the best wines to cellar or consume at home or in the bar. We have installed Enomatic wine dispensers, so our customers can pull up a chair and sample a variety of global styles of wines without buying the bottle; both those initiatives have proven very popular.

I have learned from talking to so many successful businesspeople, that success comes from getting people to do the work you don't want to do, so you have the time to focus on doing more of what you do better. And that's what Murray does so well. But no matter what he does spare time is always in short supply in Murrays time bank. In 2010 it was no different but what little spare time Murray did have, Neale Fong, Chairman of the West Australian Football Commission (WAFC) had just the place where he could spend it.

[Murray] Neale had asked me on a couple of occasions to put my hand up and take a position on the board of commissioners – I kept saying, "No, I'm really not that interested".

But then he asked again, "Look, I've only got a year to go, would you please put your hand up."

Because of the new stadium coming up, I could foresee that football would have a major say in it and so the job would be interesting – or so I thought, yeah okay, now I'll stick my hand up.

I got straight into it and was immediately elected deputy-chairman and Frank Cooper, former Fremantle Dockers board member, stepped in as chair.

With the location and plans for the new stadium still very much under discussion we created a new entity; a subsidiary of WAFC called Perth Stadium Management (PSM) to allow us to bid for the new stadium management and other venues like the WACA ground and nib Stadium. We'd been doing it for years at Subiaco Oval anyway but PSM took over the total running of it.

We changed all the staff, the caterers, we changed everything and gave it an absolute fresh-ness to show that we were even better than we had been before.

I chaired the entity. My specialist area at the WAFC was to work towards getting the manage-ment of the new stadium. If we didn't get it the WAFC would really miss out on an income that it had been making from catering and holding events at Subiaco Oval. CEO Gavin Taylor and I worked together to get some very strong international partners like Delaware North, Ticket-master and Live Nation.

Live Nation is the biggest content provider in the world, hence we got Adele, we got U2 – if you want content you need to work with Live Nation. Delaware North is the biggest caterer in the world. They are family owned, with their own sporting teams, their own stadiums, they do the Hub in Singapore, and Rod Laver Centre and Etihad in Melbourne. Then Ticketmaster is the biggest ticket organisation in the world. So, they all have the financial muscle to handle the ups and downs, and if we ever needed capital, they could put it in. So, we had very strong partners.

Each of those partners contributed an equal share to the bid of the stadium management and over the journey it cost us half a million dollars to make that bid.

Despite everything – the costs involved, the opportunities, the experience we brought to the table and the strength of our partners – our bid was totally disregarded by government. I be-lieve this was always their intention but they allowed us to spend that kind of money because they didn't have the balls to say, don't bid. They knew if they had done so there would have been an uproar from the public, so they chose to remain silent with the view that we should run football and not stadiums.

That government regime owes football an apology, however we are not wasting time waiting and they were thrown out of office just before the new stadium was completed in any case.

Until the stadium was built there were very few facilities in Perth that were up to standard, and so we would often miss out on entertainment acts. There's huge cost in moving equipment, stages and seats, and so with the economics and the logistics of moving them around, the acts are very selective on what states they visit. And without good facilities it's difficult to attract the star performers. Having Live Nation as our partner provided us the opportunities to get some of the world's best to Perth – but the government didn't look at that.

WAFC has run football and the stadium for years, and because we run both at the same time, for every dollar we get in, we have to spend 20¢ on maintaining the stadium and 80¢ to keep WAFL, country football and AusKick going, and for that we are condemned – that's totally wrong.

Football was given the lease of Subiaco Oval back at the end of 1989 when there was a two and three-tier stand and a rickety old stand on the wing. We started making improvements from the start of the 1990 football season and together with the government's help, we turned the whole stadium into a colosseum that holds 42,000 people.

On top of that, football moved from being totally broke at the beginning of 1990 – AFL, well VFL back in those days, was broke, WAFL was broke, Eagles were down to their last few hundred thousand dollars and Fremantle hadn't even entered the game. Today, football is in an extremely healthy position and that credit, in my opinion, goes to Peter Tannock and Graeme Edwards and the shareholders of IPL who agreed that football must own football.

By 2013 Murray's time was certainly being consumed with his endless obligations, and so when he received a phone call from Gary Steel inviting him to a function in Sydney, he declined the invitation. A second call, a few days later, from Antoine Billecart (pronounced Bilcar) the owner of the revered Champagne house Billecart Salmon, called for a rethink on that decision. Antoine explained to Murray, in his rich French accent, that he should attend the function. He had put Murray forward to be knighted as Chevalier for his contribution to the Champagne houses of France.

As modest as Murray might be, there was no denying that to receive such an acknowledgement was a huge honour. He booked his flight immediately. A formally attired Murray arrived at the Sydney Opera House where dinner was served to 400 guests at long elegant tables adorned in linen, silverware and crystal. The Champagne houses of France had sent magnums of their best and most prized Champagnes across the oceans, as a show of respect and appreciation for those who were to receive knighthoods that evening. For Murray it was an acknowledgement he was proud to accept and a night he will always remember – but as soon as the night was over, it was back home and back to business as usual.

In Perth, Murray's football commitments stepped up a notch or two when he accepted the role of Chairman of the West Australian Football Commission. After months, probably years of a very much publicised discussion and dispute, the decision had finally been made to replace football's outdated home of Subiaco and build a new stadium on the river foreshore at Burswood. With construction to begin the following year in 2014, the role of chairman required someone capable and willing to execute change and make some very difficult decisions.

[Murray] I knew it wouldn't be an easy role but changes were needed and I was prepared to make them. That included, rightly or wrongly, a change in CEO. In all honesty I felt there was someone better to do the job and as it has turned out the newly appointed CEO Gavin Taylor has proved himself to be worthy of the position.

He brought an energy and enthusiasm to the Football Commission which was badly needed. Working with him we have been able to take communication within the whole football family – from country football to WAFL – to an entirely new level and it's made a huge difference. Previously, it was a regular practice for the presidents of the individual clubs to go straight to the newspapers to vent any of their complaints and frustrations. That isn't good for the sport. But we have to remember people in football are passionate, and whilst we appreciate and understand where they're coming from, we can't have them venting directly to the newspapers. To try to stem this behaviour we installed an independent chair of the WAFL presidents. He set up an agreement with the nine presidents that if they had a complaint, they must go through him. He would then pick up the phone and ring me or someone else at WAFC and we would sort the problem out.

To support this, I decided every month I would attend each club's board meetings to talk to the entire board, not just the president on his own. If he then had a hothead board member wanting to have a slinging match at the commission, I'd be there to answer his questions civilly.

We started out at South Fremantle, and as expected I had one of these hotheads turn up. Eventually I turned to the chairman and said, "Look, Mr Chairman, if you can't control your board members then this won't work. You're the chair, this is your meeting, I'm just here to help. If your director there keeps going the way he's going, I may as well leave now."

Boom! It reset the standard and so then we rolled it out around all the clubs. Since these initiatives were introduced, we haven't had a single complaint in the newspapers from WAFL clubs which I thank them for.

I knew it wouldn't be an easy role but changes were needed and I was prepared to make them.

As far as moving to the new stadium it was a pretty bumpy ride. The government had agreed to the principle that football would not be worse off by going there. But that's not the way it went. They spent $1.6 billion and then decided what return they wanted, but when they realised there wasn't enough in it for them, they expected us to accept the shortfall. We were not about to accept that and so football's move to the stadium came to a halt.

We saw the problem being the government taking out $24 million to pay for the maintenance, upkeep, interest payments and to pay off the stadium. However, of that $24 million, $18 million was football generated. Our two AFL clubs were to get their slice but the government wanted to take $18 million leaving us, the WAFC, with $10 million instead of $11 as expected.

After months of negotiation and a lot of help from the AFL, the new government and football settled the financial conundrum to all parties' satisfaction, which was a huge relief for all concerned.

The land that Subiaco Oval (Domain Stadium) sits on is vested to the City of Subiaco. Back in the late 1980s it was leased to football on a peppercorn lease for 99 years; in 2016 we still had 70-odd years to go. However the then government wanted us to relinquish the lease but we only ever intended to cede it back to the City of Subiaco, who didn't want us to go anyway. This was happening as the change in government was taking place in 2016 and so we refused to relinquish the lease just prior to the change of government.

At that time, we didn't have a home to go to because the agreement of football moving to the new stadium was at a standstill. So where was the WAFC going? Where was our home? Do you sell your home without having another one to go to? NO.

The WACA ground was an option supported by the Barnett Government, however the government simply didn't have money to spend on the WACA and the incoming McGowan Labor Government did not see this as a viable option.

To this day I cannot understand why as Premier, Colin Barnett did not address football's requirements post the move to the new stadium.

That included not addressing the requirements of West Coast, who wanted to remain at Subiaco. Subsequently however, in frustration with a lack of communication, West Coast are now in the final stages of building a wonderful new facility at Lathlain Park.

Over six years, we rolled out plans and ideas to Colin Barnett who would then proceed to do nothing, which was very frustrating to football not to mention the time and money spent.

We all applaud the Barnett Governments vision for what is now Optus Stadium. However, their transparency to the major user in football left a lot to be desired, so much so that football was never able to reach agreement with the Barnett Government to play AFL at the new stadium.

Eventually, with a new government and a new AFL Commission chairman, Richard Goyder, in place, the answers came, and finally we were able to move forward.

The galvanised football family were so supportive of each other it made the case to the McGowan Government compelling, and today the success of the stadium for all parties proves what AFL football generates to the West Australian economy.

I had massive support from my commissioners, in particular, deputy Stuart Love and CEO Gavin Taylor who were all so steadfast throughout these negotiations.

We then restructured football for the long term; we rewrote WA's whole football agenda for the next twenty years from constitution of the commission to how the competition will be run. Within that revamping the WAFL is being restructured with greater direction coming from WAFC to make the competition not only more exciting but also more professional. To safeguard that we were headed in the right direction we spent $300,000 with the Boston Consulting Group, which made a series of recommendations that will be implemented over the coming years.

With the Fremantle Dockers moving to Cockburn it has opened the possibility for Fremantle Oval to become the home ground for both East Fremantle and South Fremantle. They still have their own training grounds but they both use Fremantle Oval for their home games – so one week it's East Fremantle at home and the next week it's South Fremantle at home. Not only is this more economically viable, it's a better facility, and because it's in a tourism precinct, Fremantle Council and all the restaurateurs in the area are very happy to see a game played there every Saturday throughout winter – unlike before when it was only every second week. We've taken a similar path with the amalgamation of home grounds for Subiaco and East Perth at Leederville Oval, which is also in an entertainment precinct.

As it turns out Joondalup-West Perth FC has been rebuilt, as has Claremont. Lathlain Park, Perth FC and Swan Districts are about to get upgraded facilities and Rushton Park down at

Peel was done some years ago, and each has very good facilities. These changes are all significant improvements that will allow football to move forward – so all in all, it's looking pretty good but as I said before it's been a bumpy ride to get there.

The role as WAFC chairman takes time, however it is enjoyable as it is a break from your business and is always one that is seeking to advance and improve the game and its facilities – and that's important to me.

> *The role as WAFC chairman takes time, however it is enjoyable and is always one that is seeking to advance and improve the game and its facilities - and that's important to me.*

Murray had a very clear vision of what needed to be done to put football in Western Australia in the best position for a mighty future. Not everyone agreed with his vision but as Bill Gates said – Vision without execution is daydreaming. Well Murray is not a daydreamer; he got on with the job, he took action and made changes. Admittedly his position on the popularity ladder dropped a few rungs as he encountered the naysayers and the obstacles along the way. But making friends or gathering a healthy collection of opponents along the way was of no interest to him – realising his vision of securing football for the long term, was. He has achieved what he set out to do and so now maybe he will sit back and relax...

[Murray] No, I'm not going to relax. I like being busy, I can't sit around, there's nothing worse than sitting around; I've never been able to sit on a beach for more than ten minutes. Movies are okay because you have to concentrate – but just sitting around, no that's not for me.

I used to go to Rottnest Island a fair bit – it was my dropout zone. It's where you look back at the mainland and go, I'm in a good place over here. It's one of the best assets WA has, particularly being right next to the city, to have this little island that we all call our own.

Neil Hamilton, Paul Kempthorne and I had a boat called Double Blessing that we could take to Rottnest. It was 40 foot, a decent size without being ostentatious. We had it for about seven years but in the end we were only using it once a year, which was crazy, so we sold it.

Still, some days I get up and see the calmness on the water and go, "Shit, I wish I had the boat so I could just take off," but at the end of the day, I've got enough mates with boats who regularly invite me. 90 per cent of the time I say no anyway because I'm heading south to the winery. I remember when Peter Laurance had his winery and was selling his own boat, he wrote a note saying, "I'm selling my boat because I've worked out if you own a vineyard you can't own a boat". That comment has stayed with me because Peter was 100 per cent right – I work in the vineyard and the winery and I love it, and whilst I love boats, I don't have time for both. As I've said before I'm a farmer at heart and that's where I really want to spend my time. Wine, and trying to be the best at it, is my passion.

I'm a farmer at heart and that's where I really want to spend my time. Wine, and trying to be the best at it, is my passion.

To be the best you must have great winemakers. We started off with David's daughter Freya as our winemaker, and when she left to have children in 2007 her partner, Ryan Walsh, stepped in and completed the 2008 – 2011 vintages. Then in 2012, AFL player Trent Carroll took over his role. Trent is an amazing winemaker but he and his wife Amanda were very passionate about producing raw organic kombucha, a sparkling probiotic drink, so they started their brand Rok. When it took off, Trent resigned. He found us a new winemaker, Julien Grounds, who was also fantastic because not only is he a natural winemaker he's also business driven, so, I had a great balance. In 2017 Julian was awarded Dux of the Len Evans Tutorial. Understandably, his profile attracted interest from others and that eventually saw him make a move to New Zealand's Craggy Range, a much larger and commercial wine brand. While we were disappointed to see him go, we accepted it was a move he wanted to make.

Japo Del Cani, a young Italian winemaker, has been our senior winemaker for our contract winemaking, which is where we make wines for different people like Rob Bowen wines. When Julian departed to New Zealand, Japo was naturally appointed as the principal winemaker with McHenry Hohnen from the 2019 vintage onwards.

Japo is extremely passionate and very focused on grape quality in the vineyard with our biodynamic approach to producing the very best fruit which he can make into extraordinary wines. I have great faith in him and trust this will be a relationship for many years to come.

Am I a bit over-geared down there? Most probably but you know, I think for the service we give ourselves, let alone[to our] contract people, it's the best service they can get – and I'm happy with that.

Our wines have won a lot of awards which is important to the winemakers. It's a little bit like being involved in football – the players get the grand final not the board; we are there to help them do it, that's the way I see it. From a branding point of view, it's good that your wines are up there, although I refuse to put those medals on our bottles – that's just advertising and personally I think the best advertising is word of mouth.

You can't advertise that kind of thing, most people wouldn't believe you, but they will believe a friend who's been and experienced it.

We gave a young sommelier from Sydney the opportunity to experience working for four days in vintage. You can't buy that experience but it's one that she will probably never forget. She's been taught everything from harvest through to the fermenting, to the finished product. She works at a Sydney restaurant called Bibo, and her partner is the manager of Rockpool, so it's a good network opportunity. It's not ostentatious, it's nice and simple but she is now walking around as an encyclopaedia for us.

We don't do that kind of thing often but it certainly adds that personal touch. We have a bunch of guys who call themselves the Three Fat Kings. They wanted to make a wine so we organised for them to buy a new barrel so they could then come down to the farm and pick the Cabernet to go into it. We got them to stomp it because it was only 500-700kg of grapes – it was then fermented before their barrel was filled with it. Now the Three Fat Kings barrel sits at our winery in a barrel hall and every time the guys come to Margaret River they come and have a look at it. Eventually, in about two years, it will be ready for bottling. Knowing these guys, they'll want to have a heavy Three Fat Kings type of wine, so we'll need to make it a bit richer, a longer oak.

Those little projects can be a pain in the arse but geez, it's good fun doing them because of the connection you have with people, plus all they do is talk about it. They come down to the winery and they see how precise we are, how natural we are, no chemicals anywhere and they spread that gospel. You can't advertise that kind of thing, most people wouldn't believe you, but they will believe a friend who's been and experienced it.

That's why good branding is so important – it can have such an impact on a wine label.

Look at Phil Sexton who created Matilda Bay Brewing Company. He has the Giant Steps wine label and then he created a second one called Innocent Bystander. I think his Giant Steps Moscato was his biggest product and he got that up to such a level that Brown Brothers had to buy it because it was eating into their market share of Moscato. Whatever they paid him they paid him and now he's back to just Innocent Bystander, but he could create another label tomorrow and do the whole thing again.

Howard Park has Mad Fish which could be sold off. They could say, "Look, we don't want to be involved in millions of cases, we want to go back to being earthy winemakers." Devil's Lair could get rid of Fifth Leg. Well we're no different. We could build Rocky Road up to a quantum and then somebody could say, "I want to buy that".

I didn't think that way at the start. The passion for me is in every wine we make, but I've seen what's happened to others and so I thought we should at least position ourselves in the same way – so that's why we grabbed the name Rocky Road.

We had it trademarked the day we bought the property because it was on Rocky Road and the name was available. Initially we called the vineyard Rocky Road but changed it to Hazel's because we wanted to use the name Rocky Road as a brand. Our proper brand of course is McHenry Hohnen and that's where our series wines are. Whilst Rocky Road is a series wine, it won't be once we push it into being a brand in its own right. So, if we wanted to get out of making 10,000 cases of $25 wine, somebody could buy it off us and we would go back to pottering around doing smaller amounts. We're not planning that at the moment but it's what we could do.

Everybody knows viticulture doesn't make money. Consequently, the best thing you can do is break even and make a small bit but you're not going to get rich. The only way you can get rich in viticulture is if some big tycoon comes in and wants what you've got. But in saying that someone recently asked me, "What's your last asset standing?" And I said, "The winery." I wouldn't sell it.

> *What's your last asset standing? The winery, I wouldn't sell it.*

I say that but when things get very tight you do think along those lines. But I've learned over the years that if you don't want to be in the position where you're forced to sell something, maintain a healthy relationship with your bank. The biggest thing in life is communication, so my advice is to communicate with your bank and they will work with you. If you don't communicate and you go into hiding, they won't bother looking for you, they'll just shut you down. Because of the relationship I've built with my bank they know I don't walk away from things and they know I'm still working. If I was off gallivanting around the place or not talking to them, they would probably say, "Hang on a minute, we shouldn't support a guy like that." If you are in business or not, it's important to have that open communication – it can make all the difference.

> *I've learned over the years that if you don't want to be in the position where you're forced to sell something, maintain a healthy relationship with your bank. The biggest thing in life is communication, so my advice is to communicate with your bank and they will work with you.*

There isn't a single person in this book who hasn't mentioned how critical it is to have that open communication with your bank; but how many times do we hear of people who will do anything to avoid those conversations. In movies you always see the so-called failures in life ducking out the back door to escape the creditor or ignoring their phone calls.

Few people enjoy confrontation, feelings of discomfort, guilt or despair when times are tough. But one thing is certain, facing up to a problem, dealing with an issue and accepting responsibility for it is truly an empowering experience - because you have taken control.

So, whatever the obstacle, don't run from it, find a way around it – go over it, under it or straight through it – all the while knowing another obstacle will be just around the corner. But, as they say, what doesn't kill you makes you stronger – exactly what you need to be in business.

[Murray] I've been very fortunate in that I've always done what I've wanted to do – my family will often have a go at me for it and I can't disagree – I just don't do what I don't want to do. But there is a time when you have to say, I don't want to keep doing all these things forever. So, for the last ten years I've been thinking about my exit strategies and succession planning. I'm fortunate I don't really have to worry about succession planning but it is important in families. It can put a real burden on the younger person because there's almost an expectation. Have a look at James Packer; the expectation – is he as good as his dad – all that sort of crap. You see a lot of generational people in business, particularly in wineries; some of them work really, really well and others are disasters. I don't want to be a disaster in that respect, and while I had always thought my niece Freya, who is involved in the business, would have been the ideal successor, it isn't what she wants.

Freya and her husband Ryan Walsh have created their own brand, Walsh & Sons, which is their combined passion and direction, so we have sensibly decided to do our own thing. But it does throw up a few hurdles around succession which I had not contemplated occurring. However, as with other experiences I will take this on with the team we have and enjoy the challenge to seek a sustainable pathway for the brand we have poured a lot of heart and soul into.

What's important to me now is to see that the people in my immediate family are in a comfortable space without taking away their own drive. I don't want to silver spoon anybody but at the same time I want the best for them.

> *I don't really have to worry about succession planning, but it is important in families. It can put a real burden on the younger person because there's almost an expectation - look at James Packer.*

[Murray] Although it's probably far-fetched I'd love to see my daughter Stephenie (spelt that way because of my Dad's name) become involved in what we have created here because it's a nice business to be in and perhaps become a local lawyer in Margaret River. If we can make the wine business sustainable and not something that requires continual funding then I'd love her to be involved; the opportunity would be there, but I'm not going to demand it. We'll see where it all lands.

The properties are getting close to a reasonable maturity, although there's never a day that you don't see an opportunity to improve something but most improvements cost money and you've got to know where that's coming from. I'd just like to make sure we're in the position over the next couple of years to fall into that space where the business down there is providing enough income to support our lifestyle rather than eating into the asset. A bit more work to do yet but we're getting close to it.

Then, what I really want to do is spend 80 per cent of my time down there, to enjoy it more. I don't want to leave Perth totally but I'd certainly like to have a choice of where I spend my time each year. It's not complicated, I like the simple things – the land, country life. I don't set myself to be humble but if that's the way it is then that's the way it is. I dress the way I want to dress, I don't walk around in suits, I'll put one on if I have to but I prefer not to. What you see is what you get. I don't spend time trying to impress people, that's not me. I just do what I do and if that doesn't suit people, it doesn't suit them. It's not that I don't care, it's just I don't think it matters what other people think. Some people probably have a view on me but to be honest I'm actually not interested in hearing it.

Murray is very clear and direct about where he stands, how he sees himself and his life. He won't answer a question if he isn't asked – as Murray often quotes: "You can't regret saying nothing. So, keep your mouth shut." There is an honesty in him that you almost don't expect – maybe that comes with age, experience and wisdom. For all he has achieved, for all the obstacles and all the triumphs, he still speaks softly and always appears at ease – a clear example that it isn't how one presents on the outside, it is the fire that burns within the man that maketh the man. So, what next for Murray?

[Murray] To be honest, it's pretty simple, I don't have any major ambitions to climb another mountain. We've built something pretty special down in Margaret River, so I want to go and use what we have created.

Well as they say Murray – as you sow so shall you reap. But it does seem almost impossible to imagine him not climbing any more mountains. Maybe there will be a few smaller ones that will catch his eye, who knows, but I'm sure he would agree one thing is certain – wherever he goes there will always be a bottle of red close by.

Á votre santé Murray and thank you.

Steve McHenry at the Nedlands Park Hotel

The McHenry family

Murray and Sandra

Steve and Hazel McHenry

Murray 'horsing' around on a cow

Murray and Sandra on Silver

At Christ Church Grammar School

Murray at the Royal Show

Rowing

Murray in front of McHenry
Dunstan and Hurley at
Steves Hotel

Murray

The Nedlands
Park Hotel

Steves Hotel - as luxury apartments today

Chaise and Murray's wedding day 2009

Overlooking the vines

McHenry Hohnen Margaret River

Murray - Chairman of WAFC

Murray in his AFL role

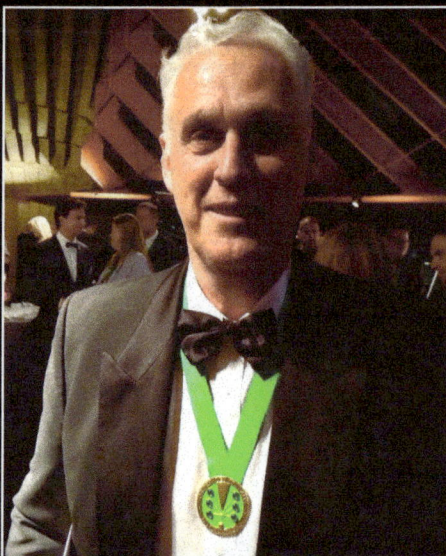

Murray inducted by the French as a *chévalier* for his contributions to the champagne industry

Murray, most at home among the vines

David Hohnen, wine writer and
critic James Halliday and Murray

Murray with his grandchildren

Murray and Chaise

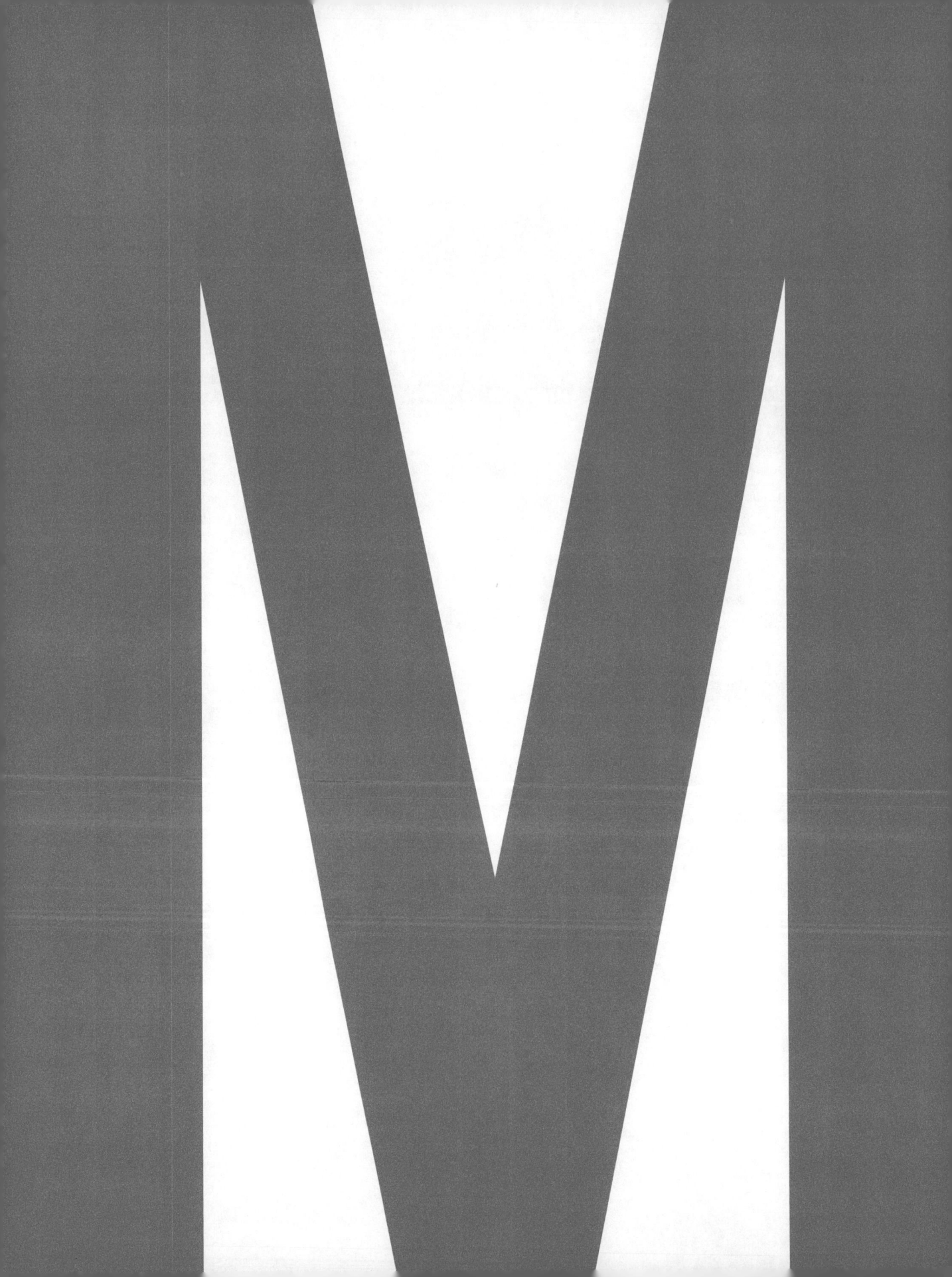

7

Pursuing an Obsession with Passion and Purpose

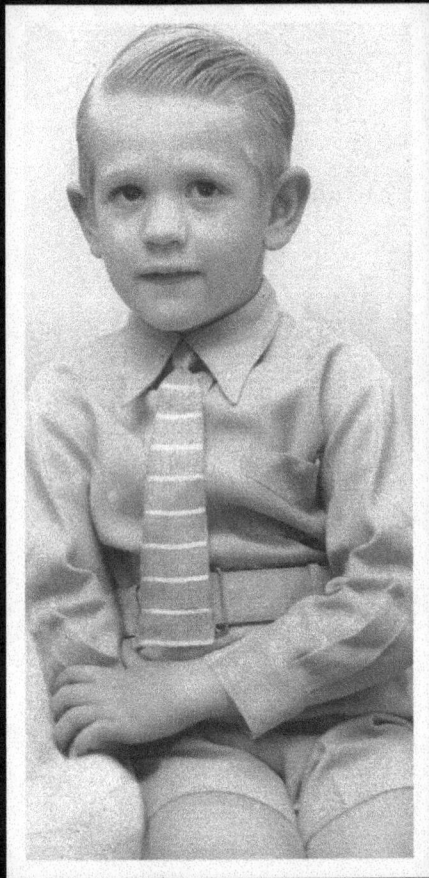

"Your health is something money can't buy.
Don't leave it until tomorrow; make
your health and fitness the two
things you work on daily."

Quiet, unassuming, very normal – that is how you might describe this couple. And for both of them life was perfectly normal – at the start that is – but it didn't stay that way for long. Their lives are testimony that even within the most ordinary, the extraordinary can lie, just waiting for an opportunity to emerge.

It took their worlds to collide to unleash that extraordinary. Whilst still in their teens, courage and the promise of freedom – and no doubt a fair amount of naivety that is kept specially for young hearts – inspired them to step into a world outside their own. Refusing to be choked by life's conformities, demands and expectations they set about exploring, developing and expanding their horizons well beyond the classrooms they had so recently left.

He was quiet but adventurous, open to opportunity and into everything fitness; she was shy but determined to challenge the system and surprisingly she had an astounding grip on numbers.

She held his hand tightly as he led the way. Both were driven but neither were sure of where they were headed. Drawing strength from each other they began to build, autonomously at first, but once they combined their strengths the extraordinary that lay within each of them was released. Together, they have come close to mastering the treadmill that carries us all, albeit very differently, through life. Now finally, after more than 30 years of building Australia's largest privately-owned fitness retail chain they are free to jump off the treadmill – but there rises yet another unexpected challenge and one they must now find a way to conquer.

They are intensely private, humble people, they are committed to promoting a healthy Australia, they are the couple behind Orbit Fitness Equipment, they are…

Peter and Lorraine Hodgson

It was the 1950s. Mr and Mrs Les and Doreen Hodgson were your typical hardworking country folk – Harvey country to be precise, where everyone knew everyone. As a truck driver in the small South-West Australian town, Les was often away from Doreen, their four daughters and their only son, Peter – the middle child.

Doreen, to help make ends meet, worked part-time cleaning at the Harvey Hospital. It was there that she was often confronted by the arrival of her concussed son after he'd been struck over the head (yet again) by one of the neighbourhood kids. But the game of cowboys and Indians was serious stuff and once released from hospital, Peter was eager to return to the streets of Harvey, ready to do his bit for the local Apaches. It was rough but that was part of the fun, and the town's kids all survived relatively unscathed. There was no, "Get inside Peter, you're not to play with that boy anymore." NO, that kind of reaction was for parents of the future.

The town's children played until dark but as soon as night fell every child's mother would stand at her back door and holler, "Tea's on the table". The children would come running from every direction; from the horse paddocks out back or the streets out front. Peter would always arrive with Rinso, his pet goat, in tow. Apparently, goats are great listeners and so with four sisters it was only natural that Rinso became Peter's greatest confidant.

Peter's schooling started at Harvey's St Anne's Catholic Primary School. A lack of teachers and space saw the need to combine grades 1 – 4 into one class. That often meant some subjects were missed whilst others were repeated. This often made it difficult for any individual brilliance to shine through. But Peter's days at St Anne's were numbered.

The State's capital, Perth, was 87 miles up the road. By the time he was nine, Peter, his mother, and sisters Maxine, Dawn, Gerry (NOT Geraldine thank you!) and Jan had made the drive one last time. Their father continued to work from Harvey but on weekends he would join them. The move into the new family home, in the inner-city suburb of Mount Hawthorn, brought an abrupt end to the freedom and life Peter knew and loved. No doubt there would have been some privately shed tears.

Peter, now in Grade 4, was sent down the road to Christian Brothers College in Leederville and his sisters to St Mary's. It was at this new school that he encountered the discrepancies between country and city curriculum. Some of the subjects he had completed in Year 3 in Harvey were only now being taught in Grade 4 at CBC. Peter was bored, and it showed. His lack of both interest and subsequent performance at school veiled the traits of the extraordinary business leader he would eventually become some 30 years down the track.

The Hodgson's settled into their new home which was located behind the local house of God. Despite being so close, young Peter would often fail to make it to early morning mass – bed was way more comfortable. This was not looked upon particularly well by the priests of St Mary's Church, nor was his stinginess with the wine he poured as an altar boy. If that wasn't enough to annoy the priests, his waving of the incense, at all the wrong times, as he walked down the aisle of the ever so quiet church, stretched their patience beyond redemption. And altar boy he was no more.

Around that same time his parents decided to separate. Upon making that decision the family home was sold and all contact with his father ceased. Doreen was left on her own to support her young family. A single mother back then was almost unheard of, and with five children to care for Doreen would surely have been fearful of what lay ahead. But with no time for fear or self-pity she rented a small house and its adjoining milk bar. It was in that milk bar, located on the corner of Scarborough Beach Road and Oxford Street that the Hodgson children first came to experience what hard work was really like. Actually, not all the Hodgson children; Peter's older sister, Maxine, had escaped into marriage, and Dawn soon decided working day and night in a milk bar was not the life for her. She moved out of home, leaving Peter, Gerry and Jan to make the milkshakes.

Helping in the milk bar was an almost unspoken rule, but if the children didn't pull their weight the shouting would start. Christmas Day was the only time their help was not expected but only because it was the one day of the year the shop closed at midday. It may have been hard for the children but as he looks back Peter realises that the discipline and learned work ethic were invaluable in the moulding of his destiny.

As Peter's teenage years progressed his days were spent between the milk bar and school with little time for anything else. By 1967, with financial struggles a daily burden in the Hodgson household, Peter had to leave school and help support the family. He was barely 15 and with little experience his job options were limited. He knew what he wanted to do but others considered his plan mere juvenile fantasy.

Peter was a great swimmer and runner; he inherited those talents from his mother. Apparently, she only just missed out on competing at the Olympics – Betty Cuthbert was chosen instead. Peter enjoyed being fit, it was in his genes, but his great passion was scuba diving – and that is what he wanted as a career. However, it wasn't to be. His mother and the staff at the CES (Commonwealth Employment Service) considered a lithograph plate maker was a far more suitable profession for a young man. As disappointing at it was, Peter may never have achieved what he has in life if he'd had his way.

He spent three months as an apprentice litho plate maker before a forward-thinking boss told him it was a dead-end job. As it turned out, he was right – there are no litho plate makers today. He suggested instead that Peter sit his exams as a communications technician – a more enduring career he believed. Peter took his advice and passed. Never one to sit around waiting for a job to come up he worked, in the interim, at the Mount Hawthorn Post Office as a telegram boy (another job no longer in existence). Peter became adept at jumping on his bike to speedily deliver a telegram. It was mostly good fun but sometimes, when there was a death in someone's family, it was up to Peter to deliver the fateful telegram. He soon learned how the different ethnicities reacted to bad news. If the recipient of the message was an older Italian woman, experience taught him that she would start wailing the moment she read it. So, Peter would run to her door, hand over the telegram and before she had time to open it, he was back on his bike, her distraught wails compelling him to pedal faster.

Not too many deliveries later Peter was offered a position as a communications technician at Post Master General (PMG), Australia's postal and telegraphic service.

Until then his mother had expected him to spend every spare moment, when he wasn't delivering telegrams, working in the milk bar. But now, finally, at 17, he was free to make his own decisions on how and where he would spend his time. With his new-found freedom and a little money came the opportunity to join American Health Studios and to participate in his work mate's favourite pastime – downing a schooner at the local watering hole. Having lunch every second Friday (pay-day) at the "Herdy" (the Herdsman Hotel) was also a must do. However, rarely did the men return to work after. It was a practice that didn't sit well with Peter, not that he didn't enjoy a beer – he just felt it shouldn't be on his employer's time. However, he was too shy and too quiet to say anything and so he simply went with the flow.

Peter may have been quiet, but he was a risk taker. It was that trait that led to him receiving the not so auspicious "Golden Screwdriver" – a PMG award for the best staff stuff-ups. It was the era before work safety laws were introduced and hence why Peter was able to lay cables in a suspended office ceiling without a safety harness. Within the roof space the tile structure was heavy and so unable to lift them Peter, balancing on the joists, crawled out. Suddenly, under his weight, the ceiling tiles parted and, with no harness for protection, he plummeted to the office floor below.

Not too long after receiving the first Golden Screwdriver Peter was awarded a second. This time the incident occurred as a consequence of him having long hair. Back then boy buns were unheard of. Unfortunately for Peter, while drilling on a work site, his unsecured hair was savagely snared by the rapidly rotating drill bit. It ripped a large section of hair from his scalp - and with that hair went a little of his dignity.

A few weeks after the scalp ripping drill incident, Peter headed across to Rottnest Island with his best mate Gordon for the March long weekend. The weekend getaway was a long-held tradition for the people of Perth, including a girl named Lorraine Luce who Peter was about to meet.

The meeting would change the course of both their lives, although neither Peter nor Lorraine could ever have imagined how significant a change it would ultimately prove to be.

Lorraine Luce was a tall, rebellious girl, quite likely the consequence of having a very strict parental upbringing. Her father Doug had endured hardships during his own childhood. He was born in Collie, a small coal mining town in Western Australia's South-West where his father, William, was the local plumber. Doug had just entered his teens when William and his wife Gwendolyn decided to move their family to Perth. On their arrival in the State's capital they purchased a delicatessen which they intended to operate together. Unfortunately, as a reservist in the Army, William was posted immediately to Rottnest Island leaving his wife on her own to run the deli and raise their young sons. Gwendolyn was from a very wealthy family, parfumiers from England, and hence had only ever known a stately existence. Alone and unaccustomed to the demands presented by her new life, she spiralled into deep depression. This is when life changed Doug. He was just 15 but as the oldest he had to step in and help run the deli, there was no one else. It wasn't an easy life for any of them, but it particularly impacted Doug and no doubt influenced the way he would later raise his own children.

As the years passed Doug went on to learn the trade of cabinet maker and to meet a young woman, Betty Peebles. The two were married and before long they welcomed their first daughter, Kerry. Lorraine then joined them, then Dianne and finally, with the arrival of Helen, the family was complete.

Life was a struggle but still Doug and Betty managed to save a thousand pounds, enough to purchase a block of land in Scarborough. Building materials were expensive and so Doug made the bricks himself and then determinedly built his family a home.

It was a small one-bedroom house, typical of the era but with six people it was decidedly uncomfortable. So again, they saved and eventually Doug built a much-needed second bedroom. Despite having the luxury of more space, four girls sharing the one bedroom was never going to be easy. The bickering was incessant. Yet again, life changed Doug. He grew increasingly strict and so did Betty.

Their second oldest, Lorraine, was an insecure but headstrong child whose greatest displeasure was school. Beyond a natural flair for maths and handwriting, Lorraine had no interest in academia. Being taller than most girls her age, at a time when being tall was not considered the enviable attribute it is today, she struggled to fit in. Her self-confidence took a regular battering and with that Lorraine began to rebel.

By the time she left Scarborough Primary School, or Deanmore as it is known today, and entered Churchlands High School she was a defiant teenager challenging the system and her parents whenever the opportunity arose.

She looked for any excuse not to go to school. Even visits to the orthodontist for the fitting of braces was a preferred experience although, no doubt, they too would have attracted the predictable resentment. But braces were expensive, and Lorraine remembers with a tinge of sadness and guilt how much harder her father had to work just so he could give his second child straight teeth.

Doug may have been strict, but he was a good man and a loyal and hard worker. When nearly 50 years old he was offered the opportunity to purchase a part ownership of the business he had joined as an apprentice so many years earlier. Lorraine was secretly proud of him but her wilful defiance masked any such emotion and she continued throughout school to give her parents much to worry about.

With average grades she only just passed her junior certificate and so Doug and Betty saw no benefit to their daughter continuing at school. Instead, they sent her to Key Personnel, a business college in the city.

Three months later she was working as a ledger machinist at Caris Brothers Jewellers earning $15.25 per week. Unfortunately, the only other ledger machinist at Caris Brothers took an instant dislike to Lorraine and her apparent inability to balance the books. Given no opportunity to defend herself, Lorraine was unceremoniously sacked.

Overwhelmed with humiliation and struggling to maintain any level of self-confidence, the fifteen year old refused to look for another job. That refusal was quickly condemned. Doug made it very clear that staying at home was not an option. He would never allow any of his children to 'bludge' on the system or on him. Defiance was pointless. So, accepting defeat a miserable Lorraine went in search of work. Fortunately, it didn't take long before she found a position at a chartered accountants office in West Perth.

She was trained as a figure typist, doing profit and loss statements and balance sheets. If mistakes were made the statement had to be redone – no erasers were allowed! Lorraine learned very quickly how not to make mistakes and as it turned out she was good at getting it right.

It's worth adding here that many who are successful in business consider that one of the most important skills you can have, if you want business success, is to know how to read and prepare a profit and loss statement.

If you are in business know how to read your profit and loss statements.

Six months after she was sacked her old boss from Caris Brothers phoned and spoke to Doug. He had discovered why Lorraine had been unable to balance the books – the other ledger machinist had been cooking the books. He wanted to apologise and ask if she would return to work for him. Although happy to have been cleared of any wrongdoing Lorraine was characteristically defiant.

[Lorraine] They could stick their job up their jumper. Anyway, by then I was earning a whopping $25 a week.

Her confidence was naturally boosted although it still wasn't enough to stop her face turning an embarrassing ruby red when anyone spoke to her. While that trait and a lack of confidence plagued Lorraine for years it never stopped her wanting to experience life – parties, boyfriends and roller-skating. Despite working full-time her parents forbade her to have that kind of fun, so she lied to them – more often than not.

Lorraine had just turned 16 when she used one of her lies to cover for a trip to Rottnest; the same weekend that Peter Hodgson and his mate Gordon were on the holiday isle (along with half the population of Perth). The weekend that would bring irrevocable change to both their lives.

[Peter] Gordon and I were staying at Tent Land on Rottnest and that's where we met Lorraine and her girlfriend.

[Lorraine] I didn't like Peter at all.

[Peter] Gordon hooked up with Lorraine's girlfriend. A few weeks later they were going to dinner at the Bullseye Steakhouse in North Perth and asked me to join them; I invited Lorraine.

[Lorraine] The Bullseye was the place to go so I accepted. I remember Peter turned up with a corsage for me and from that night we started seeing each other.

My Mother didn't like him because he was a Catholic and she was a very strict Anglican. (That's how it was in those days.)

Her parents may not have liked Peter but they soon realised they had far more to worry about when Lorraine defiantly told them, Peter and I have decided to go on an overseas holiday together. They were furious but that fury was nothing like it would have been if Lorraine had told them the truth about where they were headed and for how long. She would certainly have been forbidden to go if they had known and subsequently her life would have taken an immensely different path. However, that was never going to happen because, according to Lorraine, it wouldn't have made any difference what her parents said.

[Lorraine] I was so defiant; I was going and that was that. We had already decided we were going for three months but I told Mum and Dad we'd only be gone a short while – as it turned out we were away much, much longer.

So, Peter and Lorraine left Australia for an adventure that would first take them to a country rich in natural resources, spectacular scenery and diverse culture. It was also a country besieged with hatred and violence and where Nelson Mandela was just 10 years into his 27 years of imprisonment.

Peter and Lorraine arrived in Johannesburg, South Africa, on an afternoon in March 1973 just as 100,000 African workers went out on strike. It was the beginning of a brutal rebellion born from profound oppression, humiliation and racial segregation – the product of the apartheid legislation. But the two young travellers were oblivious to the dangers. For them South Africa was the start of what would ultimately be a character building and life changing, six-year adventure. Peter was 19 and Lorraine just 17.

[Peter] We planned to stay in Johannesburg for around three months, make some money because we didn't have much, maybe $200, and then head to the UK. Before we left Perth, we contacted this organisation which was to arrange our accommodation and set up jobs for us when we arrived. They were supposed to pick us up from the airport, but nobody showed up. We waited and waited until we were the last people there.

[Lorraine] We had already been given the address of where we would be staying so we took a taxi to Hillbrow, a suburb of Johannesburg. A few days later they called to say they'd been expecting us on a different day.

[Peter] Because I'd worked as a communications technician in Australia, I got a job as an electrician. They didn't seem at all concerned that I didn't know much about electrical work and sent me off to a mine site. I was put in charge of a team of 20 African guys in the middle of nowhere.

My next job was as auto electrician for the Municipal Transport Department (MTD). At the job interview the engineer drew a coil and said, "Where do you put positive?" And I said, "There," and he said, "You've got the job." So then apparently, I was an auto electrician, wiring up buses.

[Lorraine] Peter loved that job and I loved mine; working with an accountant at the 'Argus' which was the 'Star' newspaper. I did all of their financial statements.

One night, not long after I started at the Argus, Peter made this stew; it was revolting but we couldn't afford not to eat it. When I got paid, we bought some sausages to add to the stew but before we could someone broke into our house and robbed us. They took all of my clothes and underwear, but they also took our sausages; I just cried because we were so hungry.

It was a dangerous place and I guess there was always an underlying fear but until the robbery we didn't really think about it, not that it stopped us doing what we wanted. Mum and Dad would often write to ask if we were okay because in Australia they kept hearing about all the violent uprisings in South Africa.

[Peter] Hillbrow, where we lived, was an inner-city suburb of Johannesburg and quite cosmopolitan. It was an apartheid designated whites-only area and at the time was known to be the most densely populated two square miles in the world.

There was no TV, so we went out a lot and I trained every night. I had a life membership with American Health Studios in Perth and they had an affiliation with thousands of health clubs around the world, including one in Hillbrow. Hillbrow, being very cosmopolitan, had a lot of gyms around – most of them were like our 24-hour centres now. They were very progressive and so I learned a lot about different gyms and the practices of them – it's where my interest in the industry really started.

[Lorraine] At that age we had no fear of death; no concept of it. We just didn't think and some of the things we used to do were ridiculous. We bought an old Kombi van that we were always having starter motor issues with. Johannesburg is at 6000 feet above sea level and whenever we went somewhere different it would break down. Peter fixed it but not until after our first road trip.

[Peter] We had teamed up with friends Max, Joan and Oli and headed for Bulawayo, just inside the Rhodesian border (now Zimbabwe). Bulawayo is the second largest city in Zimbabwe, after the capital Harare.

At the time Rhodesia had so many terrorists. It was a scary place and we were all a little on edge.

We drove to Wankie game reserve (now known as Hwange National Park) which is on the main road between Bulawayo and Victoria Falls. Wankie is a massive game reserve and you could go from one base camping area to another but there could be 500-600km between them, so you had to register at the base camps. If you didn't show up where you were meant to, they would at least have some idea of where to start looking.

From there we continued on to Victoria Falls. We found ourselves on the border of Zimbabwe and Zambia which was at war with Rhodesia. Suddenly the guys at the border pulled out their machine guns and pointed them at us. I threw the Kombi into reverse and went screaming backwards, luckily avoiding any confrontation. We had real problems with that Kombi but on that day, it got us out of there.

[Lorraine] At the same time two Canadian girls were shot at and killed from across the Zambian border. They had been sightseeing at the Falls. It was a tourist destination, but it was really dangerous. The same happened to us when we went on a river cruise to see the hippos. The Zambians shot at the boat from the other side, but they couldn't quite reach us because the skipper knew how far to stay away.

So, it was risky, but we had a great life. We had lots of friends and we would have lived there happily ever after, but I got pregnant and for whatever reason we decided we didn't want to have our child born in South Africa.

Finally, after three years of what was intended to be a three-month escapade their time in South Africa came to an end. When they packed up their belongings (there wasn't much to pack) Lorraine was seven months pregnant. Most couples in the same situation would have typically returned home to the support and security of family. Not Peter and Lorraine. Instead, they headed to the United Kingdom. It was now 1976.

[Peter]   We arrived in the UK and found a bedsit near Hammersmith Station, but it was really small and expensive, so we decided to look for communal housing. I got a job with Storeacall Communications and they gave me a little Morris van to use.

[Lorraine] It was lucky Peter had that car because one afternoon I was walking home when my water broke – I had no idea what the hell was going on because we hadn't done any pre-natal classes and didn't really read anything. When Peter got home about 4 pm he realised I was about to have the baby.

[Peter]   We had never been to the hospital, so we just drove the Morris but...

[Lorraine]   We couldn't find the hospital...

[Peter]   So, we asked a policeman and he directed us and we got her in there.

[Lorraine] Barbara was born at 5:25 pm.

[Peter]   Whilst Lorraine was in the hospital, I moved our gear into a communal house in Acton, an inner suburb of London. There were about 22 people living there which was stretching the local bylaws because only 17 occupants were allowed. They also didn't allow children, so we had to sneak Barbara in.

[Lorraine] We didn't have a cot, so Barb slept in a drawer next to the bed, so when she'd cry, we'd close the... No, we didn't but sometimes I felt like it. She just didn't sleep!

[Peter] We were constantly anxious about anyone hearing her, so we were always carrying her around or taking her for a drive to get her to sleep.

[Lorraine] We finally got sprung but everyone in the house got on board and allowed us to stay; one of the boarders even gave me some mothering advice that helped me get Barb to sleep.

[Peter] We had purchased a Kombi van so decided to head over to Europe. Our budget was only a dollar a day plus fuel, so we hadn't spent anything on car maintenance and the tyres were really bald. It was hard to steer so when we were driving through Yugoslavia I decided to rotate and change them. We pulled up on the side of a cliff and when I finished the only place to wash my hands was in a stream at the bottom. So, I climbed down. It was very steep and covered in stones which began to slip. I'd almost made it when I tripped and fell, landing headfirst between two boulders. That experience ended with me being stitched up by a local doctor who couldn't speak a word of English.

We continued on and met up with two Australian couples and drove in a three-car convoy through Greece. When we got to Corfu, we were the last in the group when suddenly this car came around the corner and drove straight off the cliff in front of us. We stopped and ran down to the vehicle which was upside down. Several people were laying dazed on the ground and one lady was still in the car, so we quickly dragged her out. By then our fellow travellers had arrived on the scene with a very well equipped first aid kit, and with my first aid training we patched everyone up. What had happened was when we came around the corner the other car had moved too far to the right, the road was in such bad shape that it just gave way.

It was an unforgettable trip not only because of the chain of events that could so easily have ended in disaster, but it was on that trip they celebrated two firsts; first trip to Europe and Barb's first birthday. On their arrival back at their communal house in the UK they were met with an unexpected announcement – they had to move out. The owners had found out about Barb and were concerned she would attract the attention of child services and the local council. So, with no alternative, they were out on their own.

Still working full-time at Storacall Communications, Peter, now with a need to supplement his income, took on an additional, near full-time role, as a recreation officer and lifeguard. It was exhausting however Peter, accustomed to hard work, savoured the challenge. Lorraine also, for the first time since arriving in the UK, had to find work. She found a relatively well-paying job as a forecourt attendant (petrol pumper) earning 71p an hour (a decent income back then).

[Peter] We both had to work as everything was expensive in the UK but we still had the Kombi so we continued to go back and forth to Europe. We got to know it really well. When it came time to leave the UK we sold the Kombi but then decided we'd make one last trip. We took

Lorraine's Noddy car. It was a 1953 Morris Minor which is a very small car – hence the reason Lorraine called it her Noddy car. In Spain we started having problems with it. At first it was the exhaust valves and then the alternator went – things just kept happening. We also had our backpacks and Barb and her nappies (no disposables back then) so it was pretty uncomfortable. At the border of France and Spain I got out to stretch my legs. Just at that moment this car came hurtling down the road towards us. Suddenly it did a complete somersault and came flying through the air with the driver hanging out the window. I thought it was going to hit us, it was that close. It landed back on all fours and the driver just got out, picked up his rear windscreen off the road, threw it in the back seat, got back in and drove across the border.

By the time we got to Marcé in France we'd had enough so we drove to the train station, left the keys in the car and caught the train back to England.

That's the way we lived – we did exactly what we wanted, we had a few close calls and I guess I took a lot of risks.

Once back in England, Lorraine secured a well-paid job as a secretary for a temp company (recruitment agency for staff wanting temporary work). Barb was on the brink of turning two which meant the opportunity for her to travel free would end on her birthday. With Peter's long-held desire to see the USA, they both agreed that as he wasn't working, he would take Barb and return to Australia via the US. Lorraine would stay on in the UK for a while and continue with her temp work. And so, with Barb's birthday looming, father and daughter were soon jetting across the North Atlantic towards North Carolina.

[Peter] I met this couple on the flight who worked on a farm; he was a milker from the UK and his wife was American. When they found out that we hadn't made any plans they invited Barb and I to stay with them and I thought – why not.

Hickory Nut Gap Farm in North Carolina was like the farm off the TV series 'The Waltons', although these owners were very wealthy. The farmer was also a politician and he and his wife, who looked like a hillbilly and smoked a corn pipe, lived on the farm with their four children. The youngest was a bit crazy and would take pot-shots at tourists. The main farmhouse looked like it had been built in the civil war with hiding spots everywhere – to get away from the Yankees.

The milkers lived in a separate house and that's where we stayed. There was another house being built on the property, so I offered to wire it up with all my massive electrical skills (laughter). Barb and I ended up staying on the farm for nearly six months and that's where we celebrated Barb's second birthday.

During that time, I hitchhiked with Barb down to Florida to see some Australian friends who were there competing in a hang-gliding competition.

A man hitchhiking with a baby was a bit of an unusual sight, so we got lifts with some strange people. I remember this guy who picked us up in his truck and said, "Do you know that you can sell a blonde baby like that? You'd get a few thousand dollars for her." I didn't say much in response, but I was glad to see the back of that ride.

When the competition was over, we hitchhiked back to Hickory Nut Gap Farm. On the way, we camped overnight on Daytona Beach. The police came and wanted to know why I had Barb with me. I showed them my passport, but they wanted to separate us. After a bit of begging they took us to a hostel and the next morning we continued on our way back to North Carolina.

Meanwhile, Lorraine was still working in the UK, living with friends and enjoying work; but she was missing Peter and Barbara. It was at that point they decided she would meet them in New York and from there, together, they would fly back to Australia. Lorraine was overjoyed to touch down in New York. Finally, after so long apart they would all be together again…or so she thought.

[Peter] Barb and I had made our way to New York but when we arrived at the airport, we were told that because Lorraine had South African stamps in her passport she wasn't allowed to stay in the US.

[Lorraine] They told me I had to leave immediately – on the next plane out. I was really, really upset and just cried and cried. Fortunately, they allowed me to stay for two days to be with Peter and Barb but after that I was told I had to go...fly back to the UK.

[Peter] When that happened, I went straight in to organise Barb's and my flight back to Australia. I still had six months on my visa but when they looked at my passport they told me we'd been in the country illegally the whole time. Back when we first arrived, they'd asked where I was staying and as I had no idea at that point I just said, I'm in transit. I had an onward ticket to Australia via Hawaii and they took that to mean I was in airport transit. They didn't change my stamp, they just put a ticket in my passport, and not realising, I had simply walked out of the airport with Barb.

We didn't know what to do. They said I could try and fight it, but it was likely we'd get kicked out and never be permitted back into America. I didn't want that. Our tickets were out of LA so when Lorraine left to go back to the UK, Barb and I caught the bus to LA and then flew to Hawaii.

Lorraine returned to her job in the UK, but her New York experience had left her feeling isolated and alone. She wanted to go home. She booked a flight and within two weeks she was back in Australia.

Lorraine had been away for five years. Over that time, she had experienced so much and changed so much. She was now a mother and an independent woman. Experience had helped her understand and accept that at 22 years old, she alone was responsible for her own life and for the decisions she made – right or wrong.

[Lorraine] Being away really changed me. I didn't have much empathy for others before we went away but being on our own helped me realise I wasn't the only one who found things a bit difficult. I guess for the first time in my life I started to think of my glass being half full and not half empty like I'd always done.

I realised I could do things without my parents' help. Although I had Peter as support, sometimes it was really hard with Barb, but I learned to solve problems on my own, and if things went wrong to just get on with it.

I hadn't realised how much I'd changed until we got back to Australia. It was when I saw my parents, still doing so much for my sisters, that I realised how dependent I had been and how independent I had become. Being away when you are so young, and having to take responsibility for everything, and having no one else to blame, makes you resilient and more capable. It made me strong.

> *Being away when you are so young and having to take responsibility for everything with no one else to blame makes you resilient and capable. It makes you strong.*

Lorraine arrived in Perth on a Saturday and immediately went to stay with Peter's sister Jan. By Tuesday she had two jobs; one as a waitress at the Floreat Hotel and the other at Federation Insurance. Lorraine recalls having no time to see her parents but admits it was probably fear of how they would react that delayed their reunion. She needn't have worried.

[Lorraine] I eventually went to see Mum and Dad. They weren't home, so I sat on the front steps and waited. I wasn't sure what to expect but when they got home, they were so happy to see me – they just hugged and kissed me. When I told them that Barb and Peter were on their way back to Perth, they were so excited. They couldn't wait to meet their granddaughter. I was so happy after that visit but when I got back to Jan's place there was a really upsetting telex waiting for me. It was from Peter.

[Peter] We'd made it to Hawaii okay, but when we got there I was told Barbara wasn't allowed to leave. She wasn't naturalised and had a UK passport while mine was Australian. Because I wasn't the mother, I needed written approval from Lorraine to get Barb out of the country and into Australia. Telexes were the only way to communicate back then and that took ages; it was pretty stressful. Eventually, they allowed us to leave but then, by the time we got to Sydney, I'd run out of money. I was ready to hitchhike across Australia with Barb, anything just to get home, but Lorraine's dad paid for us to fly to Perth.

Peter and Lorraine were so young and naïve when they left Perth. Six years later, after numerous life changing encounters, they returned equally as resilient, resourceful and responsible as the other. Without that time away they may never have developed into two people capable of achieving great business success.

It was October 1978. Peter was 25. He was independent and with the skills gained from living and working abroad, he was very capable and very ready to get on with his life. Like Lorraine, he was eager to work. He took on a few jobs; as a bouncer at the Floreat Hotel, casual labouring and a short stint as a sales rep for Allwest Towing. However, always searching for the ideal job, he found an advertisement for a position recruiting staff for a newly opened health club and applied.

[Peter]   Laurie Potter's was a chain of health clubs that was an icon of the '70s and '80s. In 1979 I started working at their Cannington club as a membership consultant. I found I really enjoyed selling health – talking to people about their health, their fitness and helping them achieve their fitness goals.

By 1980 Lorraine and I had saved enough money to buy a house in Craigie. It was a long way from my work in Cannington, so I left Potter's and got a job at Healthworld Whitfords as their health club manager.

I worked there for a couple of years. Over that time, aerobics had become the in-fitness trend of the day with some places holding classes with hundreds of followers. I thought it would be a good thing to get involved in, so I started looking around for a venue. I approached the owners of a company called Indoor Cricket Arenas (ICA) with an idea to run aerobic classes in the centres when they weren't playing cricket. During our discussions they asked if I would consult on a huge warehouse health club project they were working on in Subiaco with the opportunity to manage the finished club. I liked the sound of it and so left Healthworld and started work. It was a big project and a very new concept for Perth.

We opened in 1983. The club was called Lords, and as a privately owned, multi-sports facility it was unique. The gym was large with separate spa, sauna and change rooms for men and women. So, while most other gyms at the time had to have men and women on alternate days, we were able to mix it and open seven days a week.

We were the first mixed gym in Perth and soon everyone else was trying to copy what we were doing but they didn't have our facilities, so it was difficult for them.

During the initial stages of the project I supplemented my income by starting a company, ICAROBICS Pty Ltd, having seen there was a growing demand for aerobic teachers and gym instructors. I contracted a couple of university students studying physical education to write and run the courses for me. The courses were the first of their kind in Perth and so there was quite a lot of interest. With Lords in the development stage and my initial employment package tied to the club's membership fees, it was the only way I could survive and still see the project to completion.

When Lords opened, we had signed up over 300 members in our pre-sales blitz. The club is, still to this day, one of the most successful in Australia.

With the development stage completed, Lords appointed a new general manager to oversee the operation, with me managing the health club side. We clashed and so I started to look for a new challenge elsewhere. Opening my own health club had become appealing and so with my mind made up I left Lords and started to look for a suitable location.

Opening my own health club had become appealing and so with my mind made up I left Lords and started to look for a suitable location.

I found the ideal site; a large purpose-built roller-skating rink in Morley that had never opened because the investors had run out of money. I knew it would make a great gym; it had the space and location. I wanted to call it Checkers and spent a lot of time working on the project. I was in negotiations with the agent when they revealed that they were now looking at several larger operators to invest in their own gym project on the site. One of those operators was Laurie Potter. Because I had worked previously for Laurie, I contacted him to discuss the possibility of working as a partner with an interest in the business. After several meetings Laurie told me that he was interested in the possibility of a new club but wasn't interested in any partners. Instead he offered me a position managing his club in Piccadilly Square, in the same complex as head office.

I accepted the position but never stopped wanting to have my own business. I realised for that to happen I had to set my sights lower – not the big health club I had planned to open in Morley. I started thinking about a new business venture, one that I could afford. A retail store selling exercise equipment was a business I could start without a lot of capital or requiring someone to back me; I'd already found the site.

It happened by chance. Whenever we had a staff meeting at Laurie's Hay Street City Club, I would pass this vacant shop in Milligan Street. I thought it would make a good retail store as the city was the ideal location to attract customers from both north and south of the river.

It was during that time that Tony Butler, a guy I'd met previously, started working for Laurie. One day Tony and I were chatting, and I told him I didn't think the gym industry was going to survive and so I was going to leave Potter's and start selling home training equipment. As it turned out it was something he'd always wanted to do too. I told him about the shop in Milligan Street and that I was about to sign the lease. I'd already registered the business name, Orbit Mobile Gyms. So, we both left Potter's and formed a partnership. I would have preferred to do it on my own, but I didn't want Tony as a competitor nor did I have much money – in fact I basically had nothing.

Tony and I pooled our money – $11,000. Out of that we bought a vehicle each and had "Orbit Fitness Specialists" printed down the sides along with our slogan, "To help you survive the '80s". The rest of the money went on a desk, a bit of stock, the first month's rent and some paint – we painted it ourselves. We couldn't afford a fridge or air conditioning and our till was a petty cash tin.

Selling people home equipment and supplements was becoming the new thing in America. Opposite our shop was Brian Mackey's Karate Academy, around the corner was my old haunt, American Health Studios and a few other gyms, so I could see there was a big market right there. We opened for business in early 1984 selling equipment, supplements and protein powders.

Our very first sale was a pair of ankle weights, but Tony was so excited he sold them for less than what we purchased them for. Every sale we made was noted in an exercise book with three columns headed; Buying Price, Selling Price and Profit Made. At the end of the day we would calculate the profit we'd made.

Every sale we made was noted in an exercise book with three columns headed Buying Price, Selling Price and Profit Made. At the end of the day we would calculate the profit we'd made.

With a lack of funds and industry knowledge we searched the Yellow Pages to find out where we could buy stock. We contacted York, a fitness equipment company, which had an agent in Perth and purchased a home gym, weights and bars; we also got exercise bikes from Repco and Ricardo.

We were then approached by Nordic Health, an importer, wholesaler and retailer of exercise equipment. They had a large range but only offered us a limited selection to sell because they didn't want us competing on some of their exclusive imported products. That was eventually the catalyst that sent me searching for a direct overseas supplier — just so I didn't have to rely on agents or wholesalers.

We were always trying to work out the best way to do things more cost effectively because it was hard to make money at the start. We were working at least 70 hours a week earning around $2 an hour — not that we minded, we had a lot of fun and it was what we had to do.

We were working at least 70 hours a week earning around $2 an hour - not that we minded, we had a lot of fun and it was what we had to do.

[Peter]   I spent a lot of time on the road delivering and installing equipment, but we also shared time on the showroom floor because the store was open five and half days a week. I delivered product after hours including Saturday afternoons.

One day I was on my way to buy punch bags from a supplier in East Perth and I drove past a warehouse where I noticed a home gym sitting on the loading dock — It wasn't one I'd seen before.

I went in and spoke to the owner. The company was Oxford Sports who were distributors for Olympic Pro, a brand from the eastern states which mainly supplied Myer. Then and there I organised to buy equipment from them and agreed to do all the product installations for Myer.

[Lorraine] For $24 for delivery and installation!"

[Peter]   No $22! And I would sometimes rock up at 8 or 9 pm to drop off a gym to someone and be there until midnight putting it together.

No one in Perth held a lot of stock so when we bought product that came from the east, we were always waiting for it to arrive. Problem was, our customers didn't want to wait. So, we would buy a lot of stock but then we needed a place to store it.

[Lorraine] Our family room at home became our storeroom.

[Peter]   The Olympic Pro was a good seller for us and so I decided to buy direct from Taiwan where it was produced. I contacted the factory in Taiwan and they agreed to sell to us but only if I had approval from David Gray. David was the Australian importer of the Olympic Pro, who owned the brand in New South Wales.

I rang David and he said, "Yep, that's fine," which is unusual because most people want to hold onto their product and make you buy through them. But not David.

I remember when our first container was dropped off outside our house; we were still using our family room to store stock. I unloaded it myself. It was so heavy it cracked the driveway. It's surprising it didn't crack the family room floor because we stored everything in there for quite some time.

Then I decided to go and visit the factory in Taiwan. I used the Yellow Pages at my hotel in Taipei to find the address. I didn't know where I was going and ended up walking down all these alleyways. I knocked at a door and this guy came out and spoke in very broken English. "What you doing here?" When I told him who I was he invited me in. I organised to buy equipment from him and now 30 years later I still buy from those guys.

We didn't have the internet back then and so it was difficult to find information, but I found out about the Taiwan Sporting Goods Show where you meet suppliers and see product. I still go and even now every trip is a bit of an adventure.

It was at my first show that I saw this gym in the show catalogue. It was for the home, but it was so different, more like a gym you would have in a health club. I wanted to meet the supplier, so I phoned the number from the catalogue and arranged to catch up with him at the show. We met and then drove to the Joong Chenn factory in Taichung, which is about three hours from Taipei.

We ended up at the Joong Chenn factory which made the Weck brand. Weck means absolutely nothing but they thought it sounded like a strong word which was good for gym equipment. They later changed the name back to Joong Chenn, manufacturers of the international product, Body Solid. They also have their own brand, Steel Flex.

I walked around the factory which was a small shed with mud floors at the back of a property. Several ladies were squatting next to a chroming facility painting cast weight plates. Next to the shed was a small paddock with several pigs feeding in the mud. From that day on I nicknamed it the pig farm. (Today, Joong Chenn's factory is state of the art and the owners dress in suits.)

Next to the shed (factory) were pigs feeding in the mud. I nicknamed it the pig farm. Today, the factory is state of the art and the owners dress in suits.

The next day at the show I met Dennis Lan, an agent who represented several factories. Dennis spoke good English. He had a small booth at the show and we got talking. He showed me a brochure with a similar home gym to the one I'd seen the day before and I was excited, especially when Dennis quoted me a cheaper price. After the show we headed again to Taichung and to my surprise he took me back to the same factory but this time he introduced me to the owners.

When Dennis explained how he worked I was comfortable to have him as my agent. For his commission, we agreed he would pick me up from the airport and take me to the factories to check out the quality of the product. I would place my orders with him and then his office would arrange shipment. If we had any issues, I would contact him direct and he would deal with the factories.

When we received the first shipment from Joong Chenn it was okay but the second was really bad; paint peeling off and so many other issues.

It was completely unacceptable, so I phoned the Joong Chenn factory, but I couldn't get any sense out of anyone. I decided to fly back to Taiwan to speak to Dennis and together we went to the factory. We found out that they had been moving and had subcontracted the work out. Dennis did the negotiating and we got it sorted – not that we got our money back. They'll never give you your money back because they believe you won't deal with them again – they want to keep you as a buyer. So, we were compensated but it was over our next four or five containers. Eventually, the bad lot was completely replaced, and in that way, they didn't lose face.

Without Dennis it would have been near impossible to sort it and that's why it's really important to have an agent if you are dealing in Asia. He's your go-between. People think they can go to Asia and do it on their own, but I don't know anyone who does good business in Asia without an agent. You definitely need someone on the ground who knows the language and how to negotiate – it's money well worth spending.

We've continued to deal with Joong Chenn who are now quite large and very efficient. In the early days we would often receive a container and something would be missing, and you'd ring them and ask where it is. "Don't know," was the most common answer. So eventually you'd go back to their factory and find the missing part sitting in some corner.

People think they can go to Asia and do it on their own. I don't know anyone who does good business in Asia without an agent - it's money well worth spending.

Over the years I've learned how to manage those kinds of problems but at the time we were so new to the game; a lot of our money had gone into that second container. That meant we needed to turn it over to get enough money to buy more stock. We couldn't send it back, so we had no choice but to spend more money, money we didn't have, pulling it apart, fixing it up, re-powder coating just to sell it off cheap. But what seemed so bad at the time turned into something good because it forced us to consider other options. We decided we would rent out any equipment that arrived that wasn't good enough to sell. As it turned out in those early days rentals became our saviour. We were soon pushing three-month rentals instead of one month and by doing that we doubled our income with the same number of clients. As we expanded, we used to say that our rental income would pay for any mistakes we made...and let me tell you, we made a few!

When we first started everything was a real learning curve. We didn't know about quality control but we learned pretty quickly that it's critical. We didn't know about F.O.B which is free on board, we didn't understand about money or transfers or sending out letters of credit – it was all alien to us. We had to learn from the bottom up – and we still make mistakes – but rarely the same one twice.

We didn't know about quality control but we learned pretty quickly...it's critical.

Whilst Peter was busy learning about business and building Orbit, Lorraine had taken a job in the insurance industry and was rapidly moving up the corporate ladder.

[Lorraine] Insurance was a hard industry and I imagine it still is. I started as a typist and moved up, but it wasn't easy. I remember I got a promotion that included a parking bay at the back of the office. One of the bosses came up to me and said, "Over my dead body are you going to get that car park." He felt, because I was female, I shouldn't have one. I also got a pay increase of $1 per week. That was an insult as far as I was concerned and so I resigned.

Lorraine wasn't out of work for long before she was offered the position of executive assistant to an insurance broker and owner of the company. The role came with great responsibility, but she enjoyed the challenges presented. It was her dream job. However, like so many working women Lorraine began to worry about the time she was spending away from her daughter.

> [Lorraine] I was happy with my own career path, but I wanted to spend more time with Barbara. With both Peter and I working, Barbara basically only caught a glimpse of us in the morning. In the afternoon when I picked her up from after-school care, I was often late because of the traffic. One night I discussed it with Peter and he suggested I work part-time for Orbit. It sounded ideal, so I resigned from my insurance job and started working in the business.
>
> I'd never worked in retail so wasn't used to dealing with customers face to face. Peter had promised that I would spend the majority of my time working on the books, or on the phone dealing with hire enquiries. But being a small retail store, I often had to step up and help out. It didn't take me long to gain my confidence and very soon I was talking the same language with a sales ability that matched the guys.

During our interviews Lorraine spoke often about the impact working in retail had on her self-confidence; how it so positively changed her. She believes that for anyone with a similar struggle getting a job in retail is an ideal solution. Retail is all about communication. Having to talk to the customer, to find out what they want and then sell it to them, isn't easy for someone a little unsure of themselves. But when it's a requirement of the job you have no choice. An employer can't afford to keep you if you can't sell. So it is - learn to communicate or its out the door. For Lorraine it was the catalyst that empowered her to become a great salesperson but more importantly, a woman of confidence.

> [Peter] When Lorraine joined us, I'd been having talks with Tony. I wanted to grow the business, but he was never comfortable with either taking on debt or my ideas of expansion. He was happier working for himself in a small business. In 1985, not even two years after we opened, Tony asked me to buy him out, which I did. So then it was just Lorraine and me.

Orbit Fitness was now a family owned business and with that transition came a renewed energy; there was no holding back. While Lorraine manned the store, Peter was able to search through Taiwan looking for new product; product they could call their own. However, with the arrival of every new shipment came the reminder that their so-called storeroom (their family room) was becoming grossly overcrowded. The ever-growing stockpile of gym equipment was now starting to spill out into the rest of the house. They had to find another solution! They did; a warehouse unit at 396 Scarborough Beach Road, Osborne Park. Unlike others in similar situations, they made the decision not to lease the space but to buy it. That decision was the turning point of their financial future. The warehouse was the first in what would become both a highly desirable commercial property portfolio and the spine of their business empire.

> [Lorraine] When we bought our first warehouse the variable interest rate was 22 per cent. Our

accountant at the time believed that the rate would remain for some time and suggested we fix the rate at 15 per cent for five years. We took his advice. The next year, rates plummeted well below 15 per cent leaving us stuck with our fixed rate for another four years. It was an awful blow, but you learn from those kinds of mistakes.

[Peter]   We purchased the warehouse because we needed storage space and we never intended to use it for anything else. However, we decided to try opening the warehouse to the public on weekends and when people started going out there rather than to Milligan Street, we started selling from there during the week as well.

In 1988 when the Milligan Street lease came to an end, we decided to close it down and move our retail business to the warehouse. Once out there we set up our warehouse direct program. It was the late '80s – a really tough time to be in retail but we were also off the main strip and at the back which made it even tougher. Customers couldn't find us. We upped our advertising but it was still a struggle. We would always get phone calls asking, "Where are you?"

We had to do something. Our only options were to restructure or do what others were doing – get out of retail, a bit like what's happening today.

[Lorraine] At that time retail was only five and a half days a week and so we decided to open Sundays. We were one of the first to do that, but it was exhausting working seven days a week.

[Peter]   We were also trying different ways to advertise and had experimented with several mediums. We were getting good results creating weekly sales events using radio. We had a couple of containers arriving with some popular new products so with our warehouse open on Sundays I decided we should try a one-day, Sunday only, sales event to coincide with the delivery. We used television to advertise and just bombarded the space with ads – there was no preamble, it was just concentrated. It gave us a strong presence and created a bit of a frenzy.

[Lorraine] On the Sunday morning we had people lining up trying to get into the warehouse and another line, maybe a hundred feet or so, of people purely waiting to load their cars with what they had just bought.

There were groups trying to buy the same piece of equipment, shouting, "I want one". They were given an invoice to take to the counter where I was putting through the sales and from there, they had to collect the item. The guys were just exhausted from continuously getting stock down.

Back then there weren't a lot of bank cards so after the sale we had a briefcase filled with cash – around $100,000 in notes. It was a Sunday night; the banks were closed, and we were taking all the staff out to dinner to celebrate. We didn't want to take the money to dinner with us, so we took the briefcase over to my Dad's place; he sat there guarding it all night. The next morning, we picked up the briefcase and took it into the bank; the bank manager wasn't half as excited as we were.

[Peter]   We duplicated that same sale from then on. Through trial and error, we found we could only hold one about every six to eight weeks – any shorter time period was just too close.

We then started rebranding equipment under Orbit. I would go to Taiwan and work with the factories tweaking the design and stay until I felt it was working as it should. When your name is on the product you have to make sure it's good and so by us taking the time to get it right and giving the attention to detail made Orbit a very strong and recognisable brand. That branding move was instrumental to our success. However, when you are dealing with overseas factories it isn't always smooth sailing – even if you have a mature product that has been 100 per cent reliable. That might be because the factory is trying to save money and so sources a cheaper part, but we only find out there's a problem when we start having issues and unhappy customers. In the early days every problem fell on my shoulders, but we now have one of the largest service divisions in the country, with thousands of parts. We have a quality control inspection prior to every shipment; our team randomly assembles and checks an item in each shipment to catch any product problems before they are sold.

A lot of this was, and still is, about staying in front of the curve; trying new things. Sometimes we got it right, not always, and sometimes we were ahead of the trends. We initially followed the health clubs; we imported steppers and any other product that was popular in the gyms. But a big switch came when we decided to sell treadmills.

In 1988 Oprah Winfrey celebrated, on air, her weight loss of 67 kilos by going on a liquid diet and exercising on a treadmill. From that day on everyone wanted a treadmill.

In 1988 Oprah Winfrey celebrated, on air, her weight loss of 67 kilos by going on a liquid diet and exercising on a treadmill. That revelation came just as we received our first container of Orbit branded electric treadmills. The very next day the phone started ringing with people wanting one and it hasn't stopped since.

Back then gyms didn't have treadmills but suddenly the treadmill that we had developed and designed for domestic retail became a gym product. We realised then that we could lead the market trends instead of following, and since then we've spent hundreds of thousands of dollars searching the world for products that we could sell under the Orbit brand.

There were so many opportunities out there and we – well, probably mainly me – just wanted to do everything. Lorraine made more calculated decisions based on the figures and would sometimes say, "No, we can't afford it". Sometimes I would listen and sometimes I would just do it and then she'd have to find a way to pay for it.

In 1992 we bought another warehouse unit in the same group at 396 (Scarborough Beach Road) because I wanted to manufacture our own equipment for health clubs. We didn't have a manufacturing background, so it was very stressful and was consuming a huge amount of our time. I wasn't enjoying it and it was putting lots of stress on everyone concerned but we didn't want to fail, so we persisted. A lot of work came in and so to meet deadlines we subcontracted a lot of it out and that is where we ran into problems. Some of it was substandard work which created delays, and so then we had to deal with unhappy customers. That took our focus off our core retail business. It wasn't good for us, so we took a long hard look at what we were doing and where we were going and that's when we made the decision to close down our local manufacturing arm. Today there are only a few Australian equipment manufacturers; the majority of manufactured goods are imported from Taiwan or China.

We had to learn from the bottom up - and we still make mistakes - but rarely the same one twice.

It was disappointing, but from the mistakes, lessons were learned, hence enabling Lorraine and Peter to continue to build on their warehouse direct sales. They finally reached the point where they felt they had found the magic formula. But as so often happens, yet another obstacle emerged.

[Peter]   One day one of our managers up and left us and went to the opposition. Suddenly they had opened around the corner on Scarborough Beach Road and were duplicating everything we were doing.

With that kind of competition up the road, we decided it was time to get back into mainstream retailing and started looking for a site south of the river. We found Cannington was an affordable location, and so that was where we purchased our second store — well, really it was our first store because Osborne Park was only a warehouse.

We sensed we had some real competition and were worried they may try to open next door to us in Cannington. Owning the store helped us control who purchased units in the complex. The opposition then opened their second store in Morley, we opened our third in Myaree, a store we leased, and they opened their third in Rockingham.

While our focus was on opening new stores, we were still having great success on Sundays with our big one-day warehouse sales but when we opened our fourth store in Joondalup we were forced to give them up. Back then, once you had more than three stores you weren't allowed to trade on Sundays, and for us that meant lost opportunity and lost income. We tried a few different options, but none had the same impact.

In the early days we were the only retailer advertising fitness equipment; now there're loads. But that advertising has been a major key to our survival and success and still is, although these days it's a lot more complicated with social media. You've got Facebook, Google ads, Google Shopping, search engine optimisation (SEO) and SEM — search engine i-marketing. There's also dynamic remarketing which is when a product that someone has been searching for on the internet is recreated in an ad that suddenly starts to appear whenever they go onto their computer or phone.

Advertising in this way (digitally) is so convenient and affordable but it's constantly evolving so it's confusing – especially if you were born before the 80s. But if you want to survive you have to keep up with the changing trends.

Over the years we've also come to realise that to not only survive but to have a successful retail business there's a critical level of stores you need to enable the business to support itself financially, depending what business you're in of course. For us having one store was relatively easy; when we opened our second and third stores Lorraine and I struggled but it became easier when we opened the next five. When you expand you need more people, more staff to support and run the stores, more middle managers to run operations, more warehouse and delivery people to handle stock, and that all means more customer and staff issues and more people taking sick days and holiday leave. On top of that, with growth, comes the need to make more sales and that requires more advertising.

Over the years we've come to realise that to not only survive but to have a successful retail business there's a critical level of stores you need to enable the business to support itself

It was in the late '90s that we were wrestling with our expansion. We had three retail locations, a hire business as well as importing and wholesaling our own products. The business was successful, but Lorraine and I found it very difficult to manage our growing team, so it was also very stressful. We asked for help but some of the advice took us from the frying pan into the fire.

One suggestion was to change our business model, so we did. Another recommendation was to move from our warehouse in Osborne Park into a showroom on Scarborough Beach Road – we did that too. It was a big move in terms of expense. Not only did we spend in excess of $200,000 on the internal design and build but we went from basically a zero rent to a rent of over $300,000 per year. All these changes added to our growing expenses. Lorraine and I became so consumed with worry that we were barely sleeping.

[Lorraine] It was so close to being really disastrous for us. It was such a big financial burden and something we regretted at the time, but we continued working at it, probably because we didn't have an option not to. But we didn't give up, and fortunately as it has turned out, it's been a good thing. But it was touch and go.

> *We eventually came to realise that we were the masters of our own destiny and that we needed to take ownership of our own game.*

[Peter] We eventually came to realise that we were the masters of our own destiny and that we needed to take ownership of our own game. We made the decision to revert back to what had been a successful marketing and sales model, however, the new Osborne Park retail location was still a big drain on our resources. To bring in extra income we went on another expansion program; we added stores in Joondalup, Midland and Malaga to our group.

We were looking at a further location in Mandurah when we were approached by a sporting goods store that we were wholesaling to. They asked if we would consider giving them a franchise. As Mandurah was getting further away from our home base we agreed and added our first franchise store to the mix. We were planning to open another two franchised stores, Rockingham and Bunbury, but we were finding it difficult to get the Mandurah franchise anywhere near the income of our company stores, so, we changed our mind. Instead, we opened them as company stores.

Operating any business is never going to be smooth sailing, especially when you are in uncharted waters. Ours can be harder because we import all our product from overseas suppliers. To give you an example, when the US dollar dropped to an all-time low of 49¢ it had the potential to devastate our business. The cost of goods increased 20 per cent overnight which had a huge impact on our profit margin. In retail it is almost impossible to add those extra costs onto existing products. They have been purchased with unique features to meet certain price points that are acceptable to a customer base and are competitive with what is being offered by the opposition. So, when the dollar dropped it had a devastating effect on our whole importing program which led to a huge shortfall in our overseas purchasing facility.

From the time we started our business we had a great relationship with our bank. So, on this occasion we contacted them and told them what was going on. They didn't let us down. They allowed us to change our financing package and add more funds to our facility and that enabled us to maintain our import volumes. Part of the finance restructure was an overdraft facility to help us out in the short term. Fortunately, we had sufficient assets to support those facilities but today it might be more of a struggle to get that level of support from a financial institution.

[Lorraine] Everyone in business should have that kind of relationship with their bank. We might not have been able to get through without it. You have to keep talking to them, telling them what you're doing, build a relationship – they will be more willing and able to help if they've been part of your journey.

[Peter] Developing the same kind of relationship with your suppliers can be just as important. Often cash flow can get tight, but most suppliers will help if you're honest with them. If you're having a tough month, make the call well before you are due to pay and say, "Sorry, we're a bit tight this month, is it okay if I put you out for 15 days?" If they agree don't abuse it, make sure you pay at the agreed time. When they know you're not going to muck them around you build a relationship, a trust.

[Lorraine] Having that communication is really important when you first start out because things can go bad very quickly, and when creditors are chasing you for money it's like you freeze, you don't think straight, and you can start making bad decisions. I know! We've made plenty of mistakes but we've learnt from them.

As the saying goes, 'The cheque's in the mail,' isn't something you want to become known for. When you promise to pay a supplier, pay them or let them know when you are able to pay and then follow up on your promises. We established our business on that philosophy right at the start and that enabled us to grow and keep growing.

We also reinvested the majority of our profits back into the business; not only in stock holdings but also in property. That was our way of future-proofing ourselves, although in hindsight, we could have done the warehouses better – we should have bought one big complex rather than a series of smaller ones.

Lorraine and Peter's commercial property portfolio didn't stop at warehouse units; they also had a number of stores. After purchasing the Cannington store, they added Booragoon and then Nedlands, and in between they went on a spree of leasing and opening new stores.

[Lorraine] We've had opportunities to expand across to Sydney and Melbourne. There's a part of us that would still love to do it but it would take our focus away from what we are doing here. It would also be much harder to manage because finding the right staff is a problem we already face – every day.

[Peter] We could send our best people to do Melbourne but who would to do Sydney? Then we'd have to find someone else here to keep an eye on the day-to-day management anyway. If we didn't find the right person things would start to fall apart and so we'd have to spend more time trying to pull it all back together.

[Lorraine] Even when we first opened our Bunbury store, a two-hour drive was a long way to go. We now have a good manager down there but if we had to be there every five minutes or fly over to Melbourne or Sydney...it would just make it a tough gig.

So, we don't regret our decision to stay local where we can maintain control. Our opposition, the ones that were aggressive in their expansion, are the ones that have faltered and died. For us it wasn't worth that risk.

[Peter] We still take risks, but we qualify everything now. We have a lot more to lose than when we first started, including our lifestyle. But when we were young, we took every opportunity. The jobs we took in South Africa and England...we didn't have any real skill level – I certainly didn't have any experience in what I did but I still took the job.

Admittedly it was hard when we got back after being away for so long – most of our friends already owned houses and we were way behind the eight ball. But that became a driving force to get to the next level, so we caught up very quickly.

[Lorraine] We both worked several jobs and saved every penny. We stayed with Peter's mum until we were able to save enough money for a deposit on our first house. When we moved in, we didn't have any floor coverings except in the two bedrooms. There was no table and chairs, we just made do with a folding card table and milk crates. Peter and his mate Gordon did the landscaping and eventually Peter tiled the rest of the house. But it all took time, we just did the work slowly while we saved enough money to buy more materials.

[Peter]   We started the business with very little money, but we were used to that. We had always watched what we spent, we had saved, and at the start we only invested in our stock. We also knew that being in a small business we didn't have the luxury of allowing people not to pay their bills on time; we had commitments and suppliers to pay. So, Lorraine posted the invoices out on time every month. We didn't just send out payment reminders, Lorraine would ring the customers – even late at night.

Some people could have far more successful businesses but they don't do the basics. I've seen it so often when people do a job but then forget or can't be bothered to send the account, or they send it months later. You can't run a business like that! It's not just about giving quotes or being the cheapest; it's the follow up and then as soon as the job is done it's about sending the invoice. The point is, no matter what, you're in business to make money so you have to be tireless, you have to stay focused and you have to get paid.

[Lorraine] Who can afford to have a backlog of unsent invoices? We couldn't. In those early days I'd be sitting working at one, two o'clock in the morning, sending invoices or following up on debtors – a bad debt is a bad debt at any time of the day.

The point is, no matter what, you're in business to make money so you have to be tireless, you have to stay focused and you have to get paid.

[Peter]   After Lorraine started working in the business, we were able to save more so we decided we would sell our little house and buy a larger one in a better area. We searched around and eventually bought a 4x2 house with a swimming pool, a garage with an attached workshop as well as a massive games room that doubled as our stock room. Then we went a little crazy. We were visiting friends for a Sunday breakfast when owning a holiday home came up in conversation. So there and then we all decided to drive to Mandurah to look at some. By the following week we'd bought a holiday home together.

[Lorraine] I was terrified. I thought how are we going to pay for all this? It cost us $16,000 for the holiday home per couple! But it was fantastic and became a great retreat where we would get together with friends on weekends. We got our money's worth and still own the beach shack with the same friends.

[Peter]   During school holidays Lorraine and I would holiday with Barbara down at Falcon. We would take turns opening the shop.

[Lorraine] Being unable to take time off together was the tough part, but it was the motivating factor behind our decision to expand and take on staff.

From that first warehouse purchase Peter and Lorraine spent the next 20 years substantially adding to their property portfolio. By doing so it enabled them to grow their chain of Orbit Fitness stores to 11, positioning them as the largest independent gym equipment retailer in the country.

During that time, they have opened and then closed a few stores, including one in Midland. The Midland store was doing well, but the burden of finding good staff became too great and in the end the decision to close was not a difficult one to make.

> [Lorraine] We hadn't bought the site in Midland, so when it came time to renew the lease, closing it down instead wasn't a hard decision. The location was getting tired as well. It wasn't a right or wrong decision, but we've found since that, whilst we've saved the costs off the bottom line, we haven't been able to recover the lost $1.5 million in turnover.
>
> We expected that our Midland customers would go to our neighbouring stores in Cannington, Malaga or Joondalup which aren't that far from Midland, but they didn't; so, we did lose a lot of customers. One day we may reopen out there but it would be in a different position.

With their ever expanding retail and commercial business, warehouse space was an ongoing issue. They knew that eventually they would need to find a more suitable and permanent solution.

Success in business is about continually evolving and trying new things to survive and thrive in a rapidly changing marketplace.

> [Peter] We were using several warehouses, so it was almost impossible to access stock quickly and easily. The process became more and more time consuming for our storeman who often had to move half the warehouse just to get to stock stored at the back.
>
> A friend, a wholesaler from the east, was using a contract warehouse in Kewdale so we decided to move some of our stock out to that location. We used contract delivery trucks to deliver the stock from Kewdale, but we were also delivering stock to the same stores from our Osborne Park warehouses. The double handling and extra contract storage/delivery was costing us approximately $250,000 per annum.
>
> We trialled it for about 12 months but eventually dropped the Kewdale storage company because of the expense and found a local Osborne Park company to do the same. The big cost saving then was being able to use our own delivery people, plus if we ever needed stock from the overflow facility it was just down the road. We'd only been using the Osborne Park company for about 12 months when they told us they were moving out to Kewdale. Obviously, we didn't want to go back to that same arrangement, but it meant we only had a month to find new premises for all our stock. We wanted to stay in or around the Osborne Park area and so when we took a lease on a 2000 square metre site at $300,000 a year it was all very rushed.
>
> A few years later rents started going down all over the place but not ours. So we asked for a

rent reduction. Over Christmas a letter arrived giving us a couple of weeks to object to a rent increase, but we were away and missed the deadline. Because of that we made the decision we would move out at the end of the lease. We looked to purchase land to build a warehouse/office complex where we could bring all of our departments under the one roof.

We bought land in a newly released industrial area in Gnangara, called the North Link Industrial Park – an extension of the Wangara Industrial area. We thought great, a new area, a new start. But when you go into these new areas you don't realise how much infrastructure still needs to be done. We did our research and followed all the correct procedures but when you deal with government departments everyone tells you something different. One day we were told we could have NBN and the next we were told we couldn't. It was everything from Telstra pits to NBN pits, which they insisted couldn't be put together. Then we were told there's no copper out there, so we couldn't have traditional phones or security systems. It took up so much time and effort that sometimes we wondered what we'd got into.

Wading through the quagmire of obstacles that were put before them had been costly, frustrating and exhausting but now with all four departments finally under the one roof Peter and Lorraine hoped all their problems were behind them. Realistically, like anyone in business, they knew that was not possible, but what they didn't expect was their greatest challenge was yet to come.

Our first container arrived and with that container came disastrous news.

[Peter] We'd just moved in after investing nearly $5 million on a site where the idea had been to not only save the money we were spending on rent, but also bring everyone together under the one roof – so it felt good to finally be there.

Our first container arrived and with that container came disastrous news. It turned out that the entire Wangara Industrial Extension Area that everyone, including the developer and the City of Wanneroo, had been told was zoned industrial was in fact, according to the Federal government, zoned rural.

We didn't realise at first the ramifications – we thought it was just a minor discrepancy – until they told us exactly how it would affect us.

Quarantine laws demand that if any container from overseas or interstate is to be delivered into rural areas it must first be taken to a checking station where it is decided if it needs to be washed out.

This means that a trucking company has to collect the container from the wharf, drop it to the checking station and then pick it up and deliver it to the warehouse. This operation was going to cost us around $600,000 extra per year and all because we were not in an industrial area as we had been advised. It meant disaster for us.

[Lorraine] You should have seen our gin supply go down!

[Peter] Everyone we spoke to thought the whole thing was ridiculous and hard to believe but the Federal government, which owned the land, had it listed as rural and there was nothing we could do.

For us it was a game changer.

We were advised to engage a lobbyist and after a few meetings and expensive quotes a friend mentioned someone he knew that could help. We arranged a meeting with him; we liked what was said and it was free, so we engaged his help.

[Lorraine] We were a little sceptical at first, but he had contacts and with the help of a former member of Federal Parliament he started to shake things up.

[Peter] He asked us to ring around all the local businesses to find out if there was any interest in getting everyone together to push for the change from rural to industrial, which is what we had all thought we were buying into in the first place. We made loads of calls to local business-es and discovered that a lot of our new neighbours were in a similar situation.

[Lorraine] Eventually, the lobbyist called a meeting at our warehouse with the City of Wan-neroo, the different government departments, the stakeholders – anyone who was involved.

Halfway through the meeting he came up to us looking concerned and whispered.

"It's not looking good; this could go on for years."

His words just hit us like a lead weight. Bang. We felt absolutely deflated. We didn't know what we were going to do. In just one month it had already cost us $20,000 extra in container delivery costs.

After the meeting I wanted to go to the pub and get smashed, but Peter just wanted to get stuck into work to get his mind off things.

We'd only been back at work a short while when Peter came running out of his office jumping up and down and yelling. He rarely shows any emotion so we all thought he'd gone crazy because of what had happened at the meeting.

[Peter] I'd just received a phone call – it was from Canberra. This guy says, "I'm in charge of rubber stamping and I'm looking at your paperwork here. I thought I would give you the word that it's been approved. We're changing the zoning. It will come up within two days."

It was so out of the blue. This had been going on for weeks and weeks not just a few days; after everything we'd been through – the process, the anxiety – I was just ecstatic.

[Lorraine] Our lobbyist had been pushing buttons and so our little application had started to move up the line. Also, one of the stakeholders was an importer based in Melbourne and their transport company had already applied for an application to get it rezoned. So, it was already in the system but the pushing from our side made it happen quicker.

At the end of the day, the challenges don't stop. One day you think fantastic and then bang, another obstacle – no day is plain sailing.

[Peter] At the end of the day, the challenges don't stop. You think, okay, we are at this level now, brand new warehouse, it's going to make everything really fantastic, and then bang, something else hits something else; another bang, another obstacle – no day is plain sailing.

[Lorraine] That's why you need to have people to turn to or know who to turn to in different situations. We've sure learned the power of the lobbyist and that there are people out there who can and are willing to give support – but you have to ask.

[Peter] So, with that out of the way and everyone finally under the one roof we were able to get back to focusing on the business.

Again, it's about continually evolving and trying new things to survive and thrive in a rapidly changing marketplace.

I look back to the '80s, the days when places like the Mediterranean restaurant in Subiaco were booming. No one worked on Fridays because they'd go there from 11 am onwards. The staff would park your cars and everyone who was anyone would be there – not often us because we just didn't stop working.

[Lorraine] ...thank goodness because we'd be dead by now. There's no way we could've kept up with that lifestyle but plenty of our friends did. Everyone that was around back then remembers it – it was an amazing era.

[Peter] Then the government decided to introduce a fringe benefits tax and all the lunches stopped. It probably sent a lot of restaurants and bars broke because they relied on that business trade. But all change is going to have some impact on your business; sometimes it's negative and sometimes it's going to be positive.

There have been many changes and obstacles since they opened for business in the late '80s but Lorraine and Peter have managed to duck and manoeuvre their way forward. By doing so their business has become stronger and they have become wiser. But, as is often the way, it took a tragic loss for them to stop and acknowledge that there is more to life than working hard in business. They now realise it is all about balance and making the most of and appreciating every moment life gives you.

[Lorraine] By the mid-nineties we had built the business to a level where we could have stopped and reaped the rewards, we could have chosen to just enjoy life, but we kept working.

It was around 2001 when I started thinking, what the hell are we getting out of this? Then suddenly one of our friends, Geoff Crowthers, died of cancer. That's when we realised what life is worth. He had just retired and had told us he was going to spend the rest of his life enjoying it and being happy and then three months later he was dead. That's when we said, "Right, that's it, we want to enjoy our lives as well."

[Peter]   That's when we built our house on the land we'd had for years – it was a big investment but it's been worth it. About the same time, we joined the Channel 9 Golf Club as part of our advertising program. The people we have met on those trips have become some of our greatest friends.

> *When one of our friends suddenly died that's when we realised what life was worth and that's when we said, "Right, that's it, we want to enjoy our lives as well."*

[Lorraine]   I think the friends we've made along the way has been one of the most rewarding things to come out of having our business. A lot of them, and I'm talking overseas as well, are still very good friends, some we don't even do business with anymore because they've closed their factories. Those friendships are really important to us.

[Peter]   Lorraine and I were lucky that we were able to work together – it's been good for us. We've been able to put our resources together, whereas otherwise they would have been dispersed. We don't have conflict because we both bring something different to the business; we have the same friends, the same dreams and once your dreams start to align, that's when the momentum grows.

> *The secret of our success is that we never give up on our dreams or each other.*

[Lorraine]   We still have big ideas about what we could do next, but we've achieved almost everything we wanted to. Our biggest challenge now, and I mean big challenge, is finding an exit plan – we don't have one.

[Peter]   Our daughter Barbara would be the right person to take over and run the business. She is a great operations manager and knows the business back to front. We have discussed the possibility of her taking the reins, but it is something she runs hot and cold on because she knows the daily challenges we face and the pressure we are constantly under.

Lorraine really wants to retire so at times I've said, "Okay, well let's just sell up", but it's not that easy – it's too big. We'd have to break it down to be more accessible to buyers. We're an importer, we're a retailer, and then we have the service business, the hire business and the commercial business – so we have all these businesses within the business.

[Lorraine] You know, it's not like we haven't thought about this over the last 20 years. We used to go to seminars to get ideas, but our business was always bigger than the ones they were talking about, like the local deli or newsagency.

[Peter] We could just say, well, the next plan is we'll just close – but we have 64 staff who rely on us.

[Lorraine] With the current retail marketplace here in WA the best plan is to downsize.

[Peter] Over the past few years our retail business has been getting hammered. We have seen a big drop in spending by consumers. Everyone talks about the effect of the internet on bricks and mortar businesses but from my experience customers still want to buy from local businesses, they still want personalised attention, and if they have a problem, they want to talk to someone face to face. So even though there's the growing expense of rents, rates and taxes, we still need good, well-trained people who are ready and able to help customers.

We have to reduce our overheads and the only way to do that is look at some of our slow or non-performing stores and downsize some of our larger super stores. If we reduce the number of stores, then we will need to shrink our total business. Although we aren't lovers of the franchise model, we could possibly offer the retail stores to the managers who have invested 15-plus years in the business and who have proven records of achieving results.

But then the question is, what are we going to do after? I suppose we might take a deep breath, but then are we going to be happy just playing golf? I know Lorraine would be happy lying on a beach somewhere in Portugal.

[Lorraine] Yes, I would for a while but then I'd get bored and I don't want to get old in my mind. There are still things I want to do but the fact is, it's tiring dealing with staff and all the problems that come with running a business.

When you're young you never think you're ever going to be as old as 60 or 70 – I don't think your focus goes that far.

[Peter] When we started out, we never thought about an exit plan. At 19 or 20 or 25 we didn't even have any great vision – any goals we did have were different to what they were at 30 and 40...they've evolved. When you're young you never think you're ever going to be as old as 60 or 70 – I don't think your focus goes that far. At the end of the day the things that drove us early in life – the new house, the new car – are no longer as important.

So, whilst Peter and Lorraine built a complex and multi-layered business of significant proportions, they, like so many others, never gave great thought to the need for an exit plan. They are now living with the consequences; a confronting position to find themselves at this stage of their journey. However, they are not alone in their dilemma. There are countless business owners who believe their time is better spent elsewhere in the business rather than on developing an exit strategy. Peter and Lorraine's experience would suggest otherwise. Now, having learned the lesson, they are working through this challenge, and whilst there will be others, for today, exit planning is their focus.

[Peter] No matter how old you are, health and fitness are central to enjoying life, but when you get to our age, the focus obviously becomes more about your health. Mentally, we all think we are still 19 so it comes as a shock when you can't do the things you used to do on a daily basis.

But you still want to look good, you want to present well, all those sorts of things, and while money can get you most of that, your health is something money can't buy. So, your health is something you need to work on daily.

[Lorraine] Fitness and health are Peter's hobbies and he loves talking to customers about how they can improve their health and fitness, so it's not like we've got to our age and just started thinking about it now – we've lived and breathed it – but you never know...

[Peter] I don't think we ever thought about where we wanted to be or ever expected to be where we are today. It was never about the money; it was just about being the best – and survival. For people wanting to be in business there are still plenty of opportunities out there – you just have to stay focused, motivated and trust yourself and the people you choose to do business with. There are plenty of good people but there are also some ruthless ones, and even though sometimes you do have to be ruthless to survive, you have to realise that if you're in the same game you're in the same pool and if you can't learn to live together you will be devoured.

Well, they haven't been devoured. Peter and Lorraine have learned how to compete in the field; they've learned how to live with their competitors but it's taken years and it's taken its toll.

It was never about the money; it was just about being the best - and survival.

So now it is time to slow the treadmill but it's not time to stop it, because staying motivated, focused and fit is in their DNA. It has been the major key to the success of their business journey and why they are where they are today. It took the sudden loss of their friend Geoff to realise it would be somewhat of an anticlimactic finish if they were to work relentlessly hard, only to arrive exhausted (if at all) at their destination. That realisation led to yet another. It wasn't reaching the destination that provided the greatest experiences – the achievements, the joys and the friendships – it was the journey along the way. That is why Lorraine and Peter won't stop the treadmill and why the desire to learn, to grow, to stay healthy and fit and to motivate others to do the same, continues.

Life is about making the time to enjoy the journey, and for this formidable duo, the attainment of that wisdom is one of their greatest successes yet.

Lorraine and Peter, thank you.

Peter with his sister Gerry

Lorraine, Peter and Barb London, 1976

Peter in a Healthword ad

ICArobics - early 80's

The first Orbit Store - Miligan Street
Perth City 1984

Demonstrating the latest equipment out on Milligan Street

Daily News, Monday, June 29, 1987

Fitness in your home

WITH the collapse of health clubs in Perth and in the Eastern States over recent years many people are now looking for alternatives to the clubs and the life memberships many of them offer.

One such alternative could well be buying or hiring their own equipment for use in their own home.

Training in the privacy of your own home and at your own convenience is a sensible alternative to joining a health club says Peter Hodgson.

The proprietor of Orbit Mobile Gyms, Mr Hodgson has more than 15 years experience in the health and fitness industry both here and overseas.

He says that they have a large number of successful clients now training in the privacy of their own homes and at very reasonable cost.

"It only takes about 20 minutes of training every second day.

You can find Orbit Mobile Gyms in Milligan Street, Perth, or telephone 481 1172.

• Peter Hodgson demonstrates some of the equipment at Orbit.

ADVERTISEMENT FEATURE

od '87
EISURE

Home gym

MANY people shy clear of health clubs due to the feeling of being intimidated by working out in a gym full of "super fit" enthusiasts.

This shouldn't be a deterrent to actively seeking fitness and exercise, because it can be done at home with equipment from Orbit Mobile Gyms.

Peter Hodgson of Orbit, who has 16 years experience in the health and fitness industry, both in Australia and overseas, said that there was an increasing demand for quality home training equipment.

"We hire and sell equipment to suit specific needs and provide continuous training and nutritional advice," said Peter.

"The equipment you use depends on what you aim to achieve physically."

For reducing body fat and remaining toned, multigyms aerobic exercise equipment provide all the health club facilities in the one unit and station type equipment is proving to be very popular.

Orbit Mobile Gyms in 36 Milligan Street, Perth, can be phoned on 481 1172 for details of their equipment and services.

Lorraine Hodgson, Tony Butler and Peter Hodgson of Orbit Mobile Gyms.

Inside the first store 1984

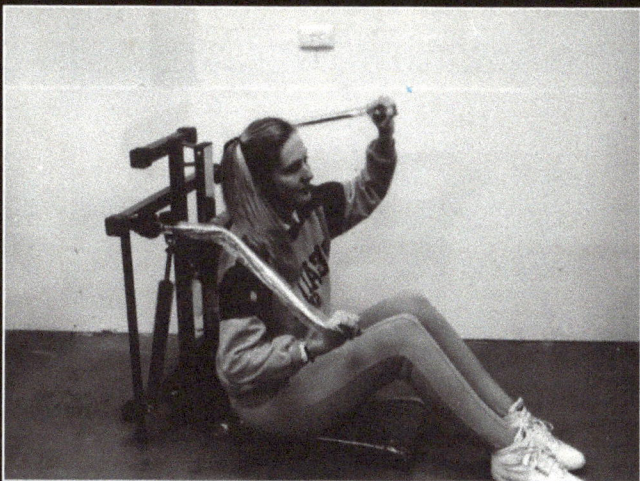

Lorraine demonstrating equipment

Barb with the 'Orbitron'

Equipment stored in Family Room

Start of Sunday trading

The warehouse 1991

The showroom in 1991

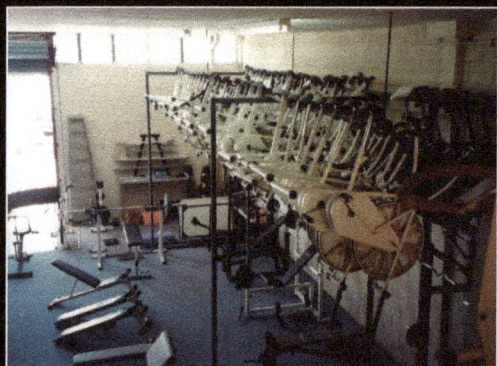
The warehouse 1991

The first Orbit showroom Osborne Park 1997

The new Orbit showroom Osborne Park 2018

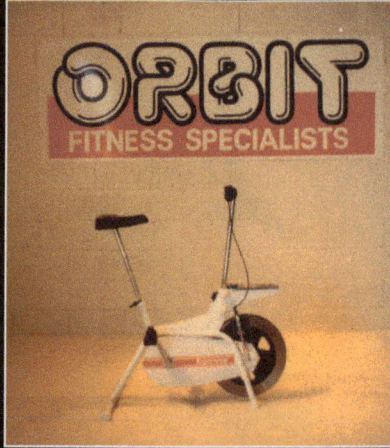

Exercise Bike – 1995 and today

The Gnangarra Warehouse 2017

The Warehouse 2018

Peter and Lorraine 1973

2016 Peter and
Lorraines wedding day
- more than 40 years
after their first date

"We all dream; some continue to dream
and some talk about the dream.
Unless we decide to live the dream,
a dream is all it will ever be."

L J Hinchliffe

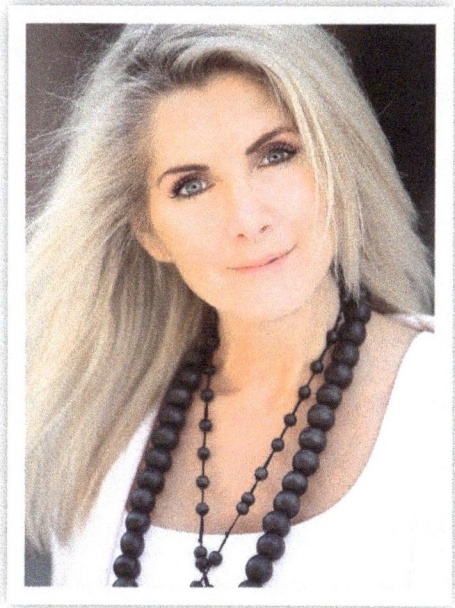

Lesa J Hinchliffe (nee Allen) was born in Perth, Western Australia. At 16 and while still at school, Hinchliffe read the book, Think and Grow Rich by Napoleon Hill, and in doing so, a lifelong interest in the psychology of business success was born. Whilst her career commenced in cartography and architectural design, Hinchliffe, compelled by aspirations for business success, moved between numerous roles and start-up businesses over the ensuing years.

Her ambitions eventually saw Hinchliffe progress into the media and to establish her own production company where she spent her time in front of the camera and behind it writing, directing and producing. Her interest in writing had begun as a child but life's commitments never allowed the opportunity to do so full-time. Finally, at 54, a long-held dream to write a book crystallised.

The journey began with trepidation and a degree of self-doubt about making it through to completion. It would prove to be a challenging task; however, the journey was to end with an unexpected outcome. From doing the research, interviewing each of the megapreneurs and the subject itself – how to achieve business success – Hinchliffe emerged as a person greatly empowered but more importantly, in terms of this journey, with an understanding of why achieving great business success can and does elude so many.

Today, Hinchliffe's words as a writer and professional speaker are driven by a desire to see everyone achieve their dreams and to live a life that is the best it can be.

Lesa J Hinchliffe